Educating for Sustainability in Japan

T0300130

Education for Sustainable Development (ESD) approaches are holistic and interdisciplinary, values-driven, participatory, multi-method, locally relevant and emphasise critical thinking and problem-solving. This book explains how ESD approaches work in the Japanese context; their effects on different stakeholders; and their ultimate potential contribution to society in Japan. It considers ESD in formal, non-formal and informal education sectors, recognising that even when classroom learning takes place it must be place-based and predicated on a specific community context. The book explores not only 'Why ESD', but why and how ESD in Japan has gained importance in the past decade and more recently in the wake of the triple disaster of March 2011. It considers how ESD can help Japan recover and adapt to disasters and take initiative in building more resilient and sustainable communities.

This volume asks the questions: What are some examples of positive contributions by ESD to sustainability in Japan? What is the role of ESD in Japan in activating people to demand and work towards change? How can schools, universities and non-governmental organisations link with communities to strengthen civic awareness and community action? After an introduction that elucidates the roots and recent promotion of ESD in Japan, part one of this volume looks at the formal education sector in Japan, while part two examines community-based education and sustainability initiatives. The latter revisits the Tohoku region five years on from the events of March 2011, to explore recovery and revitalisation efforts by schools, NGOs and residents.

This is an invaluable book for postgraduate students, researchers, teachers and policy makers working on ESD.

Jane Singer is Associate Professor at the Graduate School of Global Environmental Studies, Kyoto University, Japan, where she co-supervises the Environmental Education study area. Her research focuses on human migration and displacement, community resilience, campus sustainability and tertiary-level education for sustainability.

Tracey Gannon was a lecturer and later a tenured associate professor in environmental communication at the Graduate School of Global Environmental

Studies, Kyoto University, Japan, from 2003 to 2014. She currently divides her time between Japan and the UK, combining freelance editorial work and sustainability teaching with ongoing research into environmental education and eco literacy.

Fumiko Noguchi has been working in the field of environmental education and ESD for nearly twenty years. She has been working for the Japan Council on Education for Sustainable Development (ESD-J) as the International Programme Coordinator since 2004. She is currently a researcher at the Centre for Global Research, RMIT University, Australia.

Yoko Mochizuki is Head of the Rethinking Curriculum Programme at the UNESCO Mahatma Gandhi Institute of Education for Peace and Sustainable Development in New Delhi, India, which she joined in 2015 from UNESCO Paris.

Routledge Studies in Sustainable Development

This series uniquely brings together original and cutting-edge research on sustainable development. The books in this series tackle difficult and important issues in sustainable development including: values and ethics; sustainability in higher education; climate compatible development; resilience; capitalism and de-growth; sustainable urban development; gender and participation; and well-being.

Drawing on a wide range of disciplines, the series promotes interdisciplinary research for an international readership. The series was recommended in the *Guardian*'s suggested reads on development and the environment.

Implementing Sustainability in Higher Education
Matthias Barth

Emerging Economies and Challenges to Sustainability
Theories, strategies, local realities
Edited by Arve Hansen and Ulrikke Wethal

Environmental Politics in Latin America
Elite dynamics, the left tide and sustainable development
Edited by Benedicte Bull and Mariel Aguilar-Støen

Transformative Sustainable Development
Participation, reflection and change
Kei Otsuki

Theories of Sustainable Development
Edited by Judith C. Enders and Moritz Remig

Transdisciplinary Solutions for Sustainable Development
From planetary management to stewardship
Mark Charlesworth

Measuring Welfare beyond Economics
The genuine progress of Hong Kong and Singapore
Claudio O. Delang and Yi Hang Yu

Sustainability and Wellbeing
Human-Scale Development in Practice
Mònica Guillen-Royo

Universities and Global Human Development
Theoretical and empirical insights for social change
Alejandra Boni and Melanie Walker

Educating for Sustainability in Japan

Fostering resilient communities after the triple disaster

Edited by Jane Singer, Tracey Gannon, Fumiko Noguchi and Yoko Mochizuki

Taylor & Francis Group

LONDON AND NEW YORK

from Routledge

First published 2017 by Routledge

2 Park Square, Milton Park, Abingdon, Oxfordshire OX14 4RN
711 Third Avenue, New York, NY 10017

Routledge is an imprint of the Taylor & Francis Group, an informa business

First issued in paperback 2018

British Library Cataloguing-in-Publication Data
A catalogue record for this book is available from the British Library

Library of Congress Cataloging-in-Publication Data
Names: Singer, Jane (Professor of environmental education), editor.
Title: Education for sustainability in Japan : resilience to disasters for
    sustainable communities / Jane Singer, Tracey Gannon, Fumiko
    Noguchi, and Yoko Mochizuki.
Description: Abingdon, Oxon ; New York, NY : Routledge, 2017.
Identifiers: LCCN 2016020499| ISBN 9781138885233 (hbk) |
    ISBN 9781315715582 (ebk)
Subjects: LCSH: Sustainable development—Study and teaching—Japan. |
    Community education—Japan. | Environmental education—Japan. |
    Education—Environmental aspects—Japan. | Disasters—Social
    aspects—Japan.
Classification: LCC HC465.E5 E39 2017 | DDC 338.952/07071—dc23
LC record available at https://lccn.loc.gov/2016020499

ISBN: 978-1-138-88523-3 (hbk)
ISBN: 978-1-138-61517-5 (pbk)

Typeset in Times New Roman
by Swales & Willis Ltd, Exeter, Devon, UK

Contents

Figures

Tables

Contributors

Katsue Fukamachi is an associate professor at the Graduate School of Global Environmental Studies, Kyoto University. Her research topics include determining key factors and changes in the relationship between people and nature in *satoyama* landscapes, and project proposals for the conservation and productive use of characteristic cultural landscapes.

Shinobu Goto is an associate professor at the Graduate School of Symbiotic Systems Sciences, Fukushima University, with a specialism in environmental planning. He has written several books for public education on the issue of nuclear power and radiation, taking a critical viewpoint in the wake of the Fukushima nuclear accident.

Makoto Hatakeyama is the vice-director of the non-profit organisation *Mori wa Umi no Koibito* (The Forest is the Lover of the Sea), established in 2009 in Kesennuma, Tohoku. Since narrowly surviving the Great East Japan Earthquake and tsunami of March 2011, he has worked to achieve ecologically sustainable post-disaster community development.

Tsubasa Iwabuchi is a programme officer at BirdLife International Tokyo, responsible for developing an evaluation tool for biodiversity and ecosystem services. Before joining BirdLife in 2015, he was an assistant professor of Toyo University, where he was involved in assessing the ecological impact of the Great East Japan Earthquake.

Tadashi Izumitani is a teacher at Kindai University Senior and Junior High School. He is researching English education, second language acquisition and education for sustainable development (ESD). In the area of ESD, his focus is on international understanding.

Binxian Ji is a PhD student at the Graduate School of Global Environmental Studies, Kyoto University. Her research interests include rural revitalisation activities for sustainable development, the utilisation of *satoyama* and *satoumi* and rural landscapes. Her recent topics include resource utilisation and land use.

Toshiya Kodama is a professor at the School of Life and Environmental Science, Azabu University. His recent publications in the field of ESD include 'A study of capacity development through ESD practice in schools' (in Japanese) in *Kankyou Kyouiku* (Environmental Education) 2015.

Benjamin McLellan is an associate professor in the Graduate School of Energy Science at Kyoto University. He has more than 10 years' experience in research relating to the sustainability of the mineral and energy sectors. His current research examines the potential for resource limitations on clean energy technologies – the minerals-energy nexus.

Koichi Nagashima is an architect and urban designer and an honorary member of the Japan Institute of Architects. He headed the Union of International Architects' work programme, Architecture of the Future, from 1996 to 1999. He is currently a member of the Committee for a New Comprehensive Plan for Zushi.

Yoshiyuki Nagata is a professor at the University of the Sacred Heart, Tokyo. He has been a member of UNESCO's Monitoring and Evaluation Expert Group for the past decade. His research focuses on ESD and alternative education and his recent work includes *Alternative Education: Global Perspective Relevant to the Asia/Pacific Region*, published by Springer.

Shizuo Nakazawa is a professor at Nara University of Education. His research focuses on ESD and social studies education. He coordinates ESD lessons and programmes for schools, designed to raise awareness of the issues involved in working towards a sustainable society.

Sarajean Rossitto has worked with non-profit NGOs in Japan for more than 20 years, facilitating workshops and programmes aimed at developing knowledge, skills and organisational capacity. She has served as the Tokyo representative for a number of organisations and teaches about NGOs at Sophia University, Tokyo, and Temple University, Japan Campus.

Aiko Sakurai is an associate professor at the International Research Institute of Disaster Science, Tohoku University. She has worked in international educational development in Yemen and Vietnam and has conducted research on education recovery and disaster education in Japan and other Asian countries since the 2011 Great East Japan Earthquake.

Toyoshi Sasaki is the founder and chief representative of Kurikoma Kogen Nature School in Miyagi prefecture. He established the school in 1996 to provide outdoor education and environmental education for children and young people. He received a PhD in education from Miyagi University in 2015.

Rajib Shaw is a former professor at the Graduate School of Global Environmental Studies, Kyoto University. He is currently the chair of the United Nations Asia Regional Task Force for Urban Risk Reduction, and the president of the Asian University Network of Environment and Disaster Management.

Takako Takano is a professor in sustainability studies at Waseda University, Tokyo. She also chairs an educational charity, which provides sustainability education programmes to a wide range of people in and outside Japan, and serves on the committees of a number of governmental and non-governmental organisations linked to environmental policies and outdoor and environmental education.

Noriko Takemoto is a visiting professor and senior business adviser at Tohoku University Ecosystem Adaptability Centre. After setting up her own IT education company, she joined Catalog House Ltd as a director before accepting a professorial post in 2008. She now works with business, government and NGOs on economic sustainability.

Miki Yoshizumi is an associate professor at the Educational Unit for Studies on the Connectivity of Hills, Humans and Oceans, Kyoto University. She received a PhD in global environmental studies from Kyoto University in 2006. She conducts research on sustainable communities and ESD in Japan and Vietnam.

Yi Zhou is a master's student at the Graduate School of Global Environmental Studies, Kyoto University. Her research interests are environmental education, ESD and pro-sustainable awareness and behaviour. She received a joint bachelor's degree from the Jilin Huaqiao Foreign Language Institute in China and Hokuriku University in Japan.

Editors

Tracey Gannon is a programme-specific associate professor in environmental education at the Graduate School of Global Environmental Studies (GSGES), Kyoto University. She is also the international adviser on a Japanese government-sponsored sustainability education project for 15- to 18-year-olds at Shiga Prefectural Moriyama High School. She joined GSGES in 2003 to develop *Sansai: an Environmental Journal for the Global Community* and later founded the *Sansai* online newsletter and a research unit for GSGES students majoring in environmental communication. Gannon also led the Kyoto University Tertiary Education for Sustainable Development Initiative from April 2011 to December 2014. Dividing her time between Japan and the UK, she combines freelance editorial work and sustainability teaching with ongoing research into eco criticism, environmental film and eco literacy.

Yoko Mochizuki has been the head of the Rethinking Curriculum Programme at the UNESCO Mahatma Gandhi Institute of Education for Peace and Sustainable Development in New Delhi, India, since 2015. She has been engaged in the global implementation of ESD since the beginning of the United Nations Decade of ESD, first as an ESD specialist at the United Nations University-Institute of Advanced Studies and then as a programme specialist in the Section of ESD at UNESCO Paris. She has a PhD in comparative and international education with a disciplinary specialisation in sociology from the Graduate School of Arts and Sciences of Columbia University, New York.

Fumiko Noguchi has more than 20 years' practical experience in non-formal and informal environmental education, education for sustainability and ESD for local communities. She specialises in working with socially marginalised people, focusing her research on the critical role played by non-governmental organisations (NGOs). Noguchi worked as an international programme coordinator for the Japan Council on ESD throughout the UN Decade of ESD. As well as facilitating workshops and seminars, she has been involved in networking Asian NGOs, conducting case studies and providing policy advocacy to the Japanese government and international communities. She is currently a researcher at the Centre for Global Research, RMIT University, Australia.

Jane Singer is an associate professor at the Graduate School of Global Environmental Studies, Kyoto University. She has a master's degree in international affairs, specialising in economic and political development, from the School of International and Public Affairs, Columbia University, New York, and a PhD in environmental studies from Kyoto University, focusing on development-forced displacement. Her principal research focus is migration and displacement, primarily in Southeast Asia. She also conducts research on campus sustainability and tertiary education for sustainability. A long-term resident of Japan, Singer has three decades of professional experience as a journalist and editor of newspapers, journals and magazines.

Introduction

Top-down and bottom-up ESD – divergence and convergence of Japanese ESD discourses and practices

Yoko Mochizuki

> Japan, a country poor in natural resources, has grown to be what it is today on the strength of its human resources. It has attached paramount importance to education as the basis of development.
>
> My government, together with Japanese non-governmental organisations, has proposed that the United Nations declare a Decade of Education for Sustainable Development . . .
>
> In the process of achieving economic growth, Japan experienced a period of serious pollution which caused ill health and even the loss of lives . . . The greatest contribution we can make to the realisation of sustainable development is to share the lessons we have learned so that our friends will not repeat the grim experience.
>
> Excerpts from a speech made by the then Prime Minister of Japan, Junichiro Koizumi, at the World Summit on Sustainable Development, 2 September 2002, Johannesburg, South Africa (Ministry of Foreign Affairs Japan 2012)

In 2002, the United Nations (UN) General Assembly adopted a resolution to declare a UN Decade of Education for Sustainable Development (DESD) from 2005 to 2014, acting on a Japanese government proposal made in partnership with Japanese non-governmental organisations (NGOs). Throughout the DESD, the Japanese government contributed to the global implementation of education for sustainable development (ESD) through its significant financial contribution to the lead agency of the DESD – the UN Educational, Scientific and Cultural Organisation (UNESCO) – and to the UN University (UNU) headquartered in Tokyo, which, in 2003, established an ESD programme with funding support from the Ministry of the Environment, Japan. There is a long-standing debate on the definition of ESD, but UNESCO defines it broadly as education that 'empowers learners to take informed decisions and responsible actions for environmental integrity, economic viability and a just society, for present and future generations, while respecting cultural diversity' (UNESCO 2014, 12) and explicitly acknowledges that ESD is 'intended to encompass all activities that are in line with the [ESD] principles irrespective of whether they themselves use the term ESD or – depending on their history, cultural context or specific priority areas – environmental education, sustainability education, global education, development education, or other' (UNESCO 2013, Annex I, 2).

Redeeming the original intent of the DESD

The DESD came to a close in 2014 and the world embarked on a new set of Sustainable Development Goals (SDGs) in 2015. The SDGs, comprising 17 goals and 169 targets formally adopted by heads of state, include in Target 4.7 'education for sustainable development and sustainable lifestyles, human rights, gender equality, promotion of a culture of peace and non-violence, global citizenship and appreciation of cultural diversity and of culture's contribution to sustainable development' as a means to equip all learners with knowledge and skills to promote sustainable development by the target year of 2030 (UN 2015). This speaks to the international recognition of the importance of values-based and transformational education in enabling a global transition to sustainability. At this historical juncture, a closer look at ESD in Japan offers an opportunity to shed light on the value and relevance of ESD in the context of the ongoing reconfiguration of relations between the state and civil society and accelerating demographic, geo-political, technological and environmental change and associated risks – including natural and man-made disasters.

ESD's enshrinement as an SDG target suggests the DESD was a success in laying the foundation for ESD implementation on a wider scale in the post-2015 global development agenda. If the purpose of the DESD for Japan was to share lessons learned from Japan's past 'mistakes' in prioritising economic growth at the expense of environmental sustainability and human wellbeing, however, the DESD has singularly failed to fulfil its original intent. This book can be understood as an attempt to fulfil, albeit quite modestly, the original purpose of the DESD as envisioned by the Japanese state and NGOs by introducing the diverse practices of what is termed ESD in Japan. We also discuss the value and relevance of school-based and community-based approaches to ESD in addressing concerns of the twenty-first century – ranging from post-disaster recovery and reconstruction, disaster risk reduction and nuclear power generation to environmental conservation, community revitalisation and civic participation. The case of Japan is particularly informative given the '3.11 triple disaster' – the Great East Japan Earthquake and Tsunami and Fukushima nuclear accident that struck the country on 11 March 2011.

The structure of the book

The volume starts with an outline of the origins and development of ESD in Japan, followed by an overview of the contributed chapters. Part I of this volume then looks at ESD in the context of 'formal education', defined as an institutionalised system spanning early childhood to higher education. Primary and secondary schooling constitutes an important part of formal education and is the main focus. Part II, on the other hand, examines ESD in 'non-formal' and 'informal' learning contexts.

Non-formal education can be defined here as an organised learning activity carried out by NGOs and other groups outside the framework of the school system, while informal learning refers to unstructured learning that takes place in the family, at work, through peer interactions, the media, volunteering and any other social activities. Chapters in Part II focus on community-based education and sustainability initiatives, including recovery and revitalisation efforts by schools, NGOs and residents in the Tohoku region following the 3.11 triple disaster.

As a global education initiative coordinated by UNESCO, ESD is a global agenda to be translated and articulated in local – both national and sub-national – terms and to be implemented in formal and non-formal education at all levels. From this perspective, many ESD efforts aim to mainstream, embed or integrate ESD into the education policy and curriculum, as discussed in chapters in Part I. At the same time, as a transformative proposal for rethinking the purpose of education towards a more sustainable and just society, ESD can provoke a questioning of the role of education in modernisation (which involves westernisation in non-western societies) or 'development' that is often neither equitable nor sustainable. In other words, in its more radical form, ESD involves the critical questioning of the role that education has played in 'distributing opportunity' and 'fostering faith in the vaguely defined ideals of "modernity" and "progress" that underpin the nation-building project'(Kumar and Vickers 2015, 1). Chapters in Part II illustrate various efforts to empower civil society, either directly or indirectly countering the project of self-strengthening nation-building and, in some cases, implicitly critiquing the education system's failure to foster active citizenship and sustainable local communities.

Understanding the role of the Japanese state in promoting ESD

Most academic and policy writing on ESD refers to the global milestones of sustainable development – such as the 1987 report of the World Commission on Environment and Sustainable Development (commonly known as the Brundtland Report) or Agenda 21, established at the 1992 UN Conference on Environment and Development (the 'Earth Summit') as a global blueprint for sustainability – and introduces ESD as an externally induced reform for achieving a sustainable future. Rather than treating ESD as something new or exogenous, this chapter attempts to make bridges between Japanese endogenous social change movements and current ESD discourses and practices. Before doing so, this chapter considers the role the Japanese government played in putting sustainable development and ESD on the global agenda and its implications for the promotion of sustainable development in the domestic context.

Progressive Japanese state?

The report of the World Commission on Environment and Sustainable Development (1987), *Our Common Future*, provided the well known definition of sustainable development as 'development that meets the needs of the present without compromising the ability of the future generations to meet their own needs' (43). Whereas it is generally known among Japanese ESD circles that the DESD was a Japanese proposal, it is a little known fact that the Brundtland Commission was also a Japanese proposal and the commission's work was supported financially by Japan covering half of its total cost of US$6m (with the rest provided by Canada, Denmark, Finland, the Netherlands, Norway, Sweden and Switzerland) (Hashimoto 2007). Saburo Okita, former minister of foreign affairs and the Japanese member of the Brundtland Commission, regarded supporting the commission as Japan's responsibility because it was a country that had achieved economic prosperity. He also saw it as an opportunity for the Japanese state to demonstrate its 'dignity' vis-à-vis its commitment to environmental issues (Ibid.). Ironically, Japan was at the height of the bubble economy when the Brundtland report came out in 1987 and it was understood by Japanese politicians as an effort to address global environmental problems, such as destruction of rain forests and desertification, far from home rather than encourage reflections on unsustainable development in the country (Hara 2007).

It is obvious from this recounting that there is a gap between the Japanese state's commitment to progressive initiatives and worthy causes – demonstrated through its generous financial support extended through the UN mechanisms – and what it promotes domestically. It follows that the Japanese government's being the most important international sponsor of the DESD does not automatically translate into exemplary ESD policy and practice in Japan. Given that DESD was a joint proposal by the Japanese government and NGOs, ESD has been extensively discussed by diverse stakeholder groups and various initiatives have been taken to promote ESD in Japan. Although the phrase 'top-down' often carries negative connotations for many, certain top-down measures are essential to create an enabling environment for implementing a new cross-cutting initiative such as ESD in the formal education sector. The intention of this book is not to paint a dichotomous picture of ESD as being either top-down or bottom-up but to present multifaceted Japanese efforts to promote formal and non-formal ESD.

Monolithic Japanese state?

As in the cases of 'sustainable development' and ESD, Japan has been a major sponsor of 'human security' through its financial contribution to the UN, but it has largely treated it as irrelevant to the domestic context (Bacon and Hobson 2015). This is to be expected, perhaps, because human security is associated with development assistance and promoted by the Ministry of Foreign Affairs and the Japan International Cooperation Agency (JICA). The 3.11 triple disaster, however, has revealed the various forms of 'human insecurity' at home – some created but many merely exacerbated by the disaster – encouraging a group of human security scholars to demonstrate the applicability of the concept of human security in addressing vulnerabilities faced by contemporary Japanese society (Bacon and Hobson 2015). In a similar way, this volume aims to demonstrate the significance of ESD in addressing patterns of unsustainability and vulnerability in Japan five years after 3.11. It is important to note here that the Japanese government is far from monolithic, and policy incoherence between disaster recovery projects and ESD approaches has been one of the major obstacles in enabling a sustainable recovery process (see Postscript).

Power relationships within the Japanese government affect the implementation of ESD both domestically and internationally. The Ministry of Education, Culture, Sports, Science and Technology (MEXT) has promoted formal ESD through measures to integrate ESD into the education policy and curriculum in Japan as well as through financial contributions to UNESCO, while the Ministry of the Environment has promoted community-based ESD through non-formal ESD measures and financial contributions to the UNU. Although these voluntary financial contributions to UNESCO and UNU, which amounted to several million dollars annually over the DESD, are significant, they are miniscule compared to Japan's Official Development Assistance (ODA) disbursement, which amounts to several billion dollars per year. Apart from a few exceptions, such as a school-based ESD project in Mongolia funded by the Swiss Agency for Development and Cooperation, ESD was rarely implemented in developing countries with bilateral assistance.

During the DESD, ESD implementation's weak association with the preceding global development frameworks of the Millennium Development Goals (MDGs) and Education for All was often seen by ESD advocates as a drawback in promoting ESD as a global agenda. Seen from a different perspective, however, it has also been a blessing. Without being relegated to the field of development assistance, which bifurcates the world into donor and recipient countries, ESD has been promoted as a universal agenda equally relevant to both developed and developing countries. As chapters in this volume show, ESD has resonated deeply with various stakeholders in Japan in their efforts to improve formal education and to create more sustainable local communities, as well as to develop horizontal partnerships on ESD with their counterparts in other countries.

Convergence of Japanese ESD discourses

Partly as a result of the strong ownership of the DESD exercised by the Japanese state, local governments, NGOs, academics and individuals, Japanese ESD is characterised by a mix of predominantly top-down directives coming from the centralised state and varied bottom-up responses. Top-down and bottom-up Japanese ESD discourses converge, however, on their view of ESD as constituting a *machizukuri* or community development process (Mochizuki 2010). As Table 0.1 shows, the importance of community-based approaches to ESD is clearly acknowledged in an official account of 'features of ESD in Japan' (Interministerial Meeting on the UN DESD 2009). Many factors can account for this, including the creation of institutional mechanisms for ESD promotion to be discussed later in this chapter, but there is also a deep-seated sense of crisis about the future of Japan, which underlies this convergence in Japanese ESD discourse. The remainder of this chapter builds the foundation for a better understanding

Table 0.1 Features of ESD in Japan as defined by the Japanese government

Approaches

- Activities addressing participatory, problem-solving learning from the perspective of 'building a better society' have been conducted not only in schools but also in institutions of higher education, social educational facilities, communities, enterprises and other venues even before the start of the UN DESD.
- Efforts are being made to advance this approach in diverse educational fields, including environmental education, human rights and welfare education, peace education and development education, while incorporating environmental, economic and social perspectives.
- These have evolved into *actions for partnerships and integration of ESD that take root in communities and develop into efforts to build sustainable communities by linking the wisdom of traditional lifestyles with natural, industrial and cultural resources and also with the school curriculum.*
- In line with the development of ESD, these activities are increasingly pursued through partnerships involving schools, community centres and other local government bodies, NGOs/NPOs, institutions of higher education, enterprises and others.

Effects

- ESD in school education has led to the cultivation of 'zest for living (vigorously in difficult times)'.
- ESD rooted in local communities is a powerful tool for building and revitalising communities. *It enables residents to discover the qualities of their community, nurtures affection for and pride in the community and raises people's awareness as members of the community.*

Source: Excerpts from the Interministerial Meeting on the UN DESD 2009, 1–2, emphasis added.

of how ESD is deployed, both in the context of Japan's self-strengthening nation-building project (including improving Japan's self-image as a respectable country that upholds the ideals of ESD) and in efforts to reclaim what has been lost in the process of rapid development.

ESD in Japan: origins and development

Japanese ESD discourses and practices encompass a wide continuum of approaches to social change, with top-down conservative approaches that in no way challenge vested interests at one end of the spectrum and bottom-up forms of activism and vibrant voluntary initiatives aimed at active civic engagement at the other. As a first step to unpack the convergence and divergence of these approaches, this section attempts to contexualise Japanese ESD practices in relation to the country's rise to industrial prominence.

The section is divided into three sub-sections. The first traces the seeds of ESD in Japanese endogenous social change movements during the Taisho (1912–26) and Showa (1926–1989) periods. The second briefly summarises the qualitative transformation of environmental education and development education in Japan, influenced by the changes in Japan's international standing as an economic power and a decade of international conferences in the 1990s following the end of the

Cold War. Chapter 36 of Agenda 21 (UN Conference on Environment and Development 1992) is widely considered a foundational ESD text, which recommended that 'environment and development education should deal with the dynamics of both the physical/biological and socio-economic environment and human (which may include spiritual) development, should be integrated in all disciplines, and should employ formal and non-formal methods'. It therefore outlines the evolution of environmental and development education in Japan over three decades since the 1970s to delineate the cultural, political and historical contexts within which ESD has evolved. The objective of the first two sub-sections is to highlight the diversity and richness of Japanese endogenous education movements, which have been largely overlooked in the development of official ESD policy and practice in Japan following the 2002 UN General Assembly resolution on the DESD, as presented in the third sub-section. Many practices that are not explicitly labelled as ESD or recognised as the foundations of ESD are, in fact, deeply relevant to place-based learning for sustainability in the Japanese context. The third sub-section thus highlights a divergence between these locally rooted practices and policy-driven ESD practices in the context of the DESD, in an effort to underscore the need to bridge a gap between the official discourses and practices of ESD.

Japanese endogenous education movements and community-based learning

In a recently published Japanese-language volume on community-based learning (*chiiki-gakushu*) in Japan, Sato (2015) traces its origins to three strands of endogenous educational movements: (1) the grassroots school reform movement that had its roots in a pre-World War II learning movement by way of recording notes on everyday life (*seikatsu-tsuzurikata-undo*); (2) adult education movements spread in the 1950s in the form of small-group discussions and collaborative learning at *kominkan* (community learning centres) by local women's and young men's associations to improve the quality of life and enhance local economic and cultural activities; and (3) environmental education movements to combat environmental pollution for social and ecological justice. Although the current context of 'super ageing' (Muramatsu and Akiyama 2011) in Japanese society makes a sharp contrast to that of many developing countries, where the youth constitute the majority of the populations, these endogenous education movements find echoes today in place-based learning for endogenous development, rural empowerment, or for ecological and social justice in other parts of the world, especially in the global south, and therefore merit discussion here.

Strand 1 – grassroots school reform movement

The endogenous education reform movement in the 1950s aimed to give students the capabilities to improve and support their own villages, rather than endow them with academic prowess that would encourage them to leave their villages behind to pursue higher education and, subsequently, a better life in a city. This movement saw its origin in a writing movement, which emerged in the early twentieth century and was taken up by young teachers in Tohoku and developed into the School Education for the North Movement (*hopposei-kyoiku-undo*) to empower impoverished rural villages in the 1930s (Suzuki 2014; Miyazaki 2015). Here, loss of pride in one's own local community was understood to be a corollary of the modernist marginalisation of rural villages as places of no hope, to be abandoned by those who achieve success at school.

The School Education for the North Movement is particularly relevant to this volume because of its focus on Tohoku. The current volume was conceived as a book addressing education for sustainability in Japan after the 3.11 triple disaster, which struck Tohoku most severely and exposed pre-existing patterns of unsustainability and vulnerability in Japan. While the School Education for the North Movement was repressed by the state during World War II, it was revived in the 1950s as discussed above and developed into a grassroots adult learning movement called the Farmers' College Movement (*nomin-daigaku-undo*) in the 1970s. Jin Makabe, a farmer, poet and leader of the Farmers' College Movement in Yamagata prefecture, redefined Tohoku – which had been marginalised as *henkyo* (a periphery) from a developmentalist perspective – as a *senshinchi* (advanced region) that had innovated technology and culture to overcome constraints imposed by its harsh natural conditions (Makabe 1975 as cited in Miyazaki 2015, 40–41). This redefinition resonates deeply with current community development efforts linked with ESD, which aim to restore appreciation for the rich natural and cultural resources of rural communities suffering from depopulation and ageing (see, for example, Chapters 9, 13 and 15 in this volume). These movements provided a fundamental critique of the role of modern schooling in uprooting and alienating the 'educated' from their home (*furusato*) and, at the same time, depriving those who remain in rural villages of self-respect and pride.

Strand 2 – Japanese social education practices

The Social Education Law, instituted in Japan in 1949 as part of the post-World War II education reforms under the US occupation, has promoted non-formal learning through *kominkan*. Locally rooted social education flourished in the post-war years, with local resident groups discussing and reflecting on ways to modernise and democratise feudalistic villages, but it declined quickly as the Japanese economy entered the high-growth period and outmigration of young people from rural villages to cities became the norm (Sato 2015).

Today, the city of Okayama is one of the few Japanese municipalities where *kominkan* activities still flourish. Countering the trend of the diminishing role of the city government in social education, Okayama city subsidises the costs of *kominkan* courses on priority topics, including *machizukuri* for living together in harmony. Okayama City Government's role in fortifying *kominkan* against the overall trend of delocalisation and commodification is important to understanding why Okayama was selected to host the stakeholder meetings for the 2014 World Conference on ESD – the DESD having provided an impetus for redefining and reorienting existing community-based learning activities in Okayama from an ESD perspective. In this sense, Japanese social education traditions laid the foundations for developing a model of locally rooted ESD promotion using *kominkan* in Okayama (Okayama ESD Promotion Commission and UNESCO Chair at Okayama University 2013; also see Chapter 8 in this volume).

Strand 3 – birth of endogenous environmental education in Japan

During Japan's rapid industrialisation from the late nineteenth century through to the mid-twentieth century, the desire to 'catch up' with the west prompted a disregard for environmental costs and a lack of regulatory safeguards. A series of industrial disasters came to be recognised as social problems in the late 1960s, including cadmium poisoning that caused a painful bone condition called *itai-itai* disease, life-threatening smog from petroleum and crude oil refineries in Yokkaichi, and two separate releases of methyl mercury into waterways in Kumamoto and Niigata prefectures linked to *minamata* disease, a disfiguring, often congenital, neurological condition. These four events came to be known as the major environmental scandals of the twentieth century in Japan (Hasegawa 2004).

Amid and following the high-growth period of the Japanese economy (1954–1973), Japan saw a rise in citizens' movements objecting to environmental pollution and development policies and projects. These movements mobilised local residents, including school teachers, who were both actual and potential victims of pollution and advocated for their own and others' rights to life and a healthy environment. They employed various methods, including field surveys (to assess the harmful effects of environmental pollution) and co-learning among teachers, experts, students and local residents. This led to an endogenous form of environmental education – known as *kogai kyoiku* or pollution education – which contributed to social movements to protect citizens from various forms of environmental harms and subsequent costs to human wellbeing. In the late 1960s, highly localised pollution education came to be incorporated voluntarily into the school curriculum by progressive teachers in Yokkaichi, Kawasaki, Minamata and other places (Ando 2015, 55).[1] The next section of this chapter probes why and how this endogenous form of environmental education came to be largely replaced by a less radical one in the 1980s.

Evolution of environmental education and development education in Japan

This section traces the evolution, since the 1970s, of environmental education and development education in Japan in response to domestic and international events, issues and trends, in order to lay the foundation for understanding the social and political contexts within which Japanese ESD policy transpired.

From kogai-kyoiku *to* kankyo-kyoiku

Current Japanese environmental policy and regulations are a direct consequence of the number of environmental disasters of the 1950s and 1960s described above. After years of corporate denial and government inaction, an accumulation of scientific evidence connecting chemical emissions to disease outbreaks – plus a growing willingness of victims to file lawsuits against the companies involved – led to the enactment of the first national regulations that prioritised human health over economic development in the 1970s.

The 1970s were an important period in which environmental issues moved higher on the national and international agenda. In 1971, the Environmental Agency was created in Japan. This preceded the 1972 UN Conference on the Human Environment in Stockholm, which called for environmental education to be used as a means to address environmental problems in its Recommendation 96. In 1975, this recommendation was addressed at the International Environmental Workshop in Belgrade, Yugoslavia, organised by UNESCO and the UN Environment Programme, which adopted a global framework for environmental education known as the Belgrade Charter. In the mid-1970s, there were already tensions between those who advocated *kogai-kyoiku,* based on the experience of fighting pollution-caused diseases, and those who called for a more apolitical form of environmental learning geared towards fostering pro-environmental behaviour and nature-based learning (Ando 2015). Internationally, the official launch of environmental education is attributed to the world's first intergovernmental conference on Environmental Education in Tbilisi, Georgia (then USSR) in 1977. By the mid-1980s, the term *kankyo-kyoiku*, which had been used largely as jargon among experts until then, came to be popularised among the Japanese public, reflecting the emergence of diverse civil society organisations promoting nature-based learning under the banner of *kankyo-kyoiku* (Ando 2015).

Ando (2015) observes three trends of Japanese environmental education after pollution education came to be largely replaced by environmental education in the 1980s. First, a shift in the main promoters of environmental education from resident protest groups against environmental destruction to environmental NGOs meant an increase in practices undertaken in partnership with the public and private sectors. Whereas, formerly, the main promoters of pollution education were teachers who had been affected by pollution themselves and seen it affect their students, the new promoters of environmental education were mainly actors outside the formal education sector. Second, environmental education emphasises restoring human–nature relationships through experiential learning, while pollution education aimed to develop critical awareness of – and counter – environmental destruction that directly affected the wellbeing of local populations. Third, environmental education includes global environmental issues, while pollution education focused on domestic environmental disasters. Observing the trend of the institutionalisation and depoliticisation of environmental education, Ando calls for a rethinking of *kankyo-kyoiku* as revitalising *kogai-kyoiku* as 'education for environmental justice' (68–69). This call for the politicisation and radicalisation of environmental education resonates with Huckle and Wals' (2015) call for 'global education for sustainability citizenship' which emphasises the exploration of 'structural causes' of social and environmental injustice and 'reformist and radical solutions' (495).

Development education in Japan

In contrast to environmental education in Japan, which has both endogenous and exogenous origins, development education is an imported concept. Internationally, the concept built on early efforts to raise awareness of the so-called third world by NGOs based in Europe and North America in the 1960s, often accompanied by fundraising campaigns. The concept came to take shape in the 1970s in the form of learning activities to promote the understanding of poverty, hunger and other deprivations as the problems of 'underdevelopment' in developing countries in the south, and to encourage residents in the industrialised nations in the north to help solve these problems (Tanaka 2005). In Japan, the first symposium on development education was held in 1979 in Tokyo, co-organised by the UN Information Centre, the UNU and UNICEF's Tokyo office. Following this symposium, developmental NGOs, youth organisations and UN-related associations started organising monthly meetings to study development education, leading to the establishment of the Development Education Council of Japan (DECJ) in 1982.

In the 1980s, development education in Japan came to address not only north–south inequality and the structural and root causes of development issues but also domestic issues regarding multiculturalism and international understanding in the wake of an influx of foreign workers. A turning point in Japanese development education was 1989 – the year the Berlin Wall came down – when Japan's Official Development Assistance (ODA) disbursement reached US$9bn, making Japan the world's largest bilateral donor (Kamibeppu 2002, 57). In the same year, the Courses of Study (national guidelines for teaching revised approximately every ten years) were revised to include environmental education and education for international understanding in the national curriculum, drawing school teachers' attention to them. Around 1990, development issues gained momentum in the country, raising the profile of development education (Tanaka 2009). Although, with the exception of 1990, Japan maintained its status as the largest bilateral donor between 1989 and 2000, in 1991 the country entered the 'lost decade' when the Japanese asset price bubble burst.

Partly triggered by the end of the Cold War, a series of international and UN conferences, including the 1992 Earth Summit, was organised between 1990 and 1996. These highlighted the interconnected nature of global challenges and forged an increasing international consensus on the importance of environmental sustainability, poverty eradication and human rights promotion.[2] At the same time, the negative impact of accelerating globalisation became evident, with the 1997 Asian financial crisis raising serious concerns about a finance-led economic model. Notions of 'participatory development' (OECD-DAC 1989) and 'human development' (UN Development Programme (UNDP) 1990) entered the mainstream international development discourse, profoundly resonating with the notion of sustainable development. In 1996, the Human Development Report warned against ruthless and futureless growth 'where the fruits of economic growth mostly benefit the rich' and 'where the present generation squanders resources needed by future generations' (UNDP 1996, 2).

In 1997, in light of these domestic and international developments, DECJ redefined development education as education that aims to foster individual learners' capacities to understand various development issues, deliberate on desirable forms of development and participate in shaping a more just global society (DEAR 2004, 4, author translation). In 2003, DECJ received legal status as a non-profit organisation (NPO) and changed its name to the Development Education Association and Resource Centre (DEAR). Haruhiko Tanaka (2005), who served as the DEAR representative between 2002 and 2008, has observed in retrospect that Japanese development education has essentially been ESD since development education was redefined in 1997.

In June 2005, DEAR proposed three strategies to promote the DESD: (1) infuse as many substantive contents of ESD as possible into the new Course of Study (which was to be revised in 2008) and promote the Period for Integrated Study (see Chapter 4 in this volume); (2) revise local strategies for Agenda 21 from the perspective of ESD to make them more holistic, to include not only environmental issues but welfare, child-rearing and the concerns of foreign residents; and (3) promote the Asia-Pacific network of ESD. While DEAR's activities have focused mainly on promoting development education in schools and developing pedagogical materials, Tanaka (2005) pointed out the importance of cultivating the knowledge and skills needed to participate in broadly defined public policy, such as *machizukuri*, to upgrade environmental education into ESD in the Japanese context.

Institutionalising ESD: policy-driven ESD in Japan and beyond

Given that Japan was the country that proposed the DESD in Johannesburg in 2002, its government instituted various measures to promote ESD policy and practice, including the establishment of an inter-ministerial platform for ESD implementation, comprising 11 ministries and agencies, and the development of a national action plan (see Table 0.2). Since there are already many accounts of Japanese policy development relevant to national ESD promotion (see, for example, Abe 2009, 2012; Sato and Nakayama 2013; Interministerial Meeting on the UN DESD 2009, 2014), this section focuses mainly on initiatives taken by the Japanese government and Japan-based organisations, such as the UNU, with the purpose of raising the profile of ESD in the context of the DESD.

Table 0.2 Platforms, policies and projects in support of the domestic implementation of DESD in Japan

2003	• The Japan Council on the UN DESD (ESD-J) established
	• The Law for Enhancing Motivation on Environmental Conservation and Promoting Environmental Education enacted
2005	• The Interministerial Meeting on the UN DESD established
2006	• Japan's Action Plan for the UN DESD developed
	• Fundamental Law of Education (*kyoiku kihon ho*) revised to include the principles of sustainable development in its aims and objectives
2007	• The Strategy for an Environmental Nation in the 21st Century (*21 seiki kankyo rikkoku senryaku*) approved by the Cabinet in June 2007
	• The Roundtable Meeting on the UN DESD established, comprising experts, personnel from NPOs, educational institutions and companies/specialists, educational institutions and corporate representatives
2008	• The Basic Promotional Plan for Education (*kyoiku shinko kihon keikaku*) formulated, positioning sustainable development as one of the important principles of education in Japan
	• Promotion of ESD by increasing the number of UNESCO ASPnet schools in Japan initiated by MEXT
	• Perspectives for building sustainable society included in the Courses of Study (*gakushu shido yoryo*) for elementary schools and junior high schools in March 2008
2009	• Perspectives for building sustainable society included in the Courses of Study for senior high schools in March
2011	• The Courses of Study revised, incorporating the principle of sustainable development into the curriculum in subjects such as science and social studies (perspectives related to constructing a sustainable society)
	• +ESD Project launched by the Ministry of the Environment to promote the visibility and networking of ESD activities through development of online database
	• Japan's Action Plan for the UN DESD revised

Source: Interministerial Meeting on the UN DESD 2014.

Multi-stakeholder and interdisciplinary platforms on ESD

As a designated lead agency of the DESD, UNESCO (2005) developed an International Implementation Scheme for the DESD. The scheme emphasised the importance of basic education, contributing to the MDGs and the Education for All movement as well as 'building upon the learning from years of environmental, health, peace, economic, human rights, and development education networks around the world that for many years have used innovation to deliver valuable services in difficult situations' (UNESCO 2005, Annex I, 14). As early as June 2003, the Japan Council on the UN DESD (ESD-J) was established as a consortium of NGOs, NPOs and individuals involved in various social issues (ranging from the environment, development, human rights, peace and gender) to build a shared understanding of ESD and implement it in partnership with the government, local authorities, companies and educational institutions (see Chapter 8). As far as the author – who was closely involved in the global implementation of the DESD – is aware, national platforms like ESD-J do not exist in other countries.

Edgar González-Gaudino, a prominent Mexican environmental educator and a member of an international advisory group for the DESD set up by UNESCO, observed in 2005 that 'One *de facto* problem that the implementation of the [DESD] faces is that apparently only we environmental educators have become involved in debating its pros and cons' (González-Gaudino 2005, 244). This was patently not the case in Japan, where not only environmental educators, but also academics and practitioners of development education, education for international understanding, human rights education, peace education, adult education and so on, were discussing ESD. ESD's relevance to transformative education movements beyond environmental education in Japan is evident in the establishment of ESD groups in various academic associations, including the Japanese Society of Environmental Education, the Japan Association for International Education and the Japan Society for the Study of Adult and Community Education.

At a local regional level, the UNU acknowledged six local multi-stakeholder networks – comprising formal and non-formal educational institutions, local governments, businesses, media and NGOs – as Regional Centres of Expertise (RCE) on ESD in Japan: Greater Sendai, Yokohama, Chubu, Hyogo-Kobe, Okayama and Kitakyushu. In March 2006, the Inter-Ministerial Meeting on the UN DESD adopted Japan's Action Plan for the DESD, which identified regional initiatives, with a specific reference to the RCE initiative, as one of its three priority areas along with awareness raising and higher education (Interministerial Meeting on the UN DESD 2006). As of June 2015, 138 local multi-stakeholder networks have been officially acknowledged as RCEs by the UNU across the world (RCE network n.d.).

The two host cities of the 2014 World Conference on ESD, Aichi-Nagoya and Okayama, are members of RCE Chubu and RCE Okayama, respectively. The global RCE initiative is a good example of combining a top-down policy prescription and a bottom-up approach that begins with local concerns (Mochizuki 2013). It is top-down in the sense that the UNU requires local stakeholders to follow its prescription on how best ESD can be promoted at the local level, including involving a local higher education institution in the network. It is at the same time bottom-up in that it is a purely voluntary initiative to promote local action and no funding is provided to operate each RCE. The RCE initiative can also be considered as a successful global example of an ESD recognition and networking scheme, which will be discussed below.

ESD recognition and networking schemes

In 2011, the Ministry of the Environment-Japan launched a '+ESD project'. It promoted the visibility and networking of ESD activities by developing an online database on ESD activities and organising face-to-face meetings between participants in the project. This was partly inspired by a German initiative to designate official projects to the DESD. The German Commission for UNESCO (2011) officially designated more than 1,300 projects as 'Official German Projects of the DESD' (57). As of January 2016, 184 groups and organisations are registered in the +ESD online database (Ministry of the Environment n.d.).

Since 2008, MEXT has supported measures to promote school-based ESD through the UNESCO Associated Schools Network (ASPnet). The number of ASPnet schools in Japan has grown dramatically – from 20 in 2006 to 705 in August 2014 – spreading across 44 of the country's 47 prefectures (Interministerial Meeting on the UN DESD 2014, 7). MEXT further supported the creation of ASPUnivNet, a network of 18 universities to support primary and secondary schools in applying to become ASPnet schools and implementing ESD activities after recognition as such. Japan's highly centralised education system no doubt enabled an exponential increase in the number of ASPnet schools.

ESD promotion at the higher education level is also indirectly supported by MEXT through competitive grants awarded to higher education institutions. These fund activities designed to promote education and research that builds on their unique strengths. Under the Support Programmes for Distinctive University Education – *Tokushoku* GP (Good Practice) – and for Contemporary Educational Needs – *Gendai* GP – 42 higher education institutions received competitive grants to advance their environmental education activities between 2003 and 2009 (Abe 2009, 27). With the recipients of *Tokushoku* and *Gendai* GP grants in ESD-related fields, a network called the Higher Education for Sustainable Development (HESD) Forum was formed, which has held an annual face-to-face meeting since 2007.

In addition to these national schemes, many ESD networks have been convened and coordinated by Japan-based organisations. For example, within the framework of Japan's Strategy for an Environmental Nation in the 21st Century, approved by the Cabinet in 2007, in 2008 the UNU launched ProSPER.Net (Promotion of Sustainability in Postgraduate Education and Research Network), an alliance of leading universities in the Asia-Pacific region. ESD-J contributed to networking NGOs in Asia to advocate for community-based ESD. Through the Asia Good ESD Practice Project between 2006 and 2008, ESD-J worked with six NGOs from six Asian countries to develop 34 case studies (see Chapter 8); these NGOs later came together to form a network called Asian NGO Network on ESD. The Asia-Pacific Cultural Centre for UNESCO has also contributed to creating networks of ESD stakeholders in the Asia-Pacific region, through various activities including the Centre of Excellence Programme. Before the DESD started, the Institute for Global Environmental Strategies, set up in 1998 with support from the Japanese government, took the lead in networking environmental education stakeholders in the Asia-Pacific region under its programme Environment Education for Sustainable Development (Abe *et al.* 2012, 13). These international networking initiatives reflect, at least partially, Japan's desire to establish itself as an international leader in ESD. It is important to note that all these Japan-based organisations, except ESD-J, are funded primarily by the Japanese government.

The relevance of Japanese ESD practices to today and tomorrow

While Japanese scholars tend to critique Japanese ESD policy and practice in light of ESD principles put forward by UNESCO (see, for example, Chapter 4), some European and North American scholars have characterised ESD – as defined and promoted by UNESCO – as policy driven and dismissed it as being complicit with neo-liberalism and globalisation forces (Jickling and Wals 2008; Torres 2009; Selby and Kagawa 2011; Huckle and Wals 2015). The cases presented in this volume, however, clearly demonstrate that ESD has inspired many educators, academics, civic groups and local communities in Japan to challenge the status quo and pursue an alternative path.

What may be particularly distinctive about the promotion of ESD by Japanese actors is that their activities, whether top-down or bottom-up, are often driven by a sense of responsibility – sometimes coupled with a sense of national pride – emanating from the fact that Japan proposed the DESD. The notion that Japanese ESD policy and practice should be exemplary underlies top-down initiatives focused on boosting ESD's visibility as well as biting criticisms of such top-down approaches. Connected to this, even those critics of top-down ESD are often preoccupied with putting ESD higher on the global agenda and increasing its legitimacy and authority. ESD-J, which has advocated for community-based ESD at various international forums – such as the UN Conference on Sustainable Development (Rio+20) in 2012 and the 10th meeting of the Conference of the Parties of the Convention on Biological Diversity (CBD-COP 10) in 2010 – is a case in point. Raising the profile of ESD internationally is an integral part of fulfilling this responsibility as a country that proposed the DESD. Whatever conceptual, financial and operational limitations the DESD had, dismissing it as 'business as usual' (Huckle and Wals 2015) was not a viable option for Japanese stakeholders. While this sense of responsibility and national pride in upholding the ideals of ESD definitely has had the positive effect of making Japanese stakeholders self-accountable for ESD implementation, it has also served to blur important distinctions between the self-strengthening, nation-building project and harnessing the potential of ESD in achieving societal transformation.

Despite its role in supporting the Brundtland Commission (1987), the DESD (2005–2014), CBD-COP 10 (2010) and the Kyoto Protocol, there is no denying that the Japanese government is more or less pursuing conventional 'development' patterns even after experiencing the 3.11 triple disaster. It continues to use its centralised school education system to ensure national strength in the global economy, and there is no shortage of examples of unsustainable development policies and projects that undermine the long-term sustainability of local communities or the country. More than a few cases in this volume are framed in opposition to the central Japanese government policy, exploring ways to improve policy on specific issues such as radiation education (Chapter 6), indigenous rights recovery (Chapter 12) and disaster recovery projects in the post-3.11 context (Postscript) based on grassroots practices. Other chapters provide a fundamental critique of modernisation and developmentalism that have peripheralised rural parts of Japan and contributed to turning the country into a 'super ageing' society (see Chapters 9 and 15 in particular). Ageing and depopulation are, indeed, the biggest sustainability challenges facing Japan and cannot be ignored. One thread that weaves many contributions together is a concern with the loss of vitality of local communities – both rural and urban – and exploration of how ESD can supplement community revitalisation efforts by restoring appreciation for the rich natural and cultural resources of local communities.

Twenty years after the Human Development Report predicted the dangers of unsustainable economic growth, manifestations of 'jobless, ruthless, voiceless, rootless and futureless' (UNDP 1996, 2) growth are becoming too obvious to ignore today. In the frenzy over the post-2015 development agenda, policymakers, politicians, scholars, educators and community activists alike have pursued agendas for change. Japanese ESD discourses and practices encompass a wide range of approaches to social change, from incremental, top-down and mechanistic approaches to various forms of activism that demand ecological and social justice. Going significantly beyond the legacy of *kogai-kyoiku* or pollution education, which underpinned the Japanese proposal for the DESD, the chapters in this volume provide hints as to how the ideals of ESD can contribute to achieving economically viable, democratic, locally rooted and ecologically sound development.

An overview of chapter contributions

Part I: School-based approaches reviews the pioneering efforts of educators to conceptualise and implement ESD throughout the formal education sector in Japan by applying the principles of experiential and place-based education and collaborative teaching and learning in the classroom and, increasingly, the community.

Chapter 1 serves as an introduction to ESD in the formal education sector in Japan. Singer and Nagata explain that environmental education emerged as a response to the environmental pollution scandals during the period of rapid post-World War II industrialisation and later evolved into an ESD approach aimed at providing students with the skills and attitudes to contribute to sustainability. They cite the role played by the Japanese government in helping sponsor the DESD and the ASPnet schools as notable achievements for ESD in the school sector. The chapter concludes with an interview with Nagata, who has conducted sustainability-linked dialogue and projects that link Japanese schools with schools around Asia Pacific.

In Chapter 2, Sakurai and Shaw illustrate the evolution of Japanese disaster education since the 1995 Hanshin-Awaji earthquake up to the recent post-2011 Great East Japan Earthquake and Tsunami under the international framework for disaster risk reduction (DRR). They argue that more links between DRR and ESD are required to promote collaboration between schools and communities for more effective DRR implementation in each school. The chapter concludes with recommendations for enhancing DRR in the education sector globally.

In Chapter 3, Zhou and Singer present a case study of an ESD programme in a Japanese high school. Japan's educational reforms in recent years have facilitated various initiatives that have promoted experience-based learning, sustainability themes and other ESD-linked approaches. One of these, the Super Global High School Programme (SGH), aims to cultivate global leaders who can play active roles internationally. Shiga Prefectural Moriyama High School launched a five-year SGH programme in 2014 with the theme of realising a more sustainable society. The chapter reports the results of research by the authors to assess the effectiveness of the SGH programme at Moriyama High School and its impact on students' pro-sustainable awareness and behaviour.

In Chapter 4, Kodama examines school-based ESD practices with reference to Japanese educational policies and theories of academic ability. The chapter first traces the evolution of ESD practices in schools since 2002 and identifies four trends characterising Japanese ESD, including the use of an ESD calendar to help school teachers embed ESD into all subjects in the curriculum. Kodama discusses how the development of ESD in Japan has been influenced by the Courses of Study national guidelines for teaching, which, in turn, were influenced by the Programme for International Student Assessment standards and the associated 'key competencies' notion of the Organisation for Economic Co-operation and Development (OECD). The chapter concludes by outlining the challenges and prospects for ESD in Japan, particularly in the context of pursuing the inherently conflicting goals of enabling Japanese people to survive and thrive in the global economy while constructing a sustainable society.

In Chapter 5, Nakazawa and Izumitani discuss efforts to link world heritage education and ESD in Nara, Japan's ancient capital. The chapter notes the importance of considering not only the relationship between current and future generations but also current and past generations. Viewing cultural heritage as an important clue to understanding our ancestors' intentions and aspirations to improve societal wellbeing, the chapter introduces ESD practice based on the local cultural heritage of the Great Buddha of *Todaiji* Temple. Introducing a society's familiar cultural heritage as learning material can encourage students to explore the history and significance of a particular region and help them learn to cherish the region's unique attributes. This appreciation of the local region can, in turn, increase the desire to participate in the design of a sustainably developing community.

In Chapter 6, Goto, through the lens of ESD, addresses the fairness and bias of educational materials on nuclear power and radiation distributed to schools by the Japanese government. It presents the results of a content analysis of the Japanese government's supplementary readers on nuclear power and radiation distributed both before and after the Fukushima nuclear accident as evidence of bias in favour of nuclear power. It also introduces the efforts of the Fukushima Teachers' Union and the Fukushima University Research Group to issue original, alternative supplementary readers on radiation. The chapter calls for improved educational materials to equip students with the critical thinking abilities required to engage in the national debate on energy triggered by Fukushima, and empower them to participate in democratic decision making regarding the use of nuclear power.

In Chapter 7, Gannon, Singer and McLellan provide an overview of the design and implementation of a community-based sustainability course piloted at Kyoto University, Japan, and Hue University, Vietnam, in 2013. They introduce a longitudinal evaluative framework, designed to gauge the effectiveness of the course in fostering essential sustainability-linked competencies, such as critical thinking, problem solving and collaborative decision making, and encouraging students to not only think but to act sustainably. Particular attention is paid to the issues that arise from adapting a course created by researchers in a developed country to the needs and priorities of university students and faculty in a developing nation.

Part II: Community-based approaches considers community-based education and sustainability initiatives at the local level, with a special emphasis on the efforts of citizens, NGOs, local government and educators to build sustainable and resilient communities in villages, towns and cities across Japan. It also turns to Japan's troubled north, five years after the events of March 2011, to see if the ideals and practices of ESD can help civil society, corporations and the government in the task of not just putting the country back on its feet but of putting the country onto a sustainable footing.

Chapter 8 serves as an introduction to community-based ESD in Japan. After outlining the role of *kominkan* in promoting community-based learning and the activities of ESD-J and ACCU in promoting non-formal ESD, Noguchi and Sasaki introduce nature schools. The chapter ends with an interview with Sasaki, a founder of the Kurikoma Kougen Nature School, located at the junction of Miyagi, Iwate and Akita prefectures in Tohoku, which began in 1996 as an NGO that provides adventure education through outdoor activities. Sasaki elaborates how the School identified the needs of the local community and redefined its activities to contribute to community empowerment and local sustainable development, through the Iwate-Miyagi Nairiku Earthquake in 2008 and the 3.11 triple disaster in 2011.

Chapters 9 and 10 focus on Kansai – the western region of the main Japanese island of Honshu, which is home to the ancient capitals of Nara and Kyoto. In Chapter 9, Ji and Fukamachi discuss efforts to revitalise Kamiseya, a dying village (*genkai shuraku*) in Kyoto prefecture. Motivated by the common aim of preserving the local *satoyama* (socio-ecological production landscape), both local residents and external stakeholders have taken various measures to establish contemporary systems that can cycle local resources and hand down local culture to future generations.

In Chapter 10, Yoshizumi illustrates multi-stakeholder community environmental learning programmes in Nishinomiya, Hyōgo prefecture. In Nishinomiya, sustainable community initiatives and activities have been implemented since the 1980s through multi-stakeholder community programmes. These ESD programmes aim to raise awareness of local community issues, motivate local actors (including residents and private companies) to take action on issues, and build partnerships of multiple stakeholders to ensure actions are effective. They have been developed through the collaboration of the local government and an innovative NPO that has acted as the main facilitator. The chapter explores how these programmes have been able to promote a more sustainable community.

In Chapter 11, Rossitto introduces the response of Japanese non-profit organisations to the triple disaster. The non-profit sector in Japan has expanded and evolved greatly in the past 20 years, with natural disasters greatly affecting its development. The chapter documents how two organisations, Peace Boat and Greenpeace Japan, employed the post-3.11 momentum to energise the public and open up a new dialogue on energy and disaster policy, food safety and environmental sustainability.

A loss of self-respect and pride in rural communities is an outcome of the modernist marginalisation of rural parts of Japan, as discussed earlier in this introductory chapter. In Chapter 12, Noguchi illustrates a similar case of colonialist marginalisation, in this instance of the Ainu people, who had their livelihood options reduced. Recent efforts to protect and restore their indigenous rights to natural resources can be seen as a radical form of ESD. Noguchi discusses ESD in the context of local community development, providing perspectives from an indigenous Ainu community in Mombetsu, Hokkaido, at the northernmost tip of Japan.

In Chapter 13, Iwabuchi and Takemoto outline a Tohoku Green Renaissance Project, set up after the triple disaster by Tohoku University Environmental Organisation Consortium to help rebuild the area, promote ecosystem adaptability and move towards a sustainable society. The chapter describes project activities aimed at green rebuilding or simultaneously restoring biodiversity and ecosystem services and people's livelihoods to benefit farming, fishing and other major industries in Tohoku. The chapter introduces various ESD efforts undertaken in partnership with NPOs, industries, local and national governments, civic groups and academics.

In Chapter 14, Nagashima discusses citizen participation in *machizukuri* (community building) in Zushi city, not far from the US Naval Base in Yokosuka in Kanagawa prefecture. This is the only chapter that focuses on the Greater Tokyo area. The chapter traces the evolution of *machizukuri* efforts in Zushi over the course of 35 years. They started life as Japan's first major citizens' movement to protect greenery and urban landscape in 1982 and developed into citizen participation in city policy making on *machizukuri*. Based on the case of Zushi, Nagashima points out the importance of articulating and enhancing the identity and meaning of a place through a participatory process to realise the sustainable development of a community both psychologically and physically.

The final two chapters look at sustainable community development in the Tohoku region from a post-tsunami perspective. Chapter 15 focuses on a renowned rice-producing area in Niigata and the Postscript considers Kesennuma, famous for its fishing and fish processing industries.

In Chapter 15, Takano introduces place-based education by the NGO Ecoplus, designed to revitalise rural communities in Niigata prefecture. The chapter provides an overview of the problems faced by rural communities and gives a detailed account of the Tappo Minami Uonuma School of Life and the Environment. This project explores and promotes the educational values of rural communities by bringing local residents and visiting city dwellers together to participate in various farming and village activities.

In the Postscript, Mochizuki presents the personal reflections of a 2011 tsunami survivor, Makoto Hatakeyama from Kesennuma, Miyagi prefecture, an oyster farmer and activist for ecologically integrated natural resource management. Mochizuki then considers the implications for the future of ESD in Japan. Although Japan is an industrialised nation that is small in size, it is a country of abundant forests and extensive coastal ocean. As the Japanese economy grew, rich connections between humans, forests, rivers and oceans were severed in many regions. Hatakeyama advocates the need for a sustainable recovery process to restore these connections and reflects on the role of education in such a process. The volume concludes by connecting the dots and confirming the relevance of ESD in shaping more sustainable societies in Japan and beyond.

Notes

1 In Fukushima prefecture, junior high school teachers started organising a study group to thwart the construction of the Fukushima Daini ('number two') nuclear power plant in 1968 and later incorporated learning activities for a community with a nuclear power plant in *sangyo kogai gakushu* (industrial pollution learning) in the social studies curriculum (Ando 2015, 55).
2 These conferences include the World Conference on Education for All (Jomtien 1990), the UN Conference on Environment and Development (Rio de Janeiro 1992), the World Human Rights Conference (Vienna 1993), the Intergovernmental Conference on Population and Development (Cairo 1994), the World Summit for Social Development (Copenhagen 1995), the Fourth UN Women's World Conference (Beijing 1995) and the UN Conference on Human Dwellings (Istanbul 1996).

References

Abe, O. 2009. *Jizokukano na kaihatsu no tame no kyoiku ESD no genjo to kadai* (Current status and perspectives of ESD). *Kankyo Kyoiku* (Environmental Education) 19 (2), 21–30.

Abe, O. 2012. *Nippon – ESD no genjo to kadai* (Japan – the current state and challenges of ESD), in Abe, O. and Tanaka, H. (eds) *Asia-taiheiyo chiiki no ESD: 'Jizokukano na kaihatsu no tame no kyoiku' no shintenkai* (ESD in the Asia-Pacific region: new developments of education for sustainable development). Tokyo, Japan: Akashi Shoten, 65–87.

Abe, O., Tanaka, H. and Natori, Y. 2012. *Asia-taiheyo chiiki no ESD network: Zadankai* (ESD networks in the Asia-Pacific region: roundtable talk), in Abe, O. and Tanaka, H. (eds) *Asia-taiheiyo chiiki no ESD: 'Jizokukano na kaihatsu no tame no kyoiku' no shintenkai* (ESD in the Asia-Pacific region: new developments of education for sustainable development). Tokyo, Japan: Akashi Shoten, 11–62.

Ando, T. 2015. *Kogai kyoiku kara kankyo kyoiku he saikou* (Rethinking a shift from pollution education to environmental education), in Sato, K. (ed.) *Chiiki-gakushu no sozo: Chiiki saisei e no manabi wo hiraku* (Dynamics of community-based learning for social revitalisation). Tokyo, Japan: University of Tokyo Press, 51–74.

Bacon, P. and Hobson, C. 2014. *Human security and Japan's triple disaster: responding to the 2011 earthquake, tsunami and Fukushima nuclear crisis*. London, UK and New York, US: Routledge.

Development Education Association and Resource Centre (DEAR) 2004. *Kaihatsu kyoikutte naani?* (What is development education?). Tokyo, Japan: DEAR.

German Commission for UNESCO 2011. UN Decade of Education for Sustainable Development 2005–2014: National Action Plan for Germany (www.bne-portal.de/fileadmin/unesco/de/Downloads/Dekade_Publikationen_national/Nationaler_Aktionsplan_2011_engl.pdf). Accessed 5 March 2016.

González-Gaudiano, E. 2005. Education for sustainable development: configuration and meaning. *Policy Futures in Education* 3 (3), 243–250.

Hara, T. 2007. *Bubble-keizai no sanaka de tadashiku rikai sarenakatta Brundtland Hokoku* (Message of the Brundtland Report did not get across in Japan in the midst of the bubble economy). *Gakusai* (Interdisciplinarity) 20 (/www.isr.or.jp/gakusai/20/). Accessed 15 February 2016.

Hasegawa, K. 2004. *Constructing civil society in Japan: voices of environmental movements.* Melbourne, Australia: Trans Pacific Press.

Hashimoto, Z. 2007. *Brundtland-Iinkai to Nippon iin Okita Saburo sensei: Iinkai set-suritsu no keii nado* (Four years with the Brundtland Commission and its Japanese member Mr Saburo Okita: background of establishing the commission). *Gakusai* (Interdisciplinarity) 20 (www.isr.or.jp/gakusai/20/). Accessed 15 February 2016.

Huckle, J. and Wals, A. E. J. 2015. The UN Decade of Education for Sustainable Development: business as usual in the end. *Environmental Education Research* 21(3), 491–505.

Interministerial Meeting on the UN DESD 2006 (Revised 2011). *Waga kuni ni okeru kokuren jizokukano na kaihatsu no tame no kyoiku no junen jissi keikaku* (Japan's Action Plan for the UNDESD), Kokuren jizokukano na kaihatsu no tame no kyoiku no junen kankei shocho renraku kaigi (Interministerial Meeting on the UNDESD), 1–24. (www.cas.go.jp/jp/seisaku/kokuren/keikaku.pdf). Accessed 24 November 2015.

Interministerial Meeting on the UN DESD 2009. *UNDESD Japan report: establishing enriched learning through participation and partnership among diverse actors* (www.mofa.go.jp/policy/environment/desd/report0903.pdf). Accessed 20 February 2016.

Interministerial Meeting on the UN DESD. 2014. *UNDESD Japan report* (www.cas.go.jp/jp/seisaku/kokuren/pdf/report_h261009_e.pdf). Accessed 20 February 2016.

Jickling, B. and Wals, A. E. J. 2008. Globalisation and environmental education. *Journal of Curriculum Studies* 40(1), 1–21.

Kamibeppu, T. 2002. *History of Japanese policies in education aid to developing countries, 1950s–1990s.* New York, US: Routledge.

Kumar, K. and Vickers, E. 2015. Introduction, in Vickers, E. and Kumar, K. (eds) *Constructing modern Asian citizenship.* London, UK and New York, US: Routledge, 1–28.

Ministry of the Environment n.d. +ESD Project (www.p-esd.go.jp/search_organization_list.html). Accessed 20 February 2016.

Ministry of Foreign Affairs Japan (MOFA) 2012. Speech by Prime Minister Junichiro Koizumi at the World Summit on Sustainable Development on 2 September 2002, Johannesburg, South Africa (www.mofa.go.jp/policy/environment/wssd/2002/kinitiative2.html). Accessed 15 February 2016.

Miyazaki, T. 2015. *Chiiki-kyoiku-undo ni okeru chiiki-gakushu-ron no kochiku – hopposei-kyoiku-undo no tenkai ni sokushite* (Developing a theory of community-based learning in community education movement – based on the development of the School Education for the North movement), in Sato, K. (ed.) *Chiiki-gakushu no sozo: Chiiki saisei e no manabi wo hiraku* (Dynamics of community-based learning for social revitalisation). Tokyo, Japan: University of Tokyo Press, 27–49.

Mochizuki, Y. 2010. Global circulation and local manifestations of education for sustainable development with a focus on Japan. *International Journal of Environment and Sustainable Development* 9 (1/2/3) (special issue on sustainable development and environmental education), 37–57.

Mochizuki, Y. 2013. Multi-stakeholder networking for ESD: 'Regional Centres of Expertise on education for sustainable development' in the international development and education contexts, in Okayama ESD Promotion Commission and UNESCO Chair at Okayama University (eds) *Education for sustainable development (ESD) and kominkan/Community Learning Centre (CLC)*. Okayama, Japan: Okayama University Press, 35–68.

Muramatsu, N. and Akiyama, H. 2011. Japan: super-aging society preparing for the future. *The Gerontologist* 51 (4), 425–432.

Okayama ESD Promotion Commission and UNESCO Chair at Okayama University (eds) 2013. *Education for sustainable development (ESD) and kominkan/Community Learning Centre (CLC)*. Okayama, Japan: Okayama University Press.

Organisation for Economic Co-operation and Development – Development Assistance Committee (OECD-DAC) 1989. *Development co-operation in the nineties.* Paris, France: OECD.

RCE Network n.d. RCE vision and mission (www.rce-network.org/portal/rce-vision-and-mission). Accessed 20 February 2016.

Sato, K. (ed.) 2015. *Chiiki-gakushu no sozo: Chiiki saisei e no manabi wo hiraku* (Dynamics of community-based learning for social revitalisation). Tokyo, Japan: University of Tokyo Press.

Sato, M. and Nakayama, S. 2013. Development of DESD-IIS and Japanese contribution to DESD, in Okayama ESD Promotion Commission and UNESCO Chair at Okayama University (eds) *Education for sustainable development (ESD) and kominkan/Community Learning Centre (CLC)*. Okayama, Japan: Okayama University Press, 19–34.

Selby, D. and Kagawa, F. 2011. Development education and education for sustainable development: are they striking a Faustian bargain? *Policy & Practice: A Development Education Review* 12, spring, 15–31.

Suzuki, S. 2014. Religion and education, Japanese cases: latent issues, in Wolhuter, C. and de Wet, C. (eds) *International comparative perspectives on religion and education.* Bloemfontein, South Africa: SUN MeDIA Bloemfontein, 195–234.

Tanaka, H. 2005. *Kaihatsu Kyoiku to Jizokukano na Kaihatsu no tame no Kyoiku (ESD) – Sanka-gata shakai ni muketa shakai kyōiku no yakuwari* (Development education and education for sustainable development (ESD): the role of social education for a participatory society). *Studies in Adult and Community Education* 49 (special issue on social education and lifelong learning under globalisation), 199–211.

Tanaka, H. 2009. Development education and global educations in the Japanese context (www.dear.or.jp/eng/eng05.html). Accessed 15 February 2016.

Torres, C. A. 2009. *Education and neoliberal globalisation.* New York, US: Routledge.

UN Conference on Environment and Development 1992. Agenda 21, Chapter 36. Promoting education, public awareness and training. A/CONF.151/26.

UN Development Programme (UNDP) 1990. *Human development report 1990.* New York, US and Oxford, UK: Oxford University Press.

UN Development Programme (UNDP) 1996. *Human development report 1996.* New York, US and Oxford, UK: Oxford University Press.

UNESCO 2005. *Decade of education for sustainable development international implementation scheme.* Paris, France: UNESCO.

UNESCO 2013. Proposal for a global action programme on education for sustainable development as follow-up to the UN Decade of Education for Sustainable Development (DESD) after 2014, (37c/57) (http://unesdoc.unesco.org/images/0022/002243/224368e.pdf). Accessed 1 March 2016.

UNESCO 2014. *Roadmap for implementing the global action programme on education for sustainable development.* Paris, France: UNESCO (http://unesdoc.unesco.org/images/0023/002305/230514e.pdf). Accessed 1 March 2016.

United Nations (UN) 2015. Transforming our world: the 2030 agenda for sustainable development. A/RES/70/1. New York, US: UN.

World Commission on Environment and Development 1987. *Our common future.* Oxford, UK: Oxford University Press.

Part I

School-based approaches

1 Formal ESD in Japan

Dissolving walls between classroom and community

Jane Singer and Yoshiyuki Nagata

Japanese formal education has long been lauded abroad for its rigorous, well structured curriculum, corroborated by high scores on the PISA (Programme for International Student Assessment) standardised global science and mathematics tests. However, many foreign observers may not realise that the educational sector was perceived to be in crisis in Japan at the end of the twentieth century, as test scores were eroding and social problems, such as bullying and truancy (*futoko*), came to dominate domestic media reports. The system was seen by many as overly rigid and regimentalised (Cave 2003), leading to calls for the Ministry of Education to replace its previous approach, aimed at fostering a well disciplined and effective labour force, with promotion of the creative thinking, problem-solving and foreign language skills deemed requisite in a more globalised age (Cave 2003). In response, a number of educational reforms were ushered in to the curriculum. These included time carved out for what was called integrated learning – 50–130 hours per year initially (from 2002) but declining in recent years to 35–70 hours (Xu and Nozawa 2013) for multidisciplinary, inquiry-based learning. This explores set themes, such as environmental issues, and often engages the local community with activities such as community mapping or residents' interviews by students or school visits by community members sharing traditional or local knowledge. This kind of holistic, place-based learning effectively oriented the schools for implementing the community and participatory activities that characterise education for sustainable development (ESD).

Environmental education was first instituted in the late 1960s and early 1970s in public (i.e. state) schools in Japan to teach students about pollution. It was a response to the occurrence of several well-publicised slow-onset environmental disasters, such as ocean-mercury-linked Minamata disease and severe air pollution in Yokkaichi, Mie prefecture, which emerged during the rapid post-war industrialisation of Japan (Mizuyama 2011). The learning content expanded, however, with the growth of the environmental movement and the emergence in Japan of institutional organisations focused on environmental education in the 1970s and 1980s. By the early 1990s, the Japanese Ministry of Education had created a model for environmental education based on the 1975 Belgrade Charter that had been adopted at the International Environmental Education Meeting held in Belgrade, Yugoslavia, in 1975. The charter presents the goal of environmental education as developing a global population knowledgeable about the environment and equipped with the attitudes and competencies needed to solve problems. The Ministry identified the need for students to acquire skills and attitudes to participate actively in conserving the environment and to behave responsibly with regard to the environment (Mizuyama 2011).

The Japanese government became a major proponent of the United Nations Decade of ESD (2005–2014), underlining its commitment to ESD by providing both funding and programmes. ESD was included as a cornerstone of Japan's Basic Plan on Education, a revised national educational policy promulgated in 2008, as well as a revised policy, the 2013 Basic Plan for the Promotion of Education. The 2006 policy specifically includes the objectives of fostering pro-environmental attitudes and the desire to contribute to world peace (Abe 2014) and includes an emphasis on realising a sustainable society in subjects such as social studies and science (Mizuyama 2011). The Japanese government supported an international forum on ESD, held in Tokyo in December 2008, in the lead-up to the mid-decade conference in Bonn, Germany in 2009, sponsored by the German government and UNESCO in order to discuss achievements to date and tasks for the decade's remaining years. Japan also sponsored the final meeting of the decade, the 2014 UNESCO World Conference on Education for Sustainable Development, held in Aichi-Nagoya in November 2014 (UN Interministerial Meeting 2014), which issued the Aichi-Nagoya Declaration for mainstreaming a global action programme for ESD throughout education.

One notably active approach for ESD implementation in Japan has been the UNESCO Associated Schools Network (ASPnet), which links schools that include environmental education and other ESD-linked themes in their curriculum. The number of schools in Japan that were designated UNESCO-Associated schools burgeoned to more than 900 by 2015, more than in any other single country. The schools themselves function as educational tools, with vegetable gardens, biotopes and other campus installations, complemented by student-led efforts to lower CO_2 emissions and increase energy efficiency. Several Japanese UNESCO-Associated schools have joined with schools in other Asian countries in regional projects to research themes such as rice and radioactivity, as explained below. Others have focused on local cultural heritage, as with schools in Nara (see Nakazawa and Izumitani's chapter in this volume), or on indigenous minority residents, as with Hokkaido schools studying local Ainu traditions (Mizuyama 2011).

ESD implementation in curricula or student-led initiatives at Japanese universities have lagged behind what can be found in primary and secondary schools and in universities in many other developed nations, but sustainability-linked research and green campus efforts are expanding. According to Stephens *et al.* (2008), universities (and, by extension, higher-level secondary schools) can be seen as being subject to change to become more sustainable or as being change agents in their own right. Several Japanese universities have begun operational initiatives to cut waste, CO_2 emissions and energy use, bolstered by economic imperatives. Others have introduced innovative sustainability-based courses or certificate programmes. Mie University, for example, has used nearby Yokkaichi, with an early post-war history of highly toxic industrial air pollution, as a case study for a student course, and Miyagi University of Education is linking with local schools to provide ESD curricula and teacher training. Okayama University is one of many that have collaborated with local governments, schools and non-profit organisations as part of a Regional Centre of Expertise (RCE) on ESD, established by the United Nations University as an integrative approach for sustainability education and international understanding (UNESCO 2009). Since 2005, the Okayama RCE has promoted activities such as a monthly ESD café gathering, visits to local farmers by schoolchildren, river monitoring by students and residents and international collaboration on urban waste management.

In 2014, 18 universities were part of a network supporting the activities of the UNESCO-Associated schools in Japan. The Japanese government has provided university funding for integrated projects that support both ESD and sustainability science, which UNESCO defines as approaches to science and engineering for sustainable development that are trans-disciplinary, applying traditional and indigenous as well as scientific knowledge for problem solving (Mochizuki and Yarime 2015). Increasing interest in the university's role in advocating sustainability can also be seen with the formation of a nationwide campus sustainability network, CASNet, in 2014, spearheaded by national universities such as Kyoto University and Hokkaido University. Universities can engage with communities in many ways, including policy and planning input, providing technological assistance and innovations, inviting local residents to join non-formal activities, student internships and research, and collaborative community development (Stephens *et al.* 2008). The chapters in this section offer diverse examples of how links have been forged in Japan between school and community or university and community.

One of the most persuasive proponents of the importance of engaging students in interactive and intergenerational dialogue with community members is Professor Yoshiyuki Nagata, professor of education at University of the Sacred Heart in Tokyo. Professor Nagata received his master's and PhD degrees from International Christian University, focusing on the theme of alternative education, after a stint teaching at the alternative Summerhill School in the United Kingdom in the late 1980s. From 1995 to 2007, he worked to further international cooperation in education at the government-funded National Institute for Educational Policy Research (NIER), then he joined the faculty of the University of the Sacred Heart, where he teaches and researches the sociology of education, education for international understanding and development education. He says these are all subjects that 'are related to unsustainable issues in our society, so also related to ESD'. Professor Nagata has implemented a number of ESD projects overseas, including one in Laos that brought high schoolers together with rural villagers for dialogue and joint reflection on development and community sustainability.

In the following section, Professor Nagata discusses the provenance and implications of some recent ESD projects he has implemented around Asia Pacific.

How did you become involved in ESD?

YN: At NIER, my counterpart was UNESCO and one of the last themes we worked on together was ESD. Another group that I worked with, the ACCU (Asia-Pacific Cultural Centre for UNESCO), held a conference with UNESCO Bangkok, the National Commission for UNESCO and related people from different member states in February 2006. Our first keynote speaker was Akito Arima, an ex-minister of education, haiku poet and former president of the University of Tokyo. The second keynote speaker was Sombath Somphone, director of an NGO in Laos called PADETC (Participatory Development Training Centre), who had won the Magsaysay award in 2005. That was the first time I met him.

In 2007, I moved to Sacred Heart, so ESD was one of my last projects at NIER. During my first year here as a member of the Japan Holistic Education Society, in collaboration with the ACCU we organised an international workshop and symposium on holistic approaches to ESD at this university. Based upon this, we published a book in Japanese on holistic approaches to ESD with an emphasis on the cultural aspects of sustainable development.

I would say that there are two ESDs – one ESD with capital letters and one esd with lower-case letters. The former has been mainly initiated by UN agencies such as UNESCO, governments and other large umbrella organisations with a big influence on policies. However, our focus has been on 'lower-case esd', which includes endogenous development, human-scale education and grassroots initiatives, which I really wanted to support. Many of them are in developing countries.

Please explain your recent Japanese government-sponsored project in Laos, which involved students from a town-based high school and rural villagers.

YN: Because I started to work with university students, I unconsciously started to put emphasis on how young people can be agents of change for a more sustainable society. That became my main concern. I ended up with a few youth-led ESD projects involving students here and those outside Japan, including one in Xieng Khouang, located in north-eastern Laos, about 430km from the capital, Vientiane. Although a remote area, it has experienced rapid development, so that's one reason why we selected Xieng Khouang as our project site. They are now building golf courses and hot springs, and have large-scale agricultural development. They are converting traditional rice fields into corn fields for monoculture production but they abandon the fields if they can't find an international market and don't restore the original rice paddies. So this was a good place to stop and think about development with local people. How can we get people to stop and think about which direction their community and society are heading?

I talked about this with my local partner, Sombath, the director of PADETC, a great leader and initiator. We started to involve students in conducting surveys in villages using the Compass investigatory method, which includes four directions: N for nature, E for economy, S for society and W for wellbeing.

We can apply these four elements to assess the direction society is progressing to try to make it a more sustainable, holistically developing and well balanced society.

One of the characteristics of the project was that it was mainly led by high school students. They interviewed the villagers about development and analysed the results with the Compass method. Later they made presentations to the villagers. They opened the villagers' eyes, creating opportunities to rethink development.

This was at the time of the Millennium Development Goals (MDGs). The first goal relates to poverty. In the forests in Laos, some local authorities try to escape poverty by allowing trees to be cut down but this destroys nature and the environment they had preserved for a long time. This was a contradictory aspect of development so we wanted the students and villagers to reconsider this.

How were young people involved in this project?

YN: We emphasised the youth-development aspect partly because of the philosophy of Sombath. PADETC is a centre that trains young and poor people in villages. Youth development is one of its core themes so Sombath emphasised that young people should be a central part of the project (see Graduate School of the University of the Sacred Heart, Tokyo and PADETC, 2013). I totally agreed. ESD discourses have provided a theoretical background in declarations and books, emphasising that young people should be agents of change for a sustainable future, so involving them in a participatory method was a condition for initiating the project.

Interestingly, even in Japan, many adults – teachers and professors – worry about the results if you let young people manage lessons or projects but once we leave it to young people and stop saying or guiding them too much and just attend to their direction, in my experience it will be 100 per cent all right. But there are many contradictory aspects of ESD in formal schooling. When we introduce ESD in the classroom, teachers talk too much; they stand up in front of the students and instruct them and there's too much direction from adults, I think.

There are roles for teachers and adults to take. They can be facilitators or animators, who encourage or empower students. We tend to give answers and directions too easily in the classroom but sustainability issues have no set answers so it's a challenge for adults as well. What is important is the investigative process itself. We may not find an answer to our inquiries. Finding an answer in education is very important, of course, but trying to live with deep and essential questions is also very important.

In this project, you involved young people from an urbanised area and rural villagers. Their interaction must have been very rewarding.

YN: The process is not always effective as they have totally different values but sharing different values inter-generationally is a very good opportunity for learning from each other. That's true collaborative learning. Interestingly, adults in informal situations listen to the voices of young people, I think. In this project, after the youth-led investigation, the adults in the village were ready to listen to the young people's analysis and recommendations because they knew how seriously the students had worked and interviewed them. In our daily life, it's difficult to create this kind of situation. We don't naturally do this. ESD brought opportunities for people of different generations to sit together and discuss their future.

In the DESD there was a gap, I think. Many experts and practitioners thought that ESD is for developed countries while Education for All (EFA) is for developing countries. However, this kind of dichotomous discussion is sterile and not fruitful. The real challenge is how to create ESD in both developed and developing countries. EFA started in 1990 and was intended to provide equal opportunities for all students – those in primary and secondary schools and adults improving their literacy – mainly in developing countries. They tried to increase the number of schools and classes so it was quite a quantitative challenge, I think. When we discuss ESD in developing countries people may say that first they need schools, a healthy environment, forests, then they can talk about qualitative aspects such as ESD. But the challenge for us is that we have to create opportunities for qualitative as well as quantitative aspects of education. We wanted to create a good example of ESD that addressed these challenges in Laos.

You led another government-funded regional ESD project that was also participatory.

YN: My second project, involving cross-border radiation measurement, was also youth-led (Nagata 2012). For a long time, I have wanted to conceive a cross-border project in Asian countries led by young people and teachers rather than researchers because there have been good precedents elsewhere, such as the Baltic Sea Project, in which nine countries around the Baltic Sea collaborated quite successfully to initiate EE and ESD. However, there were many difficulties in doing a similar cross-border project in Asia as political issues arose.

The experience of 3.11, although it was very unfortunate, provided a good opportunity for educators, including me, to initiate new challenges and new educational projects – and we had the Baltic Project in our minds. I was in the last year of leading a research project for creating a regional network for ASPNet Schools, also known as UNESCO schools in Japan, when the disaster hit. My team decided to launch a youth-led radiation measurement project among ASPNet high schools in China, Korea, Taiwan, Japan (Fukushima, Nara, Tokyo), Mongolia and Russia. Each school received the same type of Geiger counter and uniform instructions to measure radiation at 1m above ground and at ground level every week using the same method and to send the statistics to our Tokyo office every Monday. My students collected and collated the data. This was a project that enabled young people to lead towards a sustainable future in Asia. Interestingly, as well as collecting data and doing scientific investigation, the students also started to exchange ideas, photos and paintings. For example, some students from Russia, I think because of the experience of Chernobyl, encouraged students in Fukushima. A quite emotional exchange occurred, which was very good. Students used a scientific method but they also expressed what they found or achieved artistically so it was a well balanced educational project.

Based on these Radiation Observation Project results, I advised ACCU to lead another cross-border youth-led project, which led to the RICE project. RICE is an abbreviation for the Regional Initiative for Cooperation for ESD, which promotes ESD through the study of rice. In Japan there are many international student exchange projects but they typically feature cultural exchange; very few are inquiry-based and problem-solving in nature. In the project, students at high schools in Kanagawa, Japan and Malang, Indonesia, investigated genetically modified organisms (GMOs). The Japanese students interviewed officials from the Monsanto company in Chiba, Japan. The Indonesian students studied whether GMO products were present in their society and found that there were a lot. The headmistress of the school thanked me when I visited, saying it was the first time she had thought seriously about GMOs and that she had learned from her students. The students also spoke about this issue with their families.

Involving young people in a project also involves family and community inherently – its influence expands so it's very effective. Good ESD will always involve people in the community. It's meant to be holistic. That's why today we value a whole-school approach and a whole-community approach. A whole-school approach does not end within schools; we must make a bridge between school, family and community.

In addition, it was a challenge but ACCU decided to include primary schools in another project concerning rice paddies. The rice paddy landscape is disappearing in many parts of Asia as development replaces it with factories or monoculture agriculture. Primary school pupils in Miyagi prefecture and the Philippines made dioramas and discussed what kind of town they wanted to live in when they became adults. They then exchanged their dioramas and their ideas through Skype. Some people may think that high school or university students are best suited to problem-solving types of projects but we can include primary school pupils in problem solving to find ideas and solutions. When we made presentations, the villagers and town residents came and listened seriously, so inter-generational exchange and communication happened in Japan as it did in Laos.

In many international declarations these days you can find a sentence about youth involvement or young people as agents of change, which is very important, but the inter-generational aspect of our reality is a missing link in our dialogue or discussions. These examples show that youth-led projects will naturally bring adults around to the dialogue, which is very good.

A challenge of ESD is that, in creating school education, we have compartmentalised many things that used to be embedded naturally in our daily lives. That's why ESD should be holistic education and it should be an integrated approach, as UNESCO has said, involving environment, society, economy and culture. School education has been divided into different elements so we try to re-integrate them.

With ESD one of the dynamic qualities is the challenge to integrate compartmentalised elements of our reality, including past, present and future. As Sombath has said, we need to connect hearts, head and hands (3Hs). In modern education heads predominate. The local and global dimensions should be connected, and transformation of ourselves and society is important. Many people insist on a transformation of society without changing ourselves. We have to transform ourselves, then society, not the other way around. As Gandhi said, be the change that you wish to see in the world.

What would you say is a major contribution of ESD to education?

YN: I was part of the DESD Monitoring and Evaluation Expert Group (MEEG) set up by UNESCO headquarters so I have observed many ESD projects for nearly a decade. Based on observing the record of DESD, I think that one of its theoretical contributions is adding to the UNESCO's four pillars of learning, as proposed in 1996 by the Delores report:[1] learning to know, to learning to do, learning to live together and learning to be. ESD contributed the idea of learning to transform oneself and society, which is very important for the world. In our projects I think students were able to transform themselves and their values.

The challenge of values transformation is important. Although we position ESD as education involving transformation of values, behaviour and lifestyle towards a sustainable future most education nowadays is knowledge-based. People talk about deep active learning but achieving it is a challenge. Asking students fundamental questions is very important, as is fostering students to understand reality and to connect with the field directly. It doesn't have to be outside Japan. It's important for students to obtain a tangible feeling that they're connected with that reality, such as unsustainable situations in developing countries. Let them take action and run the project.

Note

1 The 1996 Delors report, formally entitled *Learning: the treasure within*, was the product of an independent commission tasked with discussing the kind of education needed for the society of the future.

References

Abe, O. 2014. ESD projects in Japanese schools and in non-formal education in Japan, in Lee, J. C. K. and Efird, R. (eds) *Schooling for sustainable development across the Pacific.* Dordrecht, Germany: Springer, 125–139.

Cave, P. 2003. Japanese educational reform: developments and prospects at primary and secondary level, in Goodman, R. and Phillips, D (eds) *Can the Japanese change their education system?* Oxford, UK: Symposium Books, 87–102.

Delors, J. 1998. *Learning: the treasure within.* UNESCO.

Graduate School of the University of the Sacred Heart, Tokyo and PADETC 2013. Introduction to ESD, ESD Implementation, Wisdom Box, Design for Change (www.u-sacred-heart.ac.jp/graduate/report/1304.html). Accessed 1 December 2015.

Mizuyama, M. 2011. The environment as an issue in citizenship education, in Ikeno, N. (ed.) *Citizenship education in Japan.* London, UK: Continuum International Publishing Group, 116–129.

Mochizuki, Y. and Yarime, M. 2015. Education for sustainable development and sustainability science, in Barth, M., Michelsen, G., Rieckmann, M. and Thomas, I. (eds) *Routledge handbook of higher education for sustainable development.* Oxford, UK: Routledge, 11–24.

Nagata, Y. 2012. *Youth-led cross-border radiation measurement project in East Asia.* East Asia School Network. Tokyo, Japan: University of the Sacred Heart (www.u-sacred-heart.ac.jp/nagata/Youth_Led_Cross_Border.pdf). Accessed 1 December 2015.

Stephens, J. C., Hernandez, M. E., Román, M., Graham, A. C. and Scholz, R. W. 2008. Higher education as a change agent for sustainability in different cultures and contexts. *International Journal of Sustainability in Higher Education* 9 (3), 317–338.

UNESCO 2009. ESD currents: changing perspectives from the Asia Pacific. Bangkok, Thailand.

UN Interministerial Meeting on the DESD 2014. United Nations Decade for Education for Sustainable Development (2005–2014): Japan Report (www.cas.go.jp/jp/seisaku/kokuren/pdf/report_h261009_e.pdf). Accessed 15 December 2015.

University of the Sacred Heart, Tokyo and PADETC 2011 (eds). *Basic study for building a 'broader ESD model' for developing countries with creation and dissemination of related multimedia materials* (www.u-sacred-heart.ac.jp/graduate/report/1104.html). Accessed 1 December 2015.

Xu, Y. and Nozawa, Y. 2013. The curriculum innovation in mainland China and Japan: a school-based approach, in Law, E. H. F. and Li, C. (eds) *Curriculum innovations in changing societies: Chinese perspectives from Hong Kong, Taiwan and mainland China.* Rotterdam, Netherlands: Sense Publishers, 509–517.

2 Implications of 3.11 for disaster education and education for sustainable development in Japan

Aiko Sakurai and Rajib Shaw

The one-year period between late 2014 and autumn 2015 was marked by the redefining of major international frameworks and goals for both disaster risk reduction (DRR) and sustainable development. In November 2014, the UNESCO World Conference on Education for Sustainable Development (ESD) was held in Nagoya, Japan, and the delegates adopted the Aichi-Nagoya Declaration on ESD. This was followed by the adoption in March 2015, at the Third World Conference on Disaster Risk Reduction held in Sendai, Japan, of the Sendai Framework for Disaster Risk Reduction 2015–2030, upon the conclusion of the previous Hyogo Framework for Action 2005–2015. A final milestone for the year was reached in September 2015 in New York, when the United Nations Summit agreed on the post-2015 Sustainable Development Goals (SDGs) that succeed the Millennium Development Goals in guiding global development efforts. DRR and ESD have been more closely linked to each other under the SDGs.

This chapter will apply a DRR framework to investigate the evolution of Japanese disaster education since the 1995 Hanshin-Awaji earthquake and in the wake of the 2011 Great East Japan Earthquake and tsunami (GEJET). While acknowledging improvement, the authors propose strengthening links between DRR and ESD by applying the above-mentioned new international frameworks and promoting context-specific collaboration between schools and local communities to achieve more effective DRR implementation. Based on the Japanese model, recommendations are provided for enhancing DRR in the education sector globally.

International framework for disaster risk reduction

ESD evolution

In the course of negotiating a plan for ESD implementation at the World Summit on Sustainable Development in Johannesburg, South Africa, which was held between 26 August and 4 September 2002, Japan proposed the Decade of Education for Sustainable Development (DESD). This was in response to calls from Japanese non-governmental organisations and was part of what Japan regarded as an overall policy to support ESD's mission to build a more sustainable society. A recommendation to the UN General Assembly to consider adopting this idea was included in the plan.

Later, Japan was one of 40 national governments that stated they would co-sponsor the UN DESD at the 57th UN General Assembly in 2002. The proposal to launch the DESD, starting in January 2005, was adopted unanimously following the Johannesburg Plan of Implementation. UNESCO was designated the lead agency for the decade and developed an international implementation scheme for DESD.

Despite the strong start, DESD global efforts seemed to have stalled by the middle of the decade. The UNESCO World Conference on ESD, held in Bonn, Germany, from 31 March to 2 April 2009, issued a declaration that included the following call for action: 'The progress of ESD remains unevenly distributed and requires different approaches in different contexts. In the coming years, there is a clear need for both developed and developing countries, civil society and international organisations to make significant efforts' (UNESCO 2009, 3). The statement outlined five calls for action at the policy level and 13 calls for action at the practice level. The statement welcomed the intention, announced by the government of Japan, to jointly host with UNESCO an end-of-decade world conference on ESD in 2014. In 2010, at the beginning of the second half of the decade, UNESCO identified three priorities for addressing global sustainable development challenges through ESD – climate change, biodiversity and disaster risk reduction and preparedness. These were UNESCO's key action themes for the second half of the decade (2010–2015) (Oikawa 2014).

Japan's Ministry of Education, Culture, Sports, Science and Technology (MEXT) became a leading promoter of ESD through environmental education and education for international understanding. MEXT took several steps to link existing domestic educational efforts to the DESD. ESD was included in the 2008 Basic Education Promotion Plan and the national curriculum, and MEXT strongly promoted the establishment of UNESCO-Associated schools in Japan.

Evolution of the international framework on DRR in the education sector

The Hyogo Framework for Action (HFA), which was adopted at the UN Second World Conference on Disaster Risk Reduction in Hyogo Prefecture in 2005, identifies the importance of disaster education in building a culture of safety and resilience as the third of five priorities. Within this priority, HFA stipulates the 'inclusion of disaster risk reduction knowledge in relevant sections of school curricula at all levels' (UNISDR 2005).

The HFA is a multi-sectoral framework that includes education and has bolstered efforts by disaster education researchers and education experts regarding DRR in the education sector. For example, many of the original actions suggested to achieve the five priority goals were later modified in a plan known as Education in HFA (Gwee *et al.* 2011), which enabled practitioners to assess overall efforts toward reducing disaster risk in the education sector. Two UN agencies, UNESCO and the United Nations Office for Disaster Risk Reduction, formed a global alliance to achieve DRR at the school level by formulating a comprehensive framework on school safety, including three pillars: safe learning facilities, school disaster management and risk reduction education. These efforts enhance the resilience of the education sector by aligning disaster education with disaster management strategy and policy at the national, regional, district and local school levels (GADRRRES 2012). Goto and Okamoto (2012) are among those proposing that the lessons of HFA and ESD be synthesised in the process of curriculum development in order to create a culture of safety and a sustainable society resilient to natural disasters.

Through such frameworks, disaster education has been promoted internationally, and these efforts have continued up to the present. Their success to date was attested by adoption of the Sendai Framework for Disaster Risk Reduction 2015–2030 in March 2015 at the Third UN World Conference on Disaster Risk Reduction (UNISDR 2015a).

During working group discussions, the delegates recognised that there had been significant progress made in integrating risk reduction and resilience into the education sector around the world, yet there continued to be a need to provide relevant knowledge and skills in DRR to children and young people to help them better understand exposure to hazards, opportunities for preventing natural hazards from turning into disasters and their potential contributions to assessing risks in the community (UNISDR 2015b).

At the Sendai meeting, the Global Alliance for DRR and Resilience in the Education Sector organised a working group on school safety and reconfirmed the importance of the continued incorporation of disaster risk education. It also identified the important link between DRR, education and ESD and called for closer cooperation with the actors in climate change education to help achieve the UN's sustainable development goals for education, which were adopted in September 2015. The session also underscored the importance of building on local knowledge, traditional wisdom and storytelling to foster trans-generational learning, and reaffirmed that the involvement of local communities is essential to ensure that education and awareness-raising activities can be continued in a community (UNISDR 2015c).

Although the Sendai Framework does not include a specific priority for education, education is included in the new priority for understanding disaster risk. In addition, one of the seven global targets that were introduced by the Sendai Framework was to achieve a substantial reduction in disaster damage to critical infrastructure and disruption of basic services, including health and educational facilities. Under the new framework, more focus has been placed on the safety of the learning environment, and disaster education has been situated under an umbrella of comprehensive school safety against disasters.

ESD and disaster education links

While they share many common features, it should be noted that there are discrete forms of education that are currently being implemented to enhance sustainability and resilience in different areas and in different contexts. These include disaster risk reduction education (DRRE), ESD, climate change education (CCE) and environmental education.

Shaw (2014) writes that ESD tends to be implemented more in primary and secondary education than at the tertiary level, whereas DRRE efforts can be found equally at all three levels of education. He proposes that secondary education focus more on the environment, while tertiary education should focus more on climate change because an understanding of the subject requires a strong scientific foundation. He characterises the four types of education (ESD, CCE, DREE and environmental education) at the primary level as highlighting 'community and culture', while 'action' is the key word characterising all four types of education at the secondary level. For tertiary education, ESD focuses on enhanced knowledge and understanding of sustainable development, while DRRE and CCE focus on professional development and environmental education targets behavioural change. The goal is to transform concerned students into a concerned citizens during their progress from primary to tertiary levels of education.

The impact of effective ESD and DRRE was clearly demonstrated during the 2011 GEJET, with the survival of more than 99 per cent of the school children living in Kamaishi city in Iwate Prefecture and Kesennuma city in Miyagi Prefecture. These two cities are located on the Sanriku coast and have experienced high mortality rates caused by tsunamis over the past few centuries. However, a city-wide disaster education programme was implemented in local schools in Kamaishi nearly eight years before the 2011 disaster. For example, because they had practised disaster drills and received intensive disaster education in their schools and communities, the elementary and junior high school students of the Unosumai area of Kamaishi were successfully evacuated together, and there were no casualties among students in the school compound. An ESD programme started in 2002 in Kesennuma involved close collaboration with members of the community for disaster drills and other activities, and these close relations facilitated a quick response to the disaster. Local residents helped students and teachers to evacuate to safer places so there were no reported casualties in school compounds across Kesennuma. Hashikami junior high school in Kesennuma has also, since 2005, implemented disaster education as part of its ESD programme. These examples show how disaster education and ESD helped children to think, judge and behave in such a way as to ensure their survival at the time of the 2011 tsunami – DRRE and ESD helped save the school children. As these examples suggest, an inclusive approach to education that closely involves the community may be more important than the content of the education. Content can be customised to local needs, and the local board of education or school can choose whether to prioritise ESD, DRRE or CCE in their curriculum.

Disaster risk reduction in the Japanese education sector

Lessons learned from the 1995 Hanshin-Awaji earthquake

Disaster researchers and practitioners considered the Hanshin-Awaji earthquake on 17 January 1995 to be a turning point for Japanese disaster management policy and practices, due, in part, to the magnitude of the disaster. The 6,434 deaths that resulted exceeded the number of casualties caused by all natural disasters in the previous 25 years. Before the 1995 earthquake, disaster education was limited to fire evacuation drills. The earthquake compelled authorities to apply DRR policies and practices to the Japanese education sector. Kobe City and Hyogo Prefecture, both affected by the earthquake, collaborated closely with the national government to formulate the basic framework for Japanese DRR in education.

The Ministry of Education (MOE became MEXT in April 2001 after central government reforms) examined the lessons learned from the 1995 Hanshin-Awaji earthquake and issued two reports (MOE 1995; 1996) outlining methods to enhance DRR efforts at the school level. A major finding was that schools in Japan had not been prepared for a disaster on this scale. Although no children died at school because the earthquake occurred at 5.46 am, 179 school-aged children and 11 teachers lost their lives in Kobe city. The earthquake damaged 86 per cent of the 345 school buildings in Kobe city. Twenty-one schools needed to be rebuilt, 10 required large-scale renovation and 35 needed medium-scale renovation. For two months, 218 schools were used as evacuation shelters for 63 per cent of the 180,000 evacuees in Kobe city, delaying the early resumption of education at schools. There was no clear definition of roles and responsibilities among schools and communities on how to operate the shelters. The prolonged use of schools as evacuation shelters for community members caused teaching to be suspended, which affected the quality of education.

In the aftermath of the 1995 earthquake, the MOE examination identified four major areas for improvement in school safety during earthquakes:

1   Strengthening earthquake disaster countermeasures at schools in Japan.
2   Examining measures to secure children's safety wherever they may be – home, school or travelling between the two – and enhancing disaster education.
3   Improving the earthquake resistance of school buildings and facilities, implementing safety countermeasures for non-structural items and establishing an information coordination system.
4   Specifying schools' functions as evacuation shelters and the roles and responsibilities of teachers and the school support system, and examining actions to achieve early resumption of school education activities.

Progress of DRR efforts in the Japanese education sector (1995–2011)

Based on the lessons learned from the 1995 Hanshin-Awaji earthquake, a basic policy framework was established at the national level and, at each prefectural and municipal board of education, a series of initiatives was conducted to strengthen DRR efforts at schools.

In Japan, school disaster preparedness has developed as one of three fields of school safety, which also includes traffic and household safety. Figure 2.1 shows how disaster safety at Japanese schools is organised mainly into disaster education and disaster management, in addition to activities within schools and between

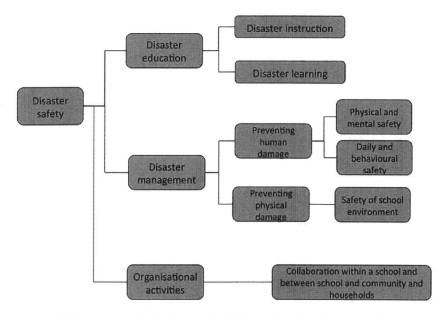

Figure 2.1 Structure of school disaster safety in Japan (based on MEXT 2013)

schools, parents and the community. The safety of the learning environment is included under school management.

In 1997, MOE issued a guidebook to schools on how to strengthen prepared-ness against disaster, entitled *Development of Disaster Prevention Educa-tion to Cultivate 'Zest for Living'* (MOE 1998). The book communicated the goals of disaster education and procedures for teaching disaster education and strengthening disaster management. The 1998 national curriculum guidelines indicated that disaster-related knowledge and information should be dissemi-nated as part of existing classes, such as social science, natural science and health and physical education. In 1998, MOE introduced 'integrated studies periods' as part of the national curriculum guidelines, including disaster edu-cation as one of the themes of this experiential and interdisciplinary learning approach. Thus disaster education in Japan was integrated into relevant sec-tions of the school curricula before the 2005 HFA identified such education as a priority.

MOE (later MEXT) developed various disaster education materials, supported teacher training on school disaster safety at a national training centre and finan-cially supported pilot projects on school disaster safety. With financial support from MEXT, the percentage of quake-resistant school buildings has substantially improved since the 1995 disaster, rising from 44.5 per cent in 2004 to 73.3 per cent in 2011 and 94.6 per cent in 2013 (MEXT 2012e).

Evolution of Japanese DRR in the education sector after 3.11

Damage to the education sector caused by the disaster

Even though the Japanese education sector has been making efforts to strengthen DRR, the 2011 GEJET caused substantial damage to the education sector. When the earthquake occurred at 2.46 pm on Friday 11 March 2011, many children were still at school, having recently finished their classes and not yet left for home. Although Japanese people have experienced many earthquakes, this was the first time Japanese schools had to deal with such a disaster on such a large scale. As of 14 September 2012, the disaster had caused 659 deaths in the education sector. Of these, 616 were children, including the 74 who died or went missing in the tragedy of Okawa Elementary School in Ishinomaki, Miyagi Prefecture. As of 28 March 2012, 241 children had been orphaned by the disaster, according to the Ministry of Welfare and Labour.

A total of 6,284 schools were damaged by the earthquake and tsunami. Of these, 930 schools (15 per cent) had totally or partially collapsed and required rebuilding. Inspections revealed that such damage was mainly caused by the tsunami rather than earthquake tremors. Although the disaster damaged many facilities, no deaths were reportedly caused by the collapse of school buildings during the earthquake; all could be attributed to the subsequent flooding. Before the 2011 disaster, 71 schools were located within tsunami inundation areas in the tsunami hazard maps prepared by the prefecture, and 53 of them (74.6 per cent) were inundated by the tsunami. The tsunami affected an additional 69 schools in the area (MEXT 2014b).

After the GEJET, many schools were used as evacuation shelters. During the peak evacuation period, 622 schools were used as shelters. Even though it was reported that education provision was disrupted at schools that served as evacuation shelters after the 1995 Kobe earthquake, after the GEJET, a larger number of schools in Tohoku were used as shelters for a longer period of time because of the scale of the damage. Six months after the disaster, 42 schools were still being used as shelters and it took almost eight months for all the school shelters to be closed. In addition to the school buildings, many playgrounds were used for temporary housing after the 2011 disaster because the amount of flat land was limited in the tsunami-affected coastal areas. Students lost the space for physical exercise, extracurricular and sports club activities (MEXT 2011a).

MEXT's response to the 2011 disaster

In response to the 2011 disaster, MEXT took immediate action to support early resumption of education in disaster-affected areas, which entailed bearing the costs of building temporary classrooms and reconstructing damaged school facilities. In addition, MEXT secured educational opportunities for affected students by distributing free textbooks, providing them with economic assistance and allowing them to go to schools in resettled or evacuated areas, reassigning teachers to schools in tsunami-affected areas and dispatching school counsellors to care for children's psychological needs.

The Expert Council on Disaster Prevention Education and Management was established in July 2011 to analyse schools' experiences during the GEJET, and to review the existing disaster education and disaster management policies. The council conducted a series of hearings and research with the affected teachers as well as schools in the affected areas and produced two reports within a year of the 2011 disaster (MEXT 2011b; MEXT 2012a; MEXT 2012b). These reports identified issues related to Japanese DRR in the education sector and made recommendations for enhancing it further. The findings from the reports were incorporated into the Five-Year (2012–2016) Plan on Promotion of School Safety, which is currently being implemented based on the lessons learned from the GEJET and the School Health and Safety Act of 2009 (MEXT 2009). The plan aims to propose practical, comprehensive school safety measures in the fields of environmental safety, education and management by building a culture of safety and reducing injuries, with the goal of zero deaths from accidents and disasters (MEXT 2012d).

Evolution of DRR in the education sector based on lessons learned from the GEJET

Enhancing disaster education

Responding to lessons learned from the 2011 GEJET, MEXT revised *Development of Disaster Prevention Education to Cultivate 'Zest for Living'* in 2013. In the guidebook, the aims of disaster education to foster children's ability to survive a disaster were redefined. Children should:

> Understand the causes of natural disasters and measures to reduce disaster risk; make proper decisions based on, and behave according to, clear thinking and precise judgement when disaster occurs and afterward.
>
> Understand and predict the risks associated with earthquakes, typhoons and other natural hazards and take actions accordingly to secure individual safety. Be prepared every day.
>
> Respect the value of their own lives and those of others; recognise the importance of creating a safe and secure society; participate in and contribute to safety activities at schools, at home and in their communities.

This definition encompasses several features. First, it places more emphasis on the link between understanding, decision-making and action, implying that disaster education should be more practical to leap the hurdle between understanding and changing behaviour. This ability is clearly linked to the approach of ESD, which fosters children's problem-solving abilities. Another feature is that the definition covers all the hazard types, not only earthquakes. Because natural hazards occur in different geographic locations and the degree of damage varies depending on the community's vulnerability, it is important to prepare for the disaster in the local context. This is an essential element of ESD, which encourages children to learn about their community and become interested in the local natural environment (MEXT 2013). Finally, the guidebook indicates that disaster education is not limited to school but occurs in daily life. Disaster education is not only for the purpose of individual survival: in addition to providing self-help during a disaster, the guidebook emphasises the importance of mutual aid by respecting others and behaving as a member of a community. These features show how Japanese disaster education has become more linked to ESD concepts. The Okayama declaration promoting ESD at UNESCO-Associated schools in Japan states:

> Through implementing ESD that makes the most of the unique characteristics of a region, children have gained a deeper understanding of how local communities are formed by people supporting each other. They have learned about the merits of communities and the issues they face. In addition, together with local people, they have considered what to hand down to future generations and what to reform, and they have learned about translating these ideas into action. ESD has also been leading to a shared understanding that the issues faced by local communities are linked to those at national, Asian and global levels and that joint efforts to overcome geographical distances and differences in generation and status enables us to create a sustainable future.
>
> (UNESCO 2014)

The above statement suggests that, to evolve further, an ESD approach is necessary for DRR in the Japanese educational sector.

Since the 1995 Hanshin-Awaji earthquake, disaster education has been promoted at Japanese schools by integrating it into existing curricula for such subjects as science, social science, health and physical education. Although there are many examples of well-conceived DRRE implementation, disaster education is still taught at a limited number of schools, mostly located in disaster-affected areas and areas of imminent disaster risk, where there are enthusiastic school principals and/or teachers of disaster education. MEXT and municipal boards of education have developed extensive teaching and learning materials but there are still many areas where the only kind of disaster education to be found is the fire evacuation drills conducted regularly at schools. Even if disaster education is implemented, the number of teaching hours is still limited. Based on the authors' experience, many school teachers believe disaster education should not account for more than 10 hours per year of instruction because additional time would reduce the teaching other subjects, which would negatively affect students' academic performance. In short, there are profound differences between schools in terms of disaster education efforts.

One reason for these differences is that teachers are rarely trained in disaster education. There are limited opportunities for teacher training since disaster education is not considered an independent subject. In addition, the multi-disciplinary nature of disaster education makes it difficult for teachers to link DRR-related knowledge and information to existing subjects according to children's development stages, and there are no established methods to evaluate children's learning about DRR. Therefore, MEXT's 2014 report proposed assigning an existing subject as a core subject for safety education and securing a certain number of teaching hours for safety education in the curriculum when the national curriculum guidelines are next revised in 2016 (MEXT 2014b). This might be an important turning point for Japanese disaster education as it evolves from being integrated into the existing curriculum to substantially being infused into the existing curriculum.

Strengthening disaster management

The lessons learned from the 2011 disaster in terms of school disaster management emphasised localising school disaster manuals for each school's context. Given that each school is located in a different geographical area, the disaster manuals and drills should be tailored to the local characteristics of each school's surroundings. To incorporate local information and backgrounds, schools are encouraged to collaborate with parents, disaster-related divisions of municipal governments and the local community. In addition, MEXT has recommended that each school disaster manual should include response procedures for post-disaster crisis management, such as shelter management and preparation efforts – including conducting evacuation drills and sharing information with parents on procedures for releasing children from schools to their parents' charge.

Responding to the review, MEXT published the *The Guide to Creating a School Disaster Manual (for earthquake and tsunami disasters)* (MEXT 2012c). The aim of the new handbook is to urge all schools to review their own existing disaster manuals and to reconsider their practicality within the school's local context. The guide also encourages schools to establish a plan-do-check-action (PDCA) cycle for disaster management when there are changes in school personnel or the local environment. Figure 2.2 shows a flowchart of disaster management that schools should follow before, during and after an earthquake.

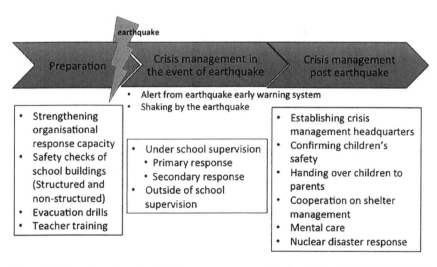

Figure 2.2 Flowchart of earthquake disaster management at schools (based on MEXT 2012c)

Improving the safety of the learning environment

MEXT considers implementing earthquake resistance measures at school facilities to be a high-priority issue and seeks to implement earthquake resistance for non-structural elements and to complete projects to increase earthquake resistance as soon as possible (MEXT 2012e). In July 2011, MEXT's working group released an urgent proposal (MEXT 2011c) for strengthening school tsunami safety measures and clarifying schools' functions as evacuation shelters during disasters, in addition to increasing the earthquake resistance of school facilities and promoting earthquake countermeasures for non-structural items such as ceiling materials. In 2014, another report proposed three tsunami countermeasures: 1) evacuating to higher places near the school, 2) evacuating to a school building, and 3) moving schools to higher elevations or building high-rise schools so students can evacuate to higher floors. In deciding which option to choose, each school's location should be thoroughly considered in terms of the altitude of the school site, distance from the sea and/or coast, geographical features of the school district, availability of high-rise buildings nearby and the expected arrival time of a tsunami after an earthquake (MEXT 2014a).

Regarding schools functioning as evacuation shelters, the report indicated that close collaboration is crucial between schools and disaster management divisions of municipal governments because the expected number of evacuees and the risks according to hazard type must be understood. Even though 90 per cent of state schools are designated evacuation shelters during disasters, schools are not always equipped with appropriate equipment such as emergency communication devices and off-grid power generation systems. The report recommends that shelter functions should be changed according to the stage of crisis, ranging from the first-response period until education resumes. The report also suggests that a school could be designed to be an evacuation shelter during disasters and as a community facility at other times – capable of hosting athletic events, festivals and intergenerational activities – to enhance the community's resilience.

In the evolution of Japanese DRR in the educational sector, one common theme is the importance of enhancing collaboration between schools, households and the community to localise DRR efforts within each school context. Since teachers are not necessarily from the community, it is not possible for them to fully understand the local community's geographical features and past disaster experiences. Given that teachers' top priority at school is to secure children's safety, they cannot take care of community evacuees when schools become evacuation shelters. Therefore, school–community collaboration is a key to effective DRR in the education sector. This is also a fundamental principle of ESD.

Nuclear disaster response and radiation education at school

MEXT's efforts after the 2011 disaster

The Fukushima nuclear power plant accident was a complex human and natural disaster that resulted from the 2011 GEJET. After the 2011 disaster, MEXT included sections on how to respond to nuclear emergencies in the *The Guide to Creating a School Disaster Manual* of 2012 and the revised *Development of Disaster Prevention Education to Cultivate 'Zest for Living'* of 2013 and it encouraged each municipal government to prepare a nuclear disaster response if any such power plants are located in the area. In the guidebooks nuclear disasters are regarded as one type of disaster. MEXT also published supplementary reading materials on radiation education in 2011 and revised them in 2014, one for elementary pupils and the other for junior high and high school students.

Fukushima Prefecture's efforts

In contrast to the efforts at the central government level, the disaster education efforts of the Fukushima Prefecture Board of Education have been mainly aimed at minimising children's exposure to radiation and its influence on their health and safety, with radiation education an important theme during the post-GEJET period. Immediately after the disaster occurred, Fukushima Prefecture prepared and distributed a teaching guidebook on radiation to all schools in the prefecture, conducted teacher training and established a study group on radiation education for teachers, where they could share information and teaching practices. By March 2014, the guidebook had been revised three times and radiation education was taught within various subjects at all of the elementary and junior high schools in Fukushima Prefecture.

The stated goal of Fukushima's radiation education is to minimise the effect of radiation on children at present and in the future, and to help them live safely in Fukushima by encouraging them to obtain accurate knowledge about radiation and to think and behave according to their own judgement. To do this, it has been linked to disaster education because both aim to foster the ability to understand risk, think and make appropriate decisions and take action. Both also emphasise practicality. The board of education has also attempted to address concerns about the possibility that disaster-affected children will suffer from discrimination. Therefore, radiation education and disaster education are both also closely connected to character education, which includes living with dignity, taking pride and feeling affection towards one's community (Fukushima Prefecture Board of Education 2014). Fukushima's approach to radiation education shares many of the aims of ESD. It intends to foster people's sense of self-sufficiency, responsibility and discernment and to encourage individuals to respect their relationships and involvement with others, the community and nature.

International implications of Japanese experiences

The Japanese experience reveals the importance of reviewing the education sector's DRR policies and practices based on lessons learned from major disasters. As a result of changes implemented after the GEJET, Japanese schools are now being prepared for tsunamis, earthquakes and nuclear disasters. Municipal boards of education have requested that schools improve their crisis management plans and evacuation drills to reflect each school's geographical and socioeconomic context. Enhancing collaboration between schools, households and the community is one of the top priorities in order to enhance the community's resilience to disasters. Discussion is under way on whether safety education should be a discrete subject with mandated teaching hours in the national curriculum and whether an evaluation system should be required to measure schoolchildren's 'zest for living'.

Analyses in previous sections found that, with the evolution of Japanese DRR in the education sector, more links between DRR and ESD are required to promote school–community collaboration for more effective DRR implementation in every school.

These experiences inform the following recommendations for enhancing DRR in the education sector globally and applying Japan's lessons to other countries vulnerable to disasters.

1   *School safety leads to resilience of the education sector.* School safety cannot be achieved at the school level alone. Schools should be supported financially and practically by local education boards and national educational authorities. Legal and legislative frameworks are necessary for schools to secure children's safety. With this support, schools can implement practical and localised disaster risk-reduction measures. A comprehensive resilience assessment of the educational sector needs to be made that measures several indicators for each school: its physical condition, human resources, the external relations between the school and its community and the natural and socioeconomic conditions of the community in which the school is located. Resilience can be fostered through long-term comprehensive school strategies.

2   *School safety leads to a culture of safety.* School safety needs to be linked to a culture of safety. Fostering children's ability to help make society safe and secure is an expected outcome of disaster education. School safety needs to be connected and customised to local conditions. Critical thinking and problem solving need to be enhanced through appropriate education. The key vision of disaster education is 'value for life' or 'zest for living' that is linked to daily life skills. These principles should be taught at school in an age-appropriate way. Disaster education requires life-long learning, and promoting a culture of safety is connected to the concept of ESD.

3   *School safety leads to holistic, community-based risk reduction.* Since community members know more about their community than school teachers dispatched by the municipal government, practical and effective DRR efforts can only be realised through close collaboration between the school and community. Schools need to be open to their communities on a daily basis. Face-to-face relations between the school and community could help foster more effective collaboration when disaster occurs. Having daily contact allows the school and community to prepare a disaster response plan and manual, conduct joint evacuation drills and identify potential hazards through learning about past disasters and geographical and socioeconomic features of the community.

Acknowledgements

This work was supported by Grant-in-Aid for Scientific Research (C) (No. 2651008) from the Ministry of Education, Culture, Sports, Science and Technology of Japan. The content was informed by discussion at a working session on disaster education at the Tohoku Forum for Creativity meeting held at the International Research Institute of Disaster Science (IRIDeS), Tohoku University on 7–8 November 2014 (IRIDeS 2014). The authors would like to thank the session participants for their stimulating contributions.

References

Fukushima Prefecture Board of Education 2014. *Hoshasen kyoiku ni kansuru shido shiryo* (Teaching material on radiation education) (www.gimu.fks.ed.jp/shidou/housyasen_kyouiku_2/). Accessed 25 April 2015.

Global Alliance for Disaster Risk Reduction and Resilience in the Education Sector (GADRRRES) 2012. Comprehensive school safety (http://preventionweb.net/go/31059). Accessed 20 December 2014.

Goto, M. and Okamoto, Y. 2012. *Building a culture of safety through education: Framework to systematize ENDPR*. Bangkok, Thailand: UNESCO Bangkok.

Gwee, Q. R., Shaw, R. and Takeuchi, Y. 2011. Disaster education policy: current and future, in Shaw, R., Shiwaku, K. and Takeuchi, Y. (eds) *Disaster Education*. Bingley, UK: Emerald Group Publishing, 23–44.

International Research Institute of Disaster Science (IRIDeS) 2014. Report of international workshop on Implementing Practical Disaster Risk Reduction, Sendai, Japan: Tohoku University. (http://irides.tohoku.ac.jp/media/files/topics/20141107_detail report_forum_for_creativity.pdf). Accessed 21 December 2014.

Ministry of Education (MOE) 1995. *Gakko Tou no Bosai Taisei no Jyujitsu ni tsuite Daiichiji Hokokusho* (Enhancing school disaster management; initial report) (www.mext.go.jp/a_menu/shisetu/bousai/06051221.htm). Accessed 20 December 2014.

Ministry of Education (MOE) 1996. *Gakko Tou no Bosai Taisei no Jyujitsu ni tsuite Dainiji Hokokusho* (Enhancing school disaster management; secondary report) (www.mext.go.jp/a_menu/shisetu/bousai/06051221.htm). Accessed 20 December 2014.

Ministry of Education (MOE) 1998. *Bosai Kyoiku no tameno Sanko Shiryo 'Ikiru Chikara wo Hagukumu Bousai Kyouiku no Tenkai'* (*Development of Disaster Prevention Education to Cultivate 'Zest for Living'*)

Ministry of Education, Culture, Sports, Science and Technology (MEXT) 2009. *Gakko Anzen no Suishin ni Kansuru Keikaku* (School Health and Safety Act) (http://law.e-gov.go.jp/htmldata/S33/S33F03501000018.html). Accessed 20 December 2014.

Ministry of Education, Culture, Sports, Science and Technology (MEXT) 2011a. *Higashinihon Daishinsai niokeru Gakko Shisetsu no Higai Jokyo* (Situation report on damage to school facilities by the Great East Japan Earthquake) (www.mext.go.jp/b_menu/shingi/chousa/shisetu/017/shiryo/__icsFiles/afieldfile/2011/06/28/1307121_1.pdf). Accessed 20 December 2014.

Ministry of Education, Culture, Sports, Science and Technology (MEXT) 2011b. *Higashi Nihon Daishinsai wo uketa Bosaikyoku Gakko Bosai nikansuru Yushikisha Kaigi Chukan Torimatome* (Mid-term report from the Expert Council on Disaster Prevention Education and Management in the wake of the Great East Japan Earthquake and Tsunami) (www.mext.go.jp/component/a_menu/education/detail/__icsFiles/afieldfile/2013/05/15/1334780_16.pdf). Accessed 20 December 2014.

Ministry of Education, Culture, Sports, Science and Technology (MEXT) 2011c. *Higashinihon Daishinsai no Higai wo Fumaeta Gakko Shisetsu no Seibini tsuite* (Urgent proposal on improving school facilities based on damages by the Great East Japan Earthquake Disaster) (www.mext.go.jp/b_menu/shingi/chousa/shisetu/017/toushin/1308045.htm). Accessed 20 December 2014.

Ministry of Education, Culture, Sports, Science and Technology (MEXT) 2012a. *Higashi Nihon Daishinsai wo uketa Bosaikyoku Gakko Bosai nikansuru Yushikisha Kaigi Saishu Hokoku* (Final report from Expert Council on Disaster Prevention Education and Management in the wake of the Great East Japan Earthquake) (www.mext.go.jp/component/a_menu/education/detail/__icsFiles/afieldfile/2013/05/15/1334780_16.pdf). Accessed 20 December 2014.

Ministry of Education, Culture, Sports, Science and Technology (MEXT) 2012b. *Higashinihon Daishinsai niokeru Gakko touno Taiou nikansuru Chousa Kenkyu Houkoku* (Research study on schools' response to the 2011 Great East Japan Earthquake Disaster) (www.mext.go.jp/a_menu/kenko/anzen/1323511.htm). Accessed 20 December 2014.

Ministry of Education, Culture, Sports, Science and Technology (MEXT) 2012c. *Gakko Bosai Manual Sakusei no Tebiki – Jishin Tsunami Saigai* (The Guide to Creating a School Disaster Manual) (for earthquake and tsunami disasters)) (/www.mext.go.jp/a_menu/kenko/anzen/1323513.htm). Accessed 20 December 2014.

Ministry of Education, Culture, Sports, Science and Technology (MEXT) 2012d. *Gakko Anzen no Suishin ni kansuru Keikaku* (Five-year (2012–2016) plan to promote school safety) (www.mext.go.jp/a_menu/kenko/anzen/1320286.htm). Accessed 20 December 2014.

Ministry of Education, Culture, Sports, Science and Technology (MEXT) 2012e. *Monbu Kagaku Hakusho* (White paper on education, culture, sports, science and technology) (www.mext.go.jp/b_menu/hakusho/html/hpab201401/1350715.htm). Accessed 20 December 2014.

Ministry of Education, Culture, Sports, Science and Technology (MEXT) 2013. *Gakkobosai no tameno Sanko Shiryo, Ikiruchikara wo Hagukumu Bosaikyouiku no Tenkai* (Revision to *Development of Disaster Prevention Education to Cultivate 'Zest for Living'*) (www.mext.go.jp/a_menu/kenko/anzen/1289310.htm). Accessed 20 December 2014.

Ministry of Education, Culture, Sports, Science and Technology (MEXT) 2014a. *Saigai ni Tsuyoi Gakkoshisetsu no Arikata nitsuite: Tsunami Taisaku oyobi Hinanjo toshiteno Bosai Kinou no Kyoka* (Report on disaster resilient school facilities: strengthening countermeasures against tsunami and disaster response for schools functioning as evacuation shelters) (www.mext.go.jp/b_menu/shingi/chousa/shisetu/013/toushin/1344800.htm). Accessed 20 December 2014.

Ministry of Education, Culture, Sports, Science and Technology (MEXT) 2014b. *Gakko niokeru Anzen Kyoiku no Jujitsu nitsuite* (Summary of discussion on enhancing safety education at school) prepared by working group on school safety under the National Council on Education (www.mext.go.jp/component/b_menu/shingi/toushin/__icsFiles/afieldfile/2014/11/19/1353563_02_3_1.pdf). Accessed 20 December 2014.

Oikawa Y. 2014. Education for sustainable development: trends and practices, in Shaw R. and Oikawa Y. (eds) *Education for Sustainable Development and Disaster Risk Reduction.* Tokyo, Japan: Springer, 15–35.

Shaw R. 2014. Overview of concepts: education for sustainable development and disaster risk reduction, in Shaw R. and Oikawa Y. (eds) *Education for Sustainable Development and Disaster Risk Reduction.* Tokyo, Japan: Springer, 1–14.

UNESCO 2009. Bonn declaration, UNESCO World Conference for Sustainable Development (www.desd.org/ESD2009_BonnDeclaration080409.pdf). Accessed 20 December 2014.

UNESCO 2014. Okayama declaration of the UNESCO-Associated schools in Japan (www.unesco.org/new/fileadmin/MULTIMEDIA/HQ/ED/pdf/ASPnetJapanDeclaration.pdf). Accessed 25 April 2015.

UNISDR 2005. Hyogo framework for action: building the resilience of nations and communities to disasters (www.unisdr.org/we/coordinate/hfa). Accessed 20 December 2014.

UNISDR 2015a. Sendai framework for disaster risk reduction 2015–2030 (www.wcdrr.org/uploads/Sendai_Framework_for_Disaster_Risk_Reduction_2015–2030.pdf). Accessed 20 April 2015.

UNISDR 2015b. Brief and concept note for working session on education and knowledge in building a culture of resilience (HFA priority 3) (www.wcdrr.org/wcdrr-data/uploads/858/Working%20Session%20Report%20-%20Education%20and%20Knowledge%20in%20Building%20a%20Culture%20of%20Resilience.pdf). Accessed 20 April 2015.

UNISDR 2015c. Working session report: commitments to safe schools (www.wcdrr.org/wcdrr-data/uploads/881/Working%20Session%20Report%20-%20Commitments%20to%20Safe%20Schools.pdf). Accessed 20 April 2015.

3 Assessing sustainability learning and practice at Moriyama High School, Shiga, Japan

Yi Zhou and Jane Singer

Education for Sustainable Development (ESD) in the formal education sector has been supported by a number of recent programmes and reform policies in Japan, including the education ministry's Super Global High School programme, which promotes internationalisation at selected high schools nationwide. These school-wide initiatives not only provide increased opportunities for implementing ESD, they can also provide the scale, focused curricula and specified time periods needed to assess the impact a specific programme has made on transforming students' pro-sustainable awareness and behaviour. In this chapter, we examine the implementation and outcomes of a Super Global High School programme focused on sustainability in a public high school in Shiga, Japan.

Background to Japan's education reform

Japan has experienced three periods of large-scale educational reform, beginning in the late nineteenth century during the Meiji Restoration (1868–1890) with the establishment of a modern, national educational system with a uniform curriculum. The second reform was the introduction of the single track 6–3–3–4 school system during the US occupation in the late 1940s. This system provided nine years of compulsory education and offered students a chance to continue study at senior high school and universities after passing entrance examinations. As academic achievement in examinations was the major criterion for secondary school admission, Japanese education became quite rigorous under this system (Fujita 2000). International achievement tests, such as the Programme for International Student Assessment (PISA), indicated that Japanese students performed particularly well in reading comprehension, mathematical literacy and scientific literacy (Ministry of Education, Culture, Sports, Science and Technology (MEXT) 2001).

However, by the late 1970s, the final years of Japan's high economic growth era, there was growing criticism of the educational system. The mass media widely covered an increase in school-linked behavioural problems such as violence, bullying and truancy, attributing them to exam pressure and overscheduled school days. In addition, there was growing concern about the ability of a centralised, top-down educational system to meet the demands of the information age and a postmodern society facing the challenges of globalisation and ageing. The Japanese also worried that many students were becoming alienated by the system's rigidity and lacked the creativity and flexibility needed in the coming years (Fujita 2000; Hamamoto 2009).

These criticisms finally prompted the third major reform of Japanese education, beginning with the establishment of the National Council on Educational Reform (NCER) in 1984. NCER published four advisory reports that established the foundation for later comprehensive educational reform, emphasising three themes: (1) the principle of respect for the individual, (2) transition to a lifelong learning system, and (3) response to internationalisation and the information society (MEXT 2001). Large-scale curriculum reform was subsequently implemented in 1998 by revising the Courses of Study, the basic guideline for the national curriculum. To improve students' motivation for learning, flexibility and their ability to learn and think independently, the revised Course of Study took measures that included:

1　Reducing the number of class hours and introducing carefully selected educational content,
2　Establishing a Period for Integrated Study,
3　Expanding elective courses,
4　Enhancing instruction to meet individual requirements throughout the entire school curriculum, and
5　Emphasising experiential problem-solving learning activities throughout the school curriculum (MEXT 2001, chapter 3, section 2.1).

Among these measures, the introduction of a Period for Integrated Study provided opportunities for the introduction of ESD into the Japanese primary and secondary curricula. The integrated study initiative enables schools to set aside time for students to study multi-disciplinary issues, such as international understanding, information technology, the environment and health and welfare. Schools and teachers were given great flexibility to determine the hours, subjects and content of learning activities based on students' interests and local characteristics.

This was not the first attempt to promote internationalisation in Japanese public education, as educational activities for improving international communication and foreign language education have been implemented at the community level for many years. For example, the education ministry's Japan Exchange and Teaching (JET) programme, which started in 1987, employs foreign recruits as assistant language teachers, coordinators for international relations or sports exchange advisers to interact with local communities. More than 90 per cent of the participants are employed as assistant language teachers, working mainly in public schools or local boards of education. Currently, there are 4,786 participants from 43 countries involved in this programme (JET n.d.). This experiment in international exchange has spurred additional reflection by the education ministry about the need to reform the traditional educational system to promote individuality, creativity and a workforce for the twenty-first century.

The Super Global High School programme

Globalisation was furthered by the emergence of the Super Global High School (SGH) programme in 2014. This was initiated by MEXT to cultivate future globalised leaders in high schools by promoting students' awareness of social issues and improving their communication abilities and problem-solving skills. Schools certified as Super Global High Schools must identify the competencies and leadership they seek to promote, and they must conduct multidisciplinary and exploratory studies in collaboration with domestic and international universities, organisations and companies. Currently there are 112 schools nationwide that have been certified as SGH schools (56 certified in 2014 and another 56 in 2015). Each SGH school proposes an original theme corresponding to the SGH guidelines, which include diverse topics such as energy, democracy, sustainability and equality. For example, the Ibaraki Prefectural Tsuchiura First High School chose as its theme 'cultivation of global human resources with a focus on developing new bio-resource businesses', while Ochanomizu University Senior High School selected the theme 'developing women's potential worldwide' (SGH Programme n.d.).

This chapter examines the Super Global High School programme that has been implemented in Shiga Prefectural Moriyama High School since 2014. This public school in Shiga prefecture was established in 1963 and launched an affiliated junior high school in 2003. It has 986 students – 237 junior high school students and 749 high school students. The students at Moriyama High School have been active participants in domestic and international events, such as the Japanese national debate contest in 2011 and the UNESCO International Education for Sustainable Development Youth Conference held in Japan in 2014. Moriyama High School focuses on international communication, establishing, in 2011, the Moriyama Overseas Study Programme (MOS-P) that has sent students to Australia and England for short-term study.

Moriyama High School decided upon the theme of sustainability for its proposed SGH project. The Moriyama Project – to Realise a Sustainable Society – encourages students to consider, discuss, research and propose ways to mainstream sustainability throughout the high school environment. The SGH programme at Moriyama High School is expected to continue for five years. The first year, 2014, focused on seven classes of first year students in the senior high school, totalling 274. To implement the project effectively, Moriyama High School planned to:

1   Coordinate with universities, companies and international organisations to enable students to carry out fieldwork or site visits and learn practically,
2   Organise sustainability-related lectures and workshops in collaboration with university faculty,
3   Conduct ongoing in-school debate activities on sustainability-related topics,
4   Assemble a topic research team of highly motivated students to visit Europe for overseas study and training, and
5   Put forward a final proposal for creating a sustainable society, in Shiga and globally, through the learning and efforts of teachers and students.

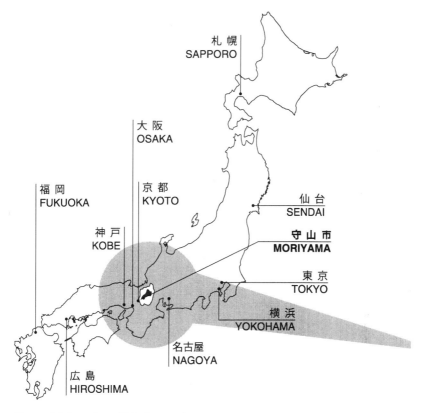

Figure 3.1 Location of Moriyama city

Source: Moriyama city website

In this way, ESD was integrated into the implementation of the SGH programme at Moriyama High School.

The SGH programme was launched on 1 October 2014. The school held an orientation meeting for all 274 students on 17 October to introduce the SGH programme, followed by a series of lectures by experts from different organisations to stimulate students' thinking about sustainability. For example, a law professor from Kyoto University gave a lecture about law and social equity, then a professor of environmental studies presented seven classes with hands-on environmental content to each homeroom in early November. Students were divided into small groups to discuss issues relating to sustainable lifestyles, such as choosing between bananas grown in Japan and those imported from the Philippines, or between breakfast at McDonald's and a traditional Japanese breakfast of fish and rice. By comparing the implications of different lifestyle choices, students came to learn about the significance of pro-sustainable behaviour and the need to act pro-sustainably.

A manager of a local housing corporation then introduced students to the concept of corporate social responsibility, the principles of 3R (reduce, reuse and recycle) and the design of environmentally friendly products, such as biomass plastic. On 17 November, a Kyoto University professor specialising in energy science explained the classification of energy, changes in energy consumption, Japan's current energy situation and future challenges. To prepare for in-school debates on eight sustainability-related topics, students received training and assistance in research skills from five graduate students of Kyoto University. Every student was involved in the debates, which began on 18 December. The topics were:

1   Shiga prefectural high schools should build dining halls in school.
2   The Japanese government should completely abolish nuclear power plants.
3   Japan should completely forbid research whaling.
4   Moriyama High School should remove all vending machines selling soft drinks on its premises.
5   Japanese youth are happy and wealthy.
6   Japan should charge for garbage collection.
7   Social networking systems hinder true communication.
8   Japan should accept more foreign labourers.

While the debates took place, lectures continued to be sponsored. On 27 January 2015, the director of the Lake Biwa Environmental Research Institute discussed the realisation of a sustainable society through development of industry and technology. Twenty-one highly motivated students were recruited to a topic research team that conducted theme-based studies and prepared for overseas study. These students joined a workshop on 7 February 2015, led by the chief executive of a global education venture, on the topic of global leadership. All the students were then provided with a talk and discussion about peace and conflict and links to sustainability. Finally, Moriyama High School sponsored a conclusive panel

Table 3.1 Timing of activities during SGH programme

Time	Activity
17 October 2014	Orientation meeting of SGH
21 October 2014	Lecture about law and social equity
4, 6 and 7 November 2014	Lectures on the principles of sustainability
10 November 2014	Presentation by Sekisui Resin Company
17 November 2014	Lecture about energy
11, 12 December 2014	Trainings on research skills
18 December 2014–28 February 2015	Weekly debates
27 January 2015	Lecture on realising a sustainable society
7 February 2015	Workshop of global leaders
10 February 2015	Workshop on peace
Early March 2015	Panel discussion

discussion in early March 2015 to summarise and present the lessons learned from the first five months of the SGH programme. The event was attended by students from both the junior and senior high school and representatives from various governments and institutions. Table 3.1 shows the timing of the activities mentioned above.

Investigating the SGH programme

Pre- and post-programme surveys

To investigate the effectiveness of the SGH programme and its impact on students' pro-sustainable awareness and behaviour, the first author conducted a five-month internship at Moriyama High School and assisted the school's assessment by implementing questionnaire surveys and focus group discussions. Pre- and post-programme questionnaires were administered to all 274 first year senior high school students. Both the pre- and post-programme surveys were divided into two parts. Part one assessed students' perspectives and understanding of sustainability and pro-sustainable behaviour in daily life. Part two identified the change in students' awareness and interest in learning about diverse social issues, their interrogative skills (including communication and problem-solving skills) and their reflections on the programme. As the objective of the SGH programme is to foster future global leaders, these indicators are helpful for assessing the programme's effectiveness and modifying further implementation. Thus the pre- and post-programme surveys shared a similar structure, although some of the content was different, as explained below.

Part one of the pre-programme survey contained seven questions about students' attitudes towards sustainability, their initial understanding of sustainability, media for learning about sustainability to date and experience of participating in sustainability-related activities, their assumption of responsibility and pro-sustainable behaviour. The survey used Likert scale assessment of statements ('strongly agree, agree, undecided, disagree and strongly disagree'). Part two of the pre-programme survey had eight questions about students' expectations of the programme, including activities, research topics and study fields that appealed to them, and their willingness to study abroad and take a job overseas. The post-programme survey also had two parts but the contents were slightly different. Part one asked students about their intentions to act for sustainability after joining the SGH programme. The other questions were the same as in the pre-programme survey to obtain comparative data. Part two of the post-programme survey contained similar questions to the pre-programme survey. Students were asked to name the activities and debate topics they had found the most interesting. Finally, they were asked to indicate the specific competencies – including communication skills, English level and critical thinking – they felt had improved as a result of the programme.

To identify students' initial perspectives on sustainability, part one of the pre-programme survey was implemented on 10 October 2014, before the orientation. Part two of pre-programme survey was distributed on the day of the orientation, 17 October, after the SGH programme was introduced to students. Because part two focused on students' perspectives of the SGH programme, students had to be informed about the programme before they could fill it out. Both parts of the post-programme survey, however, were administered on the same day, 19 February 2015. It should be noted that the SGH programme will last for five years in total but most of the student activities for its first year were concluded by 19 February 2015, when the post-programme survey was administered. For example, the sustainability-related lectures run in collaboration with Kyoto University and Seikisui Resin Company, the in-school debate contests and the global leader workshops were completed within a five-month period. This research, therefore, assessed the initial achievements of the SGH programme but was not completely conclusive.

Focus group discussions

The pre- and post-programme surveys can assess how students' awareness and behaviour change after joining the SGH programme. However, to better understand the underlying reasons for change, focus group discussions (FGD) are helpful. FDGs enable collective discussion of focused topics and permit greater flexibility in discussion than surveys, generating more extensive comments. Students were asked five main questions:

1   Do you understand 'sustainability?' Please explain sustainability in your own words.
2   Do you think sustainability is important? Why?
3   Do you think sustainability is related to you? Do you feel responsible to help make society more sustainable? Why?
4   Do you feel confident about your involvement and effort? Why?
5   Are you willing to act? If not, what prevents you from doing so?

Sixteen of the 274 first year students were selected to participate in two FDGs on 27 February 2015, led by the first author. Group one comprised eight students who were relatively inactive in the SGH programme. They were selected according to their answers in the post-programme survey, having indicated little interest in SGH activities or few feelings of responsibility for contributing to sustainability. Group two comprised eight students who were relatively active and interested in the SGH programme. They had volunteered to participate in the topic research team for concentrated studies on sustainability-related topics and additional SGH activities such as global leaders' workshops and overseas study. Students in group one were less communicative and some showed impatience because they were forced to absent themselves from their usual after-school student circle activities. The discussion finished within 30 minutes. Students in group two expressed their ideas actively, extending their discussion by 10 minutes.

Main results and discussion

This section presents the results of pre- and post-programme surveys as well as the two FDGs. As explained above, both surveys were divided into two parts. Part one assessed students' pro-sustainable awareness and behaviour while part two queried students about their expectations of, and reflections on, the SGH programme. This section will discuss several important findings.

Change in awareness of sustainability

In question two of the pre-programme survey, which assessed awareness of sustainability, students were asked to brainstorm for 60 seconds any words or phrases they associated with the word 'sustainability'. Sixty-three per cent of them could not think of any words; the remaining 37 per cent wrote down words and phrases. The author categorised students' answers into nine codes: future and future generations; limited resources; renewable resources; recycle and save; social reform; social problems; nature; environmental problems; meetings and activities on environmental conservation and protection (Table 3.2). In assessing the distribution of words by category, 31 per cent of the words related to recycling and saving, which was the most popular category by frequency of occurrence. The second most frequently occurring category was that of resources, with 26 per cent of the words, including limited resources (15 per cent) and renewable resources (11 per cent). Twenty per cent of the words concerned nature (9 per cent) or environmental problems (11 per cent). Finally, 17 per cent of the words related to social reform (11 per cent) or social problems (6 per cent).

Because students learned about sustainability topics for nearly five months, instead of simply brainstorming sustainability words (as in the pre-programme survey), students were asked in question two of the post-programme survey to write down their understanding or own definition of sustainability. The first author

Table 3.2 Students' conceptions of sustainability recorded in pre- and post-programme surveys

Pre: words by category	Rate	Post: words by category	Rate
Future generations	2%	Future generations	36%
		Continuation	24%
Limited resources/energy	15%	Reduce consumption	10%
Renewable resources/ energy	11%		
Recycle/saving	31%	Reduce waste	5%
Social reform	11%	Affluent and stable life	7%
Social problems	6%	Equality	3%
Nature	9%	Symbiosis	2%
Environment problems	11%		
Meetings/activities	4%	Cooperation	6%
		Current actions	7%

selected key words included in students' definitions of sustainability and coded them into nine categories: continuation; future generations; cooperation; reduced consumption of resources; reduced waste, including recycling; symbiosis; affluent and stable life; equality and current action. The most significant words were 'continuation' and 'future generations', mentioned by 24 per cent and 36 per cent of students respectively. Ten per cent of the students mentioned limited resources, renewable energy production and effective use of existing resources, all of which were categorised as 'reduce consumption'. Seven per cent of students wrote that we should conserve richness, diversity and stability for future generations and noted that we currently face an emergency that requires strong action. Several others mentioned such topics as cooperation, symbiosis and equality.

A comparison of the categories of words the students defined in the pre- and post-programme surveys suggests that their understanding and perception of sustainability progressed to a certain degree. In the pre-programme survey, when considering the word 'sustainability', students thought of existing environmental and social problems and concerns, such as energy depletion or food capacity. They easily connected recycling and saving activities with sustainability because the category of recycling/saving had the highest percentage of responses at 31 per cent. In the post-programme survey, however, students' responses were less linked to concerns and more to solutions and actions, such as reducing consumption and reducing waste. They identified key words of sustainability with normative implications, with 'continuation' and 'future generations' accounting for 24 and 36 per cent respectively. Rather than focusing on social and environmental problems, they regarded issues such as quality of life and symbiosis with the natural environment as in pursuit of sustainable development. Moreover, students began to attach importance to cooperation and actions for sustainability – that category accounted for 13 per cent of the responses.

Change in personal responsibility

Environmental responsibility has been defined as 'an individual's sense of obligation or duty to take measures against environmental deterioration in general, or against specific environmental problems' (Fransson and Garling 1999, 375). To get a more complete understanding of students' feelings about their individual contributions, the first author asked them to choose from the following in the pre-programme survey:

Q5) Do you think you bear responsibility for realising a sustainable society?

- Yes, I think individuals' contribution will make a change. I not only feel responsible, but also will take actions.
- Yes, but I am not confident that it will make any difference for the world.
- Yes, but I don't know what should I do.
- No, I don't think individual actions can change the world.
- No, I don't think it is my responsibility.

The five different statements show the different levels of the students' sense of responsibility. According to the results, 47 per cent had a sense of responsibility but did not know what they should or could do, while 12 per cent lacked self-confidence in their effectiveness as citizens. In contrast, 38 per cent of them understood that individual contributions could make a difference and they were willing to take responsibility for the effects of their actions. Generally, 97 per cent of the students answered that they felt responsible for contributing to promote sustainability. Only 1 per cent chose the final two statements. In other words, most of them recognised citizens' rights and responsibilities, which meant they understood the importance of exercising the rights and responsibilities of citizenship (Simmons 2014).

In the post-programme survey, students were asked the same question. The percentage of students who felt responsible for contributing to sustainable development and were willing to act was 43 per cent, five percentage points higher than in the pre-programme survey. Twenty six per cent of them felt responsible but were not confident about the effectiveness of individual actions, an increase from the response in the pre-programme survey of 14 per cent. The percentage of students who felt responsible but didn't know what they should do decreased from 47 to 29 per cent. In addition, the percentage of students who didn't feel responsible decreased to 0 per cent. All of the students indicated a sense of responsibility; although some of them lacked self-confidence or were unclear about what could be done. To conduct a t-test statistical analysis, five degrees of responsibility were coded from score 5 (= yes, I feel responsible and will take action) to score 1 (= no, I don't feel responsible). A paired-samples t-test was conducted to compare the average score of the responsibilities of students in the pre-programme survey and the post-programme survey. It should be noted that six students did not answer this question in the pre-programme survey and 12 students did not answer in the post-programme survey. Thus the sample size was 268 students in the pre-programme survey and 262 students in the post-programme survey. The result was that the average score in the pre-programme survey was 3.86 and the average score in the post-programme survey was 4.13, representing a statistically significant increase ($p < 0.01$).

According to the survey results, the majority of students reported that they felt responsible for contributing to sustainability, both in the pre-programme survey and the post-programme survey. In the pre-programme survey, 97 per cent of students said they felt responsible and 98 per cent did so in the post-programme survey. This result could have been influenced by two reasons. One is general social trends. As environmental issues and pro-environmental campaigns have been widely reported by the media, support for environmental conservation has become broadly accepted (Gifford and Nilsson 2014). Students may be affected by these prevalent norms and derive a feeling of responsibility from them. Another reason could be the environmental and cultural background of Shiga prefecture. Teachers from Moriyama High School reported that people living in Shiga prefecture tended to have a strong love of nature and desire to protect the environment. That belief is largely related to the naturally rich ecological conditions found in Shiga prefecture, including Japan's largest lake, Biwa. It is assumed that residents recognise that they accrue benefits from Biwa Lake and other natural resources. That makes them feel grateful and proud of their prefecture and to value the environment more. So it is possible that this local context is one of the factors contributing to students' high sense of responsibility and environmental awareness.

The students' sense of obligation can be divided into three levels: (1) responsible and confident about personal efforts; (2) responsible but not confident about efforts; (3) responsible but not prepared for taking pro-sustainable actions (lack of knowledge of action strategies or skills). The rate of students belonging to each group changed in the post-programme survey. Students in group (3) decreased substantially while students in group (1) and (2) increased. Without doubt, the increase in the number of students who showed responsibility and confidence demonstrated the positive impacts of the programme, because students who feel more responsible and confident will have a higher likelihood of practising pro-sustainable behaviour. The increase in students who felt responsible but were not confident cannot completely be regarded as an achievement. However, it implies that students became more conscious of what they could do but were still not confident of their skills or the results of their actions. (The role of confidence will be discussed below.)

Limited change in pro-sustainable behaviour

In question six of the pre-programme survey, students were asked whether they were performing pro-sustainable actions in daily life. Seventy six per cent of the students said they were implementing pro-sustainable habitual behaviour in daily life. Twenty three per cent of them did not. In the post-programme survey, students were asked the same question. Seventy eight per cent of students were continuing environmentally responsible actions in daily life, up two percentage points on the results of the pre-programme survey, while the number of students giving a negative response decreased from 23 to 19 per cent. Generally, students' pro-sustainable behaviour did not change dramatically. The percentage of students who had been acting pro-sustainably was already relatively high in the pre-programme survey. Even before joining the SGH programme, students sorted their rubbish by type, practised energy conservation and carried reusable shopping bags nearly every day, so no dramatic change occurred. One of the underlying reasons may relate to governmental policies. For instance, the Japanese government has, since 2007, promoted strict local requirements for sorting household waste (Ministry of Environment 2013). Citizens are required to cooperate with government regulations and currently most cities and towns in Japan follow basic waste sorting rules. We can also assume that the students were influenced by their families' following of local rules.

It should be noted that the assessment was implemented only for the first five months of the SGH programme. At this early stage of implementation, it is difficult to conduct a conclusive evaluation of the programme's effectiveness in changing behaviour. Changing behaviour is generally more time consuming than increasing knowledge and altering attitudes because it requires the students to reflect on their lives and tackle fixed habits. Strategies and activities in the first five months focused on making students aware of sustainability, understanding it and seeking to attain it. The programme did not provide specific opportunities or training that would enable students to reflect on their previous or current behaviour based on new information gained about sustainability. Without reflection, students may not seek links between themselves and sustainability and may stop at general cognition without attempting to change their behaviour. Thus, impacts on behaviour may take time to show as the programme continues.

Confidence in individual contributions

The key finding of the FDG was that most students did not feel confident about the individual contributions they could make towards achieving sustainability. In group one (relatively inactive students), five students said they lacked confidence in their ability to make individual contributions to sustainability. Two of them were unclear about their ability while one of them said he felt confident. Those lacking confidence explained that they thought personal efforts were not effective ('one person's work cannot change anything') and the number of people working for sustainability was small so sustainability efforts could not be continued for a long time. In group two (relatively active students), five students were not confident but the other three were.

This phenomenon is discussed in De Young's (2013, 27) work on environmental psychology: 'If we cast the problems faced as being at a large scale, as is often the case with environmental issues, then it is hard to imagine anything but a large-scale solution sufficing'. Environmental problems often lead people to think in a limited way about a response but the solution need not to be limited in type. As De Young continues: 'Large-scale problems may seem to demand large-scale solutions, yet the scale of the problem need not dictate the scale of the solution'. Consequently, small-scale solutions may be related to ethical issues: 'It is not your responsibility to finish the work (of perfecting the world), [yet] you are not free to desist from it either'. From this viewpoint, it can be assumed that students who are willing to engage in small-scale solutions have a sense of responsibility to support them. Conversely, students who are not confident about small-scale solutions and prefer large-scale solutions probably do not have ethical motivations.

In group two, when students were asked why they lacked confidence, most cited a perceived lack of knowledge. They repeatedly mentioned the necessity to increase their knowledge of sustainability. One student noted: 'I understand that an individual contribution can help to make a difference. But we still have to learn more. When we become adults, our ability to practise pro-sustainable behaviour will be related to how much we learn now.' Notwithstanding the actual knowledge the students have gained, they regard knowledge as a main source of confidence and their self-assessed lack of information is holding them back. Volk and Cheak's 2003 investigation into an environmental education programme disclosed similar results, revealing that students became more engaged in working to solve environmental problems when they believed they had acquired the knowledge and skills to do so (cited in Eilam and Trop 2011). It suggests there is a positive connection between students' perceived knowledge, skills and confidence.

It should be noted that the cultural context may also be an underlying reason for students' low self-evaluation. Compared with western teenagers, Japanese students tend to be more cautious and self-critical, particularly when asked to give evaluations of their capabilities. The Values in Action Inventory of Strengths was a self-assessment survey that asked respondents to assign a relative value to 24 character traits, including kindness, humour, teamwork and modesty. According to the results, young Americans endorsed leadership while young Japanese prized modesty (Shimai *et al.* 2006). Toivonen *et al.* (2011, 6) also found that 'there is a general tendency for individuals to be more risk-averse than risk-taking in interdependent cultural contexts like Japan'. They added that this tendency makes it difficult for individuals to pursue globalisation proactively, even though there may be active efforts at an institutional level. Thus the Japanese cultural background may contribute to students' professions of modesty and a purported lack of self-confidence.

Another reason why the students lacked confidence was that they felt there were many barriers to applying pro-sustainable behaviour. According to one student: 'We are doing a lot in daily life. But at the same time, even though we sort trash, we don't unplug our telephone chargers, we watch TV instead of preparing for tests, and we use computers and the internet to search for what we can do for sustainability instead of applying habitual behaviour in daily life. What we do and what we say are always different.' Another student said: 'We forget that producing a large number of flyers advocating environmental protection is a waste of paper'. They may have no idea how to overcome these obstacles due, in part, to force of habit. Numerous types of behaviour in daily life, which make a negative impact on the environment, are habitual (Roins *et al.* 1989). It is necessary to practise and persist with a new type of behaviour until it becomes a new habit (Kollmuss and Agyeman 2002). Most people fail to change the old 'frozen' behaviour (old habit) into a new one. This failure can be attributed to such constraints as a lack of time and/or money and the pursuit of convenience and comfort (Kollmuss and Agyeman 2002). However, when we explore deeply the underlying reasons for 'not having time' or 'desiring convenience', a lack of 'meaningfulness', as defined by De Young (2013), may explain this phenomenon.

De Young (2013, 24) stated that meaningfulness is a significant determinant of voluntary behaviour on both small and large scales, writing that 'the meaningfulness experienced is less about the scale of the effort and more about deriving a sense of making a difference . . . doing something judged worthwhile or making a difference in the long run are primary motives underlying voluntary environmental stewardship behaviour'. Students came across many obstacles when implementing some pro-sustainable behaviour and it made them feel overwhelmed. They thought they may never make a difference with such an ineffective approach.

In this way, their pro-sustainable behaviour lost its meaningfulness and they could not persist with it. This feeling is underlined by the statement of one student, who said: 'The results and effects of our endeavors are not easy to see. Even though we act pro-sustainably, we are not sure it is really working well and contributing.'

Conclusions

The latest round of educational reform by the Japanese government has promoted many new initiatives and programmes, including the Super Global High School programme for fostering global leaders. Moriyama High School in Shiga prefecture is one of the schools participating in the SGH programme and its focus on sustainability opens up a good opportunity for implementing ESD.

To investigate the effectiveness of the programme and its impact on students' awareness and behaviour, the first author conducted an assessment of the programme's first five months. The results revealed an improvement in students' awareness of sustainability but there was no dramatic change in behaviour. Unexpectedly, at the beginning of programme, most students already thought they bore responsibility for promoting sustainability. However, most of them did not feel confident about their own behaviour. A low evaluation of their abilities and barriers to implementing pro-sustainable behaviour, such as bad habits and feelings of uncertainty over the effectiveness of action, may account for the students' lack of confidence. Moreover, the students' lack of confidence may prevent them from instigating or persisting in pro-sustainable actions. Since the curriculum at the beginning of the programme focused on learning about sustainability rather than engaging in it, there was a positive improvement in students' cognition and awareness of sustainability. However, the authors suggest the students' investigative, evaluative and problem-solving skills should be honed by introducing more experiential learning, and that emotional learning should be included to build up solid self-confidence through the realisation of meaningfulness. This will increase the likelihood of the students changing their behaviour and engaging in sustainable issues.

Finally, it should be noted that this case study only observed the first five months of the SGH programme. This research cannot assess the total impact of the SGH programme because behaviour takes longer to change than attitudes. Thus a long-term assessment of the same students in the programme will be instructive. A sustainability-related programme should be sustainable itself. As the SGH programme will last for five years, continuous activities later on may play an effective role in changing students' awareness and behaviour.

Acknowledgements

The authors wish to thank the faculty and administration of Moriyama High School for their assistance in facilitating the research described here. They also thank Professor Tracey Gannon and Yuri Sugimoto for their advice and information in preparing the pre- and post-programme surveys.

References

De Young, R. 2013. Environmental psychology overview, in Klein S.R. and Huffman A.H. (eds) *Green organizations: driving change with I-O psychology*. New York, US: Routledge, 17–33.

Eilam, E. and Trop, T. 2011. ESD pedagogy: a guide for perplexed. *The Journal of Environmental Education* 42(1), 43–64.

Fransson, N. and Garling, T. 1999. Environmental concern: conceptual definitions, measurement methods and research findings. *Journal of Environmental Psychology* 19, 369–382.

Fujita, N. 2000. Education reform and education politics in Japan. *The American Sociologist* 31(3), 42–57.

Gifford, R. and Nilsson, A. 2014. Personal and social factors that influence pro-environmental concern and behaviour: a review. *International Journal of Psychology* 49(3), 141–157.

Hamamoto, N. 2009. Japanese middle school's adaptation of the integrated studies: a case study. The State University of New Jersey, Graduate Programme in Education website (https://rucore.libraries.rutgers.edu/rutgers-lib/26652/). Accessed 26 December 2015.

Japan Exchange and Teaching Programme (JET) (n.d.). History of JET (http://jet programme.org/en/history/). Accessed 21 February 2016.

Kollmuss, A. and Agyeman, J. (2002). Mind the gap: why do people act environmentally and what are the barriers to pro-environmental behaviour? *Environmental Education Research* 8(3), 240–260.

Ministry of Education, Culture, Sports, Science and Technology (MEXT) 2001. Japanese government policies in education, culture, sports, science and technology 2001 (www. mext.go.jp/b_menu/hakusho/html/hpac200101/index.html). Accessed 21 February 2016.

Ministry of Environment 2013. *Gomi shori kihon keikaku sakutei shishin* (Basic plan of standards for waste management) (www.env.go.jp/recycle/waste/gl_dwdbp/guideline 201306.pdf). Accessed 21 February 2016.

Roins, D. L., Yates, J. F. and Kirscht, J. P. 1989. Attitudes, decisions and habits as determinants of repeated behaviour, in Pratkanis A. R., Breckler S. J. and Greenwald A. G. (eds) *Attitude structure and function*. Hillsdale, US: Erlbaum, 213–239.

Shimai, S., Otake, K., Park, N., Peterson, C. and Seligman, M. E. P. 2006. Convergence of character strengths in American and Japanese young adults. *Journal of Happiness Studies* 7, 311–322.

Simmons, B. 2014. Essential elements of sustainability education. *Journal of Sustainability Education* (www.jsedimensions.org/wordpress/content/essential-elements-of-sustainability-education-template_2014_06/). Accessed 26 December 2015.

Super Global High School (SGH) Programme (n.d.). Outline of Super Global High School programme (www.sghc.jp/en/). Accessed 21 February 2016.

Toivonen, T., Norasakkunkit, V. and Uchida, Y. 2011. Unable to conform, unwilling to rebel? Youth, culture and motivation in globalising Japan. *Frontiers in Psychology* 2(207), 1–9.

4 Globalising school education in Japan

An investigation using the academic ability model

Toshiya Kodama

1. Introduction

The World Conference on Education for Sustainable Development (ESD), held in the cities of Okayama and Aichi-Nagoya in 2014 to mark the end of the United Nations Decade of ESD (DESD), assessed the outcomes of the decade and discussed post-DESD prospects. Highlights of the Stakeholder Meetings in Okayama included the UNESCO ASPnet (Associated Schools Project Network) International ESD Events for Students and Teachers, which hosted some 1,600 attendees, including policy makers and educators from a number of countries. Delegates at these events lauded the UNESCO ASPnet programme as one of the decade's successes, praising the rapid expansion in the number of ASPnet schools in Japan – up to 807 by the end of the decade – along with the schools' demonstration of diverse ESD practices (Asia-Pacific Cultural Centre for UNESCO 2015a, 2). The rapid proliferation in the number of schools teaching ESD across Japan gives the impression that the country is advanced in ESD practices. However, although examples of excellent ESD practices abound in UNESCO-Associated schools and non-associated schools alike, the lack of empirical research to evaluate national progress makes it difficult to claim that the integration of ESD into Japanese schools has been an unqualified success.

This chapter examines ESD practice in reference to Japanese educational policies and theories of academic ability by drawing on a literature review of Japanese educational policy and the author's notes from participation in numerous open classes. The chapter first reviews the evolution of ESD practices in Japanese schools in line with Japanese educational policy in the 2000s. It then examines the ways in which ESD's integration in schools has been influenced by Japanese government course guidelines from 2000 onwards and theories of academic ability from the same period. The chapter ends with a discussion of the challenges and prospects for ESD practice in Japan in the post-DESD era, particularly in relation to the problem of how Japan is to survive in the twenty-first-century global economy.

2. The development of ESD practice in Japanese schools

For almost 70 years, since the end of World War II, Japan's schools have remained embedded in a centralised national educational system. Curriculum content for all schools, from kindergarten through upper secondary schools, is regulated by legally binding government course guidelines that outline the national education policy and are revised once every 10 years by the Ministry of Education, Culture, Sports, Science and Technology (MEXT).

The same period has seen *Nikkyouso*, the leftist Japan Teachers Union, push forward an alternative education movement centred on teacher-led educational study and practice, in opposition to government educational control. However, the influence of the Japanese Teachers Union has decreased since the 1990s, while government control over education has gradually strengthened. The continuation of textbook censorship, the compulsory use of a national flag and national anthem in schools, and the enforcement of job performance evaluations for teachers are symbolic of the way in which the government has reasserted control. Furthermore, since 2007, MEXT has conducted a national academic ability investigation and is pushing forward a policy to evaluate the instructional activity of each school by monitoring student academic ability achievement scores.

Under the influence of recent globalisation, MEXT has promoted a new education policy that purports to answer the needs of the global economy, while maintaining domestic education policy. Hitherto, for much of the twentieth century, course guidelines had provided broad standards for study in three designated domains: subjects (including Japanese, mathematics, science, social studies and foreign languages), moral education and special activities, such as student council activities and school events. Change came at the turn of the century, with the introduction of a new period for integrated studies in the year 2000, and MEXT course guidelines and subsequent efforts to introduce ESD in Japanese schools from the start of the Decade for ESD in 2005. The period for integrated studies is used for learning activities based on teaching materials produced by schools using locally available resources, such as the local environment, culture, history and industry. Students are invited to work collaboratively on topics they have chosen, typically in areas such as international understanding, information technology, environment, welfare and health – all topics, incidentally, that lend themselves naturally to the study of sustainability. The introduction of the period for integrated studies afforded schools new discretion in determining curricula and marked the advent of a gradual but steady shift from a centralised to a more devolved teaching regime. This factor, together with an organisational culture common to many schools in Japan – in which teachers collaborate to improve their performance in the area of 'lesson studies' and schools are free to pursue their own research topics as well as to share them with the parents and teachers of other schools – has made it possible for ESD practice to thrive in Japanese schools in recent years.

The development of ESD practice in Japanese schools can be divided into three phases, starting with the initial period of ESD school practice (2002–2004) after the proclamation of the DESD at the 57th Session of the United Nations General Assembly in 2002. During this period, civic organisations, such as the Japan Council on the DESD, developed training and educational materials for individuals engaged in education, including school teachers, the staff of non-profit organisations (NPOs), companies looking to be more socially responsible and local government. Because the term 'ESD practice' was new, care was also taken to introduce the broader public to the reformation of existing educational practices from an ESD viewpoint.

The second phase (2005–2007) was a period of experimental ESD practice in some schools that enhanced the level of interest and awareness begun by the educational activities of the previous phase. Many of the best practices from this period have provided the foundation for ESD practices today. One example is the attempt by a middle school in Nara prefecture to apply ESD principles to school operations by promoting innovative classes that cut across subject areas. Others include a network of elementary and middle schools in Kesennuma city – which became part of a Regional Centre of Expertise (RCE) on ESD, acknowledged by the United Nations University, and the satellite site for the greater Sendai RCE – and a Tokyo elementary school's attempt to develop an ESD Calendar (explained below) for use in curriculum development. Other important developments in this period include Japan's Action Plan for the DESD, drawn up by the inter-ministerial meeting for the DESD in 2006, and the publication in 2007 of a *Teacher's Guide for Environmental Education* that provided schools with a manual for use when implementing ESD.

The third phase (2008–2014) was marked by the expansion and dissemination of ESD practices, boosted by the Central Education Council's decision, in 2010, to insert phrasing asserting its commitment to ESD and 'building a sustainable society' into the Basic Plan for the Promotion of Education and government course guidelines. The efforts of the UNESCO schools – which at approximately 800 schools comprised some 2 per cent of the total number of elementary and middle schools in Japan in 2014 (MEXT n.d.) – were a key characteristic of this phase, as were the increasing number of municipal governments that became bases for ESD efforts, such as the cities of Kanazawa, Nara and Tama, and the growth in the number of networks for training and education within and among local governments. Meanwhile, with the increase in initiatives, a serious search began for methods of quality improvement, such as better designs for ESD lesson plans.

During the development of the practice of ESD, four trends were identified:

1   *The development of partnerships between schools and locally based NPOs, government offices and private companies.* These saw schools collaborating with the community in diverse ways, such as inviting locally active parents to classes as instructors, developing experiential learning activities and referring to the expert knowledge provided by companies and NPOs.
2   *The increased use of the ESD Calendar to structure curricula.* This enabled educators to systematically reorganise the annual curriculum from a sustainability perspective by integrating ESD into the curriculum for all subjects in the period for integrated studies, moral education and special activities.
3   *An increase in the number of schools integrating the ESD Guidance Framework developed by the National Institute for Educational Policy Research (NIER) into their curriculum.* This framework is structured on 'ESD's constructive concepts' (diversity, reciprocity, finitude, fairness, collaboration and responsibility) and

the skills and attitudes that should be cultivated in students, namely, the ability to think critically, forecast and plan for the future, use multiple perspectives and integrate them into one's thinking, communicate and demonstrate interest in cooperating with others through respectful relationships and voluntary participation (Goto and Okamoto 2012).

4   *The structuring of ESD curricula around environmental education.* Although ESD classes should focus not only on environmental issues but also on social issues such as development, human rights, poverty and health, ESD in Japan has prioritised environmental education activities, such as taking care of and improving the environment around the school, raising animals and cultivating plants. This affords students the opportunity to learn about the local environment but does not foster the study of culture and local history required for effective ESD learning.[1]

These trends in the development of ESD in Japanese schools correspond to a reorientation, from 2000 onwards, of school education that increasingly prioritised student competence development and the consideration of local community when formulating curricula. This will be further explored in Sections 3 and 4.

3. The integration of ESD in Japanese educational policy

The development of ESD in Japan has been influenced by government course guidelines and international educational policies endorsed by the Organisation for Economic Co-operation and Development. The OECD is an intergovernmental organisation of industrialised countries that seeks to promote the social and economic wellbeing of people around the world by sharing experiences and working towards solutions at the collective level (OECD 2015). To understand how ESD has been integrated into Japanese educational policy, one must first understand the complex relationship with domestic and global educational policies throughout the 2000s that has shaped its development to date.

One important feature of the 2010 government course guidelines is that they were formulated to return Japanese education to a higher international standing after the results of the 2003 Programme for International Student Assessment (PISA) survey – an assessment of 15-year-old students' reading, mathematics and science literacy, coordinated by the OECD every three years from 2000 – reported a decline in Japanese students' reading ability. MEXT's goal 'to pull Japan back to the top level of international surveys of educational achievement' (Cabinet Office 2010, 33), in line with the 'new growth strategy' of the government at that time, is evident in the strict guidelines introduced throughout the curriculum for all subjects, including the period for integrated studies, to meet the PISA literacy standards.

The 2010 guidelines were also governed by the perceived need to educate human resources for the 'knowledge-based society' of the twenty-first century (MEXT 2008, 1–2). By the phrase 'knowledge-based society', MEXT was describing a society in which new knowledge, information and technology had become the basis and defining feature of every domain of life, including politics, economy and culture (MEXT 2005). Having determined that society in the twenty-first century would be one in which knowledge development accelerated international competition, MEXT proposed a new plan to equip workers with the skills to compete and cooperate in the global economy – for example, the flexibility necessary to continuously update their thinking with new knowledge (MEXT 2008, 1–2). Although government course guidelines before 2000 had focused on training talent for the domestic market, the 2010 guidelines were formulated to train talent to global standards. This required a new skillset, unified by a new concept called *Ikiru chikara* (zest for living), combining three elements: 'solid academic ability', evidenced in basic knowledge and the ability to think for oneself; 'strong empathy', characterised by self-control, empathy and the ability to work in a team, and 'a healthy body' (Ibid., 3). These abilities were intended to help students live in a knowledge-based society by equipping them with the capacity for life-long learning, problem solving, communication and global awareness (MEXT 2011).

This focus on key competencies – the third important feature of the government guidelines for 2010 – was largely influenced by the OECD's Definition and Selection of Key Competencies Project (DeSeCo), which set out in 1997 to define the skills necessary for a successful life and a well functioning society in a world that has become increasingly diverse and interconnected because of globalisation (OECD n.d., 4). In seeking to 'provide a sound conceptual framework to inform the identification of key competencies and strengthen international surveys measuring the competence level of young people and adults' (Ibid., 5), this PISA-linked project identified the ability to use tools such as: language, knowledge and technology for interaction; the ability to interact with groups that are different from oneself to strengthen social relationships; and the ability to act autonomously to make something meaningful to one's own life (Rychen and Salganik 2008, 200–218). Barry McGaw, head of the OECD Education Agency, has pointed out that OECD countries adopt a world view that aims for a balance between 1) sustaining the natural environment while achieving economic growth, and 2) reducing social inequality while maximising the personal success that accompanies social connections (McGaw 2008, 17). Building a sustainable society is fundamental to this world view and links the key competencies targeted in the DeSeCo projects with the theoretical foundations supporting PISA.

By integrating PISA standards into its model for increasing academic abilities through education in the core subjects and the period for integrated learning (MEXT 2008, 25), MEXT endorsed PISA as the international standard for academic ability. However, in basing its academic ability model on the need to train human resources for a knowledge-based society, MEXT deviated from the fundamental principles of OECD educational policy. By selectively importing only those elements that suit domestic educational policy, MEXT was trying to work out a compromise between two factors: 1) OECD education policies devised to transcend the barriers of borders and language by equipping workers with the abilities to compete in an increasingly mobile world labour market,[2] and

2) domestic educational policy, devised to maintain a highly skilled homogeneous labour force and retain Japan's high international standing by improving students' test scores. Efforts to introduce ESD as just one more instance of global education during this transitional period have floundered as well as flourished under the combined – one might even say chaotic – influence of these two factors.

4. The academic ability model and ESD integration

'Academic ability' is a complex concept that encompasses a student's ability to learn, learning achievement and cultivation of personality. Discussions of the concept in the field of school education in Japan since the end of World War II to the present day have encompassed definitions of basic academic ability, concerns over a perceived decline in academic ability and a wide range of positions from educators and policy makers – some insisting on 'the totality of ability and skills a child acquires in school' and others focusing more narrowly on 'the ability and skills described in government course guidelines' (Kodama 2013, 47–48). Academic ability in the twentieth century was discussed within the context of 'institutional practice which promotes "scientisation" of educational technology' (Amano 2000, 3–4), when nationalistic discourses aiming 'to integrate the nation-state' converged with the logic of industrialism to shape the discourse on education. This required an education system capable of fostering a young workforce trained to labour steadily to increase its knowledge and skills and improve the productive capacity of industry. However, in the twenty-first century, academic ability corresponding to developments in knowledge, techniques and information is required to compete successfully at an international level.

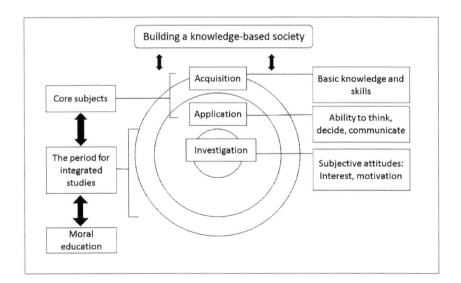

Figure 4.1 Three-level academic ability model

MEXT's efforts to cultivate a labour force that can adapt to a global economy have prompted educational reforms that are, once again, changing how academic ability is understood. Currently, MEXT is drafting 2020 course guidelines that aim to develop qualities and abilities that can adapt to an ever-changing global society. In short, 'academic ability' is a concept that changes according to the values and situation of a given time.

Kodama (2015, 137) noted that the content of the current government course guidelines for improving academic ability is best understood in terms of three levels, characterised by 1) acquisition, 2) application, and 3) investigation (Figure 4.1).

As shown in the figure, the core subjects are designed to help students 'acquire' fundamental knowledge and skills, such as an understanding of basic mathematics, and the ability to read and write in Japanese. Next, students are encouraged to 'apply' their acquired skills and knowledge in their daily life – thereby developing their ability to think, make decisions and communicate with others. The period for integrated studies subsequently offers students an opportunity to hone these skills through collaborative class- or field-based 'investigation' of issues that the students themselves have proposed. This process, known as 'investigative learning', begins with problem definition and progresses through information collection, organisation and analysis to efforts to synthesise what has been learned through the methods of summary and/or presentation.

The objective of the above model for learning is to develop students' interest, motivation and emotional engagement with the material being studied through a competency model that embraces three perspectives on learning: 'learning methodologies' (for example, the ability to gather and analyse information, and to summarise and present easily understandable findings); 'the students' needs as individuals' (for example, the ability to make decisions about one's own actions and to reflect on how one wants to live), and 'relationships with others and with society' (for example, the ability to collaborate with others to resolve an issue, being interested in participating in social activities to resolve an issue) (MEXT 2008, 25).

In the years following the guidelines of 2000, the results for the period for integrated studies were deemed unsatisfactory. Critics pointed to the difficulty of applying new teaching methods for teachers accustomed to the conventional methods used for teaching the core subjects, a lack of preparedness on the part of schools, and the lack of any mention of the academic ability model in relation to the period for integrated studies in the guidelines of 2000. Criticism from the political and economic worlds was particularly strong, with critics fearful of a decline in academic ability because the time allotted to core subjects was reduced to make way for the period for integrated studies.

However, there were also successes: many schools put together original curricula while new areas of study, such as environmental, social welfare and information technology education, gained widespread acceptance.

In the years following the guidelines of 2010, schools have built on lessons learned by creating curricula based on the three-level academic ability model described above and worked hard to connect instruction between core subjects and the period for integrated studies. Recent reports reveal that 'schools that have promoted investigative learning in the period of integrated learning have scored positively, with a high percentage of correct answers in core subjects' (NIER 2014, 3). Thus it appears that the nation's understanding of the potential of the period for integrated studies is gradually changing to a positive evaluation.

In the same period, an ESD academic ability model proposed in Japan's Action Plan for the DESD became an important guide for schools experimenting with ESD practice in the second phase of the ESD implementation process. This academic ability model identifies student competencies in terms of the desired abilities and attitudes to be developed by students, as well as on the learning methods required to foster these abilities. The requisite competencies targeted in the plan include the ability to:

- think systematically – understanding the background of problems and phenomena and considering things from multiple perspectives and in an integrated way,
- think critically and weigh alternatives,
- analyse data and information,
- communicate effectively,
- lead,
- grasp ethical concepts relating to sustainable development,
- participate fully in society as a citizen.

(Interministerial Meeting on the DESD 2006, 11.
Text adapted and translated by the author).

The plan recommends a participatory approach for learning these abilities, involving a series of processes the students can experience, feel, investigate and practice. This starts by arousing the interest of the student and proceeds through deepening their understanding and cultivating a participative attitude and problem-solving skills toward the ultimate goal: taking concrete actions (Ibid.).

At first glance, the approach appears very similar to the investigative learning method endorsed by MEXT, which underpins the period for integrated studies. However, a closer look reveals differences between the two models. The first difference is that while ESD is clearly oriented towards the cultivation of values relating to sustainable development, the period for integrated studies does not espouse a particular set of values. Most probably, avoiding a fixed set of values was deemed the most effective route to allow children to respond flexibly to a rapidly changing international society, in line with the concept of 'zest for living'.

The second difference is the aim of these two models for cultivating competency. The investigative learning method, which underlies the period for integrated studies, is based on a liberalistic theory of competency cultivation, whereby a learner in the process of resolving a given issue acquires the values included in the issue. These values then converge as the learner starts to 'think about his or her way of life' (MEXT 2008, 53–55). However, ESD practices and programmes seek to reorient contemporary society towards environmentally, socially and economically balanced development, and advocate the building of a sustainable society through action goals. In the Education for All movement coordinated by

UNESCO, for example – which was aligned with the Millennium Development Goals – ESD is grounded in the fundamental principle of equality and empowerment for all people, especially those who have been robbed of their human rights in developing countries. In ESD terms, sustainable development may be conceptualised as a successor in the lineage of 'human development' proposed in 1990 by the United Nations Development Programme (UNDP), or, in Amartya Sen's capability approach, as a process that eradicates barriers to the creation of sustainable wellbeing for people by enabling the abilities and freedom necessary for people to realise their various activities and states of being to flourish (Yoshikawa 2012, 198–204). In other words, while ESD challenges students to learn how to respond flexibly to the challenges of the global economy, it also requires them to 'transform' the reality, alienated by the global economy, to a sustainable orientation.

Without these differences being fully examined, ESD was integrated into the model of academic ability endorsed in the 2010 guidelines and the methodology proposed for the period for integrated studies. Indeed, this was done so successfully that today, ESD in Japan tends to be equated with the period for integrated studies, where it is practised in relation to MEXT's 'zest for living' initiative, rather than sustainability per se. Figure 4.2 summarises how ESD has developed in Japan at the intersection of domestic and international educational policies on the one hand, and differing models of academic ability on the other. What it cannot show are the problems and issues that have arisen as a result of the complex push and pull between these differing, sometimes contradictory, factors. These are instead examined in Section 5.

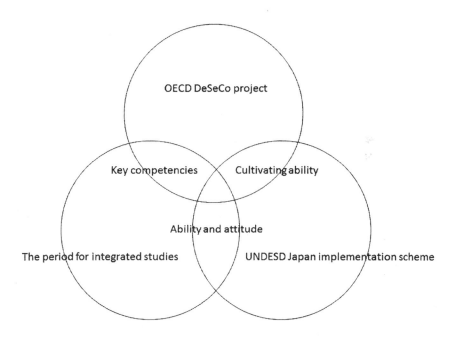

Figure 4.2 ESD practice in Japanese schools

5. Issues in ESD practice

Three problems with ESD practice in Japan may be summarised, on the basis of the discussion so far, as follows.

i. Challenges for teachers who practice ESD

As has been seen, the 2010 guidelines incorporate two fundamentally different visions for society: 1) Japan as a knowledge-based society, and 2) Japan as a sustainable society. These alternative visions are promoted in the guidelines without a theoretical investigation of either being given. In endorsing two different – one might even say opposing – visions for society, the guidelines have spawned competing educational goals that have indirectly affected the practice of ESD in schools. Specifically, schools find it difficult to move forward with educational activities with only an abstract vision of society in mind, and many educators introducing ESD are themselves at a loss to know 'what makes a society sustainable?'

ii. Challenges for ESD implementation in lessons

Discussions about ESD principles and promotion take place primarily in relation to educational policy and civic activities – two spheres in which students do not usually participate. When educational commissioners and school heads recommend ESD practices to schools and teachers in a top-down manner, teachers can find themselves practising ESD without fully understanding what it is. So far, there are few schools in which the teachers themselves have demanded to engage with ESD – something that would have led to a review of the curriculum and an engagement in lesson studies in a bottom-up manner. This situation has produced content in ESD classes that is not always appropriate for ESD. Furthermore, when representatives of these sectors talk about the 'training of human resources', there is a tendency to view students, who should be the primary learner group, as the 'targets' or the 'raw materials' of education. In this regard, Ozaki objects that the refinement of content for the concept of educational goals is moving forward without an adequate understanding of the authority and the power of the 'message' (Ozaki 2009, 25).

In short, attempts by educational commissioners, school heads and other parties collaborating with schools to promote ESD as 'something good' tend to turn ESD practice in schools into something that is far removed from students' daily lives. Furthermore, as pointed out by Kodama (2009, 39), there is a danger that ESD classes or *jyu-gyou* ('received lesson') – part of child-centred development in the school curriculum – may be replaced by classes that are part of projects or *ji-gyou* ('project/real experience lesson') determined by teachers and other adults.

iii. Difficulty of successfully teaching ESD academic ability to students

Pressure is building for twenty-first-century students to learn difficult constructs not addressed in previous courses and to acquire higher-level thinking abilities, such as the ability to think critically and integrate multiple perspectives in their studies. Whether all students can be taught such concepts and competencies is a genuine problem that must be considered. Although many Japanese schools invest an enormous amount of effort in teaching basic learning skills, such as reading, writing and arithmetic, they remain unable to overcome disparities of academic ability, as exemplified partly in a persistent child poverty rate of more than 16 per cent (Cabinet Office 2014).[3] In other words, as long as the ESD academic ability model assumes the teaching of higher-level thinking, the question will remain of whether this is something every child can be taught or whether it is content that only children with high grades can acquire. In Germany, however, ESD is part of a movement to reform education by eliminating structural inequality and ensuring a quality education for all (Takao 2010, 45). If it is indeed possible for changes in values and competencies to be taught to students with low grades, ESD practice might offer schools an opportunity not only to confront the problem of disparity but to overcome it.

It is perhaps unavoidable that these kinds of issues occur when international concepts in education are adopted at the domestic level. However, education should be understood from the student perspective as learning. Models to foster human resources and cultivate skills based on a prescribed educational policy have no inherent meaning in the classroom and, if imposed by force, may become a source of conflict between instructors and students. It is vital, therefore, when considering the development of high-quality ESD practices to put student perspectives first, before the perspectives of educational policy. This coincides with the four goals of education for learners stipulated in *Learning: the Treasure Within* – learning to know, learning to do, learning to live together and learning to be (UNESCO 1996). Given the history of ESD's development through international discussion, these principles should set the tone for the process of reviewing the quality of ESD practice in schools.

6. Perspectives for the future

The completion of the DESD in 2014 gave educators and policy makers an opportunity to review the ESD practice in Japanese schools, to assess the outcomes of the decade and consider what further steps should be taken to promote ESD in Japan's schools. Wrap-up discussions hosted by the cities of Nagoya and Okayama in November 2014 culminated on the last day of the ESD World Conference with the Aichi-Nagoya Declaration on Education for Sustainable Development, which called for 'urgent action' to strengthen and expand ESD further (UNESCO 2014, 1). Two items are of particular significance to the current discussion. Item 8 talks about the 'potential of ESD to empower learners to transform themselves and the society they live in by developing knowledge, skills, attitudes, competences and values required for addressing global citizenship and local contextual challenges of the present and the future' (Ibid., 1). Item 15a calls for greater effort to 'assess the extent to which education policy and curricula are achieving the goals of ESD' as well as for 'multi-stakeholder cooperation and partnerships between actors of the education sector, private sector, civil society and those working in the various areas of sustainable development' to reinforce efforts to integrate ESD into education. It also requests efforts be made to 'ensure the education, training and professional development of teachers and other educators to successfully integrate ESD into teaching and learning' (Ibid., 2).

I foresee five prospects for Japan, given the declaration and the discussion so far. They are as follows.

i. Improvements to ESD lesson content

In what ways can each school create lessons by linking local issues to global issues (climate change, biodiversity, sustainable production and consumption, poverty and so on)? With regard to ESD classroom practice in schools in recent years, many schools are developing lessons on themes such as 'finding something positive about the local area', 'loving the local community' and 'making a contribution to the local community'. By contrast, very few schools are working on themes designed to solve the problems faced by local communities or to 'change the local community for the better'. For schools to go forward, it is important for them to make better use of information and communications technology (ICT) in classrooms and to collaborate more fully with a variety of sectors such as NPOs, corporations and research institutes to create lessons that develop from the local to the global level. Approaches for solving the problems of the local community and/or changing the local community offer an important route to creating unique ESD in a bottom-up manner.

ii. Promoting the 'transformation' of students

In Japanese environmental education studies, 'transformation' literally means 'changing one's behaviour', but it is also used to mean 'to change one's inner life'. Teachers should create lessons that focus on the latter. For instance, Yoshida (2001, 122) argues that 'there is environmental education which focuses on and starts with what children are sad about now, happy about now, angry with now, and what they want now' – there must be 'environmental education that starts with children's voices'. He contends that transformative learning must go beyond requiring children to acquire something and change, by 'requiring the adults who are trying to educate the children to change themselves' (Ibid., 122). In short, teachers need to think about lessons that closely link what children are feeling inside to issues that deal with 'sustainability' in the local community or globally. Understanding education from the viewpoint of the children, who are the agents of learning, could be an important first step in closing the gap in academic ability.

iii. Evaluation of ESD practice

As observed in Section 2, partnerships between schools and various sectors – including companies, NPOs, governmental institutions and researchers – were enhanced over the course of the decade thanks to the introduction of ESD. Today, almost all schools in Japan are engaged in educational activities in collaboration with various sectors. In the post-DESD era, what is being questioned is the *quality* of these partnerships. In this regard, schools will have to create high-quality ESD upon full discussion with various sectors and by making the evaluation criteria for the curriculum and children's academic ability clear. To achieve this, the sectors involved in ESD need to reach a consensus on how and why evaluations are being carried out and by whom.

iv. Developing a new understanding of academic ability

In 2012, NIER proposed 'a twenty-first-century ability' model consisting of 'basic ability, the ability to think and the ability to act' as shown in Figure 4.3. This new concept of academic ability will exert an influence on the 2020 course guidelines. The model starts from the premise that the challenges for Japanese society in the twenty-first century are globalisation, finite resources and a declining birth rate in conjunction with an ageing society. It proposes a number of solutions to these predominantly sustainability-related challenges, as follows: 1) the promotion of

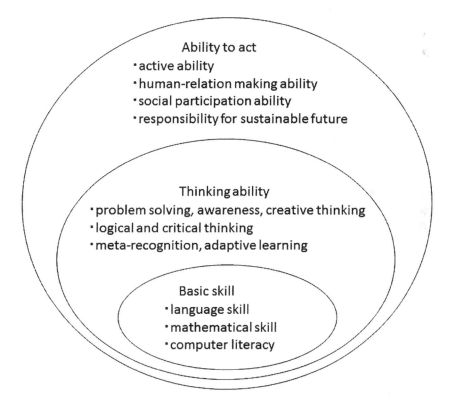

Figure 4.3 Twenty-first century ability model, proposed by NIER

a knowledge-based society, 2) the shift to a society based on community, and 3) the development and utilisation of ICT (NIER 2013, 9). 'Responsibility for a sustainable future' is placed in the 'ability to act' domain in the model and the report urges the importance of letting children internalise values through social participation (Ibid., 28–29). Although it attempts to integrate the different views on academic ability identified in Section 5, the model fails to resolve the problem of having both a 'knowledge-based society' and a 'sustainable society' in the same view. In order to develop and integrate new abilities, such as critical and systematic thinking, and values related to and integrated with new ability, the logical consistency of the two social theories needs to be examined. Furthermore, drawing on the twenty-first century ability model, a new view of academic ability, which captures characteristics of ESD, needs to be developed.

v. Setting the construction of a sustainable society as the aim of educational policy

Although it is not yet clear how the achievements of the DESD will be reflected in the 2020 course guidelines, it is possible that by rejecting its partial introduction in the 2010 guidelines and placing ESD as an aim of all educational policies, ESD will spread to schools across the country and unique educational activities that reflect the particularity of the area will be pursued. Conditions would seem ripe for such a bold move. The number of UNESCO schools in Japan has now increased to 939, according to the most recent figures available (ACCU 2015b). ESD seems set to continue to spread in the future, not only because of the effect of educational policy but because many teachers are now mining ESD's rich seam of exciting and inspiring concepts not previously seen in conventional Japanese education – such as balancing between environmental, economic and social needs – as a means to activate the local area in terms of its nature, culture and industries, with the aim of changing actions to respect individuality. However, as long as the government's economic policies exert a strong influence on education policies, the shift from 'responding to a knowledge-based society' to 'the construction of a sustainable society' will require drastic measures, such as shifting Japanese economic policies in line with a green economy. Also, there will need to be a full and frank discussion of existing problems for Japanese society, such as extensive radioactive contamination from the Fukushima Daiichi nuclear power plant accident, relief for refugees fleeing land polluted by radioactivity and the switch to renewable energy. Expanding and developing high-quality ESD will help to prepare the way for a substantial transformation of economic and educational policies as part of the process of constructing a sustainable society.

The dissemination of ESD practice in Japanese schools comes at a juncture when school education in Japan is confronted by globalisation for the first time in its history. Government course guidelines underpin an educational policy that includes neo-liberalistic and conservative thought as well as a progressive and positive response to globalisation. Although attempts to introduce the concept of sustainability to this policy through the theory and practice of ESD have not been without a certain amount of confusion, Japanese schools have everything to gain from the attempt. We stand at a turning point as to whether ESD practice in Japan will reform the former education system gently or be swallowed up by it and change in quality.

Notes

1 See Yunesuko sukuuru: Kongo 'fueru' 8 wari (Nihon Kyoiku Shinbun, 13 January 2013, 3).
2 Fukuda (2008, 51–52) argues that OECD educational policy is best understood not just as a policy of the early 2000s but as an extension of international academic strategies going back to the 1980s, the era of American Reaganomics, when research and policy development prioritised privatisation, school choice, standardisation of educational content and international testing with the sole purpose of producing human capital for the global market. Fukuda proposes that OECD policies and new orientations in educational policy, such as UNESCO's 1990 pursuit of 'Lifelong Learning for All' – promoting democracy, social cohesion and a new understanding of humans as social capital to be operated for the benefit of society – are the product of a combined political will, bent on pushing for transnational educational standards to replace old nation-based forms of policy. The expansion of European unification had exacerbated social problems such as immigration, complexity of job qualifications, unemployment and social discrimination. These problems required solutions that could transcend the nation-state framework. The DeSeCo Project – an attempt in part to guarantee the quality of labour that was freely moving within the EU countries – is one such solution.
3 The Cabinet office has reported rising trends in the relative rate of child poverty and in the percentage of elementary and middle school children receiving subsidies to attend school (Cabinet Office, Government of Japan 2014).

References

Amano, I. 2000. *Kyouiku no jissen* (The practice of education), in Amano, I. (ed.) *Kyouiku eno 'Toi': Gendai kyouikugaku nyuumon* (Questions for education: an introduction to modern pedagogy). Tokyo, Japan: University of Tokyo Press, 1–29.

Asia-Pacific Cultural Centre for UNESCO (ACCU) 2015a. *Hajime ni* (Introduction), in ACCU (ed.) *Yunesuko-sukuuru no ima: Hirogari tsunagaru ESD suishin kyoten* (UNESCO-Associated schools in Japan as bases for promoting ESD: current status and way forward). Tokyo, Japan: ACCU, 2. (www.UNESCO-school.MEXT.go.jp/aspnet-events/?action=common_download_main&upload_id=8812). Accessed 10 January 2016.

Asia-Pacific Cultural Centre for UNESCO (ACCU) 2015b. *Yunesuko sukuuru e youkoso* (Welcome to UNESCO Schools) (www.UNESCO-school.MEXT.go.jp/). Accessed 23 November 2015.

Cabinet Office, Government of Japan 2010. *Shin seichou senryaku: Genki na Nippon fukkatsu no shinario* (A new growth strategy: scenarios for reviving a healthy Japan) (www.kantei.go.jp/jp/sinseichousenryaku/sinseichou01.pdf). Accessed 10 January 2016.

Cabinet Office, Government of Japan 2014. *Kodomo no hinkon* (Child poverty) (www8.cao.go.jp/youth/whitepaper/h25honpen/b1_03_03.html). Accessed 27 September 2014.

Fukuda, S. 2008. *Guroubalizumu to gakuryoku no kokusai senryaku* (Education policy and the strategy of competencies in globalism). *Kyouiku-gaku Kenkyuu* (The Japanese Journal of Educational Research) 75 (2), 48–59.

Goto, M. and Okamoto, Y. 2012. *ESD koyuu no gakushuu-katei wo kousou shi tenkai suru tame no hitsuyou na wakugumi* (The framework needed for the proper development and formulation of ESD coursework), in Kadoya, S. (ed.) *Gakkou ni okeru jizokukanou na hatten no tame no kyouiku (ESD) ni kansuru kenkyuu saishuu houkokusho* (Education for sustainable development (ESD) for schools: final report). Tokyo, Japan: National Institute for Educational Policy Research, Educational Curriculum Research Centre.

Interministerial Meeting on the DESD 2006 (revised 2011). *Waga kuni ni okeru kokuren jizokukano na kaihatsu no tame no kyoiku no junen jissi keikaku* (Japan's Action Plan for the UNDESD), *Kokuren jizokukano na kaihatsu no tame no kyoiku no junen kankei shocho renraku kaigi* (Interministerial Meeting on the DESD), 1–24 (www.cas.go.jp/jp/seisaku/kokuren/keikaku.pdf). Accessed 24 November 2015.

Kodama, T. 2009. *Kasumigaura ryuiki-chiiki ni okeru gakkou wo kyoten toshita ESD jissen no kousatu: Ushiku shiritsu Kamiya shougakkou no jirei bunseki wo chushin ni* (The research of ESD practice at school in the Kasumigaura basin area focusing on a case study of Kamiya Elementary School in Ushiku city). *Kankyou Kyouiku* (Environmental Education) 19 (1), 29–41.

Kodama, T. 2013. *Gakuryoku* (Academic ability), in Japanese Society of Environmental Education (ed.) *Kankyo kyouiku jiten* (Encyclopedia of environmental education). Tokyo, Japan: Kyouiku Shuppan, 47–48.

Kodama, T. 2015. *Gakkou ESD jissen ni okeru 'nouryoku ikusei ron' no kousatu* (A study of capacity development through ESD practice in schools). *Kankyou kyouiku* (Environmental Education) 25(1), 132–143.

McGaw, B. 2008. *Hajime ni* (Foreword), in Rychen, D. S. and Salganik L. H. (eds) *Kii konpitenshii: kokusai hyoujun no gakuryoku wo mezashite* (Key competencies for a successful life and a well-functioning society). Tokyo, Japan: Akashi Shoten, 17–18.

Ministry of Education, Culture, Sports, Science and Technology (MEXT) n.d. *Yunesuko sukuuru e youkoso* (Welcome to UNESCO schools) (www.UNESCO-school.MEXT.go.jp). Accessed 24 September 2015.

Ministry of Education, Culture, Sports, Science and Technology (MEXT) 2005. Central Council for Education, The future of higher education in Japan: report 1 (www.MEXT.go.jp/english/highered/1303556.htm). Accessed 25 September 2015.

Ministry of Education, Culture, Sports, Science and Technology (MEXT) 2008. *Shougakkou gakushuu shidou-youryou kaisetu: sougouteki na gakushuu no jikan hen* (Commentary on the elementary school government course guidelines: the period for integrated studies). Tokyo, Japan: Toyokan Publishing.

Ministry of Education, Culture, Sports, Science and Technology (MEXT) 2011. *Genkou gakushuu shidou youryou: Ikiru chikara* (The present government course guidelines: zest for living) (www.MEXT.go.jp/a_menu/shotou/new-cs/idea/). Accessed 25 September 2015.

National Institute for Educational Research (NIER) 2013. *Kyouiku-katei no hennsei ni kansuru kisoteki-kenkyuu houkokusho 5: Shakai no henka ni taiou suru shishitu ya nouryoku wo ikusei suru kyouiku-katei hensei no kihon-genri* (Report 5 on basic research into composition of educational process: basic principle of educational process to develop the ability and quality to respond to changes in society) (www.nier.go.jp/kaihatsu/pdf/Houkokusho-5.pdf). Accessed 25 January 2016.

National Institute for Educational Research (NIER) 2014. *Heisei 25 nendo zenkoku gakuryoku gakushuu-zyoukyou chousa kurosu-shuukei kekka* (The result by cross tabulation in 2013 national academic ability investigation) (www.nier.go.jp/13chousakekkahoukoku/data/research-report/crosstab_report_summary.pdf). Accessed 25 January 2016.

Nihon Kyoiku Shinbun 13 January 2013. *Yunesuko-sukuuru: kongo 'fueru' 8 wari* (UNESCO schools will 'increase': 80 per cent of schools respond) in *Nihon Kyoiku Shinbun* (Japan Educational Press).

Organisation for Economic Co-operation and Development (OECD) n.d. The definition and selection of key competencies: executive summary. Downloadable from the Definition and Selection of Competencies (DeSeCo) page of the OECD website (www.oecd.org/education/skills-beyond-school/definitionandselectionofcompetenciesdeseco.htm). Accessed 23 November 2015.

Organisation for Economic Co-operation and Development (OECD) 2015. Our mission (www.oecd.org/about/). Accessed 20 November 2015.

Ozaki, H. 2009. *Kyouiku mokuteki-ron ni okeru 'kyouiku mokuhyou' gainen no bunseki: 'kyouiku-mokuhyou'/'kyouiku-mokuteki' kankeisei no kentou* (An analysis of the theory of educational objectives: reexamining the relationship between educational objectives and education aims). *Tohoku Daigaku Daigakuin Kyouikugaku Kenkyuu Nenpou* (Annual Bulletin of the Graduate School of Education, Tohoku University) 58 (1), 13–32.

Rychen, D. S. and Salganik, L. H. 2008. *Kii conpitenshii no teigi to sentaku* (Definition and selection of key competencies), in Rychen D. S. and Salganik L. H. (eds) *Kii konpitenshii: kokusai hyoujun no gakuryoku wo mezashite* (Key competencies for a successful life and a well-functioning society). Tokyo, Japan: Akashi Shoten, 200–224.

Takao, A. 2010. *Koukyoui-kuseido ni okeru ESD no igi no kousatu: Doitsu no 'ESD konpitenshii moderu' wo meguru giron to hyouka kara* (A study of significance of ESD in public education systems: an analysis of the discourse on 'competency models' in Germany). *Kankyou kyouiku* (Environmental Education) 20 (1), 35–47.

United Nations Education, Scientific and Cultural Organisation (UNESCO) 1996. *Learning: the treasure within. Report to UNESCO of the International Commission on Education for the 21st Century*. Paris, France: UNESCO. (http://unesdoc.UNESCO.org/images/0010/001095/109590eo.pdf). Accessed 24 September 2015.

United Nations Education, Scientific and Cultural Organisation (UNESCO) 2014. Aichi-Nagoya Declaration on Education for Sustainable Development (https://sustainabledevelopment.un.org/content/documents/5859Aichi-Nagoya_Declaration_EN.pdf). Accessed 24 September 2015.

Yoshida, A. 2001. *Holisutikku kyouiku ron* (Holistic education theory). Tokyo, Japan: Nippon Hyouronsha.

Yoshikawa, M. 2012. *Kaihatsu to kyouiku no rekishi-teki hensen to ESD* (ESD and historic change in development and education), in Sato, M. and Abe, O. (eds) *ESD nyumon* (An introduction to ESD). Tokyo, Japan: Tsukuba Shobou, 187–210.

5 Perspectives on education for sustainable development through local cultural heritage

Shizuo Nakazawa and Tadashi Izumitani

Introduction

The approach known as education for sustainable development (ESD) has been diffusing through society since the start of the UN-sponsored Decade for ESD in 2005. Under the leadership of the United Nations Educational, Scientific and Cultural Organisation (UNESCO), ESD has been applied at designated schools around the world, while companies and non-profit organisations (NPOs) have increasingly incorporated ESD into employee training, lectures and workshops. The success of these efforts can be seen in the increased public interest in global issues such as climate change, natural disasters, resource depletion, loss of biodiversity, conflict and poverty (Goshima and Sekiguchi 2010). The impact of the Decade for ESD can also be seen in the growing popular understanding of the interlinking of global issues and the fact that our lifestyles are making an impact on the present and future lives of the earth's population. Furthermore, by broadly considering the theoretical framework of ESD, we can deepen our understanding of education itself to develop ESD-based educational reform.

In this chapter, we will explore the learning theories of ESD by considering the competencies and sense of values it fosters, and will examine the possibility for ESD to promote educational reform. By introducing a case study of an ESD cultural heritage activity for primary school children, developed at Nara University of Education, we will identify perspectives that are lacking in conventional ESD approaches, consider the significance of ESD and clarify ideal future directions for realising it.

Considering the theoretical framework of ESD

Abilities that ESD can foster

The National Institute for Educational Policy Research of Japan (2012) has identified the competencies that should be stressed in ESD initiatives, corresponding to competencies suggested by Transfer 21 (Yui *et. al* 2012, 124) in Germany and by the NPO ESD-J (2007), a civic group that promotes ESD at the Japanese private enterprise level. Table 5.1 shows these abilities in terms of key competencies identified by the Organisation for Economic Co-operation

Table 5.1 Desired values and competencies for ESD identified by various organisations

	Key competency (Organisation for Economic Co-operation and Development)	Ability for formation (Transfer 21)	Target competency and behaviour (National Institute for Educational Policy Research)	Desired competency (ESD-J)
(1) Interacting in heterogeneous groups	• Ability to relate well to others • Ability to cooperate • Ability to manage and resolve conflicts	• Cooperativeness • Ability to participate • Ability to motivate others • Ability to handle dilemmas	• Ability to communicate • Ability to cooperate with others • Attitudes towards participation in groups or community	• Ability to express one's ideas • Ability to cooperate with others
(2) Acting autonomously	• Ability to act within the big picture • Ability to form and conduct life plans and personal projects • Ability to assert rights, interests, limits and needs	• Ability to reflect upon principles • Ability for voluntary action • Ability to take ethical actions • Ability to support others	• Ability to consider multilaterally and comprehensively • Ability to participate actively	• Ability to understand acceptable environmental limits • Ability to plan future society • Ability to put plans into practice
(3) Using tools interactively	• Ability to use language, symbols and texts interactively • Ability to use knowledge and information interactively • Ability to use technology interactively	• Ability to adopt other viewpoints • Ability for prediction • Ability to acquire recognition beyond specialised fields • Ability to handle complicated and incomplete information	• Ability to think critically • Ability to predict future scenarios and to plan	• Ability to criticise • Ability to feel and think by oneself • Ability to make deep insights
(4) Respecting others			• Attitude to defer to connections between people and between people and the environment	• Ability to acknowledge and respect other sets of values

Source: Author.

and Development (OECD) (OECD 2005). The reason for selecting the key competencies of the OECD as the yardstick is that the basic values that underpin the key competencies are 'respect for human rights' and 'sustainable development'.

Table 5.1 adds an important value fostered by ESD – respect for others – to the three key competencies of the OECD (interacting in heterogeneous groups, acting autonomously and using tools interactively). It shows that key competencies of the OECD have almost the same system and content as the desired values and competencies fostered by ESD.

Furthermore, the National Institute for Educational Policy Research notes that these key competencies correspond to the concept of *ikiru chikara* (zest for life), which the Japanese Ministry of Education, Culture, Sports, Science and Technology (MEXT) regards as a central theme of school education. *Ikiru chikara*, which has been the principle of the curriculum guideline for Japanese school education since 2002, refers to achieving a balance of solid academic prowess, rich humanity and health and fitness (MEXT 2011, 7). Solid academic prowess means 'to acquire the basics and fundamentals; to cultivate introspection, the desire to learn and think, independent decision-making and action, as well as the talent and ability for problem-solving'. To be rich in humanity means 'to cultivate self-discipline in balance with consideration for others and a sense for inspiration, in harmony with the spirit of cooperation', and health and fitness indicates 'health and fitness for living a vigorous life'. Thus, we can foster the desired ESD competencies by developing the learning activities, aimed at the acquisition of *ikiru chikara*, that are already being conducted in Japanese schools.

The sense of values to foster through ESD

Even if competencies are promoted, for them to function effectively we must also promote desired values. We will here examine the values promoted by ESD, based on the definition of sustainable development provided by the Brundtland Commission (World Commission on Environment and Development 1987), and considering the Decade of Education for Sustainable Development (DESD) International Implementation Scheme (UNESCO 2005) and the Education for Sustainable Development Implementation Scheme of Japan (Cabinet Secretariat 2011).

The DESD International Implementation Scheme (UNESCO 2005, 16) claims that 'the human element is now widely recognised as the key variable in sustainable development'. It further explains that it is important to promote values to realise a sustainable society, as part of the role of education. The scheme classifies education for sustainable development as essentially about 'relationships between people' and 'relationships between people and their environment'. It states that the basic values that ESD should promote include the following:

- Respect for the dignity and human rights of all people throughout the world and a commitment to social and economic justice for all
- Respect for the human rights of future generations and a commitment to intergenerational responsibility

- Respect and care for the greater community of life in all its diversity, which involves the protection and restoration of the earth's ecosystems
- Respect for cultural diversity and a commitment to build locally and globally a culture of tolerance, non-violence and peace.

It is clear that the first and fourth statements refer to relationships between people, while the third indicates relationships between people and their environment. The second can be regarded as involving relationships between people and their environment in that 'the human rights of future generations' may refer to the right to exploit resources, such as energy, to consume unpolluted water, air and food and to enjoy beautiful scenery.

On the other hand, the agenda identified for priority by the Education for Sustainable Development Implementation Scheme of Japan (Cabinet Secretariat 2011, 6) specifies two important points. The first is 'to integrate consideration for the environment into society and the economic system' and the other is 'to integrate consideration for human rights and culture into lifestyle' (authors' translation). In addition, the widely accepted Brundtland Commission definition of sustainable development (World Commission on Environment and Development 1987, 8–9) as 'development that meets the needs of the present without

Table 5.2 The sense of values developed through ESD

	DESD International Implementation Scheme (2005)	*Brundtland Commission (1987)*	*ESD Implementation Scheme of Japan (2011)*
Relationships between people	Respect for the dignity and human rights of all people throughout the world and a commitment to social and economic justice for all	Meet the needs of present generations	To integrate consideration for human rights and culture into lifestyles
	Respect for cultural diversity and a commitment to build locally and globally a culture of tolerance, non-violence and peace	Meet the needs of future generations	
Relationships between people and their environment	Respect for the human rights of future generations and a commitment to intergenerational responsibility	Meet the needs of future generations	To integrate consideration for the environment into society and the economic system
	Respect and care for the greater community of life in all its diversity, which involves the protection and restoration of the Earth's ecosystems	Meet the needs of present generations	

Source: Author.

compromising the ability of future generations to meet their own needs' implies equity between generations as well as equity within each generation. Table 5.2 recognises these desired values according to whether they refer to relationships between people or relationships between people and their environment.

This arrangement clarifies that the sense of values developed through ESD includes considerations for the environment in society and the economic system as well as respect for human rights and culture both between generations and within each generation.

Possibilities for ESD to promote educational reform

ESD aims to foster leaders who can help create a sustainable society. We must explore the nature of a person who could act as a leader for a sustainable society with reference to the difference between morality and ethics, the basic criteria that define right and wrong in our daily lives. Morality and ethics are not the same: morality is regarded as a model that is conceived to suit a specific society, while ethics are universal principles that all human beings share (Fujita 2013, 22).

Considering the sense of values we want to promote in ESD, it follows that the ideal leader of a sustainable society is an ethical rather than a moral person. If a sustainable society has been realised for all people, it should be both moral and ethical. However, our current society is an unsustainable one. In this case, the ideal leader should be an active person, who tries to reform an unsustainable society in accordance with universal principles shared by all people at a particular time and between generations. This should not be a person who follows rules that promote or result in an unsustainable society (for example, by giving priority to economic growth).

Next we must review whether today's formal education is effective in fostering such an active person. To do this, we need to consider whether the current education system is effective in terms of the teachers' and students' roles and classroom learning approaches.

According to convention, a teacher is a person who has knowledge while a student is a person who does not; a teacher is a person who teaches while a student is a person who is taught (Nakazawa 2009). This static relationship is established on the premise that the teacher has the answer to a question the student wants to ask. However, a teacher cannot put ESD into action for students if this paradigm is applied. Although the teacher may be aware of various global issues, he or she lacks the knowledge of complete solutions. ESD is designed to foster leadership for a sustainable society: it does not require students to memorise answers to global questions. What is demanded in ESD is not the transmission of knowledge from teacher to student but the transmission of attitudes for trying to design a sustainable society.

In Japan's current formal education system, the common learning approach involves lectures, in which a teacher communicates his or her knowledge to all students in the classroom. In Japanese schools, this approach becomes more common as students proceed from junior high school to senior high school. In the classroom, the teacher does most of the speaking while the students take notes in silence. Although this is the typical classroom approach, it is not effective for ESD. It allows a teacher to identify global issues but not to explain them sufficiently or suggest solutions. This prescriptive approach is ineffective because the steps required depend on individual and societal values and goals.

Although it is important for students to have knowledge of global issues in ESD, it is more important for them be able to investigate with their peers possible measures to help address global issues, to think about what to do and to carry out strategies. In this collaborative research, the role of the teacher is as an expert researcher. Because there is no single answer to the challenge of realising a sustainable society, we must remove the wall between a teacher who teaches and a student who is taught. Through experience in drawing on each other's strengths and cooperating in group research, students will become active citizens who continue to learn and investigate.

ESD through cultural heritage

ESD aims to alter people's behaviour in relation to the environment, economy and society to realise a sustainable future for the environment, economy and society (Cabinet Secretariat 2011, 4). ESD provides people with two avenues for positive behavioural change on an individual level. One is to change their lifestyles, for example by saving electricity, water and energy, and the other is to participate in civil activities for creating a sustainable society in their communities. In addition, the impetus for changing behaviour is linked to appreciating one's community. People devote themselves to what they appreciate.

One way to encourage people to appreciate their community is to promote a community's cultural heritage (see Figure 5.1). Local cultural heritage gives children opportunities to pay attention to their communities. At Nara University, we implemented an ESD initiative based on this learning theory (see Table 5.3 for details).

Revival of the great statue of Buddha in Todaiji Temple

Nara University of Education is located in Nara city, Nara prefecture, in the western Kansai region of Japan. This historic city was the capital of Japan

Figure 5.1 ESD strategy through cultural heritage

Table 5.3 Outline of cultural heritage-based ESD initiative

Purpose	• To recognise that every generation's wish for a sustainable society can be realised by a committed community • To discover the values of the local cultural heritage
Theme	To investigate the role of the Great Buddha in *Todaiji* Temple with the motivation to design a sustainable society
Content	To understand the role of the Great Buddha in *Todaiji* Temple with the motivation to design a sustainable society by learning about the history of the initial construction and reconstruction of the Great Buddha
Participants	Fifth-grade students from all (47) primary schools in Nara (n = about 1,000)
Procedure	After reading at school about the reconstruction of the Great Buddha, students visit *Todaiji* Temple. There, seeing the difference in colour between its body and face, the many patches in its body and the line drawings carved on the lotus petal on which the Great Buddha sits, students understand about the history and significance of the fabled and repeated reconstruction of the Great Buddha over the years. After that, students examine the cultural heritage of their community and seek to convey its values to others
Targeted specific outcomes	The participating children: • Become aware of the universality and timelessness of the desire to realise a sustainable society • See that the seemingly impossible can be accomplished by cooperating with others
Assessment of the programme	In this initiative, it is important to give advice to participating children and to improve their willingness to take further action. Programme assessment involved examining behavioural change among students, including increased interest in learning more about *Todaiji* Temple and their local cultural heritage, and increases in the number of children participating in sustainability activities, such as cleaning the river or disaster drills
Role of Nara University of Education	Created ESD initiative, conducted teacher training for implementing the initiative among teachers from participating schools in Nara
Framework with educational committee	The educational committee in Nara has created a textbook for all fifth-grade primary school students in Nara about the Great Buddha

Source: Author.

1,300 years ago, when it was known as *Heijokyo*. In Nara, many wild deer can be found grazing peacefully in a very large park just 10 minutes from the main Nara railway station. The deer in Nara have been valued as messengers of God for more than 1,000 years so they are well accustomed to people. Many tourists, including families and foreign visitors, come to Nara Park to feed the deer biscuits and take their photographs. Although Nara has many tourist attractions besides Nara Park, the biggest draw for tourists is *Todaiji* Temple. Enshrined in *Todaiji* Temple is a statue of Vairocana Buddha, known familiarly as *Nara no daibutsu*, the Great

Buddha of Nara, which is 14.98m high and weighs 500 tonnes. *Todaiji* Temple has been registered as a UNESCO World Heritage Site.

Every primary school child in Nara city visits *Todaiji* Temple as part of the ESD curriculum promoting Nara's cultural heritage. Tourists from all over Japan and the world can be seen at the temple, which features a number of attractions, including *Daibutsuden*, the hall where the Great Buddha has been enshrined; *Nigatsudo* Hall, which is famous for an event, *Shunie*, that has been held annually for the past 1,000 years; *Kaidando* Hall, which holds the statue of *Shitenno*, a national treasure; *Shosoin* Repository, where artefacts from Emperor Shomu are kept and *Tegaimon* Gate, which dates from the Nara era (about the eighth century CE). However, it is *Daibutsuden* that almost all tourists visit. A survey by Nara city (Nara City 2012) revealed that, in 2012, 13.32 million people visited Nara city and 1.43 million of them stayed there and went sightseeing. A total of 56,000 international visitors came to Nara for sightseeing. Furthermore, another survey (Nara Prefecture 2012) found that 53 per cent of the visitors from overseas in 2008 visited *Todaiji* Temple, making it the favourite destination for foreign visitors. As part of the ESD initiative, primary school students ask people why the great statue is such a great attraction. The children interview tourists as well as the staff of *Todaiji* Temple and gradually discover appealing information about the Great Buddha.

The Great Buddha in *Todaiji* Temple was first constructed by Emperor Shomu in 752 CE. This was an extremely unstable era in East Asia because the allied forces of the newly established Tang dynasty in China and the Silla in the Korean peninsula fought and conquered the other two Korean kingdoms, Baekje and Goguryeo. The domestic situation in Japan at that time was also severe, with the spread of smallpox, a massive earthquake and prolonged drought. In response to these calamities, Emperor Shomu decided to construct a Great Buddha in 743. His intention was expressed in an imperial edict issued that year that read: 'I want to make a world where all animals and plants shall flourish' (authors' translation). The edict also explained how the Great Buddha should be built:

> If I were to command it, the Great Buddha would be completed in no time, given my wealth and power. But a Great Buddha built in such manner will have no heart. It will only bring suffering to the people. Instead, gather what each can give, however small that may be. Give everyone a chance to contribute to the creation of the Great Buddha if he wants to, even with a blade of grass or a clump of earth.
>
> (Nishiyama 2004) (authors' translation).

That was what Emperor Shomu wished for. With the help of 2.6 million people, who responded to his call to 'make a world where all animals and plants shall flourish', the Great Buddha was completed in 752 CE.

However, 428 years later, in 1180, the Great Buddha in *Todaiji* Temple was caught up in warfare, which spread from rival samurai conflict in nearby Kyoto, and it was destroyed by fire. Some local townspeople attempted but failed to rebuild it, concluding that, as a document of the time stated, 'it is beyond the reach of human power' (Nara National Museum 2006) (authors' translation). A Buddhist monk named Chogen Shonin felt differently: he publicly declared: 'Even if you all say "I can't do it," I shall do it'. Chogen Shonin travelled through Japan with an entourage of 50 people, asking everyone to 'contribute to the construction of the Great Buddha, whether with a length of cloth, an iron nail, a twig or small coins' (Nara National Museum 2006) (authors' translation). In the same way as Emperor Shomu, he tried to build the Great Buddha by collecting what each could give, however small that may be. Thus the Great Buddha was reconstructed in 1185.

The Great Buddha was destroyed by fire once again during samurai warfare 400 years later. This time, the public again tried to reconstruct the Great Buddha but they were unable to gather enough material because the entire country was at war. The body of the Great Buddha was completed but, since they were unable to place a heavy head upon it, the head was made from wood and covered with sheets of copper. The *Daibutsuden* that sheltered the statue could not be built so the Great Buddha was exposed to the elements for the next 120 years.

In the seventeeth century, the monk Kokei Shonin volunteered to reconstruct the Great Buddha. One rainy day, when he was just 13 years old, he went to *Todaiji* Temple and visited the Great Buddha with his master to bow beneath it. Kokei Shonin reportedly said: 'I have an umbrella but the Great Buddha I bow down to suffers beneath the rain. I will definitely reconstruct the Great Buddha.' (Nara National Museum 2005) (authors' translation). When he was 35 years old, Kokei Shonin travelled alone throughout Japan, soliciting donations for recon- struction. He called on the people to 'contribute to the construction of the Great Buddha, even if with a single needle or a blade of grass' (Nara National Museum 2005) (authors' translation). Like Emperor Shomu and Chogen Shonin, he tried to build the Great Buddha by collecting whatever each contributor each could give, no matter how little. At first, no one would cooperate with Kokei Shonin because they didn't believe he could reconstruct the Great Buddha. However, even when forced to travel alone, he held on to hope. Eventually, people began to co-operate and this evolved into a successful national effort to reconstruct the Great Buddha. The current statue, reconstructed in 1692 in *Todaiji* Temple, is the result of contributions collected from all over Japan.

Observed carefully, the surface of the Great Buddha in *Todaiji* Temple appears as fractured as its history. The pedestal upon which the Buddha sits dates from the time of Emperor Shomu, the torso was reconstructed by monk Chogen Shonin and monk Kokei Shonin reconstructed the head. Each time it was rebuilt, the statue represented the wishes of the many people who sympathised with Emperor Shomu's statement: 'I want to make a world where all animals and plants shall flourish'. The true charm of the Great Buddha in *Todaiji* Temple is its continued existence over 1,250 years – thanks to the wishes and actions of so many people.

Revival of the Great Buddha in Todaiji Temple and ESD

From the reconstruction of the Great Buddha in *Todaiji* Temple, we can learn three things concerning the design of a sustainable society. The first is the importance of holding on to belief, the second is the meaning of the wishes represented by the Great Buddha and the third is the importance of passing down our cultural heritage and conserving traditions.

Kokei Shonin began the reconstruction of the Great Buddha alone. He must have worried about succeeding and must have wanted to give up at times, but he kept faith in his mission and finally achieved the seemingly impossible reconstruction of the Great Buddha. Today, have we given up on the creation of a sustainable society? When confronted by the large numbers of people who express little concern for the impact of corporate economic activities and the implications for future generations, we may feel powerless to realise plans for a sustainable society. However, we should be determined to create a sustainable society for the children of the future. The power to reconstruct the Great *Todaiji* Temple attests to the importance of joining forces with others and ardently attempting to create a more sustainable society. Learning such as this, based on historical facts in one's own community, can touch people's hearts. This kind of place-based education began in Nara city in 2009 so it may be too early to expect noticeable outcomes. However, after 10 or 20 years of continuing education, we can expect increasing numbers of local residents to promote sustainable development in their communities.

We also learn about the aspirations represented by the Great Buddha. The Brundtland definition of sustainable development (World Commission on Environment and Development 1987) refers to the needs of present and future generations, but this anthropocentric orientation omits any reference to plants and animals. Animals and plants exist autonomously and are exploited by human beings. However, 'a world where all animals and plants shall flourish' connotes a robust ecosystem with healthy biodiversity; in other words, a sustainable society. We flourish as a result of ecosystem services – provisioning services (food and raw materials); regulating services (temperature regulation, water retention and carbon sequestration) and cultural services, such as relaxation and recreation in natural settings. A human being is part of an ecosystem, so when we destroy an ecosystem, we are strangling ourselves. We can learn the importance of maintaining a harmonious balance between human activities and natural environments from Emperor Shomu's concept of 'a world where all animals and plants shall flourish'.

This concept has another meaning: a world of peace. The Great Buddha has been destroyed by fire twice in war. Nothing, no matter how impressive or admired it may be, can be passed on to the future unless peace prevails. War causes the greatest environmental disruption, as attested to by the wholescale destruction of plant, animal and human life caused by the atomic bombs dropped on Hiroshima and Nagasaki in 1945. Thus the phrase 'a world where all animals and plants shall flourish' means to value natural environments and to build a culture of peace. Certainly, the ability to value the natural environment and peace is one of the main objectives of ESD.

The third lesson concerns the importance of passing on a cultural heritage and traditions to ensuing generations. Children who understand and are impressed by the rich meaning of the *Todaiji* Temple can continue their learning by researching their local cultural heritage and traditions. We can find many examples of cultural artefacts, practices and traditions that live on, irrespective of the length of their history, because local people have carefully conserved them and passed them on. Cultural heritages that are neglected do not survive (Hyogo Prefectural Board of Education 2000). Elements of one's cultural heritage have been passed down from one generation to the next and there are those who actively conserve them.

There are four reasons why learning about one's cultural heritage is important for a community (Nakazawa and Tabuchi 2008; 2014). The first is that learning about local cultural heritage can heighten residents' interest in local history and the community's current situation, which leads to greater civic engagement. The second is that residents come to appreciate the richness of their local culture and the value of their community. The third is that residents learn that their modern community has been shaped by the efforts of – and difficulties faced by – past generations and that this history is also part of the local cultural heritage. By understanding this, residents will naturally feel a sense of responsibility for conserving their heritage, improving it and passing it down to the next generation. Finally, residents will come to realise that their modern local community is a fragile creation that they can recreate by themselves as past generations did, which should spur them to act to realise a desirable future. This sense of responsibility for passing on the local culture, and a future inclination towards autonomously recreating their local community, should generate a change of behaviour that will enable the realisation of community sustainable development.

A re-examination of ESD through the implementation of cultural heritage initiatives

By applying ESD to the study of a local cultural heritage, we can reconsider the definition of sustainable development, while evaluating the effectiveness of the ESD approach.

Re-examining the definition of sustainable development

The definition of sustainable development as 'development that meets the needs of the present without compromising the ability of future generations to meet their own needs' may be widely accepted, but it can be regarded as incomplete in some respects. As mentioned before, it refers to equity between generations and within each generation. Consideration of fairness within a generation refers to equity with people living in the same period, whereas equity between generations necessarily includes only those living after us, which connotes a lack of consideration of people living earlier than ourselves. Another difficulty with this definition is that 'needs' can be thought to mean physical 'necessities'. However, needs should also be construed as including non-material aspects such as intentions and aspirations. When we regard needs as referring to cognitive concepts, fairness within the generation would also imply respecting intentions and aspirations for all people to improve their lives, which shows the values of respect for human rights and culture that are the objectives of an ESD approach. On the other hand, fairness between generations can also imply responsibility between generations. We inherit a society that has resulted from the efforts and difficulties of past generations and their intentions and aspirations to improve their lives and communities so that future generations can live better lives (Nakazawa 2014).

Our cultural heritage supplies us with clues for understanding the efforts and difficulties of past generations. Using our cultural heritage as learning material has two types of significance. One is that learning about the problems and efforts of past generations encourages us to take a more measured and patient approach to working to achieve a more sustainable society. For example, the abbot Ganjin, who came to Japan from China, constructed *Toshodaiji* Temple, another ancient temple in Nara that has been recognised as a World Heritage Site. In response to a request by the Japanese that he bring Buddhist teachings from China, he and his disciples risked their lives repeatedly in efforts to travel to Japan. Saying: 'We must not spare our lives for Buddhism', (Nara National Museum 2009) (authors' translation), they made five attempts over a 12-year period, losing 32 disciples and the abbot's eyesight in the process. Finally this persistence prevailed; the abbot settled in Japan and founded *Toshodaiji* Temple as a place in which to learn about Buddhism. By visiting this temple and studying its history, and by recognising that society is constructed as part of an historical process, we can understand the importance of persistent effort and co-operation to realising a sustainable society. Another important implication of studying the local heritage is that it promotes collaborative action with local people. In the mountains east of Nara city is the town of Oyagyu, which used to sponsor an annual traditional event, the *Taiko odori*, a ritual of dance accompanied by *Taiko* drumming. A decline in the town's population forced the event to stop in 2013. However, local junior high school students began studying the *Taiko odori* tradition and they interviewed local residents, who were familiar with the local cultural heritage and traditions. By asking them for details, the student researchers gave the local townspeople an opportunity to re-examine and re-appreciate their local cultural heritage, traditions and events. The students learned that the *Taiko odori* had started more 500 years ago as a way for the people to beseech God to provide ample water – it was an event expressing people's wishes for stable weather for good harvests. The community now periodically sponsors meetings to study the *Taiko odori* and the local residents' association is planning to collaborate with the junior high school to restore the event. By making the local cultural heritage the basis for an ESD approach, we can integrate residents' autonomous learning with children's formal school education, which will help bring about the creation of a sustainable community.

Assessment of an ESD initiative

Near Nara Park, famous for its deer, is an area called *Naramachi* (Old Town of Nara city), with streets that retain the appearance of the Edo era (1650–1867). As part of the primary school cultural heritage ESD initiative, third-grade students interviewed people who work to conserve the city of Nara and recorded their impressions. The children learned that some residents regard automobiles as unsuitable for the district's narrow streets and are planning to introduce *jinrikisya*, manual rickshaws that are propelled at low speed and emit no waste, as the main form of transport. Other residents are renovating the Edo-era buildings by reinforcing the structure and retaining the traditional façade, while modernising the interior. Still other residents have remodelled an old home to create the Nara *Rakugo* Museum, which conserves the local tradition of Japanese *rakugo* (storytelling). The students were impressed by these efforts, writing such comments as: 'I was amazed at the idea of making a *Rakugo* Museum to maintain the atmosphere of *Naramachi*', 'Rickshaws are quiet and environmentally friendly as they emit no gas, which I think is perfect for Nara city' and 'In order to conserve Nara city, I thought it was a good idea to carry out contemporary renovation just on the inside'. One pupil wrote just one word: '*uketsugu*' (inherit). How can we assess the thinking reflected in this one word? A one-word comment like this, although it implies that the student identified with the town as her own community, might normally be given a low evaluation when compared with the more effusive comments of other students. However, this approach to evaluation would be a problem. ESD respects diversity, valuing the different priorities placed on different issues in varied countries and regions. Diversity is also the keyword for the values fostered by ESD, including respect for biodiversity, respect for cultural diversity and the participation of various stakeholders. Nevertheless, predetermined and standardised evaluation criteria are typically used for assessment, contradicting the ideal of diverse assessment of ESD. If ESD seeks to change attitudes to help realise a sustainable future and sustainable community, then evaluators should aim to produce this outcome by assessing the learning situation of each person by interviewing or working with them and giving advice about future activities that will improve engagement.

Conclusion

In this chapter, we interrogated the concepts behind the education for sustainable development approach developed during the UN Decade of ESD, concluding that it includes values promoting human rights, culture and the environment. ESD was seen as an avenue for fundamentally changing the process of teaching in schools because this approach is incompatible with the traditional top-down mode of knowledge transmission. With ESD, teachers and students need to explore a challenge co-operatively. Considering the significance of ESD through one's cultural heritage, we noted that the accepted definition of sustainable development by the World Commission on Environment and Development (1987) includes individuals' intentions for creating a sustainable society (for example, consideration for the environment in society and the economic system, respect for human rights and culture between and within generations) as well as needs, indicating that it is possible to connect the past, present and future using 'responsibility' as a keyword. We also proposed evaluating ESD activities according to the improvement in people's willingness to participate in the creation of a sustainable society.

We then introduced an ESD case study for primary school children, implemented by our university as an example of ESD through a community's cultural heritage. The activity concerned the reconstruction of the Great Buddha in *Todaiji* Temple, which is registered as a World Heritage Site. A community's cultural heritage need not be recognised officially in this way, of course; it does not even need to have a long history. It is important to rediscover often overlooked local cultural traditions and to foster an appreciation for one's community. Local cultural heritage exists anywhere. By promoting an ESD approach through cultural heritage, we can cultivate future leaders for constructing a sustainable society.

Acknowledgement

We are grateful to Dr J. Singer and the editorial team for support and comments on the earlier versions.

References

Cabinet Secretariat 2011. *Waga kuni ni okeru 'kokuren jizoku kanona kaihatsu no tame no kyoiku no 10-nen' jisshi keikaku* (Japanese implementation scheme for the UN-sponsored Decade for Education for Sustainable Development) (www.cas.go.jp/jp/seisaku/kokuren/keikaku.pdf). Accessed 6 September 2015.

ESD-J 2007. *Jizoku kano na shakai no tame no hito dukuri* (Fostering human resources for sustainable society) (www.esd-j.org/j/documents/esd-j_ref.pdf). Accessed 8 September 2015.

Fujita, M. 2013. *Tetsugaku no hinto* (Hints for philosophy). Tokyo, Japan: Iwanami Shoten.

Goshima, A. and Sekiguchi, T. 2010. *Mirai wo tsukuru kyoiku ESD: Jizoku kanona tabunka shakai wo mezashite* (ESD, education for creating the future: aiming at a sustainable and multicultural society). Tokyo, Japan: Akashi Shoten.

Hyogo Prefectural Board of Education 2000. *Jisedai eno keisho to atarashii bunka no sozo no tameni* (For passing on to the next generation and creation of a new culture). Hyogo, Japan: Hyogo Prefectural Board of Education.

Ministry of Education, Culture, Sports, Science and Technology (MEXT) 2011. The revision of the course of study for elementary and secondary schools (www.mext.go.jp/english/elsec/__icsFiles/afieldfile/2011/03/28/1303755_001.pdf). Accessed 7 September 2015.

Nakazawa. S. 2009. *Kosei shugi ni motoduku gakushu riron e no tenkan: shogakko shakaika ni okeru jyugyo kaikaku* (Conversion to learning theory based on constructivism: class reform in social studies in elementary schools), in Imatani. N. (ed.) *Jinsei sekkei noryoku wo sodateru shakaika jyugyo* (Social studies lessons to foster a life design capability). Nagoya, Japan: Reimei Shobo, 83–112.

Nakazawa, S. 2014. *Sekai bunka isan to gakusei no sankagata gakushu: totsukawamura michibushin ESD taiken boranteia wo toshite* (The world's cultural heritage and student participatory learning: through Totsukawa Michibushin ESD volunteer activities), in the Japanese Society for Environmental Education (ed.) *Kankyo kyoiku to ESD* (Environmental education and ESD). Tokyo, Japan: Toyokan Publishing, 84–89.

Nakazawa, S. and Tabuchi, I. 2008. Educational practices of world heritage education as the form of regional studies. *Bulletin of Nara University of Education: Cultural and Social Science* 57(1), 129–140.

Nakazawa, S. and Tabuchi, I. 2014. Sense of values and the ability that we want to bring up in education for sustainable development. *Bulletin of Centre for Educational Research and Development* 23, 65–73.

Nara City 2012. *Nara shi kankou irekomi kyakusu chosa houkoku* (Report on survey of visitors in Nara city) (www.city.nara.lg.jp/www/contents/1347582712483/files/H24irekomi.pdf). Accessed 8 June 2016.

Nara National Museum 2005. *Todaiji Kokei shonin: edo jidai no daibutsu hukko to nara: tokubetsuten* (The priest Kokei: the reconstruction of the Great Buddha and the city of Nara in the Edo period). Exhibition Catalogue. Nara, Japan: Nara National Museum.

Nara National Museum 2006. *Daikanjin chogen: todaiji no kamakura fukko to aratana bi no soshutsu: goonki 800nen kinen tokubetsuten* (Priest Chogen and the rebuilding of *Todaiji*: the *Kamakura* era, an age of artistic revival and innovation). Exhibition Catalogue. Nara, Japan: Nara National Museum.

Nara National Museum 2009. *Kokuho ganjin wajoten: tosho daiji kondo heisei daishuri kinen* (*Ganjinwajo*: national treasures from the *Tenpyo* period: commemorating the *Heisei* renovation of *Toshodaiji* Temple's *Kondo*). Exhibition Catalogue. Nara, Japan: Nara National Museum.

Nara Prefecture 2012. *Nara ken gaikokujin kankoukyaku jittai chousa kekka houkokusho* (Debriefing report of a survey of foreign visitors to Nara) (www.pref.nara.jp/secure/92571/houkokusho-main.pdf). Accessed 10 June 2016.

National Institute for Educational Policy Research 2012. *Gakko ni okeru jizoku kanona hatten no tame no kyoiku (ESD) ni kansuru kenkyu saishu hokokusho* (Final report on studies on education for sustainable development (ESD) in schools). Curriculum Research Centre report.

Nishiyama, A. 2004. *Shomu tenn: daibutsu zoritsu ni kometa negai* (Emperor Shomu: hopes included in construction of the Great Buddha). Nara, Japan: Todaiji.

OECD 2005. Definition and selection of key competencies. Executive summary (www.deseco.admin.ch/bfs/deseco/en/index/02.parsys.43469.downloadList.2296.DownloadFile.tmp/2005.dskcexecutivesummary.en.pdf). Accessed 7 September 2015.

UNESCO 2005. Decade of Education for Sustainable Development international implementation scheme (http://unesdoc.unesco.org/images/0013/001399/139937e.pdf). Accessed 8 June 2016.

World Commission on Environment and Development 1987. *Our Common Future*. Oxford, UK: Oxford University Press.

Yui, Y., Urabe, M., Takao, A., Iwamura, T., Kawada, T. and Konishi, M. 2012. *ESD competency: Gakko no shitsutekikojo to keisei noryoku no ikusei no tame no shido shishin* (ESD competency: guiding principles for schools' qualitative improvement and capacity building). Tokyo, Japan: Akashi Shoten.

6 An investigation into fairness and bias in educational materials produced by the Japanese government to teach school children about nuclear power and radiation

Shinobu Goto

Those who cannot remember the past are condemned to repeat it.
George Santayana, *The Life of Reason,*
Volume 1, 1905

1. Introduction

In March 2011, the Fukushima Daiichi nuclear power plant became the site of the worst nuclear accident to occur since Chernobyl 25 years earlier. It suffered a triple meltdown after being struck by a 13m-high tsunami triggered by the Great East Japan Earthquake. Before the accident, the Japanese government had promoted nuclear power for the generation of electricity over several decades, devoting vast resources to public relations (PR) to persuade the public that nuclear power was both safe and necessary (Onishi 2011). These resources included government-sponsored advertisements in newspapers and on television and public educational materials such as a supplementary reader on nuclear power for school children. Consequently, many Japanese people believed the nuclear power plants in Japan would be safe even if a large earthquake and tsunami occurred – a notion now known as 'the myth of [nuclear power plant] safety' (Investigation Committee on the Accident at Fukushima Nuclear Power Stations of Tokyo Electric Power Company 2012, 43).

One of the most important lessons from the Fukushima nuclear accident is that fairness, accuracy and balance in the government's discourse with the public on nuclear power are essential to prevent the spread of myth and promote the Japanese people's critical thinking. Education for sustainable development (ESD), endorsed by the Japanese government since 2002, when it proposed the United Nations Decade of ESD (2005–2014), positions critical thinking as an important competency to be promoted in formal, non-formal and informal education (UNESCO n.d.). Given its commitment to the decade, one would expect the Japanese government to provide *model* energy education materials for schools, giving children a balanced presentation of the issues surrounding nuclear power and energy policy and encouraging their capacity for critical thinking, in line with ESD's stated goals. However, this has not been the case.

This chapter focuses not on the technological lessons from the Fukushima nuclear accident but on the educational lessons. It begins with an introduction to Japan's nuclear energy policy and the educational materials promoted by the Japanese government for use in formal education by teachers working in structured school settings. This is followed by an objective and quantitative content analysis of the Japanese government's supplementary readers on nuclear power and radiation, which reveals the readers to be inherently biased. An account of various stakeholders' activities in criticising the unfairness of the government's educational materials comes next, with special attention paid to an original, alternative supplementary reader on radiation published by a research group based at Fukushima University. The conclusion calls for improved educational materials to equip students with the critical thinking abilities required to engage in the national debate on energy triggered by the Fukushima nuclear accident, and empower them to participate in democratic decisions regarding the use of nuclear power.

2. Promoting nuclear energy through policy, PR and formal education

2.1 Nuclear energy policy and public education in Japan

The Japanese government has, since the 1950s, promoted nuclear power as a national energy policy – a strategy propelled mainly by the Liberal Democratic Party, the dominant party in Japanese politics for most of the post-war period. Nuclear power's importance to Japan derives primarily from the country's lack of fossil fuels – Japan imports 84 per cent of its fuel for energy requirements – and subsequent need to enhance energy security (World Nuclear Association 2015). On the eve of the 2011 Fukushima disaster, there were 54 nuclear reactors in operation, producing about 30 per cent of Japan's electricity (Ibid.). Japan has the third largest number of nuclear reactors in the world after the United States and France.

The Japanese government has deployed diverse media, including pamphlets, supplementary readers, poster contests, websites and video programmes accessible online, to promote nuclear power to the general public through PR campaigns and the education sector.[1] Several newspaper groups and the nine major regional electric power companies have worked alongside the government in these efforts. For example, Matsutaro Shoriki, the owner of the Yomiuri Shinbun group and a member of the lower house of the Diet from 1955, used his media group to sponsor an Exposition on the Peaceful Use of Atomic Energy in Hibiya, Tokyo in November 1955 that attracted some 350,000 visitors (Anzai 2012, 27–8). The nine major electric power companies in Japan spent a combined ¥2.4trn (US$27.6bn) between 1970 and the 2012 fiscal year on advertising nuclear power (*Asahi Shinbun* 2012).

In terms of public education, the Ministry of Education, Culture, Sports, Science and Technology (MEXT) and the Agency for Natural Resources and Energy (ANRE) are the main governmental bodies in charge of nuclear education in formal education in Japan. Although nuclear power is included in the courses of study determined by MEXT every 10 years as broad standards for all schools, implemented to ensure a fixed standard of education throughout the country, the authorised textbooks used in Japanese schools provide relatively little information on nuclear power. The various media described above, therefore, play a large part in informing the Japanese public about nuclear-related issues, along with the supplementary readers (used alongside textbooks by many schools) described in more detail in Section 2.4 of this chapter.

2.2 Textbook Examination Procedure and its standards in Japan

The Textbook Examination Procedure for textbooks used in Japanese schools allows publishing houses to create their own textbooks and submit them for official examination and approval by MEXT. Textbooks approved by MEXT are then placed on display in local communities for public view. The final decision on which books to use rests with local boards of education, in the case of public (i.e. state) schools, and with the schools themselves in the case of private institutions. Once schools have decided which textbooks to use, orders are placed with the publishers and printing and distribution begins. The entire process takes a considerable amount of time and most textbook projects run for at least three years, from the appointment of the writing committee to the actual use of books in classrooms (Ministry of Foreign Affairs of Japan 2014).

In contrast, the supplementary readers used in schools are not required to go through the Textbook Examination Procedure on the grounds that they are educational materials but not textbooks. There are no strict criteria governing the publication of supplementary materials (MEXT 2015), which may be produced by teachers, educational boards, publishing houses and also the government, which issues its own supplementary readers to disseminate contents related to important aspects of national policy. Supplementary readers issued by the government are distributed to almost all schools. Although the use of these materials is optional, with teachers given discretion over whether or not to use them, they are used widely by teachers to supplement the material offered in authorised textbooks.

This chapter focuses on the 'fairness' or 'unfairness' of the government-produced educational materials for schoolchildren in formal education dealing with nuclear power and radiation, with a special focus on the supplementary readers. Here, 'fairness' is defined in reference to the Textbook Examination Procedure used by MEXT to screen textbooks 'in an appropriate and fair manner based on the relevant examination standards' (Ministry of Foreign Affairs of Japan 2014) – a procedure that is not, as explained above, used to screen the supplementary materials used in Japanese schools. The procedure sets out standards and conditions for the selection, organisation and amount of material featured in textbooks as follows:

> Chapter 2: Selection/treatment and organisation/amount . . .
>
> Fairness in selection and treatment
>
> - There should be no bias towards specific subjects, phenomena or fields, and an overall balance should be maintained.
> - One-sided views should not be included without adequate safeguards.
>
> (MEXT 2014a; Ministry of Foreign Affairs of Japan 2014)

These points are important for defining fairness or unfairness as they are understood in this chapter, with 'unfairness' defining any situation where there is bias, a one-sided perspective or lack of balance or emphasis in the selection and treatment of information in educational materials. Although not all 'bias' is intentional – it can be both conscious and unconscious – the examples of 'unfairness' presented in this chapter represent the explicit intentions of the Japanese government to influence and distort the discussion of nuclear power.

2.3 The Japanese government-sponsored contest on nuclear power

The unfairness is illustrated by some examples of public education and PR, mainly targeting school children. The government sponsored short essay contests on the theme of nuclear power between 1969 and 2010, and poster contests between 1994 and 2010. Figure 6.1 shows three of the 12 prize-winning posters from 2009.

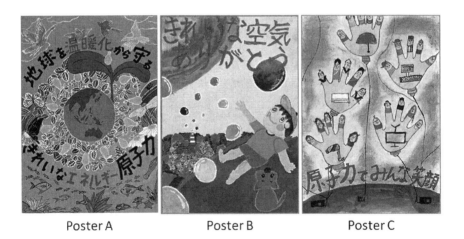

Poster A   Poster B   Poster C

Figure 6.1 Prize-winning entries in the government-sponsored nuclear power poster contest 2009

Source: MEXT and ANRE 2009.

All the posters featured in Figure 6.1 praise nuclear power. Poster A, earning first prize among applicants from all age categories, was created by a 13-year-old student from Saitama prefecture. It states: 'Nuclear power is clean energy preventing global warming'. Poster B, securing second prize in the under-12 category and created by a student living in Ibaraki prefecture, says: 'Thanks for clean air from nuclear power'. Poster C, winning third prize in the under-12 category and produced by an 11-year-old student from Fukushima prefecture, says: 'Nuclear power makes everybody smile'. The hands shown in the poster represent happy families enjoying the benefits of various electrical devices powered by clean, green, nuclear power.

Many Japanese would find poster C particularly ironic, given the aftermath of the Fukushima nuclear accident, which has torn families apart geographically and economically as a result of evacuation zones, differences in vulnerability to radiation caused by age, loss of livelihood and voluntary and involuntary displacement. In Fukushima prefecture and the surrounding areas, many families in which two or even three generations had hitherto lived together under one roof were sundered by the accident, with approximately half of all evacuated households having to live their daily lives separated from family members with whom they had previously cohabited (Fukushima Booklet Publication Committee 2015, 25). Of course, the students themselves are innocent of any blame in producing their artwork: they were simply responding to encouraging 'hints' for participants – such as 'nuclear power generation supports our life' – that appeared in the poster contest's application guidebook. The hints in the guidelines for the following year were particularly leading in this respect, informing participants that 'nuclear power plants generate important electricity', 'nuclear energy is kind to the earth' and 'five protective layers keep nuclear plants safe'. These are just three of nine hints in the 2010 guidelines, which referred students solely to nuclear power's positive aspects 'for reference when preparing posters' (MEXT and ANRE 2010a).

These posters were praised widely and deployed in PR across various media – such as pamphlets, supplementary readers and websites – up until the time of the Fukushima nuclear accident. They were then withdrawn and the contests discontinued following broad criticism from the general public, including a petition demanding the contests be stopped.

2.4 Supplementary readers on nuclear power and radiation

Figure 6.2 presents an overview of educational materials and books on nuclear power and radiation disseminated in schools before and after the Fukushima nuclear accident by various actors. These include supplementary readers published before and after the accident by the Japanese government and nuclear-related educational materials issued for the first time in November 2011 by the Fukushima Prefectural Board of Education, modelled on supplementary readers published by the Japanese government in October 2011. The figure also shows 'alternative' materials issued by the Fukushima Teachers Union and the Fukushima University Research Group – a group of lecturers based at Fukushima University, the author among them – in 2012 and 2013.

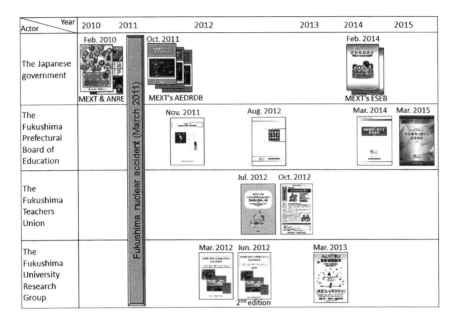

Figure 6.2 Educational materials on nuclear power and radiation issued by various actors before and after the Fukushima nuclear accident

Note: AEDRDB = Atomic Energy Division of Research and Development Bureau; ESEB = Elementary and Secondary Education Bureau.

The supplementary readers on nuclear power for elementary and junior high school students published by MEXT and ANRE in February 2010 (MEXT and ANRE 2010b; 2010c) were withdrawn within months of the Fukushima nuclear accident. This was because they included inappropriate information on safety that was proved wrong by the accident, such as 'Nuclear power plants are designed to withstand large earthquakes and tsunamis'. Other material presented in the readers was clearly biased. For example, one page in the reader on nuclear power for elementary school students, which compared the characteristics of thermal power plants and nuclear power plants, depicts the thermal power plant with a scary facial expression in contrast to the nuclear power plant, shown with a gentle and benign face (see Figure 6.3). In the same figure, CO_2 emission is represented as waste from the thermal power plant, but radioactive waste is not shown below the illustration of the nuclear power plant. This biased information indoctrinates students to accept nuclear power.

New supplementary readers focusing on radiation rather than nuclear power were issued by MEXT (without ANRE) to all Japanese elementary, junior high and high school students in October 2011, at a cost of approximately ¥340m. The readers contained few facts or lessons learned from the Fukushima nuclear accident – beyond eight lines in the preface describing the disaster – and, although lavishly illustrated,

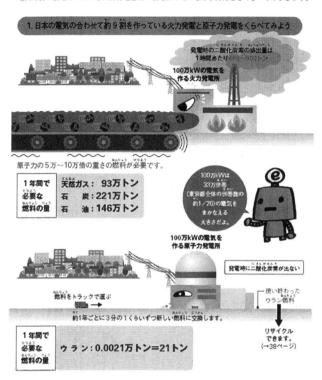

⑦ これからも電気を使いつづけるために

かぎりあるエネルギー資源、ふえる世界のエネルギー消費、地球温暖化…。わたしたちが
大人になってからも電気を安定して使いつづけるにはどうしたらいいのでしょうか。日本の
電気の約6割を作っている火力発電と約3割を作っている原子力発電をくらべてみましょう。

1. 日本の電気の合わせて約9割を作っている火力発電と原子力発電をくらべてみよう

発電時の二酸化炭素の排出量は
1時間あたり400～900トン

100万kWの電気を
作る火力発電所

原子力の5万～10万倍の重さの燃料が必要です。

1年間で必要な燃料の量	天然ガス：93万トン
	石　炭：221万トン
	石　油：146万トン

100万kWは
33万世帯
（東京都全体の世帯数の
約1/20）の電気を
まかなえる
大きさだよ。

100万kWの電気を
作る原子力発電所

発電時に二酸化炭素が出ない

燃料をトラックで運ぶ

約1年ごとに3分の1くらいずつ新しい燃料に交換します。

使い終わった
ウラン燃料

リサイクル
できます。
（→38ページ）

1年間で必要な燃料の量	ウラン：0.0021万トン＝21トン

Figure 6.3 Comparing the characteristics of thermal power plants (above) and nuclear
power plants (below)

Source: MEXT and ANRE 2010b.

they did not feature photographs of the accident. Furthermore, they made no
mention of children's vulnerability to radiation exposure – a perplexing omission,
given widespread public concern about this issue after the accident. Concerned parents across Japan formed more than 300 social movement organisations seeking to
protect children from radiation (Holdgrün and Holthus n.d.) while food distributors,
consumer groups, daycare centres and anxious parents monitored food for radioactive
contamination themselves (Anzai 2012). Even so, the Fukushima Prefectural Board of
Education modelled its own educational publication about radiation on the Japanese government's supplementary readers in November 2011. Students could not be
expected to learn important lessons from Fukushima using these supplementary readers.

3. Content analysis of the Japanese government's supplementary readers on nuclear power and radiation

In order to objectively and quantitatively clarify the characteristics of the Japanese government's supplementary readers, especially their accuracy and fairness, content analysis was applied to the supplementary readers of 2010 and 2011 (Goto and Sugawara 2013). Methods of text mining and sentiment analysis (opinion mining) were applied using KH-Coder text mining software, developed by Koichi Higuchi (Higuchi n.d.).

The procedure for text mining is as follows:

1   Pre-process text data of documents.
2   Extract the 150 words that appear with the greatest frequency in each supplementary reader.
3   Specify compound words and unnecessary words.
4   Create a co-occurrence network and clusters among the extracted 150 words based on subgraph detection.
5   Code the word clusters.
6   Create co-occurrence networks around specific words, in this case, *genshiryoku* (nuclear power) and *hoshasen* (radiation).

Table 6.1 ranks the top 10 of the 150 words that appeared with the greatest frequency in each supplementary reader. The words in bold type represent the specific words *genshiryoku* (nuclear power) and *hoshasen* (radiation) or compound terms including these specific words. The specific words and related compounds terms appear frequently in the readers. In the 2011 readers, only *hoshasen* (radiation) and its compound words are ranked. This is because descriptions of *genshiryoku* (nuclear power) were largely omitted in the later reader, which focused primarily on radiation.

Figure 6.4 shows the co-occurrence network for the word *genshiryoku* (nuclear power) in the 2010 supplementary reader for elementary school students. The word *genshiryoku* (nuclear power) is included in the reader's title – *Waku waku*

Table 6.1 The 10 most frequently appearing words in the Japanese government's supplementary readers for 2010 and 2011

Rank of appearance	The 2010 supplementary reader		The 2011 supplementary reader	
	For primary school students	*For junior high school students*	*For primary school students*	*For junior high school students*
1	*Denki* (electricity)	**Genshiryoku-** *hatsuden* **(nuclear power generation)**	**Hoshasen** **(radiation)**	**Hoshasen** **(radiation)**
2	*Tsukau* (use)	*Energy* (energy)	**Hoshasei-** *busshitsu* **(radioactive material)**	**Hoshasei-** *busshitsu* **(radioactive material)**

3	*Energy* (energy) *Tsukuru* (generate)	**Hoshasen** **(radiation)**	*Aru* (exist)	*Riyou* (use)
4	*Nenryou* (fuel)	*Aru* (exist)	*Ukeru* (receive)	*Ukeru* (receive)
5	*Aru* (exist)	*Tsukau* (use)	*Ryou* (quantity)	*Aru* (exist)
6	*Dekiru* (can do)	*Dekiru* (can do)	*Riyou* (use)	*Dekiru* (can do)
7	**Genshiryoku-** *hatsudensho* **(nuclear power** plant)	*Uran* (uranium)	*Tsukau* (use) *Deru* (out) *Dekiru* (can do)	**Hoshanou** **(radioactivity)**
8	**Hoshasen** **(radiation)**	*Nihon* (Japan)	*Hakaru* (survey)	*Shiraberu* (investigate), **Hoshasen**-*ryou* (quantity of **radiation)**
9	*Uran* (uranium)	**Genshiryoku** **(nuclear** **power)**	*Dasu* (emit) *Hito* (human) *Mono* (matter)	*Fukumu* (contain)
10	**Genshiryoku-** *hatsuden* **(nuclear power** generation)	*Nenryou* (fuel)	*Iroiro* (various) *Shiraberu* (investigate)	*Ekkusu* (X)

Note: All words in bold type represent the specific words *genshiryoku* (nuclear power) and *hoshasen* (radiation) or compound terms including these words.

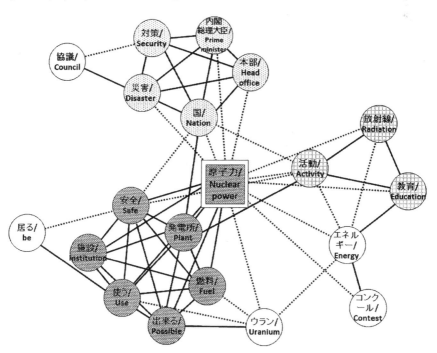

Figure 6.4 Co-occurrence network for the word *genshiryoku* (nuclear power) in the 2010 supplementary reader for elementary school students

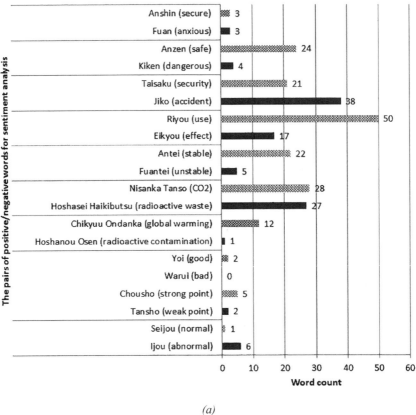

Results of sentiment analysis in the supplementary reader for junior high school students issued in 2010

(a)

Figure 6.5 Positive/negative word counts from a sentiment analysis of Japanese government supplementary readers for junior high school students in 2010 (a) and 2011 (b)

genshiryoku rando (The exciting world of nuclear power). In the figure, strong co-occurrences between any two words are shown by a bold line. Words appearing in circles with the same shading belong to the same clusters. For example, *genshiryoku* is seen to have a strong co-occurrence with the positive word *anzen* (safe) in the same cluster. This result clearly indicates that the 2010 supplementary reader emphasised the safety of nuclear power.

The procedure for sentiment analysis is as follows:

1 Set up a framework pairing positive/negative words in relation to chosen terms, in this case, *nuclear power* and *radiation*.[2]
2 Count the appearances of each word and compare them in each pair.

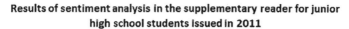

Results of sentiment analysis in the supplementary reader for junior high school students issued in 2011

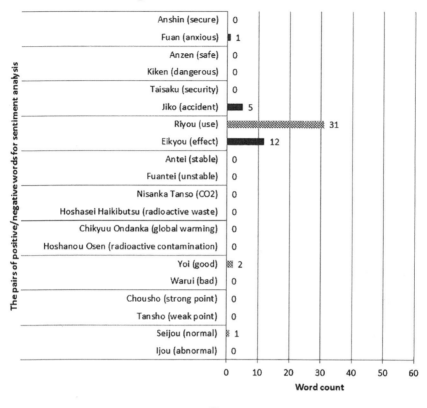

(b)

The sentiment analysis revealed a number of pairs of positive/negative words such as safe/dangerous, of which 10 key word pairs are depicted on the left hand axis of the two bar graphs shown in Figure 6.5. Here, bar graph (a) presents word pairings for the 2010 supplementary reader for junior high school students, while bar graph (b) presents word pairings for the 2011 reader. Dotted shading is used to represent the positive word count and bold shading represents the negative. In the 2010 supplementary reader, the positive word count exceeded the negative in seven pairs, indicating that the 2010 supplementary reader was biased toward the promotion of nuclear power. In the 2011 supplementary reader, the count for these words decreased when general descriptions of nuclear power were omitted, owing to the reader's new focus on radiation. In 2011, the level of fairness had improved relatively but the positive aspect of radiation (*riyou* or use) was still emphasised more than the negative (*eikyou* or effect).

4. Criticism of the Japanese government's supplementary readers

The Japanese government's 2011 supplementary readers were criticised, not least by the Fukushima Prefectural Assembly. In March 2012, the assembly adopted a resolution calling for the readers to be revised considering the gravity of Fukushima's situation in light of the nuclear accident and radioactive contamination. The Fukushima Teachers Union also took a critical stance, publishing an alternative book on radiation in July 2012 and issuing alternative material for teachers in October 2012 (see Figure 6.2). Hisako Sakiyama, a member of Fukushima Nuclear Accident Independent Investigation Commission, publicly criticised the supplementary readers and the accompanying guidelines for the teachers, which recommended that teachers help students to understand that there is no clear evidence that radiation levels lower than 100mSv cause disease (Sakiyama 2012, 1,118). Jumpei Ryu, a professor of Kagawa University, questioned the readers' value as science education. He compared a number of British science higher-level student textbooks with the Japanese government's supplementary readers, considering their respective contributions to science literacy and the public understanding of science (Ryu 2012). Notably, the Japanese Society of Environmental Education held special sectional meetings on nuclear power and environmental education every year from 2011 to 2013, focusing specifically on how to improve the contents of nuclear power education.

Anand Grover, Special Rapporteur to the United Nations Human Rights Council on people's right to enjoy the highest attainable standard of physical and mental health, reported on the Japanese government's response to the Fukushima nuclear accident after visiting Japan between 15 and 26 November 2012. In a report released in May 2013, Grover reserved special criticism for the Japanese government's presentation of radiation-related health issues in the supplementary readers:

> The supplementary reading and presentation materials mention that there is no clear evidence of excess risk of diseases, including cancer, when exposed for a short time to radiation levels of 100 mSv and below. This gave the impression that doses below 100 mSv are safe. As noted above, this is not consistent with the law in Japan, international standards or epidemiological research. Additionally, the Special Rapporteur notes that the textbooks do not mention the increased vulnerability of children to the health effects of radiation. Such information may give children and parents a false sense of security, which may result in children's exposure to high levels of radiation.
>
> (Grover 2013, 17)

In March 2012, the author and colleagues formed the Fukushima University Research Group of Supplementary Readers on Radiation to create an original, alternative supplementary reader on radiation to controvert the Japanese government's supplementary readers (see Figure 6.2). This new reader included a detailed presentation of the facts and lessons learned from the Fukushima nuclear accident, as well as a discussion of the problem of unfairness in Japanese public education and PR on nuclear power. It included an explanation of why children are particularly vulnerable to radiation exposure and introduced various arguments to ensure a balanced presentation of issues and promote students' critical thinking abilities with regard to scientific uncertainties, such as the effects of exposure to low doses of radiation. Initially printed in 2,000 copies and issued online in PDF format to make it accessible to more people, the reader was generally well received in terms of its content. At the same time, the reader attracted some criticism owing to a number of minor errors, which were amended before its reissue online three months later, in June 2012, as a revised and enlarged second edition (Fukushima University Research Group of Supplementary Readers on Radiation 2012). The reader has gained broad support from the general public and the Fukushima Teachers Union, which has distributed it to all its members. The authors have received many offers of support from educators across Japan, who are now using the reader in classrooms and seminars. They also have the support of municipal boards of education in a number of prefectures, which are using the reader as a reference when preparing their own educational materials. The reader was published as a book in March 2013 (Goto 2013).

MEXT issued a second revision of its supplementary readers on radiation in February 2014 (MEXT 2014b; 2014c) at the cost of approximately ¥290m. MEXT's more neutral Elementary and Secondary Education Bureau (ESEB) took over responsibility for the readers from the previous bureau, MEXT's Atomic Energy Division of Research and Development Bureau (AEDRDB). Professional school textbook examiners were included in the editing process for the first time.

The revised 2014 supplementary government readers showed significant improvement in terms of the fairness and balance of the information presented. Descriptions of the Fukushima nuclear accident were improved and neutral, and more careful expressions were used when dealing with uncertain problems, such as the effect of exposure to low doses of radiation. Significantly, the readers mentioned the vulnerability of children to radiation exposure for the first time.

Undoubtedly, these improvements emerged following widespread criticism from the general public and scientific community in Japan, as well as actions such as the Fukushima University Research Group's publication of its reader and book on radiation, which directly criticised the unfairness of the Japanese government's supplementary readers. Today, the Fukushima University Research Group, the Fukushima Teachers Union and various citizen groups continue to work to improve the content of the government's supplementary readers, focusing on the following problems, which have yet to be solved:

1 The readers do not provide adequate information on the radiation dosage levels in the evacuation zones in Fukushima (20 mSv per year), the dosage limit in radiation-controlled areas in Japan (5.2 mSv per year) or the dosage limit of radiation for the general public (1 mSv per year).

2 They do not include adequate explanation of deaths related to nuclear accidents and radiation exposure. These include the 2,007 deaths (estimated

by Fukushima prefecture) that resulted from the Fukushima nuclear accident (*Tokyo Shinbun* 2015) and the deaths caused directly by the accident at JCO Co. Ltd. (formerly Japan Nuclear Fuel Conversion Co.), a nuclear power plant in Tokai, Ibaraki prefecture, in 1999 (International Atomic Energy Agency n.d.).

3   The provision of information relating to children's vulnerability to radiation exposure is insufficient.
4   They do not provide any consideration of the Japanese government's responsibility for the Fukushima nuclear accident.
5   They lack content addressing the pros and cons of nuclear power – content that is needed for the purpose of democratic decision making.

5. Positioning nuclear energy science in the context of ESD

5.1 Questionnaire survey of science teachers from Fukushima prefectural junior high schools

To better understand the state of nuclear power and radiation education in Fukushima prefecture in terms of content, educational materials available and concerns expressed by educators, I conducted a questionnaire survey of junior high school science teachers working in Fukushima prefecture in December 2013, in collaboration with students from my laboratory (Iino and Goto 2014). There were 231 junior high schools before the nuclear accident but three closed as a result of the disaster. Therefore, questionnaires were sent to 228 schools, of which 125 responded (response rate: 55 per cent). In response to the question: 'Do you feel anxiety about nuclear power and radiation education?' 79 per cent (99/125)

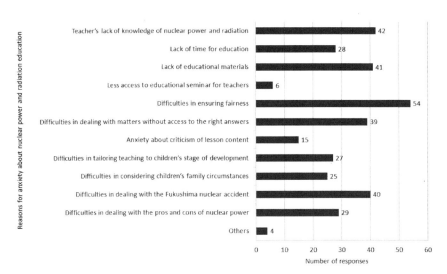

Figure 6.6 Results of a survey among science teachers of Fukushima prefectural junior high schools, which asked: 'Please provide your reasons for anxiety.' (n = 99, multiple answers allowed)

of teachers chose 'anxious' (81/125) or 'very anxious' (18/125). The reason (multiple answers allowed) most commonly given for anxiety was 'difficulties in ensuring fairness' (54/99) followed by 'lack of knowledge' (42/99), 'lack of educational materials' (41/99), 'difficulties in dealing with the Fukushima nuclear accident' (40/99) and 'difficulties in dealing with matters without access to the right answers' (39/99) (see Figure 6.6).

For the question: 'What do you think are the issues in nuclear power and radiation education?' (multiple answers allowed), the following were the most frequently chosen: 'to increase teachers' knowledge about nuclear power and radiation' (81/125), 'to ensure educational materials' (69/125), 'to secure time for education' (52/125), and 'to improve the contents of supplementary readers' (49/125).

These results indicate that more accurate, fair and balanced educational materials on nuclear power and radiation are required by the science teachers in Fukushima prefectural junior high schools.

5.2 Responsibility of the Japanese government in proposing the UN Decade of ESD

As mentioned previously, the Japanese government proposed the United Nations Decade of ESD in 2002. Critical thinking is recognised as an important competency in ESD by the United Nations Educational, Scientific and Cultural Organisation (UNESCO), along with 'imagining future scenarios and making decisions in a collaborative manner' (UNESCO n.d). Providing model ESD educational materials that help students develop the critical thinking necessary to first envision and then work collaboratively towards achieving the most sustainable future for their society is something that all government signatories to the decade should be aiming for – Japan most of all, given its key role in proposing the decade.

Evidently, the Japanese government's supplementary readers on nuclear power and radiation cannot be models because of biased, inadequate information and a refusal to refer to important lessons from the past. This is particularly disappointing, given that other governments have created good models for ESD educational materials that deal with energy issues. One supplementary reader on nuclear power, published in 2008 by the German Federal Ministry for the Environment, Nature Conservation, Building and Nuclear Safety (*Bundesministerium für Umwelt, Naturschutz und Reaktorsicherheit*), received official commendation from UNESCO for its contribution to ESD, not least because of the way it dealt fairly with the pros and cons of exiting nuclear power.

5.3 What is the real bottom line of sustainable development?

Figure 6.7 shows two commonly accepted models that are used to explain sustainable development based on a 'triple bottom line' methodology. The 'three pillars' model of sustainable development is often used to represent the importance of interconnections within social, economic and environmental spheres. However, this representation has been criticised for failing to convey their interdependence.

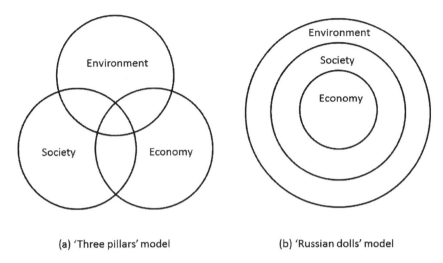

(a) 'Three pillars' model   (b) 'Russian dolls' model

Figure 6.7 Models explaining sustainable development based on 'triple bottom line' methodology

The 'Russian dolls' model uses a systems view to clarify that the economic system emerges from the social system, which is a part of the wider environmental system (Lipscombe 2009, 16). While this may seem an anthropocentric viewpoint, it acknowledges the fact that both the economy and society can only exist within a healthy natural environment (Chambers *et al.* 2000, 5).

The Fukushima nuclear accident proves the validity of the Russian dolls model, for which environmental sustainability is the real bottom line. An evacuation zone of approximately 1,150km^2 remains off-limits to residents, owing to high levels of contamination by radioactive materials. As recently as December 2015, four years and nine months after the accident, government sources reported that some 99,946 people remain in a state of evacuation, unable to return to their homes (Fukushima Prefecture n.d.) – a figure that may well be higher. At the most fundamental level, the unsustainability of a degraded environment has left people unable to live and perform socioeconomic activities in an area that was once their home.

Bearing in mind that, in the past, the developers of nuclear power plants such as the Fukushima Daiichi plant courted local governments with promises of investment, jobs and social infrastructure for the communities in which they were placed, ESD in the years since the Fukushima nuclear accident offers Japanese students an opportunity to consider and discuss not only the interdependence of the social, economic and environmental aspects of the triple bottom line, but also the dependence, priority and trade-offs among them. Here, it is important for students to understand that *the answer* is not necessarily required. Rather, it is the process of questioning, critical enquiry and collaborative thinking that is important, enabling them to participate in decisions made on energy and other important areas.

5.4 Imagining future scenarios and making democratic decisions

Various opinion polls show strong and persistent public opposition (about 60 per cent) to the restarting of nuclear power plants – however, this has not been reflected directly in Japanese voting behaviour. Voter turnout was low, at 59.32 per cent, in the Lower House elections in December 2012 and the Liberal Democratic Party regained control of the country as the ruling party, despite its staunch promotion of nuclear power, seemingly because other concerns, such as the economy and national security, were uppermost in voters' minds. Since then, the Abe administration has pushed forward its nuclear power agenda. On June 1 2015, it approved the draft of a new energy mix scenario for 2030, which allotted a 20–22 per cent share to nuclear power (World Nuclear News 2015), and in the same year it restarted two reactors at the Sendai nuclear power plant. The Takahama and Ikata nuclear power plants will restart in 2016. Although the regulatory standards for nuclear power plants have become stricter, 'the myth of nuclear power plant safety' would seem to have been reinstated.

From the viewpoint of democratic decision making, the contents of education on nuclear power and radiation affect people's critical thinking abilities, their capacity to imagine future scenarios and their voting behaviour in the short, medium and long term. The legal voting age in Japan will be lowered from 20 to 18 years in June 2016. Both informal and formal education in schools are now of vital importance in terms of learning lessons from the Fukushima nuclear accident.

6. Conclusion

This chapter has assessed, through the lens of ESD, the fairness of the Japanese government's educational materials on nuclear power and radiation for formal education. A content analysis of the government's supplementary readers on nuclear power and radiation gave evidence of bias towards the promotion and use of nuclear power. After the Fukushima nuclear accident, the 2011 supplementary readers continued to emphasise the positive aspects of radiation more than the negative. As a consequence of broad criticism, re-revised supplementary readers on radiation were issued in 2014. Although problems in the context of ESD still remain, the readers' fairness has improved significantly.

The Japanese government is required to fulfil its global responsibility in the context of ESD and as a country in which a nuclear disaster has occurred. One of the most important lessons learned from the Fukushima nuclear accident is that fairness in public education and PR regarding nuclear power is essential to promote critical thinking and public engagement with energy issues to ensure development is participatory and mistakes like the Fukushima disaster do not recur. It is to be hoped that this work will contribute to the improvement of fairness in education and democratic decisions regarding the use of nuclear power in Japan.

Acknowledgement

A part of this research was supported by the Grant-in-Aid for Young Scientists B (No. 24710043) of the Japan Society for the Promotion of Science.

Notes

1 The special websites on nuclear power, including video programmes accessible online, existed before the Fukushima nuclear accident. These included *Atomin* (Information for nuclear power education, www.atomin.go.jp), produced by the Ministry of Education, Culture, Sports, Science and Technology (MEXT), and *Naruhodo! Genshiryoku A to Z* (Let's learn about nuclear power from A to Z, http://enecho.meti.go.jp/genshi-az/) by the Agency for Natural Resources and Energy (ANRE). Although these websites were deleted after the Fukushima accident, it is possible to access them through the Web Archiving Project (WARP) of the National Diet Library (http://warp.da.ndl. go.jp/). Similar video programmes on nuclear power are still accessible on the *Saiensu channeru* (science channel) of the Japan Science and Technology Agency (JST), one of the independent administrative institutions of MEXT (https://sciencechannel.jst.go.jp/, accessed 2 March 2016).
2 The KH-Coder software does not include a function for sentiment analysis. For this reason, we referred to the results of text mining and argument points for the use of nuclear power and radiation in other studies, such as the Deliberative Poll on Energy and Environmental Policy Options by the Japanese government held in July 2012 (Executive Committee of Deliberative Poll on Energy and Environmental Policy Options 2012) in setting up the framework pairings for our sentiment analysis.

References

Anzai, I. 2012. *Genpatsu jiko no rika shakai* (Scientific and social aspects of the Fukushima nuclear disaster) Trans. Suloway, S. Tokyo, Japan: Shinnihon Shuppansha Co. Ltd.

Asahi Shinbun 2012. *Genpatsu hoyuu 9 sya koukoku 2.4 chouen* (Nine major electric power companies spent more than ¥2.4trn to sell public on nuclear power). *Asahi Shinbun*, 28 December 2012.

Chambers, N., Simmons, C. and Wackernagel, M. 2000. *Sharing nature's interest: ecological footprints as an indicator of sustainability*. London, UK: Earthscan Publications Ltd.

Executive Committee of Deliberative Poll on Energy and Environmental Policy Options 2012. Report of deliberative poll on energy and environmental policy options (www. cas.go.jp/jp/seisaku/npu/kokumingiron/dp/120827_01.pdf). Accessed 25 December 2015.

Fukushima Booklet Publication Committee 2015. Ten lessons from Fukushima: reducing risks and protecting communities from nuclear disasters (http://fukushimalessons.jp/ assets/content/doc/Fukushima10Lessons_ENG.pdf). Accessed 25 December 2015.

Fukushima Prefecture n.d. *Shinsai higai jokyo sokuhou* (Preliminary report on disaster damages and victims) No.1598 (www.pref.fukushima.lg.jp/site/portal/shinsai-higaijo kyo.html). Accessed 23 January 2016.

Fukushima University Research Group of Supplementary Readers on Radiation 2012. *Hoshasen to hibaku no mondai wo kangaeru tame no fukudokuhon. kaiteiban* (The supplementary reader to learn about radiation and the issues of radiation dose. Revised edition) (www.ad.ipc.fukushima-u.ac.jp/~a067/index.htm). Accessed 25 December 2015.

German Federal Ministry for the Environment, Nature Conservation, Building and Nuclear Safety 2008. *Einfach abschalten? Materialien für Bildung und Information* (Switch off simply? Materials for education and information) (www.schule-der-zukunft.nrw. de/fileadmin/user_upload/Schule-der-Zukunft/Materialsammlung/downloads/atomen ergie_de_gesamt.pdf). Accessed 25 December 2015.

Goto, S. 2013. *Minna de manabu houshasen fukudokuhon* (The supplementary reader on radiation for everybody's learning). Tokyo, Japan: Godo-shuppan.

Goto, S. and Sugawara, Y. 2013. *Content analysis of the Japanese government's supplementary readers on nuclear power and radiation.* Abstract. Paris, France: The MacroTrend Conferences.

Grover, A. 2013. Report of the special rapporteur on the right of everyone to the enjoyment of the highest attainable standard of physical and mental health (www.ohchr.org/ Documents/HRBodies/HRCouncil/RegularSession/Session23/A-HRC-23–41-Add3_ en.pdf). Accessed 25 December 2015.

Higuchi, K. n.d. KH-Coder index page (http://khc.sourceforge.net/). Accessed 25 December 2015.

Holdgrün, P. and Holthus, B. n.d. Gender and political participation in post-3/11 Japan. Working paper 14/3. *Deutsches Institut für Japanstudien* (www.dijtokyo.org/publica tions/WP1403_Holdgruen_Holthus.pdf). Accessed 25 December 2015.

Iino, S. and Goto, S. 2014. Status and issues of nuclear power and radiation education in Fukushima prefecture: a questionnaire survey among the science teachers of Fukushima prefectural junior high schools. *Conference proceedings of the 25th Annual Meeting of the Japanese Society of Environmental Education.* Tokyo, Japan: The Executive Committee of the 25th Annual Meeting of the Japanese Society of Environmental Education, 77.

International Atomic Energy Agency n.d. Lessons learned from the JCO nuclear criticality accident in Japan in 1999 (www-ns.iaea.org/downloads/iec/tokaimura-report.pdf). Accessed 23 January 2016.

Investigation Committee on the Accident at Fukushima Nuclear Power Stations of Tokyo Electric Power Company 2012. Executive summary of the final report. (www.cas.go.jp/ jp/seisaku/icanps/eng/final-report.html). Accessed 25 December 2015.

Lipscombe, B.P. 2009. Extra-curricular education for sustainable development interventions in higher education (http://hdl.handle.net/10034/109413). Accessed 25 December 2015.

Ministry of Education, Culture, Sports, Science and Technology (MEXT) 2014a. *Gimukyouiku shogakkou kyoukayou tosho kentei kijun* (Textbook examination standards for compulsory education) (www.mext.go.jp/a_menu/shotou/kyoukasho/1260042. htm). Accessed 18 February 2016.

Ministry of Education, Culture, Sports, Science and Technology (MEXT) 2014b. *Shogakusei no tame no housyasen fukudokuhon* (The supplementary reader on radiation for elementary school students). Tokyo, Japan: MEXT.

Ministry of Education, Culture, Sports, Science and Technology (MEXT) 2014c. *Chugakusei to koukousei no tame no hoshasen fukudokuhon* (The supplementary reader on radiation for junior high and high school students). Tokyo, Japan: MEXT.

Ministry of Education, Culture, Sports, Science and Technology (MEXT) 2015. *Gakkou ni okeru hojyokyouzai no tekisetsu na atsukai ni tsuite (tsuchi)* (Notification for the proper treatment of the supplementary educational materials in school) (www.MEXT. go.jp/b_menu/hakusho/nc/1355677.htm). Accessed 24 January 2016.

Ministry of Education, Culture, Sports, Science and Technology (MEXT) and Agency for Natural Resources and Energy (ANRE) 2009. *Dai 16 kai genshiryoku posutaa kontesuto sakuhinshuu* (The portfolio of the 16th poster contest on nuclear power). Tokyo, Japan: Japan Atomic Energy Relations Organisation.

Ministry of Education, Culture, Sports, Science and Technology (MEXT) and Agency for Natural Resources and Energy (ANRE) 2010a. *Dai 17 kai genshiryoku posutaa kontesuto oubo youkou* (The application guidebook of the 17th poster contest on nuclear power). Tokyo, Japan: Japan Atomic Energy Relations Organisation.

Ministry of Education, Culture, Sports, Science and Technology (MEXT) and Agency for Natural Resources and Energy (ANRE) 2010b. *Waku waku genshiryoku rando* (The exciting world of nuclear power). Tokyo, Japan: MEXT and ANRE.

Ministry of Education, Culture, Sports, Science and Technology (MEXT) and Agency for Natural Resources and Energy (ANRE) 2010c. *Charenji! genshiryoku warudo* (Challenge! Everything you need to know about nuclear power). Tokyo, Japan: MEXT and ANRE.

Ministry of Foreign Affairs of Japan 2014. Japan's School Textbook Examination Procedure (www.mofa.go.jp/policy/education/textbooks/index.html). Accessed 25 December 2015.

Onishi, N. 2011. 'Safety myth' left Japan ripe for nuclear crisis. *The New York Times Asia Pacific*, 24 June 2011.

Ryu, J. 2012. On nuclear power problem in science education in Japan. *Kagaku* 82(10), 1,132–1,141.

Sakiyama, H. 2012. Public education on the health effects of low dose radiation: why the government underestimated the risks. *Kagaku* 82(10), 1,116–1,123.

Tokyo Shinbun 2015. *Fukushima shinsai kanrenshi 2000 nin cho* (Disaster-related deaths number more than 2,000) (www.tokyo-np.co.jp/article/feature/tohokujisin/list/CK2015122902000197.html). Accessed 23 January 2016.

UNESCO n.d. Education for sustainable development (ESD) (www.UNESCO.org/new/en/education/themes/leading-the-international-agenda/education-for-sustainable-development/). Accessed 25 December 2015.

World Nuclear Association 2015. Nuclear power in Japan (www.world-nuclear.org/info/Country-Profiles/Countries-G-N/Japan/). Accessed 25 December 2015.

World Nuclear News 2015. Plan sets out Japan's energy mix for 2030 (www.world-nuclear-news.org/NP-Plan-sets-out-Japans-energy-mix-for-2030–0306154.html). Accessed 16 January 2016.

7 Collaborating for change

Teaching and assessing a university community sustainability course in Japan and Vietnam

Tracey Gannon, Jane Singer and Benjamin McLellan

1. Introduction

Sustainability now has a much higher profile in higher education discourse, policy making, research and curriculum development than it did at the beginning of the United Nations Decade of Education for Sustainable Development (UNDESD) in 2005 (Sterling and Maxey 2013, 5). In recent years, many higher education institutions have succeeded in promoting environmental stewardship and sustainability curricula on campus, putting building design on a 'green' footing and engaging students in the community beyond the campus (Barlett and Chase 2004, 2). Yet, as Sterling and Maxey point out, 'the picture is mixed', with many institutions prioritising efforts to 'green' their operations and estates – in terms of 'saving energy, reducing [campus] carbon footprints, of developing green travel plans [for staff and faculty members], local purchasing and so on' (Sterling and Maxey 2013, 6) – ahead of reforming the curricula of higher education institutions that remain 'the most difficult area of sustainability practice in which to gain traction' (Ryan and Cotton 2013, 151).

Indeed, a daunting number of problems impede progress in the provision and embedding of sustainability education in universities. These include the organisation of institutions around departments and disciplines and the large scale of campuses, which 'can lead to silos that hamper efforts to build significant curriculum change across a campus' (AASHE 2010, 4). There is an urgent need for innovative and empowering pedagogies that target 'not just the "what" but the "how" of education' (Ryan and Cotton 2013, 152. See also Kagawa 2007 and Eilam and Trop 2011). As Barlett and Chase note, there are 'extreme burdens [placed] on faculty and administrators', who are obliged to decentre their own expertise to work across boundaries and connect disciplines – often without key skills and training in institutional change and lacking key support from institutions and peers – when promoting and creating sustainability courses (2004, 12). The traditional disparity between funding for research and funding for education, the academic career 'value' placed on each of these activities – which weighs typically in favour of more readily quantifiable research outputs in research related to disciplines (Ibid., 10–11) – and a lack of viable, proven sustainability assessment tools to assess the importance of education, research and outreach activities in higher education institutions (Yarime and Tanaka 2012) also discourage progress.

This chapter describes a course created by the three-year, Japanese government-funded, Kyoto University Tertiary ESD Initiative (hereafter TESDI). It was established in 2011 by an interdisciplinary group of researchers, based primarily at the Graduate School of Global Environmental Studies (GSGES), Kyoto University. TESDI had two main goals: first, to devise a model, widely replicable approach to tertiary-level community sustainability education for use in developing and developed countries and, second, to create an evaluative framework to assess the effectiveness of the course in fostering essential sustainability-linked competencies – such as critical thinking, problem solving and collaborative decision making – and encouraging students to not only think but act sustainably.

This chapter is a positivist case study assessment that provides 1) a description of the process by which a model sustainability course was created, implemented and replicated for use abroad and 2) an assessment of the course's efficacy in transforming behaviour for students in Japan and Vietnam. Section 2 examines the efforts to develop the course and evaluative framework in Kyoto from 2011 to 2012, followed by the implementation of the course in Kyoto and Vietnam in 2013. Section 3 considers the course's efficacy in transforming sustainability knowledge and competencies into pro-sustainable action, based on results obtained using the evaluative tools described in Section 2. While the analysis has been largely qualitative and empirical, requiring a certain degree of interpretation, two general conclusions can be drawn. First, the students' prior knowledge of sustainability was an important influence on course effectiveness. Second, fieldwork was the most important of the various trialled elements in converting theoretical knowledge to practical understanding, while social networking had limited success as a learning tool. The chapter ends with an examination of the issues of ownership and equitable collaboration in tailoring a course made in one context for use in another, the course's contribution to capacity building for teachers and students and the logistical as well as ethical issues that arise when a course created for use in a developed country is transferred to a developing one.

2. Designing and implementing the course and evaluative framework

2.1 Developing the course and parallel assessment tools

2.1.1 Course design

TESDI's multi-disciplinary team of 11 international and Japanese academics set out in October 2011 to establish the course's aims during a one-week series of workshops, entitled 'Defining "Our" ESD'. Participants – including academic experts in ESD and related environmental disciplines, government and non-governmental organisation (NGO) representatives, architects and planners, students and local residents from all over Japan – discussed the building of sustainable communities over the week. The exploration opened on campus with a workshop hosting presentations from guest speakers and TESDI project members. It was followed by four days of fieldwork in Kyoto city, in Kamiseya (a tiny mountain village in northern Kyoto prefecture) and in the seaside resort of Miyazu, also in northern Kyoto prefecture. The workshop series ended with a day of discussion to ascertain the components of 'our' ESD. The workshop defined the approach as one that:

1   Gives 'students a broad understanding of how global or national processes and policies can affect local attempts to foster sustainable development and vice versa',
2   Addresses sustainability issues in cities, sustainable development in mountain communities and sustainability of coastal areas 'from diverse perspectives', and
3   Promotes dialogue between teachers, students and local people and experiential learning processes to 'foster a new generation of graduates that are systems and team oriented, ethically conscious and open to local and international exchange'.

(Neef 2012, 9).

These and other defining principles, established during the week of workshops, ultimately underpinned the content and method of the Building a Sustainable Future: Principles and Challenges (hereafter, BSF) course, designed to incorporate:

- *A community-based approach to sustainability.* This was devised to encourage students to identify the links and interdependencies between urban, mountain and coastal communities and environments.
- *A modular approach.* The new course examined global issues relating to sustainable development, ethics, food, water and energy, followed by campus-wide, city-wide and rural and/or coastal fieldwork addressing sustainability issues in a community-specific context.
- *Collaborative course development.* Core team members from varied disciplines designed the course, with assistance from guest lecturers and teaching assistants.
- *Collaborative teaching.* Teaching methods included interdisciplinary and integrated approaches and team teaching, led by core team members and/ or guest lecturers, including professors and practitioners from local government, NGOs and local citizens' groups. Guest lecturers and practitioners also supported fieldwork. Teaching assistants helped to create and implement classroom activities for students and organise and guide fieldwork.
- *Collaborative learning.* All modules maintained a balance between classroom and fieldwork elements with an interactive approach retained, even in classroom-based teaching, through group work and peer feedback. Students were put in teams and tasked with developing questions and probing assigned topics relating to community sustainability.

2.1.2 Developing the course and evaluative framework in 2012

In 2012, the first year of its implementation, BSF was developed as a modular course combining interactive and interdisciplinary learning in the classroom with community-based sustainability-themed fieldwork in campus, city, rural and coastal communities. The course comprised five modules, beginning with general principles ('What is sustainability and why does it matter?') and global issues such as food, water and energy in Module 1, followed by three 'fieldwork modules' (Modules 2–4), each with a tripartite structure, embracing classroom/ fieldwork/feedback-based classes, applied to each of the three communities. Module 5 introduced a final project, requiring students to work in groups to design a practical campus sustainability proposal involving different community scales. The course could be regarded as embodying a 'third-stage' approach to 'education as sustainability'. Mochizuki and Yarime (2016, 18) define this as 'a carefully designed process where multiple actors can share knowledge and perspectives and develop an understanding of one another's interests and concerns, which in turn open opportunities for them to reach a shared diagnosis of a specific sustainability challenge as a foundation for deciding on particular interventions or solutions'.

The evaluative framework was developed and applied to assess the effectiveness of course elements and the course as a whole in enhancing students' eco literacy and fostering environmental action. This is consistent with the tradition of ESD assessment, for which 'inscriptions of competence and implicit theories of change have become infused into ESD curriculum discourses' (O'Donoghue 2016, 224). The assessment initially comprised pre- and post-course questionnaires that incorporated opportunities for self-grading; fieldwork diaries generated by students during the three community-based fieldwork modules; teaching assistant and teacher observation of student participation in group work; and qualitative

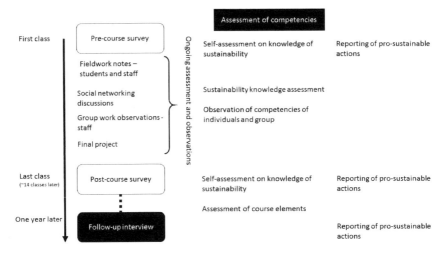

Figure 7.1 Assessment framework applied to the course

assessments of student engagement in an online bulletin board system. It also included in-depth, semi-structured interviews with approximately half the students, conducted two weeks after the course ended.

A revised approach was applied in 2013, consisting of pre-and post-course questionnaires and follow-up interviews to be conducted one year after the course, to provide a more longitudinal assessment, as well as an online discussion forum and fieldwork evaluation diaries. The framework for assessment of knowledge and competencies is described in Figure 7.1. The data collected for the 2013 course was used for the analysis described here.

2.2 Piloting a replicable approach to community-based sustainability

The course and revised evaluative framework were piloted at Hue University, in central Vietnam, and at Kyoto University (KU) in 2013. The Hue pilot comprised five weeks of classes held three times a week in evening sessions, which were extra-curricular for attending students. In contrast, classes for the Kyoto pilot were held once a week over the 15 weeks of the regular academic semester, and graduating students were awarded credit for taking the course. The Hue cohort was solely Vietnamese, with 13 students aged 21 to 23. The Kyoto cohort comprised 19 short-term international exchange students aged 20 to 30 from 12 countries. In both cases, the students were from multiple disciplines.

TESDI team members worked closely with researchers affiliated with the Centre for Agricultural Research and Development (CARD) at Hue University of Forestry and Agriculture (HUAF) in two preparatory workshops. Prior relationships with researchers at CARD expedited the discussion process, with members swift to determine how to adjust the course content and implementation to local conditions. This ensured not only the replicability of the course but its utility when used in a very different context to the one in which it had been developed, in terms of generating student outcomes. Discussions covered the choice of teaching personnel, course modifications in line with teaching capacities, the timing of the course, the recruitment process for the participants and logistics. Team-based teaching was decided upon, with TESDI members teaching global issues and core sustainability concepts and HUAF's youngest teaching faculty members teaching local issues and leading community fieldwork. In comparison to the Kyoto course, which used a popular social networking site (SNS), the Vietnam team created an online course support (OCS) website to offer students access to background readings and lecture materials ahead of the course, as well as the chance to communicate online about course content.

Figure 7.2 demonstrates the general course configuration and summarises important commonalities and differences between the two pilots in content, structure and scale. Most elements in the framework were modular so the course could be readily adapted to the context and capabilities of an alternative host institution. Using the same framework regardless of teaching context also allowed comparability, which was necessary to determine whether the course transferred effectively from one country to another in improving students' knowledge and moving them towards taking greater practical action for sustainability in their daily lives.

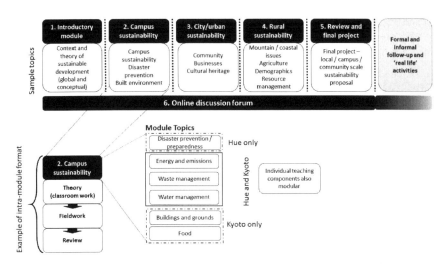

Figure 7.2 Structure of the course showing modular configuration

3. Evaluating the course's efficacy in fostering pro-sustainable outcomes

3.1 Carrying out the assessment

The assessment used the 'knowledge-action' spectrum to understand how students progressed from the beginning to one year beyond the end of the course in terms of improving their knowledge of sustainability issues and moving towards taking greater practical action for sustainability in their daily lives. As with most ESD courses, the goal here was transformative learning through praxis or what Wals *et al.* (2016, 30) refer to as 'a cyclical iterative journey of reflection and action'. The assessment of data obtained through the evaluative framework was conducted as a training and collaboration exercise. It involved two social research students interning for the PACE (Professional and Community Engagement) programme at Macquarie University, Australia, who were supervised in their assessment of the project by TESDI researchers. It set out to answer two key research questions:

RQ1) How have the students developed over the course with regards to knowledge of sustainability, sustainability-related competencies and pro-sustainable action? and

RQ2) What have been the most effective elements of the course?

Table 7.1 demonstrates the needs–outcomes framework that was used as a basis for evaluating the course. The framework describes the key desired characteristics at each level of the hierarchy, the major research questions that applied to each level, sources of data and the indicators used, where applicable.

Table 7.1 Outcomes hierarchy applied in the assessment

Outcomes hierarchy		Questions	Information source
Ultimate outcomes	• Sustained changes in individual behaviour • Uptake of programme/course in other countries • Inform future ESD courses in terms of structure, content, delivery • Guide decision-making processes of university administration	How have the students developed over the course with regards to their knowledge of sustainability, sustainability-related competencies and pro-sustainable action? What have been the most effective elements of the course?	Follow-up interviews
Intermediate outcomes	• Promotion of pro-sustainable behaviour in short term, small changes that demonstrate new understanding and awareness • Transfer of understanding/knowledge/awareness into action • Personal behavioural/attitudinal changes	What have been the most effective elements of the course?	Comparison between pre- and post-course surveys
Immediate outcomes	• Students pass course, build eco literacy, awareness of triple-bottom-line sustainability • Skills in communication, leadership, etc. • Interpersonal skills (from fieldwork) • Appreciation of local and global sustainability issues • Students from non-environmental backgrounds given opportunity to learn about sustainable development (through classroom-based activities and lived experience) • Students questioning status quo, thinking how the current state of things could be improved/approached better	What have been the most effective elements of the course?	• Comparison between pre- and post-course surveys • Fieldwork reflections • Comparison of what students expected to learn on fieldwork; anything students found interesting; what they actually learned
Activities/ outputs	• Course resources • Fieldwork guides • Final presentations proposing ideas to improve sustainability		
Needs	• A programme that responds to the need for ESD that can be implemented across various countries/cultures; flexibility of delivery without compromising core content • Deliverable/accessible to students from a range of disciplinary backgrounds • Course that does not just deliver environmental knowledge/content, but also fosters eco literacy, pro-sustainable activities, ability and skills to act on knowledge and apply it to solve problems • Course that builds key competencies that are not ESD specific e.g. leadership, verbal and written communication, English skills		

The BSF course generated large amounts of qualitative and some quantitative data that could be analysed. NVivo software was used for qualitative data analysis. First, the pre- and post-course surveys, fieldwork activity sheets, online discussion threads and follow-up interviews were imported into the program for coding. Each data set was read closely and words and short passages indicating students' knowledge, skills, actions and perceptions of the different course elements were coded. Similar ideas were labelled using the same code. This led to the emergence of general trends in the progression of student knowledge, skills and action and their perspectives on the most effective aspects of the course.

A second round of coding was then applied to identify links between existing codes. Through this process, connections between different course elements and developments in students' knowledge, skills and actions emerged, which provided an indication of which elements of the course were most effective at improving understanding and inspiring pro-sustainable action among students.

3.2 Research results

As indicated in Table 7.1, many of the course's outcomes could be considered intermediate outcomes, achieved within the term of the course itself. These were assessed using pre- and post-course surveys and observations from fieldwork and class activities. The ultimate outcomes of the course were evaluated solely from the follow-up interviews and aimed to clarify the ongoing impact on students' lives.

3.2.1 RQ1: How have the students developed over the course with regards to knowledge of sustainability, sustainability-related competencies and pro-sustainable action?

Knowledge

Students' self-assessments of how much they knew or understood about sustainability (scaled from 1 = very little to 5 = very much) were solicited before and after the course. Their responses are shown in Figure 7.3. The responses shown do not represent the full student cohort – only those students from each cohort who completed both surveys (10 out of 13 in Vietnam, and 13 out of 19 in Kyoto). The quantitative data was only a small proportion of the total assessment and because the sample size for those taking the survey was small, it is difficult to argue any statistical significance. With a less than one full point change across the two cohorts (average increase from 2.98 to 3.78), the results cannot be argued clearly. For the Vietnam cohort, a greater than one-point increase on average across the sample was recorded, with two students showing a two-point increase and one showing an increase of three points.

Qualitative and empirical evaluation of the full data sets for both student cohorts suggests the course successfully realised its aim of developing students' knowledge and awareness of sustainability issues. A comparison of the use of key words and phrases relating to sustainability, listed by students as part of a sustainability brainstorming exercise in the pre- and post-course surveys, helps

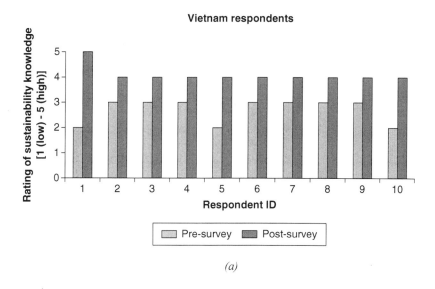

(a)

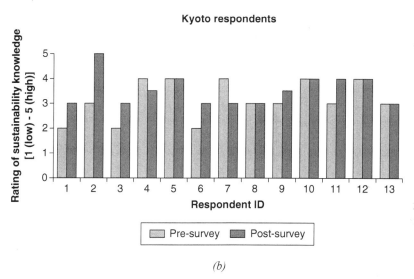

(b)

Figure 7.3 Students' responses before and after the course explaining how much they understand sustainability

to clarify the progression of knowledge. In Kyoto, for instance, one student associated the words 'clean energy', 'green', 'reusable', 'long-lasting', 'efficiency' and 'conserve' with sustainability before the course. However, course participation prompted her to conclude that 'sustainability isn't just about making things green' but about 'finding the right balance between many different factors and aspects'

(Student 8, Kyoto cohort). A similar progression was discernible for the Hue students. One initially associated words such as 'use', 'enough', 'save', 'future' and 'awareness' with sustainability but, after completing the course, referred to the 'balance among economic, social and environment' and the need to 'reduce your ecological footprint' (Student K, Hue cohort).

These findings were bolstered by an analysis of student postings on the online discussion forums, reflections on their fieldwork and follow-up interviews to plumb their acquired normative knowledge – defined by Wiek *et al.* as incorporating concepts such as intergenerational justice, equity, socio-ecological integrity and ethics (2011, 209). Student 14 of the Kyoto cohort argued for food systems based on buying locally and seasonally 'because buying food from local farmers could help reduce carbon output, caused by long-distance food transport, and stimulates the local economy'. Student 5 of the Hue cohort described personal health problems during a brief stay at a friend's house close to an industrial zone in the city of Danang, Vietnam, saying: 'That scared me. Just think about the people who work in those factories. Who work every day in the industrial zone.'

Together, these results reveal a general shift away from one-dimensional, environmentally biased conceptualisations of sustainability to multifaceted, multidisciplinary understanding with an increased awareness of the scale and complexity of sustainability-related issues. The tendency of students, who are unfamiliar with sustainability concepts, to conceive it initially in terms of environmental aspects and actions, rather than its social, economic, political and cultural dimensions, has been well documented by Summers *et al.* (2004) and Azapagic *et al.* (2005). In this context, the students' trend towards an increasingly 'holistic (multi-dimensional) interpretation' (Kagawa 2007, 335) of sustainability concepts is evidence of a growth in sustainability knowledge in general and normative knowledge in particular.

Competencies

The data sets also show the course to have been effective in developing existing key competencies in sustainability, defined here as 'complexes of knowledge, skills and attitudes that enable successful task performance and problem solving with respect to real-world sustainability problems' (Wiek *et al.* 2011, 204). As part of the post-course survey, students were given a list of 11 skills, which included many of the 'regular' academic competencies (basic capacities in critical thinking, communication and pluralistic thinking) that 'serve as the foundation of academic sustainability education' (Ibid., 211–212), and asked to identify those they possessed. The results are summarised in Figure 7.4. It is important to note that students were not required to distinguish between the skills they possessed before the course and those they had after it. Opportunities to differentiate between existing and acquired skills were instead provided in subsequent questions, which asked students to underline any new skills and reflect upon what might have triggered the perceived changes.

As indicated in the figure, many students in Kyoto defined themselves as flexible, open to other views and compromise and skilled at synthesising ideas. Students also professed to be good listeners, collaborators, persuaders and able to take responsibility and lead. In fact, of the 13 Kyoto students who completed the

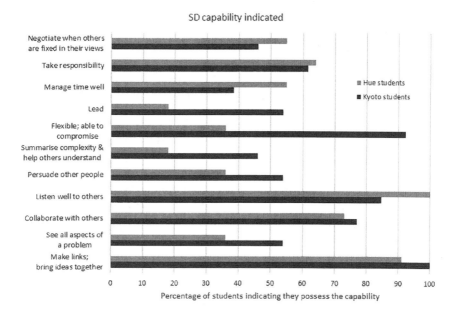

Figure 7.4 Competencies developed by students (both cohorts)

post-course questionnaire, only one expressly indicated that he had acquired a new skill (the ability to make links and bring ideas together) as a result of the course. Instead, students in the Kyoto cohort reported that participation in the course had *strengthened* their existing skills. Student 8 commented on her improved ability to 'become a bit more flexible to others' views and opinions, since sustainability really is a complex thing and it can work differently for every case'. Student 1 emphasised the course's role in developing his ability to be flexible and open to other views, previously 'one of my weakest points'.

This result contrasts with results for the Hue cohort, many of whom reported the development of new abilities, particularly those relating to communicating in groups. Eleven students believed they had gained the ability to listen well to others, while 10 reported the ability to make links and draw ideas together. Student E summarised her personal development in communicative competence as a persuader and negotiator as follows:

> The new skill for me is persuading other people. Our class has many members com[ing] from different [schools of the] university and different grade[s]. That make[s] [it] hard for me to share ideas and persuade other member[s] [in] the group. However, in this course, we had many chance[s] to learn and work in group[s], so I gradually did know how to make them agree with me.

For both cohorts, the attained or enhanced capacities fall into two main competence categories: systems thinking competence, defined as 'the ability to collectively analyse complex systems across different domains (society, environment, economy, etc.) and across different scales (local to global)' (Wiek *et al.* 2011, 207), and interpersonal competence, defined as the 'ability to motivate, enable, and facilitate collaborative and participatory sustainability research and problem solving', including advanced skills in communication, deliberating and negotiating, collaborating, leadership, pluralistic and trans-cultural thinking and empathy (Ibid., 211). Mining the data sets for the fieldwork evaluation guides and online entries to the SNS community or OCS also showed a marked development in normative competence – defined as the capacity 'first, to collectively assess the (un-) sustainability of current and/or future states of social-ecological systems and, second, to collectively create and craft sustainability visions for these visions' (Ibid., 209) – for many students from both cohorts. This competence is based on normative knowledge, which enables students to evaluate current and future states of sustainability with reference to values and leads students towards anticipatory competence – defined as the 'ability to collectively analyse, evaluate, and craft rich "pictures" [stories, images] of the future related to sustainability issues and sustainability problem-solving frameworks' (Ibid., 207–209) – and strategic competence – '[t]he ability to collectively design and implement interventions, transitions, and transformative governance strategies toward sustainability' (Ibid., 210) – as seen in the following comment from Student I from Hue:

> I think Hue is ready for sustainability. To achieve this goal, we need a multi-solution, which combine[s] a lot [of] policies as well as collaboration among the agents, organisations, authority and residents. Of course, it will cost dramatically, it may even slow the rapid speed of economic growth as well. But we must move forward towards this goal [sustainability], step by step, to the greatest extent possible.

Student I's comment is mirrored by others in her cohort, who were able to identify a standard their government should be working towards and suggested action they believed should be undertaken to reach the ideal state. Student C said raising people's environmental awareness was 'more important than simply making more regulations'. In such cases, the 'interlinking' of key competencies offers a pathway to future change, with the increase in normative knowledge triggering the changes in values, attitudes and motivation that form a potential basis for future action.

Action

The course was shown to be particularly effective in empowering students in Kyoto and Hue to take pro-sustainability action in the immediate aftermath of the course. Eleven out of the 13 Kyoto students, who returned both surveys, reported engaging in some type of new pro-sustainability behaviour as a result of their participation in the course – most commonly transforming their behaviour in relation to their consumption of food and other resources, such as paper, energy and water. For example, students reported changes in their food habits, such as reductions in their weekly meat consumption and efforts to reduce waste.

Responses from the eight students in the Kyoto cohort who responded to TESDI's request for follow-up interviews suggested that most of the continued pro-sustainability activities were along these lines – taking public transport, walking, recycling, using less electricity and reducing food waste. Some students had successfully followed through with planned reductions for resource use cited in their post-course surveys. For example, Student 8 had proposed and followed through on taking shorter showers, while Student 18 had reduced electricity by spending more time at the public library to avoid air-conditioning his apartment and had reduced his paper consumption by using electronic documents.

Although six of the eight Kyoto interviewees reported sustaining most (if not all) of the pro-sustainable behaviour initiated during the course, some students had not changed their behaviour long term, while few students reported intensifying their pro-sustainable efforts in the 12 months after the course. Student 18 reported that hills and dangerous traffic conditions made cycling a less viable means of daily commuting after returning home to Hong Kong. Where possible, he said he tried to walk instead of using public transport. Student 13 experienced difficulty in changing his eating habits after moving to the US, where meat is widely available and inexpensive. However, he did express a commitment to returning to more pro-sustainable levels of meat consumption upon returning to Germany, his home country.

Significantly, these and other students' responses displayed an awareness of the actions they could and should be taking, with barriers (both real and perceived) reducing their capacity to maintain pro-sustainable actions. Equally important, although individual actions had not always been sustained, many students reported promoting sustainable behaviour to others after returning to their home countries in the 12 months after the course. Student 14 said she had 'taught my mum about careful selection of food when shopping in the market. Eating locally and going organic are now [a principle] my family upholds.' Meanwhile, Student 13 of the Kyoto cohort 'became the annoying guy urging people to recycle paper or turn their lights off when leaving at night' – confident or, rather, 'pretty sure that bringing up the one or other statistic or giving people funny looks when they behave too unsustainable for my taste raised some awareness here and there'.

The Hue students also increased the scope of the pro-sustainable actions they carried out before the course, such as recycling and conserving water and energy, by reducing their motorcycle use and using more public transportation by the end of the course. In all, five students reported favouring more sustainable transport options instead of motorbikes, with Student I commenting on the OCS bulletin board as follows:

My parents want to buy a new motorbike but I opposed. I suggested buying a bicycle for me instead. My father was really surprised. 'Do you want to stop sharing your motorbike with me? Will you ride to school [?]' I just said: 'Why not? My school [is] nearby and I'm planning to lose weight.'

As with the Kyoto cohort, a small number of students followed through on pro-sustainable initiatives proposed at the end of the course. Students C and E attempted a form of vertical farming using recycled plastic bottles to grow plants and food organically for family consumption. This was inspired by a final presentation on a hydroponics-based vertical farming scheme to grow produce for the campus cafeteria. Student C succeeded in growing various kinds of vegetables, including cabbage, chilli peppers, onions and traditional red-leafed vegetables, through this method.

These and other Hue students were carrying out a high number of proactive sustainable actions even one year after the course, with activities increasing in variety, complexity and scale. Student J engaged in extra-curricular tree planting for the first time after the course and Students E, I and J volunteered for city-based activities such as a recycling group, campaigning house to house on waste recycling and cleaning up litter. Student C started vegetable farming after approaching her grandparents (formerly farmers) for advice on how to nurture the hitherto neglected family plot of land. She used a combination of chemical and organic fertilisers and sold part of the harvest to increase her family's income. Student M worked with Student E to grow plants hydroponically, which were marketed online as gifts for Women's Day and to create 'green spaces' in workplaces. Most students promoted pro-sustainable behaviour to other students both socially – peer to peer – or by working through the university-based Youth Union or student circles. They also talked to their families, colleagues and wider social circles about sustainability as their growing knowledge fired their passion.

3.2.2 RQ2: What have been the most effective elements of the course?

Four tools were used to deliver the course: lectures, group discussions in class, fieldwork and the online course support and discussion forum (SNS or OCS). Students were asked in the post-course survey to rank these elements in terms of their usefulness in teaching and solving sustainability issues. The most effective elements, as ranked by students from both cohorts, were fieldwork and group discussions (see Table 7.2). Representing a vastly different approach to conventional 'non-natural' classroom-based learning (Orion, cited in Eilam and Trop 2011, 46), these aspects enabled students in both cohorts to engage actively with course content and their peers. The fieldwork, in particular, allowed them to place sustainability problems in different, local and often unfamiliar contexts. Experiences with rural communities, in particular, gave meaning to topics students had learned about in class: '. . . [lectures] really make sense only when we understand that there are people behind these matters, and meeting them teaches a lot' (Student 11, Kyoto cohort). Students became empowered by first-hand experience of sustainable solutions, in some instances, while learning about problems directly from those experiencing them in others. In both cases, learning 'directly from someone who knows a lot about that topic makes it easier for us to learn' (Student 10, Kyoto cohort). The combination of cognitive and emotional learning afforded by fieldwork as a 'multidisciplinary

Table 7.2 Rating of successful and unsuccessful elements of the course

Site	Elements by level of effectiveness		
	Most effective	*Least effective*	*Neutral*
Kyoto	Fieldwork	Online discussion platform	Lectures
	Group discussions		
Vietnam	Fieldwork	Online discussion platform	
	Group discussions		
	Lectures		

and multidimensional learning experience' helped students to 'cognitively understand connections between systems and their effects on human lives in the present and in the future' (Eilam and Trop 2011, 56) and added an emotional dimension to their learning experience that fuelled changes in attitudes, motivation and action.

Students' reflections upon what might have triggered the perceived changes in personal competence seen in Figure 7.4 strongly support their individual ranking of course elements. Significantly, as stated above, students from both cohorts said fieldwork and group discussions contributed most to the strengthening of existing skills or acquisition of new skills. They cited the importance of listening to the views of their peers and engaging in debate as a major factor in their self-development, along with the importance of coming into contact with different perspectives. Student 14 of the Kyoto cohort said he 'learned a lot from the discussions with students from different cultural backgrounds' and found it 'inspiring to listen to and share our unique points of view with each other in such a harmonious learning atmosphere'. Likewise, Student H from Hue attributed his increase in knowledge to the group discussions and feedback sessions in class, which offered 'chances for us to review what we learned in fieldwork and to know the thinking of other people. Because each person has [a] different point of view . . . we can see totally different opinions.'

For both cohorts, but particularly for the students in Hue, negotiating complex, multi-faceted issues while collaborating and communicating with peers generated the keen desire to transfer course knowledge into everyday life through the pro-sustainable actions already noted. While less effective at fostering competencies and motivating action, the course's lectures provided basic and essential knowledge to students in both cohorts while encouraging them to rethink their understanding of sustainability and pro-sustainability behaviour.

When considered independently of the other elements of the course, the online-based content and discussion platform were ranked least effective by both cohorts. Evidently, although both tools still had value in reinforcing the knowledge and skills gained through other aspects of the course, they provided little in the way of new knowledge and understanding.

3.2.3 Results summary

The course was able to improve the sustainability knowledge, competence and actions of the students of both cohorts. This suggests that cross-cultural transferability of the course was achieved, although the results suggest it was particularly successful when students were relatively new to the concepts being taught and/or the teaching method, which was the case in Hue. Of the various methods trialled for effectiveness, fieldwork and group discussion came out top for both cohorts. Overall, there are strong indications that students' gains vary, depending on their respective starting points as individuals, the cultural, social, economic circumstances in which they live or have been raised, and their familiarity with the content and pedagogy being used to teach them. Even so, the course retained meaning for all students – even those who already had some experience of learning about sustainability – by encouraging them to develop and share their knowledge while inspiring change in others, starting with their peer group, families, local community and scaling up to larger society. Significantly, even in the absence of sustained individual action – as observed, for example, with some students in the Kyoto cohort – most students promoted more sustainable behaviour to others in the 12 months after the course.

Individual students' ability to sustain change in the long term was facilitated by the availability of supportive networks and favourable environments in which to act, as well as by individual circumstances. For the Hue cohort, the continued support of networks of family, friends, other students and amenable colleagues in bolstering students' enthusiasm to change actions locally – in their homes, at school and in the workplace – emerged as an important factor for sustaining pro-sustainable behaviour. Where these support networks are diminished – which was the case for many Kyoto students, who lived in environments that were either new to them or less conducive to carrying out pro-environmental actions than Japan, or for some Hue students, who were entering the workplace after graduation – students may feel less inclined to take or continue pro-sustainable action or may feel unable to maintain the momentum and motivation built up during the course. This is consistent with previous research, which notes 'multiple factors' and 'a complex socio-cultural process' inhibit the process of facilitating behavioural change towards pro-sustainable action (Kagawa 2007, 333–334, drawing on Folke 2003; Kolmuss and Agyeman 2002; and Darnton 2004). 'External social, political and economic barriers can thwart the best intentions' (Schultz and Oskamp 1996 cited in Short 2010, 14).

The aspect of motivation preceded by growth in normative knowledge, changes in values and the subsequent development of normative competence emerges as an important bridge between knowledge and action for all students taking this course. As mentioned, one Kyoto student reported on geographical and cultural barriers to change but expressed the intention to change in different, more settled circumstances. In addition, many students reported talking to others and inviting them to change rather than taking direct action to change their own actions. Finally, although some students continued to voice reservations about the capacity of individuals to affect change, the comments of many students suggest a general shift towards a sense of responsibility and empowerment, and

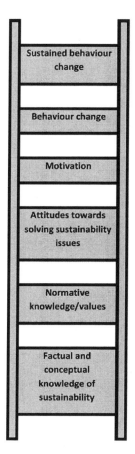

Figure 7.5 Conceptual ladder model of progress from knowledge to sustained behavioural change

the realisation that not only authorities but individuals and communities can play a role in sustainability efforts. Student 14 from the Kyoto cohort posted the following on the SNS discussion platform:

> Although it is cheaper if we choose to buy ordinary vegetables sold in the big market or mass-produced bio-engineered food . . . if we are willing to pay a bit more for organic food, we can contribute to sustainability development. It is often heard that individuals can barely help the development of sustainability in the community. But if everyone is the advocate and at the same time supports others' sustainability initiatives, we can help change the world.

Such statements are consistent with reaching at least the 'motivation' rung of the ladder of progress from knowledge through motivation to sustained behavioural change, shown conceptually in Figure 7.5. Students who report taking more proactive sustainable actions, even one year after the course, as well as fostering change in others can be assumed to have reached the top of the ladder – and beyond.

4. Discussion

By demonstrating the course's effectiveness in leading students from knowledge to action in Hue as well as Japan, Section 3 also demonstrates its replicability. We close with an examination of some of the course's wider implications as a toolkit for educators, which is usable in very different contexts to build teacher capacity and prompt wider change at the curricular level, while visiting some of the challenges that arise in implementing courses of this nature.

4.1 Ensuring cross-cultural transferability of the course

Identifying local concerns and ceding course ownership to partners at HUAF in replicating and adapting the course for use in Vietnam was the determining factor in ensuring the course's cross-cultural transferability (Singer 2015). This entailed being cognizant of the reasons motivating HUAF administrative personnel, faculty members and students to provide or participate in the course. At the administrative level, both KU and HUAF welcomed an English-language course that accorded with both institutions' professed commitment to internationalisation. Participating faculty members from both sides also shared an interest in opportunities for interdisciplinary research and international collaboration. However, the desire to enhance pedagogical skills by exploring interactive teaching methods provided an additional stimulus for faculty members at HUAF. Likewise, although students in both institutions were driven by an interest in sustainability and a desire to study in English, a graduation certificate for participation proved attractive to attending students in Vietnam, who – unlike students in Kyoto – were unable to claim credit for taking the course.

The modular construction of the course also emerged as a primary factor in facilitating its adaptation and modification for use in Hue. Its construction enables the substitution or elimination of components and/or modules to tailor the course for use in any higher education institution. This means it can be adapted according to the capacities of teaching staff, requirements for courses either inside or outside a given curriculum and important factors such as class size, students' age and academic level, opportunities for fieldwork and funding constraints. To date, the authors have incorporated elements and approaches from the BSF course in other courses offered by KU and there is potential for introducing the course into dual degree programmes or other academic exchange programmes between KU, HUAF and other partner institutions in South East Asian countries, such as Cambodia, Laos and Thailand. This suggests the course has considerable potential as an ESD 'toolkit' or as 'take and use resources' (Desha and Hargroves 2014, 40) that can be made available through an online portal and adapted for use anywhere, in any context, by teachers working to local conditions. In this, it relieves overburdened faculty members of the necessity to 'reinvent the wheel', not only in developing countries such as Vietnam, where funding for higher education sustainability programmes is limited, but in developed countries 'while they wait for program-wide, department-wide and institution-wide strategies [for sustainability curriculum renewal]' (Ibid., 83).

4.2 Opportunities for building capacity

Although building capacity is essential for improving sustainability education at the tertiary level in all countries, it is particularly important in the case of universities in developing countries, where ESD's uptake in higher education is often compromised by weak tertiary institutions, inadequate funding and human resources, and a lack of prioritisation for sustainability in the curriculum and teacher education (Kieu *et al.* 2016). Faculty members at HUAF benefited as much as the Kyoto teaching team from working with colleagues from other disciplines, collaborative preparation of lesson materials, skill sharing and exchanging teaching methods in the classroom and in the field. However, they also claimed to have learned a great deal from working with teachers versed in interactive teaching methods rarely deployed in Vietnamese classrooms, where the prevalence of top-down teaching approaches and traditional teaching styles with an emphasis on knowledge-based teaching are one of the main obstacles for effective ESD implementation (Ibid.).

Opportunities to build capacity were also afforded to the course teaching assistants. In Japan, three KU graduate-student course teaching assistants presenting at the Higher Education for Sustainable Development Forum – an academic forum for researchers and academics from all over Japan – held at KU on 18 November 2012, recounted valuable experience gained as ESD educators providing input into course design, leading fieldwork and, on some occasions, contributing to classroom teaching (Gannon *et al.* 2012). In Hue, young administrative staff from HUAF gained from playing an instrumental role in an English-language teaching environment, assisting in fieldwork, contributing to the development of classroom materials and preparing a 15-minute film, accessible on the university website, which documented the course and its impact on attending students.

Finally, as already shown, student capacities and competencies improved in areas such as engagement, leadership, collaborative ability and the key sustainability competencies required for working towards finding solutions to various sustainability problems. Students in both cohorts assumed a leadership role by teaching friends, family and workmates about sustainable consumption. Many students reported changed lifestyles and pathways. Two students in the Kyoto cohort undertook internships and pursued further studies in sustainability-related fields. Several students in the Hue cohort chose sustainability-related topics for their graduation theses and applied for international scholarships to study themes related to sustainability. Four Hue students made sustainability-linked presentations in Japan, during a summer exchange trip to KU in 2013, while four Kyoto students attempted to put their final project proposal into effect, with weeks of effort in the summer vacation attempting to persuade the KU cafeteria to provide a vegetarian lunch option. This brings the BSF course in line with DESD goals to promote education that creates a more dynamic, diverse, responsible cohort of future global leaders who are trained in sustainability concepts (see Chapter 4).

4.3 Logistical difficulties in sustaining the course and its replication

As mentioned, although Hue University hosted the course, with students recruited across different schools of the university, HUAF took a leading role in providing teaching expertise and technical support for implementing the course outside the conventional curriculum. TESDI team members' existing relationships with key figures on the HUAF team played a fundamental role in smoothing the transition process, along with funding, provided by the Japan Society for the Promotion of Science (JSPS), for TESDI's activities. Funding for the course in Kyoto was also provided by the JSPS, in addition to the Kyoto University International Education Programme hosting the course. In both cases, financial support was used to fund the hiring of teaching assistants, travel arrangements during fieldtrips and honorariums for guest lecturers and guides during some of the fieldwork. When financial support was cut and then finally stopped, the feasibility of an intensive course, heavy in fieldwork and with a high faculty-to-student ratio, was effectively negated.

It is clear that as long as courses such as this remain innovative – or, in the words of Desha and Hargroves (2014, 85), 'opportunistic, faculty-driven, ad hoc'– initiatives that have been 'bolted-on' instead of being 'built into' (Sterling and Maxey 2013, 6) the undergraduate curriculum, their longevity remains at risk. Their impact is also at risk, given that they have a reduced chance of reaching the broader student cohort. Recent years have seen a surge in the number of higher education institutions offering sustainability education and in the funding available for sustainability-related courses and research (Wiek *et al.* 2011, 203–204; Desha and Hargroves 2014, 50–52). However, problems are sure to persist as long as interdisciplinary courses offered outside the formal university curriculum are not supported within the whole-university context – particularly if governmental interest in promoting educational initiatives of this nature subsides and, with it, governmental subsidies. This is particularly problematic in Vietnam and other developing countries, where greater vulnerability to the worsening impacts of climate change and natural disasters makes ESD an especially important approach for achieving sustainable development (Kieu *et al.* 2016) and the problem of who can pay for this kind of academic intervention is as acute as their need.

4.4 More and better assessment needed to confirm the efficacy of sustainability courses

Ranking and assessment systems are increasingly influential in guiding the activities of higher education institutions and proof of success is necessary to justify the integration of sustainability courses into university curricula (Yarime and Tanaka 2012). Without such proof, sustainability educators will always be at a disadvantage when pushing for inter-departmental and interdisciplinary programmes and whole-university change.

This is awkward for sustainability courses in general, given the long-contested question of whether acquired environmental knowledge and attitudes necessarily result in an increase in pro-environmental behaviour (Eilam and Trop 2011, 47, drawing on Hines *et al.* 1987; Hungerford and Volk 1990; Marcinkowski 2004), and additional difficulty in measuring behavioural change in terms of the impacts of those actions on environmental quality (Short 2010). Appropriate quality assurance is also needed to assess not only the 'fitness for purpose' of new pedagogies, in terms of their taught content and research outputs, but also ultimately their 'fitness for transformation as a key driver for sustainable development and societal change' (Fadeeva *et al.* 1, 2014).

It is also awkward for the BSF course in particular, given that larger sample numbers are undoubtedly needed to achieve the key goal of assessment, answering our research questions. As mentioned, only 13 out of the 19 students in the Kyoto cohort completed both the pre- and post-course questionnaires, while only eight students from among the same cohort responded to the request for a follow-up interview by email. This naturally makes it difficult for the assessors to confirm or disprove sustained action – small or otherwise – for the Kyoto cohort and compromises efforts to compare results for the two cohorts. The course is also relatively recent, requiring further longitudinal follow-up to show longer-term outcomes.

In addition, further work is required to successfully integrate motivation into the knowledge-action framework presented in this chapter and to identify the thresholds needed to change behaviour. Although we introduced changes in motivation into the spectrum of observed changes, after identifying more emotional and intuitive aspects, such as values, acting as a bridge between students' understanding and practical activity, our observations came too late to be built into the assessment from the outset. Exploring this aspect requires a more detailed analysis of all parts of the data set. Fieldwork evaluation sheets, documenting students' thoughts before, during and after the fieldwork, and conceptual diagrams of sustainability, drawn by students, offer the possibility to chart changes in attitudes as well as relevant triggers. A closer investigation of discrete words and phrases implying an urge towards change, action and knowledge – to identify normative words and phrases such as 'ought to', 'should', 'wrong' and 'right' in students' survey responses, fieldwork feedbacks and the semi-structured interviews – through deeper NVivo coding analysis is also needed to plot an increase in motivation for many students.

4.5 A question of ethics

'Sustainability organises our knowledge and directs our activities according to some conception of what is good, of what ought to be sustained' (Parker 2012, 7). Since it is above all 'an ethical concept, aiming for justice and equity for all humanity at present and for future generations' (Dahl 2014, 187) and involving judgments 'of better and worse, right or wrong' (Parker 2012, 7), faculty members may shy away from 'teaching for values' (Howard 2012, 151) and feel trepidation about crossing a line between pedagogy – with the teacher facilitating student-driven actions – and demagogy – with the teacher a coercive advocate (Eilam and Trop 2011, 54; Short 2010, 13). Curricular models that 'promote critical thinking over knowledge transmission, investigation over indoctrination, and collaborative, local, science-based solutions over advocacy-driven measures' (Short 2010, 8) are essential for facilitating student-driven actions and precluding teacher bias (Ibid., 19), as are educator protocols 'for documenting student action planning and the impacts of their actions to better protect practitioners against allegations of advocacy' (Ibid.).

Replicating a sustainability course designed in a developed country for use in a developing one also puts course organisers in the uncomfortable position of appearing to preach from the pulpit of one of the many industrialised nations that has not practised the sustainability gospel it preaches. Discomfort in challenging the way things have been done increases exponentially if we take into account the fact that things are done differently, and values are weighed differently, in different countries and at different times. It is hoped that the approach and pedagogy derived from our longer experience of providing education for sustainability with more generous funding can be transferred to the other university while the course's content and focus are tailored to reflect the concerns and exigencies of the host institution. By doing this, we can foster interest and ownership by faculty and staff, making it more likely that the course (or some iteration of it) can be integrated into the host university's regular curriculum and exert expanded influence on its curriculum as a whole.

Acknowledgements

This research was supported by the Japan Society for the Promotion of Science Grant-in-Aid for Scientific Research project no. 23300285. The authors thank Professor Andreas Neef for his guidance in developing the course design, core lectures and evaluative framework in the first two years of the TESDI project and all TESDI members, guest lecturers and fieldwork guides for their help in implementing the course in Kyoto and Hue. Special thanks are owed to teaching assistant coordinators Melina Sakiyama, Yuri Sugimoto and Holger Schaefer and to all our teaching assistants in Kyoto and Hue for their invaluable support during the course implementation. We also thank Thi Kinh Kieu for interpreting and translating the follow-up interviews in Hue in March 2013, and PACE interns Sarah Borkman and Emily Mander for their work on the assessment presented in this chapter.

References

Association for the Advancement of Sustainability in Higher Education (AASHE) 2010. *Sustainability curriculum in higher education: a call to action.* Denver, US: AASHE (www.aashe.org/files/A_Call_to_Action_final%282%29.pdf). Accessed 11 March 2016.
Azapagic, A., Perdan, S. and Shallcross, D. 2005. How much do engineering students know about sustainable development? The findings of an international survey and

possible implications for the engineering curriculum. *European Journal of Engineering Education* 30, 1, 1–19.

Barlett, P. and Chase, G. W. 2004. Introduction, in Barlett, P. and Chase, G. W. (eds) *Sustainability on campus: stories and strategies for change (urban and industrial environments)*. Cambridge, US, and London, UK: MIT Press, 1–28.

Dahl, A. L. 2014. Sustainability and values assessment in higher education, in Fadeeva, Z., Galkute, L., Mader, C. and Scott G. (eds) *Sustainable development and quality assurance in higher education: transformation of learning and society*. Hampshire, UK: Palgrave Macmillan, 185–195.

Darnton, A. 2004. The impact of sustainable development on public behaviour: report 1 of desk research commissioned by COI on behalf of DEFRA. (http://collection.europarchive.org/tna/20080530153425/, www.sustainable-development.gov.uk/publications/pdf/desk-research1.pdf). Accessed 4 June 2016.

Desha, C. and Hargroves, K. C. 2014. *Higher education and sustainable development: a model for curriculum development*. London, UK, and New York, US: Routledge.

Eilam, E. and Trop, T. 2011. ESD pedagogy: a guide for the perplexed. *The Journal of Environmental Education* 42 (1), 43–64.

Fadeeva, Z., Galkute, L., Mader, C. and Scott, G. 2014. Assessment for transformation – higher education thrives in redefining quality systems, in Fadeeva, Z., Galkute, L., Mader, C. and Scott, G. (eds) *Sustainable development and quality assurance in higher education: transformation of learning and society*. Hampshire, UK: Palgrave Macmillan, 1–21.

Folke, C. 2003. Social-ecological resilience and behavioural responses, in Biel, A., Hansoon, B. and Martensson, M. (eds) *Individual and Structural Determinants of Environmental Practice*. Aldershot, UK: Ashgate, 226–42.

Gannon, T., Sakiyama, M., O'Connell, M., Kato, Y., Noro, T. and Ozaki, Y. 2012. *Henka suru tame ni korabo suru: 'jizokukanou na mirai wo kouchiku: kihongensoku to chousen' koosu shoukai* (Collaborating for change: introducing the Building a Sustainable Future: Principles and Challenges course). Presentation delivered at the Higher Education for Sustainable Development Forum, 18 November 2012, Kyoto University.

Hines, J. M., Hungerford, H. R. and Tomera, A. N. 1987. Analysis and synthesis of research on responsible environmental behaviour: a meta analysis. *Journal of Environmental Education* 18, 1–8.

Howard, P. 2012. Who will teach the teachers? Reorienting teacher education for the values of sustainability, in Bartels, K. A. and Parker, K. A. (eds) *Teaching sustainability/ teaching sustainably*. Sterling, US: Stylus Publishing, 149–157.

Hungerford, H. R., and Volk, T. L. 1990. Changing learner behaviour through environmental education. *Journal of Environmental Education* 21, 8–21.

Kagawa, F. 2007. Dissonance in students' perceptions of sustainable development and sustainability: implications for curriculum change. *International Journal of Sustainability in Higher Education* 8, 3, 317–338.

Kieu, T. K., Singer, J. and Gannon, T. 2016. Education for sustainable development in Vietnam: lessons learned from teacher education. *International Journal of Sustainability in Higher Education*. Scheduled for publication in 2016 in vol. 17, issue 6.

Kollmuss, A. and Agyeman, J. 2002. Mind the gap: why do people act environmentally and what are the barriers to pro-environmental behaviour? *Environmental Education Research* 8, 3, 239–60.

Marcinkowski, T. 2004. *Using a logic model to review and analyse an environmental education programme*. Washington DC, US: North American Association for Environmental Education.

Mochizuki, Y. and Yarime, M. 2016. Education for sustainable development and sustainability science: re-purposing higher education and research, in Barth, M., Michelsen, G., Rieckmann, M. and Thomas, I. (eds) *Routledge handbook of higher education for sustainable development*. Oxford, UK: Routledge, 11–24.

Neef, A. 2012. Summing up: identifying challenges and making achievements while defining 'our ESD'. *Sansai Newsletter,* 2, 8–9.

O'Donoghue, R. 2016 Evaluation and education for sustainable development: navigating a shifting landscape in regional centres of expertise, in Barth, M., Michelsen, G., Rieckmann, M. and Thomas, I. (eds) *Routledge handbook of higher education for sustainable development*. Oxford, UK: Routledge, 223–237.

Parker, K. A. 2012. Introduction: Sustainability in higher education, in Bartels, K. A. and Parker, K. A. (eds) *Teaching sustainability/teaching sustainably*. Sterling, US: Stylus Publishing, 1–16.

Ryan, A. and Cotton, D. 2013. Times of change: shifting pedagogy and curricula for future sustainability, in Sterling, S., Maxey, L. and Luna, H. (eds) *The sustainable university: progress and prospects*. London, UK, and New York, US: Earthscan Routledge, 151–167.

Schultz, P.W. and Oskamp, S. 1996. Effort as a moderator of the attitude behaviour relationship: General environmental concern and recycling. *Social Psychology Quarterly* 59 (4), 375–383.

Short, P. C. 2010. Responsible environmental action: its role and status in environmental education and environmental quality. *The Journal of Environmental Education* 4 (1), 7–21.

Singer, J. 2015. Assessing the effectiveness of an undergraduate course taught in Japan and Vietnam on fostering pro-sustainable outcomes. Presentation at AASHE 2015 Conference: Transforming Sustainability Education, Minneapolis, US, 27 October 2015.

Sterling, S. and Maxey, L. 2013. Introduction, in Sterling, S., Maxey, L. and Luna, H. (eds) *The sustainable university: progress and prospects*. London, UK, and New York, US: Earthscan Routledge, 1–16.

Summers, M., Corney, G. and Ghilds, A. 2004. Student teachers' conceptions of sustainable development: the starting-points of geographers and scientists. *Educational Research* 46, 2, 163–82.

Wals, A. E. J., Tassone, V. C., Hampson, G. P. and Reams, J. 2016. Learning for walking the change, in Barth, M., Michelsen, G., Rieckmann, M. and Thomas, I. (eds), *Routledge handbook of higher education for sustainable development*. Oxford, UK: Routledge, 25–39.

Wiek, A., Withycombe, L. and Redman, C. L. 2011. Key competencies in sustainability: a reference framework for academic programme development. *Sustainability Science* 6 (2), 203–218.

Yarime, M., and Tanaka, Y. 2012. The issues and methodologies in sustainability assessment tools for higher education institutions: a review of recent trends and future challenges. *Journal of Education for Sustainable Development,* 6 (1), 63–77.

Part II
Community-based approaches

8 Community-based, non-formal and informal ESD in Japan

Where top-down and bottom-up approaches meet

Fumiko Noguchi and Toyoshi Sasaki

Japan is one of a very few countries where both government and non-governmental/non-profit groups have been actively committed to community empowerment through non-formal and informal educational approaches over the past 70 years. Since the enactment of the Social Education Act of 1946 (Government of Japan 1946), the government has actively established *kominkan* or community learning centres (CLCs), libraries and museums at national, municipal and local community levels. *Kominkan*, in particular, which numbered 17,143 nationwide in 2005 (Ministry of Education, Culture, Sports, Science and Technology of Japan (MEXT) 2011), have played a central role in providing non-formal learning opportunities to community residents. They employ qualified social education coordinators and/or non-formal education specialists, many from non-profit organisations (NGOs), who organise learning activities for local residents, and they provide space for residents' activities.

Besides government-driven, non-formal education, NGOs have made indispensable efforts in enabling community empowerment in Japan. Both non-formal education agents and community/rural development non-profit groups have laboured to make rural and local communities more sustainable and resilient culturally, economically and environmentally. Particularly, many of them have focused on marginalised groups – such as young people, women, the disabled, small-scale farmers and indigenous/minority residents – by sponsoring learning and community activities to address their issues. Legislation entitled Establishment of Implementation Systems and Other Measures for the Promotion of Lifelong Learning, which was subsumed under the Social Education Act of 1990 (Government of Japan, 1990), sought to enhance non-formal learning activities provided by NGOs and the corporate sector (Noguchi *et al.* 2015).

During the UN Decade of Education for Sustainable Development (UNDESD) (2005–2014), the initiative's political and economic priorities facilitated the active participation of formal education stakeholders in ESD. Yet the voices of those in non-formal and informal education were seldom heard. In Japan, however, there were two organisations that laboured to fill the gap between formal and non/informal education in the international theoretical and political discourse over ESD: the Asia-Pacific Cultural Centre for UNESCO (ACCU)[1] and the Japan Council on Education for Sustainable Development (ESD-J).[2] One of their major contributions was in reviewing existing efforts by non-formal education organisations and community development organisations in Japan and the Asia-Pacific region from the viewpoint of ESD and highlighting the effectiveness of this education in achieving sustainable development. A central goal was to raise awareness of the importance of non-formal and informal education in achieving sustainable development. Such efforts encouraged some *kominkan*, non-formal education NGOs and community organisations to reflect upon and revise their activities by applying the framework of sustainable development and community empowerment.

ACCU widely promoted ESD through non-formal education activities in community learning centres in the Asia-Pacific region, including *kominkan* in Japan. It conducted projects that focused on non-formal ESD, such as HOPE[3] and the COE programme for ESD,[4] and sponsored occasional workshops and conferences. These were attended by representatives from networked non-formal education organisations in Asia, community educators, governments and international organisations, such as UNESCO. ACCU invited educators from key *kominkan* in Japan to participate in their regional and international conferences. These occasions contributed to a positive reappraisal of the existing non-formal education activities by *kominkan* and expanded the understanding of ESD in the *kominkan* context. Such efforts resulted in hosting the Okayama Kominkan-CLC International Conference, which was held before the UNESCO World Conference on ESD in 2014 (Okayama city 2016). Okayama *kominkan* stakeholders developed a localised version of the Okayama Commitment to serve as a final joint statement of the Okayama Kominkan-CLC in order to promote ESD after the UNDESD (*Sanyo Shimbun* 2014).

ESD-J has taken two approaches to the promotion of ESD: community based and multi-stakeholder, spanning formal, non-formal and informal education sectors. The group networks with stakeholders across Japan and Asia, including schools, non-NGOs, national, municipal and local governments, business and researchers. It also reports on existing community-based activities from the perspective of ESD. Its reports have helped to clarify the important role NGOs play in empowering community residents and to redefine ESD in a community development context. By doing so, ESD-J has helped to advocate for the inclusion of an NGO-driven, community-based approach to ESD in the policies of governments and international bodies.[5] Through initiatives such as the Asia ESD Good Practice Project (AGEPP), which reported on 34 NGO community development practices across Asia (ESD-J 2016b), the group has reported on the importance of adopting a community-based approach in ESD, particularly for informal ESD in community and rural development.

The UNDESD highlighted the role of non-formal education, governmental institutions such as *kominkan* (which tend to follow government priorities when selecting teaching content) and themes such as literacy education, expansion of basic education and disaster and climate change education. However, non-formal education and community/rural development NGOs received little press. These non-profits tended to be outside of UNESCO and educational or environmental ministry dictates. They often work on issues – such as human rights, peace, security, gender and poverty – that are either beyond the scope of international organisations or government or are not seen as priorities because of political sensitivities and/or economic considerations.

Other important actors in addressing these issues in Japan are nature schools, which have worked mostly in the field of environmental and outdoor education as non-profit entities. According to Sasaki, there were 3,696 nature schools in Japan in 2010 (2015).[6] He identifies the following features as being common to nature schools in Japan.

1   They contribute to forging strong links between humans and nature, humans and humans and humans and society to create a society in which people can live in harmony with nature.
2   They deliver safe and enjoyable educational activities that include experience of nature and community development under the guidance of specialists.
3   They possess administrators, instructors, a fixed address, curricula, activity sites and participants.

The interview that follows discusses the efforts of one such facility, the Kurikoma Kougen Nature School. It has been successful in identifying the needs of the local community, which had not been served by government policies, and in transforming its activities to achieve community empowerment and sustainable development.

Kurikoma Kougen Nature School is located at the south-eastern foot of Mt. Kurikoma (1,627m), which lies at the junction of the three north-eastern Honshu prefectures of Miyagi, Iwate and Akita. The nature school is an NGO that provides adventure education to children through outdoor activities, such as river touring, snow camps, trekking and horseback riding. Toyoshi Sasaki founded the school in 1996 after spending 15 years studying and practising field/adventure education.

The school is notable for more than its outdoor education activities – it has put much effort into helping the surrounding community overcome various socio-economic problems and become more sustainable and resilient. In the following interview, founder and principal Toyoshi Sasaki explains how the school has transformed its activities following the major earthquakes of 2008 and 2011.[7] The two earthquakes afforded a critical opportunity for Kurikoma Kougen Nature School to respond to the disasters by using life skills nurtured at the nature school, and to strengthen the staff's ability to deal with local community issues in the post-disaster period. The experience changed the direction of the school and gave it a new role – to establish a sustainable regional industry through a philosophy based on ESD.

You have said that Japan's nature schools are unique. Please explain how.

TS: Nature schools in Japan go beyond the conventional role of outdoor education, which often includes activities such as hiking, rafting and rock climbing. Nature schools are often located in small rural communities and take unique approaches; most have built a strong relationship with local communities. Some organise workshops for adults living nearby. They do not just facilitate outdoor activities but are also proactively involved in community development and creating small-scale, community-based industries, particularly in forestry and agriculture (Sasaki 2015).

Japan's nature schools have gained recognition as successful local business entities, particularly since the Earth Summit in 1992. They have contributed to the local community by solving local problems and functioning as a community hub. They have played a particularly important role in creating space for practising ESD and closely linking with local primary industries, which rely heavily on local natural and human resources.

Does your school programme also engage with societal issues?

TS: Yes. Kurikoma Kougen Nature School functions as a refuge for young people with serious social adjustment problems, including severe depression and truancy. These include students who refuse to go to school and adults in their 20s and 30s who could be designated as NEET (not in education, employment or training). It is said that, in 2014, there were more than 120,000 truant students in Japan, including those in primary and middle schools. It is also said that there are more than 700,000 NEETs in Japan. These students and young adults find it hard to engage with people socially and they may spend months – even years – secluded in their bedrooms.

These students often feel overwhelmed by the standard Japanese school system, which focuses on rote learning from textbooks. However, they will often respond much better if they are encouraged to develop tacit rather than explicit knowledge. Experiential and hands-on learning activities, such as farming (looking after domestic animals or a vegetable garden) and other everyday tasks, are a better foundation for young people with learning difficulties than learning via the formal education system. Through such learning activities, nature schools can initiate a cyclical process of on-site training, discovery and self-realisation. In our summer camp programmes, we have had a number of young adults (about 70 participants by 2008) who could be characterised as NEETs. Since 2006, we, in close collaboration with the Ministry of Health, Labour and Welfare, have sponsored a programme targeting these young adults and some of our participants have gone on to become staff at the school.

Your nature school has been affected by two serious earthquakes. Please explain what happened.

TS: The Iwate-Miyagi Nairiku Earthquake hit the Tohoku area on 14 June 2008. The epicentre was only a few kilometres north of the school. We had to evacuate everyone from our mountainside site in compliance with a government evacuation order. Despite being affected by the earthquake themselves, the staff of the nature school tried to support communities nearby by providing food, clothing and other daily necessities and helping to clear wreckage and landslide debris. Over time, these efforts expanded into innovative projects that contributed to the recovery and revitalisation of the region.

Two years and nine months later, we were subjected to another massive earthquake, the Great East Japan Earthquake and Tsunami of 11 March 2011. This time, the school staff promptly headed to the hardest-hit areas to offer assistance. A few days after the quake, we established a volunteer centre for support and relief activities. The experience of the Iwate-Miyagi Nairiku Earthquake enabled Kurikoma Kougen Nature School to play a significant role in supporting the survivors of the 3.11 disaster.

Please explain in detail your experience of the first earthquake.

TS: When the earthquake hit in 2008, there were 20 people at the school: 10 staff members and 10 boarding students living in the Koei dormitory. Fortunately, we didn't suffer any casualties and, although our facility incurred serious damage and lost its telephone, water and electricity supplies, we could access water from mountain springs and had camping lanterns and a power generator. After contacting the students' parents to let them know their children were safe, we tried to maintain essential services and repair the damage caused by the earthquake. All the staff stayed at the school. All the roads to the Koei district of Kurikoma where our school is located were blocked but we did not feel isolated.

On the third day after the quake, the government ordered us to evacuate. We were moved to an evacuation site by a Japanese Self-Defence Forces helicopter. For the next two years, we were unable to operate the school in Koei. Half of the students went home but the rest continued to stay at a temporary house that our school rented. That was a big challenge for us. We lost homes and livelihoods and had to live in the unfamiliar and difficult environment of a temporary housing shelter, where privacy was lacking and toilet facilities were overcrowded. No one knew when we could go home or could predict what would happen next.

How did you make use of your nature school expertise after the earthquake?

TS: At Kurikoma, we understand 'adventure' as being something that takes one out of one's comfort zone. It's unknown, dangerous, unpredictable and, since we're unaccustomed to it, we may feel insecure and challenged. No result is guaranteed and one never knows whether one will succeed. The opposite experience to adventure is what we call a 'C-zone' experience, which is a comfortable, secure situation in which one feels safe. One can predict incoming situations and can easily handle them in a C-zone experience. The two earthquakes provided an experience similar to an adventure in that people's daily lives were full of unusual experiences and they were forced to confront severe challenges. The evacuation sites and refuge centres, on the other hand, could be considered C-zones. The school decided to go beyond the C-zone. Once everyone had become familiar with the evacuation site, we changed the circumstances to promote the personal growth of the staff and students. This idea was integrated into the management of the relief centre.

The staff found that their work in the aftermath of the earthquake forced them to take on new roles and tackle new challenges, which gave them an opportunity for personal growth. At the volunteer centre, our main focus was to find out what the affected people needed and to help them in any way we could. But we also had to assess situations where we could not help, investigate why and instigate changes for better assistance. Volunteer work is, in itself, adventure education – the concepts and practices of adventure education can be put to use fully and the volunteering staff develop a stronger sense of confidence as their life skills and coping abilities are strengthened by overcoming challenges.

In this situation, one needs to consider different perspectives, collect information and materials and then communicate. 'Life skills' enabled us to react to situations more flexibly than is the norm in Japan and our experiential learning activities provided the foundation for an approach by staff to facilitate relief efforts through open communication, engagement with others and problem solving.

What did your school do?

TS: Early on, a lack of transport hampered mobility for some evacuees and they lacked daily necessities. Everyone who had been evacuated from the mountain had left most of their possessions behind. With every road off the mountain sustaining damage, all of the disaster victims were without cars. I called for cars to be donated via my online blog, which was only communication tool I had that time. Within a week, five cars had been donated, which enabled the volunteers to help the elderly with shopping and visits to local hospitals.

All 10 staff spent every day at the evacuation site. We established a volunteer centre at one evacuation site with 120 residents. I became the manager of the centre and every day we tried to identify the problems affecting the residents and decide on the right courses of action. For example, the earthquake had hit just before local farmers were to ship the first harvest of strawberries, a vital cash crop for their economic recovery, but they weren't allowed to access the strawberry fields on the restricted mountain site. After we pressed the government, it allowed the farmers and their families to return to their homes, providing a military helicopter to transport them, but it insisted the farmers could only carry back essential items, not harvested strawberries. We responded creatively by securing one third of the helicopter seats for volunteers, who filled their backpacks with 400kg of strawberries they had harvested from the mountain fields, enabling the farmers to at least salvage some of their critical harvest.

How would you assess the impact of the two earthquakes on your school?

TS: Two earthquakes hitting our region presented severe challenges for Kurikoma Kougen Nature School but they also represented a crucial opportunity for rethinking the value of forest resources as a sustainable source of energy. I believe that creating new industries around renewables can help solve the energy and environmental problems of this country, while helping to revitalise the forest-rich Tohoku region of north-eastern Japan. We now have also remodelled our school as an experimental village for eco-friendly living, based on an 'eco village' plan. We use firewood for heating and hot water, and our goal is to achieve a balanced coexistence of farming within nature.

The evacuation after the earthquake in 2008 forced us to halt operations of the nature school for two years. At that time, the school established the NPO Japan Forest Biomass Network (JFBN) to start projects for planting and using forest resources. JFBN aims to use local forest resources and realise the coexistence of our local society and the surrounding natural environment. We weren't sure how we could link our educational institution with this unfamiliar business sector but we hoped to create an opportunity for creating something new.

Why did you decide to work with forest resources?

TS: Used efficiently, forest resources leave no waste. Wood can be used for houses, furniture or other woodcraft and wood chips as the raw material for pulp. Wood waste from construction and woodworking can be used as fuel. If we can use local resources to fuel local demand, we can reduce the import expenditures of ¥20 trillion that Japan is said to be using for fossil fuels annually. The forests in Japan, however, are facing many problems. Of vital importance is the need to find a way to access, process and market the enormous potential of under-used forest resources.

How did your NPO use the forest?

TS: The evacuation area where we were relocated was predominantly forest. I thought if we could use the forest, we could create a new local industry that would also contribute to easing Japan's over-dependence on fossil fuels, while reducing environmental pressures and local forest degradation. In 2008, we received a grant from the national government's Rural Revitalisation and Wellbeing programme for our proposed forest activities – the Japanese government was, at that time, starting to focus on how to revitalise rural areas of the country.

We began work on the project in 2009. A local group, the Committee to Examine the Utilisation of Forest Resources, became the parent body for JFBN. Kurikoma Kougen Nature School, together with local lumber mills and building firms, became the centre of forest resource utilisation activity. We worked mainly on the local promotion of pellet heaters and on expanding sales to other prefectures. Pellet heaters are a highly efficient form of combustion heater that use pellets created from scrap wood and sawdust. Pellet heaters are said to achieve upwards of 80 to 90 per cent combustion efficiency. The promotion and development of this network involved opening communication channels between pellet stove manufacturers, pellet producers, building firms, carpentry factories, saw mills and architects around the country. We needed to collaborate with companies and fields previously unknown to us as a nature school. Now we have integrated the activities of the educational institution with these sectors, which are usually separate from education.

One of our activities involved a young local woodworker, whom we have known since the school's founding. He produces an innovative, non-toxic timber as an alternative to building materials that cause 'sick house' syndrome. He smoke-seasons the timber to make it insect proof and render it mould resistant. To reduce carbon dioxide emissions, he uses the woodchips from timber mills as the fuel for the smoking process. Although his effort resulted in smoke-seasoned non-toxic timber, we learned that after it was shipped it was often used in combination with ordinary wood and toxic paint.

The story behind this timber simply was not reaching carpenters and construction firms. To bolster awareness of his sustainable timber and put our communication and educational skills into practice, the Kurikoma Kougen Nature School organised a 'forest class'. The 30 participants, from all over Japan, included building firm employees, carpenters, architects, editors of architectural magazines and people who were planning to build houses. During the day, we toured a clear-cut area, a tree plantation and a primeval forest of Japanese beech, all located at the base of Mt. Kurikoma. In the evening, back at the school, we discussed deforestation and safe and healthy housing. We also visited the smoke-seasoning plant and held a woodcraft class, where participants made small low platforms that allow air to flow under bedding in closets, under computers or other household items. The participants took them home as souvenirs after painting them with non-toxic paint. This event became a unique opportunity to bring together producers and consumers under the banner of safe, healthy and eco-friendly housing. Many of the participants later said that, after our workshop, they felt they had a greater appreciation of the forest resources they encounter on a daily basis. The event also gave them an opportunity to learn, for the first time, about timber production processes and current problems facing forestry. This experience enabled the nature school to strengthen its role as a place for people to connect with, and learn about, forests and forestry issues. The forest class provided crucial insights necessary for the establishment of the JFBN, which was consolidated formally in 2012.

What was the impact on the school of the second earthquake?

TS: The 3.11 disaster further highlighted the enormous potential of forest resources and their sustainable utilisation. Immediately following the earthquake, a cold snap hit the region while we were without electricity and fuel distribution had not yet begun. It should be noted that 92 per cent of the 20,000 casualties of 3.11 were people who had drowned as a result of the tsunami. Sadly, the other 8 per cent were preventable deaths of people who had survived the tsunami but later died of hypothermia. Given the seriousness of the situation, JFBN asked network members across Japan to deliver pellet stoves and wood pellets to the evacuation sites.

JFBN grappled with other problems, too. The prefabricated temporary housing provided for disaster victims was unsuitable for the severe cold of Tohoku winters and temporary housing was not being built fast enough to shelter people. Therefore, we proposed to Minami Sanriku Town Office that we would build temporary wooden housing in cooperation with local carpenters, using local timber to benefit the local economy. Unfortunately, Japanese law required work on temporary housing to begin within one month of a disaster. This inflexible time restriction meant many small companies and organisations that wanted to help, including us, were unable to procure sufficient materials or human resources within one month and so were not allowed to build temporary housing. A massive building company network, the Prefabricated Building Network, was one of the few that could start construction within one month. Local governments in the disaster-affected areas were in disarray and Japan's restrictive laws and conservative ways of thinking were slowing relief efforts at a time when action needed to be taken. So the JFBN began raising funds from private sources and took action. We managed to complete a revitalising, co-existent living space for victims of the disaster that we called *Tenohira-ni-Taiyo no Ie* (House of Palms Spread to the Sun), which is located in Tome City, an area next to the tsunami-affected city of Minami-Sanriku. Our main purpose was to provide support for children in the affected areas.

This house was constructed from local timber, smoke-seasoned by local carpenters who had apprenticed in traditional construction methods. They used traditional tools and the *tekizami* method of cutting timber by hand, not machine. We installed a pellet-fuelled boiler and a solar hot water system to heat water and a solar power system for electricity. We wanted it to exemplify the concept of the 'eco-friendly wooden house' and to model various types of renewable energies. At present, this facility mainly accepts families with children from Fukushima, who have been restricted from playing outside by the government because of the high levels of radiation caused by the Fukushima nuclear accident. They can stay either temporarily or long term.

We wish to continue expanding our network and enhancing our activities in these new areas to further link our everyday lives to the forests, and to encourage people to be more eco-friendly by using forest resources healthily so that, eventually, everyone can enjoy nature's abundance. We are working to establish a system that creates long-term profits for communities that co-exist with the natural environment in sustainable ways.

How do you incorporate education into your forest activities?

TS: It is necessary to increase consumer awareness of the issues in the forestry industry. It is very hard to bring about big change by merely planting trees in a forest area. However, we can make a major difference by affecting consumption. We can purchase ethical and sustainable materials and products, for example, by using locally sourced timber to build a house. Thinking about forest problems, or understanding the value of sustainably logged wood for furniture or handcrafts sold in shops, can be a start. JFBN has organised seminars with building firms and is producing furniture from wood grown in the Tohoku region.

Our mission statement says: 'We vow to contribute to the enlightenment of people and to help build a society where a sustainable, peaceful and prosperous lifestyle is achieved,' (Kurikoma Kougen Nature School 2016). Since the two disasters, Kurikoma Kougen Nature School has engaged in various forest-related activities as well as environmental education. Education for children, the next generation, is indispensable for solving the forests' problems and environmental issues. Places like our school enable children and adults to discuss, learn and think about these problems.

How do you want to develop the school in the future?

TS: The experiences of the two earthquakes gave us the opportunity to rethink how well our school's education could strengthen 'life skills' and how it could help us address the ongoing challenges of rebuilding and revitalising affected areas. Nature schools that have previously connected people with nature and people with each other through adventure education are now taking on a new role as social enterprises that can create sustainable industry. Some other nature schools have also worked for forestry conservation. However, so far, we are the only nature school that has actively promoted a sustainable forestry industry. Our experience shows that a nature school can serve as a hub that connects individuals, groups and businesses, building 'social capital' in a region to combat a wide range of issues through collaboration and partnerships with diverse sectors.

Our nature school has developed innovative approaches to integrate educational methods, facilitate networking and foster problem-solving skills. Our experience shows that nature schools can function well in challenging situations. Today, many companies conduct tree planting activities as part of their corporate social responsibility. However, we may need to improve how we use the forests as the trees mature. We would like to connect forests with corporations and consumers to achieve healthy and sustainable forest resource use and contribute to an abundant life for all in an eco-friendly society.

Notes

1 The Asia-Pacific Cultural Centre for UNESCO (ACCU) is a non-profit organisation for regional activities in Asia Pacific in line with the principles of UNESCO, working for the promotion of mutual understanding and cultural cooperation among peoples in the region. ACCU was established in 1971 in Tokyo. ACCU implements various regional cooperative programmes in the fields of culture, education and personnel exchange in close collaboration with UNESCO and its member states in Asia and the Pacific (ACCU 2016a).
2 Founded on 21 June 2003, the Japan Council on the UN Decade of Education for Sustainable Development (ESD-J) is a networking organisation dedicated to promoting education for a sustainable society, given impetus by the UN Decade of Education

for Sustainable Development (DESD). ESD-J is a gathering of NPOs and individuals involved in social issues, such as the environment, development, human rights, peace and gender, who have joined forces for the purposes of searching for and realising forms of education that can be shared by all. ESD-J also works with the government, local authorities, companies and educational institutions to promote ESD. The organisation's name changed in 2015 to the Japan Council on Education for Sustainable Development, following the conclusion of the UNDESD (ESD-J 2016a).

3 See ACCU (2016b).
4 See ACCU (2016c).
5 ESD-J promoted three key concepts to the national government and to international organisations throughout the UNDESD: 1) the importance of a community-based approach in ESD, 2) the significant role that NGOs could play and 3) the importance of informal learning in the community development process. See ESD-J (2016a).
6 According to Sasaki (2015), this number is based on a report by the Japan Environmental Education Forum in 2010. It includes both profit and nonprofit organisations which provide activities on a regular basis, and does not include governmental organisations, visitor centres, museums, libraries and others that provide interpretation depending on visitors' needs.
7 See the website of Kurikoma Kougen Nature School for details: http://kurikomans.com/en/index.html.

References

Asia-Pacific Cultural Centre for UNESCO (ACCU) 2016a. About ACCU (www.accu.or.jp/jp/en/about/index.html). Accessed 11 February 2016.

Asia-Pacific Cultural Centre for UNESCO (ACCU) 2016b. History of HOPE (www.accu.or.jp/esd/hope/index.html). Accessed 4 February 2016.

Asia-Pacific Cultural Centre for UNESCO (ACCU) 2016c. COE programme for ESD (www.accu.or.jp/esd/projects/coe/index.html). Accessed 4 February 2016.

Government of Japan 1946. Social Education Act.

Government of Japan 1990. A Law Concerning the Establishment of Implementation Systems and Other Measures for the Promotion of Lifelong Learning.

Japan Council on Education for Sustainable Development (ESD-J) 2016a. About ESD-J (http://esd-j.org/english/about-esd-j/organization). Accessed 11 February 2016.

Japan Council on Education for Sustainable Development (ESD-J) 2016b. References (http://esd-j.org/english/references). Accessed 5 February 2016.

Kurikoma Kougen Nature School 2016. Mission Statement (http://kurikomans.com/en/about/about.html). Accessed 26 February 2016.

Ministry of Education, Culture, Sports, Science and Technology of Japan (MEXT) 2011. *Kominkanno suii* (Changes of Kominkan in number) (www.mext.go.jp/a_menu/01_1/08052911/001.htm). Accessed 7 June 2016.

Noguchi, F., Guevara, R. and Yorozu, R. 2015. *Communities in action: lifelong learning for sustainable development.* Hamburg, Germany: UNESCO Institute for Lifelong Learning.

Okayama City 2016. Kominkan-CLC International Conference: Community Based Human Development for Sustainable Society (www.okayama-tbox.jp/esd/pages/5431). Accessed 5 February 2016.

Sanyo Shimbun 2014. Developing Okayama version CLC conference outcome document. *Okayama Shimbun*, 19 December 2014.

Sasaki, T. 2015. *Kankyoshakai no henka to shizengakkouno yakuwari* (Change in environmental society and the role of nature schools). PhD thesis. Miyagi University.

9 Can civil society revitalise dying rural villages?

The case of Kamiseya in Kyoto prefecture

Binxian Ji and Katsue Fukamachi

Introduction

Japan's rural landscapes, or *satoyama*, include settlements, farmland, water systems and forests with diverse tree species of various ages, which together reflect unique local natural and cultural features. *Satoyama* landscapes have been shaped by the lifestyle and land use of the local people and have changed throughout time. They can be said to reflect the knowledge and techniques of local residents, who developed systems for the sustainable use of local natural resources while also finding ways to overcome threats posed by nature, such as typhoons or other disasters. Today, however, changes in the use of resources, migration to urban areas and an ageing population have resulted in the inability of many villages to continue managing their local resources. Village functions have deteriorated, formerly managed farmland and forests have been abandoned, and the state of the traditional *satoyama* – including ecosystem services and biodiversity – has declined. The situation is particularly serious in dying villages (*genkai shuraku*), where social and agricultural functions are gradually disappearing. According to Ohno (2005, 5), dying villages are defined as 'villages in which more than half of the residents are 65 years old or older, and where it has become difficult to conduct social activities and community work, in particular, ceremonial occasions such as coming-of-age ceremonies, weddings and funerals, or maintenance work traditionally shared among villagers, such as repairs of local shrines, temples and roads'.

According to the *Survey Report on Village Functions in Dying Villages in 2005* by the Foundation for Rural Development Projects (2006), many villages in the rural Honshu regions of Hokuriku and Chugoku – where small villages with an ageing population abound – had already disappeared at the time of the survey, or were expected to disappear in the near future. In the villages that were expected to disappear, there were many cases in which agricultural activity as an income source had ceased to exist, and where residents relied on retirement pensions or payments by family members for a living. Although, in areas other than the Hokuriku and Chugoku regions, residents still conducted community work and continued to manage village farmland and forests, a clear tendency to abandon certain village functions was noted. For instance, villagers had stopped conducting traditional ceremonies, they held village meetings less frequently or irregularly and they had discontinued some other social activity. In addition, there were cases of landslides on slopes in mountainous areas or collapses of stretches of farmland, which could be thought to have occurred as a result of a lack of management.

The Ministry of Internal Affairs and Communications surveyed 64,954 inhabited villages in 801 municipalities and 522 districts nationwide – totalling 11,887,715 people and 4,679,721 households – for a 2011 report on depopulation and related issues in rural villages. It classified 31 per cent of the villages (20,113 villages) as mountainous and 29 per cent (18,830 villages) as in 'other rural areas'. Thus, about 60 per cent of all villages were in rural areas. Sorted by type, 82.7 per cent (53,704 villages) were classified as basic primary industry villages, 10 per cent (6,519 villages) were strategic villages (such as those located at intersections or junctions) and 6.3 per cent (4,080 villages) were major villages (with an administrative or other important function). About 10 per cent of the 64,954 villages were tiny, with fewer than 10 households. In 10,091 villages (15.5 per cent), more than half of the population was elderly (65 years or older). Among these, there were 575 villages (0.9 per cent of the total) in which all residents were elderly.

To address the serious challenges posed by rural depopulation throughout Japan, a number of groups, including community groups, other civic organisations, administrative bodies, universities, research institutes and business enterprises, have built collaborative networks that apply a range of approaches to attempt to revitalise dying villages. Both internal and external stakeholders cooperate to manage and employ local resources effectively. In some cases, non-residents, including villagers who have roots in a depopulated village but do not live there any more, have become key actors in these networks. For rural villages on the verge of disappearance, the support provided by civic groups has become indispensable.

In this chapter, we will explore how a network of individuals and groups aiming to revitalise a depopulated village can work by examining the case of Kamiseya. This is a small village set in a mountainous rural area on the Tango Peninsula in the municipality of Miyazu city in northern Kyoto prefecture. Motivated by the common aim of preserving the local *satoyama* landscape so that it can be passed down to future generations, various stakeholders have been working together to revitalise this rural area. Both local residents and outsiders have taken various measures to support traditional local social systems, including land tenure, resource management and use of forest commons, while also replacing some old ways with new systems when deemed necessary. Civic groups, local community members, administrative units and other entities have made a cooperative effort to preserve, revitalise and create new elements of the local *satoyama* landscape with the common aim of establishing contemporary systems that can cycle local resources and perpetuate local culture in a way that is suitable to the locality.

In the past, diverse sustainable uses of natural resources supported the life of people living in the *satoyama* countryside, which resulted in the maintenance of varied ecosystems with a multitude of functions. Different plant species appeared, depending on how the forest was managed and used, the intensity of tree cutting and the cutting cycle. This contributed to the preservation of biodiversity. In a changing landscape, the spatial distribution of species would be dependent on their biological characteristics and patterns of land use. It is necessary to consider both natural conditions and human impacts to fully understand the relationship between landscape change and its biodiversity at several spatial scales.

This chapter, therefore, examines environmental changes, the role and significance of new and long-established civic groups, and the role of local residents who have been managing *satoyama* landscapes. The Kamiseya case study sheds light on how non-profit organisations (NPOs) and other citizen initiatives can affect the long-term sustainability of local *satoyama* landscapes. It helps to illuminate the role citizen activities can be expected to play in the future and what kind of difficulties may be encountered.

Case study: the small rural village of Kamiseya

Geography, climate and population

Figure 9.1 shows major roadways and pathways in Kamiseya in 1970 and 1995. Kamiseya is a small, picturesque, mountainside village located adjacent to the sea port city of Miyazu on the Japan Sea, approximately 130km north of Kyoto. The residential area of Kamiseya lies at an altitude of 340m to 380m. The whole village comprises 650 hectares, of which 620 hectares are forested (Fukamachi *et al.* 2001). The average annual temperature for Kamiseya is estimated to be approximately 10–12°C, based on data for 1994, which show an average annual

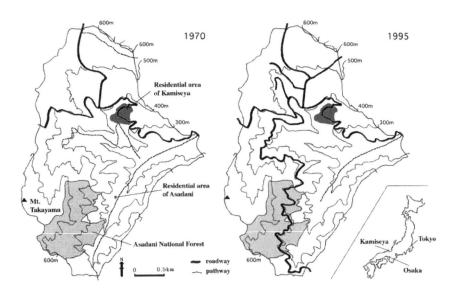

Figure 9.1 Major roadways and pathways in Kamiseya in 1970 and 1995

temperature of 13.9℃ for Miyazu city, which is adjacent but located at a lower altitude. The average snowfall is 2–3m in winter.

There were 60 households in Kamiseya in 1900, the same number as recorded in 1924 (with a total of 290 residents). However, this figure decreased to 38 households in 1970 and to only 13 households in 1995 (Fukamachi *et al.* 2010). Accompanying Japan's rapid industrialisation from the 1960s to 1990s, several factors led to a decline in population in Kamiseya, as in similar rural communities nationwide. In 1967, for example, the Japanese government implemented an acreage-reduction policy to contend with an oversupply of domestic rice that was putting severe pressure on market prices. This forced farmers to abandon some of their farmland (Ogawa *et al.* 2005). Between the 1950s and the 1990s, previously rural residents moved into urban areas to meet the demand for labour in the expanding heavy and chemical industries. At the same time, demand from the construction sector caused timber to be imported from foreign countries on a massive scale, which caused domestic wood prices to fall and weakened the Japanese forestry industry significantly (Ogawa *et al.* 2005). Finally, the expanding postwar transition to fossil fuels as the primary energy source led to the irreversible decline of the rural-based charcoal industry. The remote location and harsh winters of Kamiseya made the village even more vulnerable to these adverse impacts (see Figure 9.2).

Table 9.1 shows the changes in area of agricultural land in Kamiseya. In 1970, there were 32 farming households and the total cultivated area amounted to 3,930 acres, 83 per cent of which comprised paddy fields. However, cultivated acreage continued to shrink along with the rapid decrease in farming households. In 2005, only four farming households remained and the cultivated land amounted to a mere 438 acres. The period from 1970 to 1975 saw the proportionally largest decrease in cultivated areas with paddy fields. In 2005, areas with rice paddies

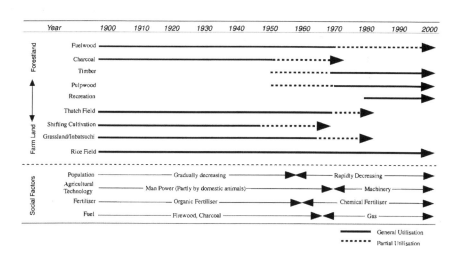

Figure 9.2 Changes in land use and social background in Kamiseya

Table 9.1 Changes in area of agricultural lands in Kamiseya

Year	Number of farm households	Cultivated agricultural lands (a)			Total	Abandoned lands (a)
		Rice field	*Vegetable field*	*Orchard*		
1970	32	3280	650	0	3930	no data
1975	22	1952	429	0	2381	1232
1980	15	1427	197	1	1625	159
1985	11	916	107	0	1023	563
1990	11	799	85	0	884	655
1995	8	590	407	0	997	613
2000	7	493	110	3	606	2
2005	4	335	103	0	438	26

amounted to only 10 per cent of the rice paddy surface of 35 years earlier. The ageing of the population and an increase in abandoned land had led to the deterioration of land and irrigation facilities, a decline in biodiversity and to fewer functions that enhance land and environment conservation.

There were 13 households with 23 full-time and six part-time residents in 2012. The 23 full-time residents included 15 local people and eight newcomers (who were not born or did not grow up in Kamiseya). More than 56.5 per cent of the full-time residents were 65 years old or older. Thus Kamiseya can be called a dying village or *genkai shuraku*. The majority of the residents were ageing local people or retired newcomers and their main source of income was state and company pensions. Although many villagers grew vegetables or other crops, most did so only for household consumption. In household surveys, most residents stated that ageing, depopulation and heavy snowfall were the main problems faced by the village.

Revitalisation activities

As in other depopulated rural areas of Japan, the main problem facing environmental sustainability in Kamiseya today stems from a lack of local farmers and hunters due to the ageing population. As a result, paddy fields have been abandoned, forests neglected and farmland has seen an increase of damage by wild animals. Where land abandonment has occurred as a result of changes in human land use, the landscape has tended to become more homogeneous. A particularly important change brought on by this simplification of the landscape has been the loss of a mixture of open and closed farm types in landscapes, in which the number of discrete species can increase. The *Red Data Books* of Japan warn that many indigenous plant and animal species associated with traditional human activities – such as man-made water systems, periodical cutting and burning for the maintenance of agricultural lands, open forestlands and secondary coppice forests – have recently become threatened with extinction (Fukamachi *et al.* 2001).

For Kamiseya, attracting new residents is imperative. Although the beautiful natural features and abundant indigenous local knowledge are attractive to newcomers, heavy snowfall and few job opportunities have deterred people from moving to Kamiseya. Members of local support groups concluded that new ways had to be found to revitalise the area. Could newcomers be attracted based on the potential of the traditional landscape and culture?

Efforts to that end have been made since the beginning of this century. In 2007, the Kamiseya area was included in the newly established Tango-Amano-hashidate-Oeyama Quasi-National Park (Satoyama Network in Seya 2013a). In 2009, the *Asahi Shimbun* newspaper and the Forest and Culture Association (a public service corporation established to commemorate the 100th anniversary of the *Asahi Shimbun*) included Kamiseya in 'Japan Hometown 100' (Forest and Culture Association 2013), a list of 100 villages considered to excel in landscape, biodiversity and human activities. Moreover, Kamiseya received some financial support for revitalisation from the Kyoto Prefecture Development Bureau for the Tango Area. It also benefitted from the Kyoto prefecture government-sponsored initiative *sato no shikakenin,* which recruited young people and dispatched them as village business initiative promoters to help solve local problems and promote regional revitalisation in depopulated rural areas. One person who had been sent to Kamiseya on this scheme later chose to relocate to the village.

In addition, a large number of community-based activities designed to revitalise the village are carried out in Kamiseya. The advanced age of most Kamiseya residents means the founders or leaders of these activities are usually people from outside, who built good relationships with locals while taking part in field activities during their college years or while working. Some of them have chosen to relocate permanently to Kamiseya.

Surveys and interviews of organisations involved in local activities, conducted in 2013 (Ji 2014), found that most participants were employees, students or young mothers who joined with their children. The reasons they cited for joining were wanting to try something new, not having had a similar experience in the past and being interested in some aspects of the activity – for example, nature, locally produced textiles or organic products, such as the organic rice vinegar produced by a local company. Participants who were parents wanted their children to experience activities such as the rice harvest. University faculty members chose Kamiseya as a field site, where their students could examine forests and soil and learn about rural sustainability issues. College students conducted activities related to their research and helped local residents carry out local landscape conservation measures, such as mowing grass and cutting bamboo.

Revitalisation activities in Kamiseya have been centered on two local institutions involved in shaping the future of the village. The Satoyama Network Seya (SNS) is an NPO that aims to pass on traditional local knowledge and restore the local *satoyama* landscapes by promoting sustainable resource use and management. *Kouryoku no Kai* (Kouryoku Club) promotes the cultivation of abandoned paddy fields and has built a venue, the Kouryoku farmhouse, for citizen group networking.

Two main community-building institutions in Kamiseya

SNS was formed in 2003 and its founding director is the president of Iio Jozo, a family business in Miyazu that produces high-quality vinegar. Members of SNS include local residents, researchers and supporters from outside the village. The NPO aims to pass on traditional local knowledge, restore the *satoyama* landscape of Kamiseya by using and managing natural resources, and provide a community for people involved in *satoyama* management activities related to food, shelter, traditional crafts, education for sustainability and recreation (SNS 2013b).

SNS activities have been subsidised by business corporations, local governments and the Furusato and Terraced Rice Field Support Project, which encourages young people to help preserve and pass on regional culture and conserve terraced rice fields (SNS 2013b). SNS accepts interns from Kyoto University and research students from Kyoto Gakuen University. Its efforts to promote environmental conservation and regeneration, economic revitalisation of rural communities, and maintenance of traditional culture and knowledge have played an important role in the revitalisation of Kamiseya (Singer 2010). In November 2010, SNS set up a research group of local residents, university researchers and NPO staff tasked with conserving the village landscape by restoring the *satogawa* (village streams) as a physical and cultural feature that would be used and maintained sustainably and reintegrated into daily village life. The group has conducted joint activities with other institutions, including the Local Council for the Seya Area, Kyoto University, Kyoto Prefectural University and the Tango Civil Engineering Office of Kyoto prefecture and Miyazu city. SNS activities include managing waterside space in Kamiseya, developing local activities and creating and displaying learning materials, such as pamphlets and videos. Field activities include looking for wild birds at the headstream in Seya, visiting beech stands of the Seya plateau, learning about *satoyama* management and organic rice cultivation, and walking tours through the *satoyama* landscape that include viewing the neighbouring Miyazu coast from the Seya plateau (SNS 2013c and Miyoshi 2013). SNS has also organised village activities such as the annual residents' sports event, cleaning the village pathways and facilities, weeding the roadsides and temple grounds and maintaining roads in the plateau beech forest. In the winter, it has recruited volunteers to help remove snow from rooftops, working with other local groups such as the *Seya no ko* (Children of Seya), Kouryoku Club and Miyazu City Ecotourism Promotion Council.

A second important institution in Kamiseya is the Kouryoku Club. It was established by a retired newcomer, who relocated to Kamiseya and bought two houses in the village, one for his family and one for community use. He named the latter *Kouryoku no ie*. *Kouryoku* is Tango dialect and may be translated as 'assistance' and *ie* means house (Kouryoku Club 2013). Some 860 volunteers helped the owner restore the farmhouse for community use. Various traditional local products, such as *fujiori* (items made of Japanese wisteria fibre) and local timber, were used in the restoration work. The house retains traditional features such as a *kamado* (a wood-burning stove made of mud and bricks) and a *hagama* (a heavy earthenware pot used to cook rice). Members of the club gather twice a year to work in the fields: in spring to plant organic rice and in autumn to harvest the rice and stack the sheaves on *tenpiboshi* racks to dry in the sun. Since the club uses previously abandoned rice fields, participants not only experience traditional cultivation methods but also help to preserve the traditional terraced landscape. The club's membership has increased from 25–30 people in 2007 to about 60 people, some of whom are children. The club has expanded from one group to three involved in planting and harvesting. The original group consists of the owner's circle of friends, the second group includes people who love the landscape of Kamiseya and enjoy painting or drawing it, and the third group comprises young mothers and children. These mothers want to teach their children, from first-hand experience, where their food comes from. *Kouryoku no ie* is also used as a base for the *Seya no ko* children's activity group and for activities related to ecotourism. Students and other visitors can also experience traditional rural life at the house. In 2013, for example, the owner taught 80 third graders from Miyazu primary school about Kamiseya traditional village customs and folk craft.

Specific activities

The two groups mentioned above are assisted by a number of other local support organisations, which sponsor a full roster of revitalisation activities throughout the year. Some of them are described here. One is Iio Jozo, a family-run company, founded in 1893, that produces vinegar using traditional methods. The company has garnered extensive media coverage, including mention in a popular adult manga, *Oishinbo*, because of its long-standing concern for environmentally friendly production and food safety, and its products are sold in prestigious national department store chains. Eighteen farmers were contracted by Iio Jozo to grow organic rice for vinegar in 2013 (personal communication with Iio Jozo staff, 2013). After the foundation of SNS, Iio Jozo employees facilitated the use of abandoned farmlands in Kamiseya for cultivating organic rice. This has enabled the company to ensure the quality of the raw materials used in its vinegar production process, while helping Kamiseya to rehabilitate abandoned fields. Two staff members commute from Miyazu for approximately five months of the year to plant, tend and harvest the organic rice. Other staff members come to help during busy times. In addition, more than 100 Iio Jozo customers from cities such as Tokyo and Osaka join the team as volunteers to help during the planting and harvesting season. Iio Jozo organises field site visits, lectures on vinegar production and tastings. It also maintains links with universities. For example, members of an agricultural student circle and community network at Kyoto University have visited the vinegar company since 2007 (Iio Jozo 2013) and helped with rice planting and harvesting. The exchange is mutually beneficial because the students learn through practice and the company gains feedback on its products for future development.

The Tango Mura Okoshi Kaihatsu Team (Tango Village Revitalisation Team), hereafter TMOKT, was founded in April 2004 by a project team from the Faculty of Business Administration at Ritsumeikan University. The group currently has 45 members, who are first-, second- or third-year students at Ritsumeikan University (TMOKT 2013a). The group's objective is to protect local landscape and *satoyama* features such as *kayabuki* (thatched roofs) in and around the depopulated Kamiseya area, promote traditional practices for local revitalisation and identify opportunities for local business initiatives.

Members of TMOKT have conducted two main activities in Kamiseya. First, the group maintains two *kayabuki* roofs, one in Kamiseya and one in the Omiyacho Ikaga district of Kyotango city. The restoration of the house in Kamiseya began in June 2004 and was completed in May 2008. To thatch the farmhouse, members harvested *sasa* bamboo leaves themselves. The group also attempts to revitalise local business activities by investigating and exploring opportunities (TMOKT 2013b). Through workshops and by engaging in commerce, TMOKT members gain business experience and gather traditional rural knowledge that is quite a contrast to their modern urban lifestyles (personal communication with TMOKT representative, 2012). Some former members of the group have returned after graduation to help out in TMOKT's activities.

In 2009, TMOKT sponsored a meeting of the University Student Regional Organisation Summit, which brings together organisations from across Japan that practice similar activities. The summit sponsored lectures, planning sessions, discussions and workshops related to topics such as *kayabuki* thatching in Kamiseya, providing good opportunities for communication between students from different groups and universities.

An example of another student activity was a series of visits, sponsored by the instructors of an undergraduate course offered at Kyoto University in the spring semester of 2012 and 2013. The course, called Building a Sustainable Future: Principles and Challenges, incorporated field work in urban and rural settings for students studying community sustainability. In 2013, four teachers (among them two international teachers) and 22 students (19 of them international students) came to Miyazu city and Kamiseya village. The students visited SNS and learned about the local situation through lectures given by professors and individuals active in village revitalisation activities. They also visited *Kouryoku no ie,* whose owner shared stories about Kamiseya life and customs, and had the opportunity to walk about the village and to talk to a local resident in her house.

Another important component of local heritage activities is the effort to conserve *fujiori,* a traditional weaving technique that uses fibres of the Japanese wisteria vine to make tools or cloth. Kamiseya is one of the few places known to still practise this unique craft but, with only a few elderly locals still practising it, the art was in danger of extinction. A few practitioners initiated a *fujiori* workshop in 1985 and in 1989 some graduates of the course established the Fujiori Preservation Society. The workshop's objective is to protect cultural heritage and pass on traditional practices and skills that are in danger of dying out. In 1991, *fujiori* was designated an intangible folk cultural asset by Kyoto prefecture. In 2010, the building that formerly housed the Seya Branch School of Hioki Junior High School (which closed its doors in the 1980s when pupil numbers declined) became a training centre for the workshops and an exhibition space for *fujiori* works, artifacts and techniques. As of late 2013, a total of 463 participants had attended the *fujiori* workshops and 162 had become members of the Fujiori Preservation Society after finishing the course (personal communication with the owner of *Kouryoku no ie* 2013).

Each course comprises seven workshops, which last for 10-and-a-half days over an eight-month period. The workshops are held periodically on seven weekends between May and December, and participants are expected to attend all of them. The course is led by volunteers, who have learned *fujiori* from Kamiseya grandmothers, or by former course alumni who come back to help workshop participants learn how to weave the wisteria vines. Participants experience every stage of the *fujiori* process: first, finding and cutting down the *fuji* vines; next, removing the bark and boiling it using *aku* (wood ash); then making the thread and, finally, weaving it into cloth. Making *fujiori* requires a great deal of time and patience.

In September 2013, the Fujiori Preservation Society was awarded the Suntory Prize for Community Cultural Activities. The ¥2m award from the Suntory Foundation recognised the achievements of the society in conserving and preserving customs and culture relating to *satoyama* for future generations. The Fujiori Preservation Society held an exhibition at Honenin Temple in Kyoto to celebrate its 30th anniversary in 2014.

Some other groups also organise revitalisation activities. A group in charge of agricultural products specialises in processing local produce and other materials. The *Seya no ko* children's activity group, a group established by a newcomer, conducts seasonal activities for children and parents and explores ecotourism projects while protecting natural sightseeing resources and focusing on environmental conservation and education.

Activities conducted in Kamiseya encourage participants to learn about rural life in Japan, recognise local problems and think about solutions. Many participants become more conscious of the food they eat and begin to consider the sustainability or desirability of their current lifestyles. In surveys and interviews conducted in 2013, participants in activities in Kamiseya reported that local food, if cooked simply with just a few seasonings, was more delicious than food prepared with many synthetic spices. Participants have also said that activities, such as rice cultivation, have taught them to treasure their food and to fully understand the arduous, labour-intensive nature of cultivation – and this has had a positive influence on their daily lives. Others have reflected on Kamiseya's agricultural model and have reappraised what is 'green' and what is safe. Students, in particular, have benefited from the precious field-work opportunities related to their studies. In interviews, local residents have stated that they now recognise more clearly than before the value and importance of their culture, which they will hand down to succeeding generations.

Summary

Thanks to citizen activities in Kamiseya, cultural features such as *fujiori* and traditional farmhouses are being preserved and handed down to the next generation, resulting in some *satoyama* resources being properly managed and used once again. In addition, local farmers, enthusiastic volunteers – and contracted workers and volunteers affiliated with Iio Jozo – are now growing rice on terraces that were previously abandoned. This has helped to boost local production substantially and has led to good management of farmland and the water system. Citizens who have moved to Kamiseya from outside or who live in the vicinity of the village have been instrumental by taking the initiative in such activities – and it is often these people who make sure the activities continue. They carry out revitalisation work for Kamiseya alongside their household and personal activities.

Civic actions in Kamiseya contribute to the conservation of *satoyama* landscapes in two ways. First, by providing direct support through the use and management of *satoyama* resources such as *fuji* vines and by cultivating farmland. Second, by providing services that benefit the landscape indirectly, such as distributing information, training staff, assisting local groups, promoting exchange visits and strengthening networks.

While local revitalisation activities change every year, there are some continuous elements:

1   Passing down the use of traditional cultural resources and preserving *satoyama* landscapes;
2   Increasing exchanges between rural and urban residents;
3   Identifying attractive rural village features and distributing related information; and
4   Establishing and making available venues in the village where internal and external actors can interact.

The members of most civic groups have diverse interests and come from a variety of professions. They collect knowledge of *satoyama* and disseminate it to others. In addition, they organise lectures to train *satoyama* guides and create opportunities for the public to experience on-site activities. Educational on-site experience programmes for people from outside the village have improved their understanding of rural issues and provided the village with much needed manpower for local resource management. In addition, eco tours in Seya have generated wide public interest and have resulted in the local landscape being registered as 'the Kamiseya Satoyama Landscape, where bamboo-grass-thatched farmhouses and rice terraces weave a harmonious landscape' in its entry in the Kyoto Prefectural Registration System for Landscape Assets (Kyoto Prefecture, n.d.). The NPO SNS has played an important intermediary role in providing legal and financial expertise to encourage young people and farmers, who were interested in starting agricultural or business ventures, to move to the village. It has also made use of subsidies from Kyoto prefecture to cut down weeds in the village, recultivate rice terraces, organise teams for shovelling snow and hold workshops on dealing with damage caused by wild animals and tackling the spread of invasive bamboo.

When civic groups find it difficult to achieve their aims because of a lack of skilled workers or technical expertise, they can consult other civil society organisations, governments, universities or businesses and forge collaborative networks. Cooperation between diverse groups has been indispensable for preserving *satoyama* landscapes and local resources. Civil society and educational activities organised over many years in Kamiseya have finally led to a greater public understanding of the value of local nature and culture. More concretely, a few young families have decided to move to the area in recent years – possibly suggesting the drastic decline in the local population can be stopped.

Civil society activities in dying villages make direct changes to the lifestyles and working environment of a village. They also play an important role in collecting and disseminating traditional knowledge that has been used, historically, to maintain natural landscapes. These activities also help people to appreciate a way of life that is in harmony with *satoyama*.

The fact that increasing numbers of civil society groups across Japan are acting as intermediaries, bringing together stakeholders in the management and use of resources, is one of the main reasons for their success. Today they play an instrumental role, buttressed by government subsidies allocated for village revitalisation initiatives, in maintaining vital village functions and supporting residents in their daily lives.

However, many issues have yet to be resolved. For instance, a solution must be found to close the gap in awareness and values between local residents and civil society groups. Although outside volunteers and NPOs may recognise the appeal of rural life, village residents often discourage their children from remaining at or returning home. They see few prospects for future economic viability. In addition, revitalisation events or activities that promise only temporary benefit – or are not really suited to a village – need to be reconsidered. Local governments must support activities, communicate more effectively and not simply adopt standardised approaches that may not be best for specific village conditions. Moreover, it is often difficult for non-profit groups to run their organisations effectively and maintain project continuity and stability when the participants and their numbers change.

In light of these obstacles, it is imperative for support groups to network and share tasks efficiently, to increase communication and to cooperate closely with local residents and administrative bodies to find ways to conserve the local *satoyama* landscape while revitalising the locality. They must assiduously investigate the history of the local natural environment and the people who have continued to inhabit it. This will enable the groups to provide the expertise and mechanisms needed to shape a future *satoyama* based on both traditional and imported values.

Finally, it must never be forgotten that residents – including children and students, who will become the leaders of the next generation – should play the main role in citizen groups. Their contributions will provide the necessary momentum and they will learn from each other while being exposed to nature, culture and traditional *satoyama* practices. One of the most important roles of civil society groups may be to provide continuing opportunities for residents to support their local environment.

References

Forest and Culture Association 2013. *Sinnrinn Bunnka Kyoukai no gaiyou* (Outline of Forest and Culture Association) (www.shinrinbunka.com/). Accessed 30 December 2013.

Foundation for Rural Development Projects, General Committee 2006. *FY 2005 Genkaisyurakuniokeru syurakukinoinojittainikansuru chosahoukokusyo* (Survey report on village functions in dying villages in FY 2005), 116.

Fukamachi, K., Ohgishi, M., Oku, H., Miyoshi, I., Horiuchi, M. and Shibata, S. 2010. Changes in the rice terrace landscape and factors playing a role in the survival of the rice terraces in a mountainous area of the Tango Peninsula. *Journal of Rural Planning Association Editorial Board* 28, 315–320.

Fukamachi, K., Oku, H. and Nakashizuka, T. 2001. The change of a satoyama landscape and its causality in Kamiseya, Kyoto prefecture, Japan, between 1970 and 1995. *Landscape Ecology* 16, 703–717.

Iio Jozo 2013. *Okyakusama no Koe* (Customer feedback) (iio-jozo.livedoor.biz/archives/cat_10006970.html). Accessed 19 December 2013.

Ji, B. 2014. Revitalisation strategies in rural Japan: a case study of Kamiseya, Kyoto prefecture. Masters thesis, Graduate School of Global Environmental Studies, Kyoto University.

Kouryoku no Kai (Kouryoku Club) 2013. *Kouryoku no Ie toha* (What is Kouryoku Club?) (http://kamiseya.com/newpage7.html). Accessed 7 May 7 2013.

Kyoto Prefecture n.d. *Kyotofukeikan shisantorokuchiku no shokai 13* (Kyoto Prefectural registration system for landscape assets introduction 13) (www.pref.kyoto.jp/toshi/sisan013.html). Accessed 19 November 2015.

Ministry of Internal Affairs and Communications, Working Group for Measures Related to Depopulation in Rural Areas 2011. *Kasochiikitouniokeru syurakunojyokyounikansu-rugenjyouhaaku chosahoukokusyo* (Survey report on depopulation and related issues in rural villages), 161.

Miyoshi, I. 2013. *Kamiseya no Satoyama Keikan ni Tyouwashita Satogawa no Soushutu to Katuyou* (Creation and utilisation of harmonious satogawa of satoyama landscape of Kamiseya) (www.youtube.com/watch?v=oxYwS3A1j80). Accessed 8 November 2013.

Ogawa, N., Fukamachi, K., Oku, H., Shibata, S. and Morimoto, Y. 2005. *Tango Hanntou ni okeru Sasabuki Shuuraku no Hensen to sono Keishou ni kannsuru Kennkyuu* (Title study on transition and succession of village landscape of Sasabuki in the Tango Peninsula). *Landscape Research Japan* 68 (5), 627–632.

Ohno, A. 2005. *Genkaisyuraku – Sonojittaiga toikakerumono* (Shedding light on the state of dying villages in Japan). *Nogyo to Keizai* (agriculture and economy), *Showado*, 5.

Satoyama Nettowaaku Seya (Satoyama Network in Seya) (SNS) 2013a. *Seya no Shoukai* (Seya introduction) (www.satoyama-net-seya.org/世屋紹介/). Accessed 29 November 2013.

Satoyama Nettowaaku Seya (Satoyama Network in Seya) (SNS) 2013b. *Danntai Gaiyou* (Community outline) (www.satoyama-net-seya.org/団体概要/). Accessed 7 May 2013.

Satoyama Nettowaaku Seya (Satoyama Network in Seya) (SNS) 2013c. *Seya no Satogawa wo Kanngaeru Kai* (Association of thinking about Satogawa of Seya) (www.satoyama-net-seya.org/里川プロジェクト/事業内容/). Accessed 8 November 2013.

Singer, J. 2010. NPO-led revitalisation of Japan's satoyama landscapes. (Unpublished paper).

Tango Mura Okoshi Kaihatsu Team (Tango Village Revitalisation Team) (TMOKT) 2013a. *Mennbaa* (members) (www.tangoweb.co.jp/tmkt/member.html). Accessed 13 November 2013.

Tango Mura Okoshi Kaihatsu Team (Tango Village Revitalisation Team) (TMOKT) 2013b. *Timu ni tsuite* (about the team) (www.tangoweb.co.jp/tmkt/team.html). Accessed 16 November 2013.

10 Multi-stakeholder community education through environmental learning programmes in Nishinomiya

Miki Yoshizumi

Introduction

The need to engage stakeholders at all levels and to realise multi-stakeholder partnerships and voluntary commitments to achieving sustainable development has been recognised at recent international conferences as well as in ongoing global conversations on the post-2015 development agenda (UNDESA 2014). Citizen participation has also been recognised as a key aspect in implementing a sustainable city (UN 1992, EC 1996, Ueta 2004). Japan has a strong history of citizen participation in sustainability efforts, particularly since the emergence of a community movement confronting government inactivity in preventing environmental pollution after the high-growth period of the 1960s (Shinohara 1977). During that time, many local residents complained of inadequate environmental policies and city planning, and residents confronted governments, seeking to improve the situation. When the Japanese City Planning Act was revised in 1980, a district planning system was introduced and the legislation recognised that public participation should be implemented at the planning stages of district plans. In 1992, a revised Act affirmed the necessity of public participation in making master plans. Since then, public participation evolved from protests and demands to a situation more conducive to participation and partnership (Nakazawa *et al.* 1995).

However, several challenges have constrained effective citizen participation. First, there are frequent conflicts between governments and residents as well as among residents themselves, particularly since residents tend to have diverse ideas about city planning. For example, if a new road is constructed, it may be a boon to some but a bane to others so support will vary. In every community there will be residents who make frequent appearances at town meetings to push for expanded government services. Second, the initiative and proactive stance of residents may vary. As Arnstein (1969) pointed out in her Ladder of Citizen Participation framework, there are eight possible levels of participation, with manipulation and therapy on the bottom rungs. Recently, the Japanese City Planning Act and similar laws have required public participation in urban planning. In Japan, however, most residents do not participate in city planning fora because they expect governments to provide city planning and members of the public often lack experience of participating in city planning activities. Communities often do little more than to facilitate ritualistic public participation and public hearings, such as eliciting public comments (Takahashi 2000).

Another difficulty for citizen participation is the realisation of broad-based stakeholder participation. Often only certain types of people – for example, retired people and local activists – tend to participate in meetings and activities while other members of the general public are reluctant to get involved. In Japan, young and middle-aged people rarely participate in local community activities because of their disengagement from local issues and long working hours. Most participants in town and community meetings are elderly. Japanese society has a system of neighbourhood associations. Traditionally, all residents were socially obliged to participate in their neighbourhood association, called a *jichikai* or *chounaikai*. Recently, however, participation in neighbourhood associations has decreased, with the percentage of residents enrolled falling from 70.2 per cent in 1968 to 12.7 per cent in 2007 (Ministry of Internal Affairs and Communications 2010). It can also be argued that Japanese culture does not reward people for expressing their opinions in public. As a result, only certain types of people join in local activities, who eventually start to feel a sense of 'saturation' and stop joining in (Rydin and Pennington 2000). Therefore, it is necessary to implement measures for the long-term involvement of various stakeholders.

Finally, there is the issue of the sustainability of community activities. Most citizen participatory initiatives wane when the immediate problem appears to be solved and the protest message seems to have been put across. Moreover, some people think that citizen participation is simply a one-off event, such as a government-led town meeting or public opinion hearing. However, to achieve true sustainability, it is important for individuals and communities to maintain their interest and to continue participating in civic sustainability activities.

In Nishinomiya city since the late 1980s, initiatives for multi-stakeholder partnerships and community activities for sustainable community development have been developed through multi-stakeholder community education based on environmental learning programmes. Nishinomiya city has been awarded internationally and domestically for its environmental communication, environmental education programmes, sustainable community development and education for sustainable development (ESD) programmes. Nishinomiya's government-linked programmes have been recognised as one of Japan's most influential ESD models by the Japanese Ministry of the Environment, while its community education activities have generated both environmental improvement and a more sustainable community (Yoshizumi 2009).

This chapter provides a case study of Nishinomiya's efforts, exploring how the city's environmental learning programmes, which were facilitated by a non-profit organisation (NPO) and later expanded as ESD programmes, have been able to promote multi-stakeholder partnerships and community activities that work toward creating a more sustainable community.

A case study of Nishinomiya city

Background

The city of Nishinomiya has an area of 100km^2 and a population of 487,128 (as of 1 March 2015). The population has increased since the Great Hanshin-Awaji Earthquake of 1995, even though the population of most Japanese cities has decreased. Nishinomiya has developed as a popular commuter town, sandwiched between Osaka and Kobe in south-eastern Hyogo Prefecture in the Kansai region of central Honshu. Most local industry consists of small and medium-sized businesses and the city is well known for sake brewing. Nowadays, Nishinomiya is the most popular city in the Kansai region in which to live and raise children, according to a survey conducted by real estate giant Recruit (2015).

Influenced by increasing worldwide concern over environmental issues, a community-based environmental learning project called the Citizens' Nature Survey was launched in 1989 through the initiative of Masayoshi Ogawa, an official with the Nishinomiya environment bureau at that time. This programme aimed to interest residents in their local environment by encouraging them to investigate it by themselves. Based on the results of the nature surveys, the Earth Watching Club (EWC) for local children was developed in 1992 by Nishinomiya city government to promote environmental learning programmes.

The Great Hanshin-Awaji Earthquake of 1995, which caused more than 6,000 casualties in an area that included Nishinomiya, was a turning point for community-based environmental learning projects such as EWC. They began to be perceived as not only an effective tool for tackling environmental issues but for issues such as crime and risk reduction – and with the capacity for use for local disaster preparedness. As a result, the EWC concepts were developed by members of the EWC secretariat and, in 1998, an NPO called Learning and Ecological Activities Foundation for Children (LEAF) was created. Masayoshi Ogawa, who was by then a department chief in the city government, initiated LEAF in partnership with other members of the EWC secretariat and his collaborators in previous environmental initiatives. LEAF was developed to contribute to the development of a sustainable society by building partnerships between citizens, businesses and the local government (LEAF 2013). Through LEAF, the Nishinomiya city government has developed various environmental policies and conducted a broad range of community-based environmental initiatives. In 2006, the Nishinomiya ESD Exploratory Committee was established by the city government to integrate several ESD-related programmes and build a multi-stakeholder network for ESD programmes in Nishinomiya. As many activities related to ESD had already been developed in Nishinomiya, these activities were reviewed in terms of ESD concepts, and all the relevant ongoing activities were reorganised as ESD programmes. New activities for ESD programmes were also developed. As a result of this initiative, Nishinomiya was selected as a model city for ESD by the Japanese Ministry of Environment in 2006. LEAF has promoted the ESD programmes by coordinating with various stakeholders, such as the local government, several community group leaders, schools and private companies.

Framework for a sustainable Nishinomiya

Nishinomiya issued the Environmental Learning City Declaration in 2003 and published an Environmental Learning City Action Charter to raise awareness among the citizens of Nishinomiya. The charter identified five general goals: learning together; participation/collaboration; promoting a harmonious existence; recycling-based society and networking. Based on these goals, Nishinomiya issued a revised environmental plan in 2005. The revised plan has two fundamental objectives: to develop communities that nurture generations through environmental learning and to build a community system that encourages multi-stakeholder decision-making to foster a more civically engaged public on all issues. Based on the objectives in the environmental plan, various ESD programmes have been developed in Nishinomiya.

ESD programmes in Nishinomiya

By the early twenty-first century, Nishinomiya had a number of separate, independent community and governmental organisations conducting activities on various themes, such as environment, welfare, gender, peace and international issues. However, sectionalism among these community groups resulted in bureaucratic complexity and inefficient administration. Nishinomiya tried to connect the issues and organisations and to promote cooperative activities for sustainable development by starting an umbrella ESD programme in 2006 and establishing the multi-partner Nishinomiya ESD Promotion Council to guide and facilitate it.

The main concept of the Nishinomiya ESD programme is to 'link organisations, issues, areas, generations and the world and build sustainable communities' (City of Nishinomiya 2007) through hands-on educational and environmental learning programmes, seminars, training programmes and the sharing of information on issues such as the environment, peace, gender and equity. As demonstrated by the seven examples explained below, these activities have been developed based on the environmental charter and goals and aim to develop a system of mutual learning and to promote citizen participation through ESD.

Eco Card system

The Eco Card system was one of the first activities developed by the Earth Watching Club and it has continued to be very successful. This project aims to forge links between schools, families and communities through Eco Actions, which include cleaning up litter, learning from the natural environment and reducing solid waste. All elementary school children in Nishinomiya receive an Eco Card each year. When children perform an Eco Action, such as purchasing an eco-friendly product or separating recyclable goods, they get a stamp from one of the 2,000 participating Eco Stamp Holders, which include local schools, stationery shops, the city hall and other member institutions or individuals. Interestingly, these Eco Stamp Holders decide by themselves whether an action by a child should be rewarded as an Eco Action. Thus, while children actively search for what might

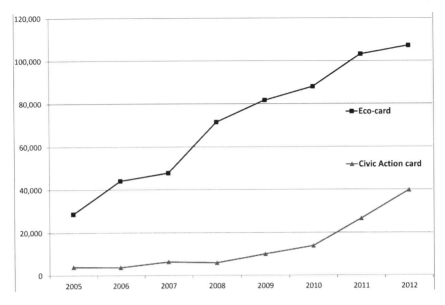

Figure 10.1 Number of people who submitted Eco Cards and Civic Action Cards
Source: Author

be considered Eco Actions, the stamp holders must also continue to learn and develop their ideas on what can be considered Eco Actions.

Initially the Eco Card system was a programme for children and students under 12 years old. The Civic Action Card was later developed for those aged 13 and older. This card aims to motivate people to act not only on environmental issues but on various community issues.

The number of activities for the Eco Card and Civic Action Card systems has increased, as shown in Figure 10.1.

After collecting more than 10 stamps on their Eco Card, children are awarded the title Earth Ranger for their eco-friendly actions. More than 2,000 children are certified Earth Rangers each year. The number of Earth Rangers has been increasing. In 2005, 1,749 Earth Rangers were certified in Nishinomiya. In 2012, 5,705 children were certified, suggesting public awareness of ESD is rising in Nishinomiya.

After more than 15 years of implementation, the Eco Card system has affected two generations, including parents and young elementary school teachers who grew up carrying Eco Cards themselves.

Safety and eco guide project

This project includes environmental and disaster-management education initiatives, based on lessons learned from the Great Hanshin-Awaji Earthquake.

The project aims to provide opportunities for each citizen to feel more confident and safe by learning about local history, nature, geography and the relationship between nature and physical safety. The Nishinomiya city government published the *Safety and Eco Guide Manual* to help community leaders and school teachers to implement related activities (Yoshizumi 2009). Subsequently, the city developed a number of 'eco community' initiatives, as explained below.

Storytellers programme

This programme, organised in collaboration with public schools, runs special classes where students can learn about environmental issues from different perspectives. One such class, entitled Storytellers, invites elderly residents to talk about what the environment was like when they were young. In the Storytellers training seminar, which was initiated in 1999, the participants take 10 different courses that cover the main aspects of the city's history and environment and learn about the geographical context of their community. By listening to what these Storytellers have experienced, school children and new residents who have moved to Nishinomiya from other cities can discover and compare the differences between the environmental conditions of the past and present. They can also learn how the natural environment has changed by taking short excursions called 'town watching' – community-based town planning in which people walk with Storytellers to various sites and identify local issues such as environmental and disaster hazards, and learn local cultural and geographical history (LEAF 2013). Through the activities, residents can understand and cultivate interest in their community while identifying issues for sustainable development. These activities have led to a growing number of eco actions and community-based activities, which are fostering an eco community. Another Storytellers programme, Nishinomiya *Furusato* (hometown) Walk for Sustainable City, has been held annually since 2007. About 450 participants joined in the event in January 2009, and 774 participants took part in November 2013.

Experience-based environmental education programme

The EWC programme has developed activities that allow residents of all ages to experience the local natural environment. The Miyamizu Senior Nature Observation Activities, for example, targets elderly residents, while several programmes for school children have been developed and are recognised as part of the school curriculum by the Nishinomiya Board of Education. Children get the opportunity to learn about local mountains, rivers and coastal environments through school excursions, hands-on games and exploratory activities. These activities have been widely recognised as exemplary environmental education, with many local governments and community groups asking LEAF to share their experience. Consequently, LEAF organises training seminars for community leaders of nature activities from all over Japan. After the training seminars, the leaders are encouraged to develop nature experience activities tailored to their own communities (Yoshizumi 2009).

Even very young children can participate in nature education. In the Child-Raising Programme in the Forest, which began in October 2013, pre-kindergarten children and their parents can experience the natural environment. The programme is particularly popular among young mothers, who get the opportunity to meet in a relaxing atmosphere outdoors. The programme aims to enable children and young parents, who do not get much opportunity to spend time in natural surroundings, to enjoy being in the forest. The programme is organised by LEAF, the Kobe Co-op grocery chain, the Fukoku insurance company and the Nishinomiya government. Past participants have rated the programme highly and have indicated an interest in continuing participation.

Environmental learning through farming

Japan only produces about 40 per cent of the food it consumes and Japanese agriculture is beset by challenges. In Nishinomiya, continuing urban development is increasing waste and turning agricultural land to residential and industrial plots. LEAF launched the Mt. Kabuto Agriculture School in 2006 to encourage residents to cultivate rice and vegetables, to promote the links between agriculture, forestry, fisheries and consumers, and to deepen relationships between humans and the natural environment. The project is sponsored by several food processing companies, a waste management company, a co-operative society and a university. LEAF organises the school programmes, seminars and hands-on events such as cultivating land, planting rice and vegetables, harvesting and cooking to enable the participants to harvest foods and connect with the natural environment (Yoshizumi 2009).

Developing a participatory biodiversity strategy

Concerned by the impacts of increasing urbanisation, Nishinomiya announced an official biodiversity strategy in March 2012, which aims to conserve an environment that is home to 3,637 discrete species of plants and animals (City of Nishinomiya 2012). The strategy includes action plans for urban, mountain, riverside and coastal areas, implemented by various stakeholders in a partnership and applied according to the PDCA (plan-do-check-act) cycle.

Several projects have been conducted as a part of the action plans, starting with the campsite-based Urban *Satoyama* project. *Satoyama* refers to the traditional Japanese agricultural landscape, which includes a mosaic of ecosystems providing resources for human life, such as rice, grass to maintain soil fertility and feed animals, and wood for fuel and as a house-building material (UNU 2013). *Satoyama* also plays an important role in religious and cultural activities, while maintaining biodiversity and ecosystem services. The project aims to identify ecosystems and vegetation on Mt. Kabuto and to use natural resources sustainably, including using local timber as firewood for the campsite. The second project published a book that presented the results of an ecological assessment in Nishinomiya. The third project was the Nishinomiya Citizen Nature Survey, whereby local residents reported wildlife sightings that they charted on a website. From June 2013 to October 2013, 7,074 residents participated in the project.

Connecting the private sector to environmental learning programmes

To encourage collaboration between the public and private sectors, LEAF provides opportunities for corporations to become engaged in developing environmental learning programmes for students and residents. Activities have included the farming programme mentioned above and educational projects for school children. Based on LEAF's coordination, schools and companies have organised educational programmes focusing on each company's particular products, such as clothing, food, housing, energy, eco-friendly stationery and bottles. Private companies dealing with environmental management, such as recycling and waste treatment, also organise eco tours. Thus private companies are able to present children with an environmental message as part of their corporate social responsibility (CSR) activities, while promoting their businesses and connecting to local communities. The eco tours have also been conducted as training programmes for school teachers and local governmental officers in Nishinomiya. LEAF and private firms co-sponsor seminars and environmental learning programmes for elementary students. These have become increasingly popular, with approximately 90 companies now participating.

LEAF tries to involve the private sector in its activities to provide companies with CSR opportunities and also allay the costs. For example, LEAF has involved food, food processing and waste management companies in the farming experience programme. Moreover, LEAF has worked on the Child-Raising in the Forest Programme in partnership with a co-operative society and an insurance company. In the Koutou eco community, a waste collection company, a company that has developed waste collection vehicles with measuring instruments and a management consultancy worked with residents and local government to reduce household garbage.

Enhancing community initiatives

Nishinomiya sponsors a number of activities at the micro level in constituent communities to improve civic engagement for sustainability. One initiative is Eco Community Meetings, which are held in each of the city's 20 junior high school districts. The members of these meetings are leaders of various community groups, such as the environmental sanitation council and social welfare council, as well as ordinary residents, representatives of schools and local businesses and local government officers. LEAF acts as a facilitator. Each area is responsible for developing its own activities for a sustainable community and Nishinomiya city government provides a small grant of ¥100,000 (about US$840) per year for each area.

The initial activity is typically conducting a town watching session, whereby the residents walk around their own area to learn about the merits of their community, such as historic buildings, beautiful natural scenery and attractive shops. They formulate specific objectives and a community action plan towards a more sustainable community. Town watching is a learning process and therefore should not be a single action but a series of continuous actions.

After Nishinomiya held an Environmental Town Planning Workshop at eight sites to promote eco community activities in 2005, six eco communities were established and two eco communities were developed in 2006. Based on the experiences of the first eco community activities, the project was extended to other local communities. By January 2015, 20 eco communities in Nishinomiya had been established.

Also at the local level, Nishinomiya established three environmental learning centres: in a mountain area, the city centre and a coastal area. Each centre provides residents with information about environmental issues and serves as a community centre, where residents can communicate with their neighbours, members of LEAF and local government, and enjoy recreation and relaxation. Each centre conducts various activities, including environmental learning programmes for local schools and residents.

In November 2009, the Nishinomiya Financial Support Programme for Sustainable Community Development was established by the Chamber of Commerce and Industry of Nishinomiya, the Nishinomiya Rotary Club and LEAF. The programme provides financial support to eco community groups for their activities, based on the amount of Eco Action points stamped on Eco Cards and Civic Action Cards in each eco community.

Building multi-stakeholder and international partnerships toward ESD

As mentioned above, after the great Hanshin earthquake of 1995 it was difficult for Nishinomiya to continue providing learning programmes that focused only on the environment – it became necessary to link them to safety and social issues. Masayoshi Ogawa had previously coordinated with Nishinomiya city government to build multi-stakeholder partnerships and establish several partnership organisations, which expand the environmental learning programmes into ESD programmes to achieve a more sustainable Nishinomiya city. One of the organisations is the Environmental Plan Promotion Partnership Meeting, which consists of citizens, businesses, experts and city government. Nishinomiya established the ESD Promotion Council as a partnership organisation to promote the Nishinomiya ESD programme. Its members are: LEAF; the Nishinomiya City Social Welfare Council; the Nishinomiya Teachers' Union; the Chamber of Commerce and Industry of Nishinomiya; Kobe Co-op, a consumer cooperative; the Nishinomiya city government; the Nishinomiya Education Board; the Nishinomiya ESD Exploratory Committee and the Kobe Newspaper Company. Nishinomiya city government tries to promote partnerships among a number of stakeholders and especially encourages community participation.

Nishinomiya has also established the Nishinomiya Environmental Learning City Partnership with eco communities, an eco network and the Nishinomiya city government. The members of each eco community are the residents of each high school district mainly responsible for promoting environmental learning programmes and participatory town planning for sustainable development. The eco network is made up of school teachers and representatives of community groups, business sectors and the city government, and tries to develop a framework for the environmental learning city and ESD programmes. Moreover, an Environmental Learning Steering Partnership Council has also been established to coordinate the ideas and activities of the eco community, eco network and city government, carried out by environmental experts and leaders of community groups, business sectors and the city government.

Nishinomiya city government also develops projects to foster global youth partnerships. It organises the Junior Eco Club Asia-Pacific Conference each year. In addition, LEAF has created The Chikyu Kids Environmental Network, an online database of children's environmental activities around the world, spanning more than 80 countries. LEAF has also coordinated joint projects between Nishinomiya and Burlington, Vermont, USA. These have promoted education for sustainability through community partnerships.

The case studies of the eco community meeting activities have been used for training courses on developing capacity in sustainable community activities. These have been used in international cooperation projects funded by the Japanese International Cooperation Agency (JICA) and other foundations. LEAF has organised JICA-funded training programmes for students, government officers and researchers in Japan, Malaysia, Chile and some Pacific island states in addition to other training programmes in China, Vietnam, Korea and the USA. These international activities are not only for international cooperation but for increasing the motivation of local communities in Nishinomiya through discussion and working with people from around the world.

Since 2010, Nishinomiya has conducted a training programme for Asian students, Women Leaders Promoting ESD Based on the Local Community, initiated by Kobe College. In the programme, female students from Asian countries study ESD through internships and fieldwork in Nishinomiya.

Key factors for promoting community activities and building multi-stakeholder partnerships in Nishinomiya

This section discusses how Nishinomiya initiatives have been successfully implemented and explains the context for the community's strong efforts toward realising sustainable community development and building multi-stakeholder partnerships.

LEAF as a facilitator for building multi-stakeholder partnerships

LEAF was established in 1998 to promote environmental learning programmes in Nishinomiya through the initiative of the Environmental Learning City Promotion division of Nishinomiya city government. To achieve its stated goal of achieving sustainable community development and a sustainable society, LEAF coordinated with schools, local communities and private companies. To realise its goal, LEAF's approach involves: (1) establishing partnerships with various civic groups, the private sector and government agencies; (2) developing respect for the environment, including nature and culture; and (3) cultivating people's 'self-learning ability' so they can learn independently of educational institutions at home and in the community. Specifically, LEAF aims to establish a system that enables people who are relatively unconcerned with environmental issues to participate in environmental activities and city planning through various public events targeting a mass audience. Through its environmental learning and ESD activities, LEAF seeks to raise people's awareness of environmental issues and community development (LEAF 2013).

When it comes to public participation, governments often have conflicts with citizens and the private sector. When governments organise workshops and meetings with residents, the residents often either complain about government inactivity/mistakes or merely file a number of wish-list requests. However, in Nishinomiya, LEAF has successfully coordinated effective discussions between the city's government and its residents.

In addition, LEAF has coordinated not only environmental learning pro-grammes but also various community activities in relation to ESD. In particular, LEAF tries to involve many types of stakeholders and individuals. In Japan, as in many other countries, environmentalists may promote environmental activities but many citizens and private companies often hesitate to join in. However, LEAF lowers the barriers to participation in such activities for students, residents and companies through the Eco Card system, training seminars and enjoyable events, publicised through leaflets and other media, including online.

LEAF's engagement of a wide range of citizens has been a critical feature in implementing ESD. Young people and children, commonly viewed as the agents of behavioural change, are the typical targets of educational programmes. How-ever, LEAF's outreach has extended beyond to sectors of the workforce and the community. The seminars organised with private companies are effective in rais-ing the awareness of the students involved and also in helping employees become more environmentally conscious and aware of important elements of sustainable development, such as the close interaction between economic activities and social and environmental consequences. This creates mutual learning opportunities for students and corporate employees.

Information sharing

Nishinomiya has produced booklets, newsletters and websites to share inform-ation about community initiatives and environmental activities in the city. One of the websites is the Eco Community Bulletin Board (City of Nishinomiya 2015, http://info.leaf.or.jp/index.cgi), developed and operated by LEAF, which promotes a range of activities and reports on each Eco Community in Nishinomiya. The website shares information about past, current and planned activities in each area.

In addition, viewers can check their Eco Card points and Earth Ranger status, and share information on meetings, increasing residents' motivation to act.

LEAF also developed a website to share photos and information about farming activities and another site explaining the objectives, links between stakeholders and many activities affiliated with the ESD programme.

Increasing motivation for community activities

In Nishinomiya, several approaches are applied to increase the motivation of local communities, including the Eco Card system and websites. For example, the website for the Kotou Eco Community displays the rate of waste reduction and a comparison of performance in different neighbourhoods to encourage competition. Participation in events, such as town watching and farming, is easily accessible to all local residents and LEAF-sponsored newsletters, websites and workshops promote information sharing and lower barriers to first-time participation.

This approach encourages the participation of a range of stakeholders, thus avoiding a common pitfall for many ESD programmes, namely the lack of a common terminology, vision or clear channels of communication.

Conclusion

As mentioned in the introduction, multi-stakeholder partnerships and voluntary commitment to sustainable development have been recognised as key aspects in implementing a sustainable city (UN 1992, EC 1996, Ueta 2004). It is also recognised, however, that there are difficulties in achieving broad citizen participation and building multi-stakeholder partnerships. These barriers include participant conflicts, an unwillingness to take the initiative and feelings of negativity among residents, limited participation and the unsustainability of community activities. A case study of efforts in Nishinomiya provides several lessons to be learned.

First, Masayoshi Ogawa had initially coordinated within Nishinomiya city government to build multi-stakeholder partnerships and establish several organisations to develop environmental learning programmes into ESD programmes. At the beginning, Nishinomiya developed environmental learning programmes led by Masayoshi Ogawa. After the Hanshin earthquake, Nishinomiya connected the programmes to others and developed various kinds of community-based ESD programmes. These were designed to interest and involve students, teachers, parents, seniors, universities, governments, business sectors and other stakeholders in discussing and jointly addressing important local issues. The ESD programmes bring together previously uninvolved stakeholders so they can learn from each other and collaborate to work for sustainable community development. Through the ESD programmes, residents have learned about their local environment as well as local issues.

Second, it is clear there is a need for a group to play a facilitating and coordinating role to promote community development and build multi-stakeholder partnerships.

In Nishinomiya, LEAF plays an important role as a facilitator for sustainable community activities and a coordinator between communities and governments. LEAF brings together residents and governments, businesses, schools and community groups. It organises successive local meetings to allow the varied stakeholders to express their views, learn from each other and gain new understanding of one another's interests to help forestall the possibility of conflict. LEAF overcomes the institutional barriers that weaken business involvement in sustainable community development by promoting the benefits of participation, including sales promotion, improved ties with the government and schools, and improved communication with local residents.

Third, to coordinate various stakeholders, it is very important to share information. Nishinomiya disseminates news of the achievements of community development, such as waste reduction efforts and eco point activity, via newsletters, websites and other media to increase motivation of participants.

To replicate Nishinomiya's success, it is important to develop unbiased intermediaries, such as LEAF, to facilitate community activities, build multi-stakeholder partnerships, share information and coordinate various opinions. The LEAF founder, Masayoshi Ogawa, has said it is important to apply a long-term approach and develop sustainable activities that a range of actors can take part in.

LEAF's success is largely attributable to Masayoshi Ogawa but the NPO has tried to foster successors to facilitate LEAF and ESD programmes in Nishinomiya. LEAF has developed retirement and other staff benefits, commensurate with those of private companies, to attract top-class personnel to continue its operations. As of 2015, LEAF has six full-time employees with this benefit package and younger officers have taken over many of Masayoshi Ogawa's roles.

As mentioned above, Nishinomiya has disseminated its model not only domestically but also through several international cooperation programmes. International interns studying at Kobe College learn about local activities and can apply that knowledge when they return to their home countries. The shared activities enable local people to work together with international visitors, which boosts their motivation.

While this examination of Nishinomiya suggests several effective and highly feasible approaches for sustainable community development, further comparative study of community development in Japan and elsewhere could yield other interesting examples. A broad-based comparison may reveal common core elements for the design of successful community development programmes across varying local contexts.

References

Arnstein, S. R. 1969. A ladder of citizen participation. *Journal of the American Institute of Planners* 35 (4), 216–224.

City of Nishinomiya 2007. Nishinomiya ESD (in Japanese) (http://esd.leaf.or.jp/). Accessed 29 June 2015.

City of Nishinomiya 2012. *Miraini Tsunagu Seibutsu Tayousei Nishinomiya Senryaku ~ Ikimonotodeai, Fureai, Manabiai* (Nishinomiya strategy of biodiversity to pass on to the next generation). Nishinomiya, Japan: Nishinomiya city government.

City of Nishinomiya 2015. Environmental learning city Nishinomiya eco community bulletin board (http://info.leaf.or.jp/). Accessed 1 April 2015.

European Community (EC) 1996. European Sustainable Cities, Brussels, Expert Group on the Urban Environment, European Commission.

Learning and Ecological Activities Foundation for Children (LEAF) 2013. *Annual action report*. Nishinomiya, Japan: LEAF Press (in Japanese).

Ministry of Internal Affairs and Communications 2010. *Jouhou Komyunikeshon Hakusyo* (white paper on information).

Nakazawa A., Narumi K., Hisa T. and Tanaka A. 1995. *Nihon niokeru Juuminsankagata Machizukuriron no Hensen ni Kansuru Kenkyu 1970–94* (A study on change of research on participatory city planning in Japan 1970–94). *Proceedings of Annual Research Conference of Architectural Institute of Japan*, 627–628.

Recruit 2015. *Kansai sumitaimachi ranking* (ranking of the best city to live in for the Kansai area) (www.recruit-sumai.co.jp/data/150317_sumitaimachi2015kansai.pdf). Accessed 18 November 2015.

Rydin Y. and Pennington M., 2000. Public participation and local environmental planning: the collective action problem and the potential of social capital. *Local Environment* 5(2), 153–169.

Shinohara H. 1977. *Shimin Sanka* (public participation). Tokyo, Japan: Iwanami-shinsho.

Takahashi H. 2000. *Shimin Shutaino Kankyou Seisaku* (residents-driven environmental policy). Tokyo, Japan: Koujin-sya.

Ueta, K. 2004. *Jizokukanouna Chiiki Shakaino Dezain* (design for sustainable societies). Tokyo, Japan: Yuhikaku.

United Nations 1992. Agenda 21 (www.un.org/esa/sustdev/documents/agenda21/index.htm). Accessed 1 June 2015.

United Nations Department of Economic and Social Affairs (UNDESA) 2014. High-level political forum on sustainable development (https://sustainabledevelopment.un.org/content/documents/1312HLPF_Brief_3.pdf). Accessed 29 June 2015.

United Nations University Institute of Advanced Studies (UNU) 2013. *The International Partnership for the Satoyama Initiative (IPSI) formulation and development*. Yokoyama, Japan: United Nations University.

Yoshizumi M. 2009. Towards sustainable community development: education for sustainable development initiatives in Nishinomiya. *SANSAI: An Environmental Journal for the Global Community* 4, 45–65.

11 From challenge to opportunity

Japanese non-profit organisations harness post-3.11 civic engagement

Sarajean Rossitto

Introduction

The multiple disasters of 11 March 2011 (known as 3.11) resulted in a large inflow of resources and a surge in civic activity in a region of Japan facing both ongoing challenges and limited non-profit sector development. The response of Japanese non-profit, non-governmental organisations (NGOs) to the disasters was wide reaching but often constrained by insufficient capacity and the scale of the devastation. While problems have been the focus of many previous articles, some organisations that were active in Tohoku were able to convert challenges into opportunities for public engagement, capacity development and public image transformation. After an overview of the development of the non-profit NGO sector in Japan and the Tohoku context, this chapter will introduce the non-profit response and the impact of the disasters on sectoral development. The focus will then turn to two organisations, Peace Boat and Greenpeace Japan, that have harnessed the post-3.11 momentum to engage citizens and to foster expanded public dialogue on the issues of energy, disaster policy and sustainability. These organisations leveraged their strengths through rapid and innovative responses, providing positive examples from which other groups may learn.

Overview of the Japanese non-profit NGO sector

Although the development of the modern Japanese non-profit NGO sector is widely seen as dating from the 1995 Hanshin Awaji Earthquake (also called the Kobe Earthquake), the public has been active in various types of associations – including neighbourhood associations and local religious groups – since long before 1995. The first non-profit corporations – public benefit organisations (PBOs) – were established to benefit vulnerable members of society requiring specific support. They came into being in 1896 under the Japanese civil code and were under close government scrutiny. Given their reliance on government funds and staff, the status of these organisations as autonomous NGOs has been questioned (Simon and Irish 2004; Rossitto 2000). From the 1930s and through World War II, other types of civic organisations, including youth groups, religious organisations and workers' associations, were codified and centrally regulated by government bodies (Amenomori 1993).

The defeat in World War II, combined with the US occupation, allowed for the resurgence of civil society. After the war, private schools, social welfare organisations and religious organisations were able to apply for approval under new laws, although some degree of government control remained. Leftist sentiment, as expressed through workers' and teachers' movements, intensified until Cold War pressures caused the occupation to suppress them, resulting in many organised workers losing their jobs or being silenced for engaging in social reform activities (Amenomori 1993).

Citizens' groups flourished in the 1960s and 70s, focusing on quality of life and social issues associated with Japan's rapid economic development, which had led to increased air, water and noise pollution (Rossitto 2004). These civic organisations entered into lengthy court battles, seeking corporate and government redress in association with major environmental scandals such as Minamata disease, caused by mercury poisoning in chemical wastewater, and severe air pollution in the industrial city of Kawasaki. These cases eventually helped strengthen environmental laws, institutions and organisations and represent successful examples for Japanese civil society, despite a lack of broad public recognition.

In the 1970s and 80s, human rights organisations attempted to gain social parity for women, *burakumin* (a Japanese underclass) and residents of Korean and Chinese descent. Becoming a signatory to international human rights treaties put pressure on the Japanese government to develop concomitant domestic legislation ensuring rights protection. Japanese NGOs became adept at employing outside pressure by focusing international attention on contentious issues (Reimann 2005) such as gender inequality, when they pushed for the creation of the Equal Employment Opportunity Law to comply with the CEDAW, the Convention to Eliminate Discrimination Against Women (Rossitto 2000; JNNC 1996).

In the 1980s, the emergence of Japan as a major donor of overseas development assistance (ODA) helped catalyse NGO development as monies were channelled through Japanese NGOs (Osa 2013). Community leaders' efforts to develop a new system for NGO registration by lobbying Diet members and sponsoring public discussion culminated in the 1998 Specified Activities Non-Profit Corporation Law (the 'NPO Law'). This is widely seen as the first case of civil society actively promoting government policy change in Japan (see Pekkanen 2000 and Schwartz 2002). Original efforts focused on developing officially recognised mechanisms for volunteer activities. However, the new government registration system implied less government interference in non-profit activities than under the previous PBO Law, so it has also provided impetus for rethinking the role of citizens in community and policy formulation. The 1998 NPO Law set out guidelines and criteria for registration, allowing organisations to apply for tax exemption status at their discretion, but the arduous application process has resulted in fewer than 200 of the more than 40,000 registered organisations being granted such status (Government of Japan Cabinet Office 2010).

Even before the non-profit law, it was estimated that there were more than 1 million unincorporated organisations, including civic groups, children's groups, senior citizens' associations and neighbourhood associations (Imidas 99, 1999). After the enactment of the NPO Law, the number of organisations seeking official NPO recognition increased rapidly, peaking at about 500 organisations per month in 2003 (Government of Japan Cabinet Office 2004). By 2010, Japan had more than 40,000 registered non-profit organisations, 50 per cent of which had less than one full time staff member and an annual operating budget smaller than US$100,000 (Government of Japan Cabinet Office 2010). After the 2011 multiple disasters, there was another rapid increase in the number of new organisations. As of June 2015, more than 50,000 organisations have been incorporated under the NPO Law and the average number of full-time staff in each organisation has increased to four (Government of Japan Cabinet Office n.d.).

Tohoku, March 2011

Before the disaster, Tohoku was already a marginalised area facing many of the challenges common to rural areas in developed nations: a rapidly ageing population, economic stagnation, limited physical access to other parts of the country and a limited number of sizable civil society organisations.

The Tohoku economy is based on fishing and agriculture and, according to the 2010 census, about 30 per cent of the fishers and farmers are over 65 years of age. Ageing industries and limited job opportunities have resulted in an outward migration of young people seeking better education and job opportunities. Approximately 24.8 per cent of the population of Tohoku is over 65 years old, higher than the Japanese average of 23 per cent, and the percentage is even greater in the coastal towns that were most affected by the tsunami (Government of Japan 2010). Given the mountainous terrain of Tohoku, where villages are separated not only by mountains but also by inlets and small fishing bays, coastal villages are often difficult to access, resulting in the evolution of distinctive lifestyles, practices and dialects among the populations. These communities had operated quite autonomously and were unaccustomed to outside interference (Japan NPO Centre 2014).

Before 11 March 2011, there were limited numbers of registered civic organisations in north-eastern Japan. While neighbourhood associations have played an active role in community-based functions such as festivals, they are not autonomous from local government or business associations. Reliance on government agencies for most, if not all, social services and a traditional patriarchal local hierarchy have been the norm, resulting in limited space for autonomous civic activities. The multiple dimensions of the disasters, coupled with the influx of resources – including funds, goods and people – have caused dramatic and ongoing changes in the way these communities function (Japan NPO Centre 2014).

The triple catastrophes of earthquake, tsunami and nuclear meltdown that hit Tohoku affected several million people. Close to 500,000 people were evacuated, 15,890 died, 2,589 went missing and 6,152 were injured. As of March 2015, 228,863 Tohoku disaster evacuees still lived in temporary housing, including those in government-sponsored interim housing, those living with family or friends and those with other irregular tenure (Asian Disaster Reduction Centre 2015).

Government employees and elected officials in Tohoku were affected directly because many local government offices were destroyed or rendered non-functional and staff were often overwhelmed by the magnitude of the public need in addition to their own losses. The accidents at the Fukushima Daiichi nuclear plant, located between Tokyo and the areas worst affected by the earthquake and tsunami, slowed the response time and affected access given concerns about radiation and the lack of accurate information. The extent of the damage, exacerbated by the nuclear meltdown and Tohoku's pre-existing social problems – demographics, weak economy, poor accessibility and limited civil society – inhibited an efficient and effective initial response by the government, civil sector and the international community (Japan NPO Centre 2014).

2011 Tohoku disaster response by civil society organisations

Emergency relief phase

Immediately after the disasters, institutions and citizens within Japan and around the world initiated drives for necessities and funds. In the early stages of the response, most non-profit organisations focused on satisfying daily needs and then expanded to include physical rehabilitation, removing debris and protecting marginalised populations (Japan NPO Centre 2014).

Hundreds of organisations and citizens' groups responded, including Second Harvest Japan (2HJ), a Tokyo-based food bank, which provided food to temporary shelters, evacuation centres and residents living in the affected areas. This continued long after the emergency relief period concluded, totalling 225 deliveries of more than 25,000 food packages containing more than 1.5 million tons of food (2HJ 2015). Kyoto-based NICCO (Nippon International Cooperation for Community Development) provided 5,900 hot meals to more than 1,600 people, ran a mobile health clinic and monitored the conditions of the elderly with door-to-door visits. NICCO has supported 30,481 people through food and goods distribution, psycho-social care programmes, child protection activities, agriculture redevelopment and livelihood support projects. It has also assisted many others less directly through pest control and streetlight projects (NICCO 2013; Yeoh 2012a; Yeoh 2012b).

Given the vastness of the disaster-affected area, coordination, assessment and information sharing were challenging. The Japan Platform, founded in 1999 to ensure a coordinated and rapid response to humanitarian crises overseas, links NGOs with the business community and the Ministry of Foreign of Affairs (Japan Platform 2015). However, there was no similar structure in place for domestic disasters. Intermediary organisations, such as the Tokyo-based Japan NPO Centre (JNPOC), established in 1996 to support civic activities and promote the growth of the non-profit sector (Japan NPO Centre 2014), took the initiative because many of its community-based non-profit members lacked access to expert personnel and funding. JNPOC and Nagoya-based Rescue Stockyard, founded in 1996 to foster disaster volunteerism in Japan, took leading roles in developing a coalition of multi-sector actors. At its peak, the Japan Civil Network for Disaster

Relief in East Japan had more than 850 member organisations sharing information and expertise, more than 21 per cent of them from within the Tohoku region (Japan NPO Centre 2014). However, this was not a formal organisation with disaster management experts and so could not take the place of a highly endowed coordination agency.

Because domestic Japanese organisations often work within a specific community, Japanese and non-Japanese international NGOs (INGOs) with experience in humanitarian response were encouraged by the Japanese government and intermediary organisations to partner locally embedded organisations. Since the local organisations did not have the capacity for large-scale operations, these partnerships were crucial. Japanese INGO staff also faced challenges because, while they were experienced and skilled in humanitarian relief, many were not accustomed to providing a response in a developed nation or did not have professional experience in Japan. Given the insular nature of Tohoku, in some communities the disaster response expertise of INGOs was seen as not applicable. Other challenges arose because the domestic organisations lacked knowledge of standardised practices, such as stakeholder needs assessment, inclusion of diverse populations in programmes and programme assessment. This sometimes made it difficult for local organisations to access overseas resources or to develop equal partnerships with larger organisations.

Health and safety concerns after the nuclear disaster resulted in fewer organisations responding in Fukushima than in other areas. However, some chose to make Fukushima a priority. When staff from the Association for Aid and Relief Japan visited a local school in Minami-Soma in April 2011, they witnessed children being served meals consisting of a single slice of bread and water. Delivery trucks refused to bring food to the region and local food production halted because of radiation fears. The organisation stepped in, providing lunches for students and food packages for the elderly and disabled along with wheelchairs and other necessary equipment (Yeoh 2012b).

Recovery and redevelopment

The move from the evacuation centres to interim housing complexes started in mid- to late 2011, marking a shift in people's needs. Non-profit NGOs responded by focusing their efforts on community building, providing food, daily necessities and services in the transition from relief to recovery. To improve the limited access to fresh, healthy food and to provide employment income for residents, some organisations organised shuttle bus services and helped establish new businesses such as grocery stores and restaurants. Eat and Energize the East and IMPACT Foundation supported business expansion by marketing new products and sponsoring skills training (D. Takahashi, Chief Administrator, Eat and Energize the East, personal communication 2014; H. Nishida, Executive Director, Women to Women Japan, personal communication 2014).

To target the needs of people living in new communities of strangers, some groups sponsored socialisation activities to bring people together and foster a sense of community. NPO Aichi-Net started with community engagement, facilitating the annual summer festival in the Rikuzentakata area, approximately 155km north-east of Sendai. By working with residents, they learned that the disruption of rice farming had affected both the food supply and the sake industry. Aichi-Net collaborated with a local sake brewery and supported its product marketing through consumer cooperatives (Yeoh and Rossitto 2013).

Other non-profit organisations sought to facilitate dialogue between interim housing dwellers and local government and share ideas about redevelopment to promote new relationships and deepen personal connections. Pacific Asia Resource Centre Inter-People's Cooperation produced community newspapers providing information on business openings, transport, government hearings and reconstruction plans while also encouraging all to take part in redevelopment hearings with government officials (R. Inoue, Chair, PARCIC, personal communication 2014).

The interim housing did not always meet the needs of single mothers and those who were elderly, disabled or less mobile. Rescue Stockyard added handrails, wheelchair slopes, storage units and benches in interim housing to improve access and conditions for all residents (Yeoh 2012b).

However, meeting physical needs proved easier than meeting the psychological needs of the many residents who had lost loved ones. The range of psycho-social needs varied from socialisation support to professional psychiatric treatment. Given the stigma associated with mental illness in these traditional communities, many needy residents did not seek support. Some non-profit organisations provided access to professional mental health services, while many others set up social events. Concerned about individuals dying alone in isolation, volunteers and staff encouraged residents to keep track of their neighbours – particularly men – to prevent them from avoiding social contact for extended periods of time due to trauma, depression, alcoholism, loneliness or boredom (Inoue *et al.* 2014).

The suicide rate in May 2011 was 19 per cent higher in the disaster-affected areas than it was in May 2010 but this significant increase was not long lasting (National Police Agency 2011). The female suicide rate increased in the short term while the increase in the male suicide rate was more delayed – in the first two years after the disaster, suicides fell overall but started to increase after that (Orui *et al.* 2014). Mental health surveys in 2013 showed that 10.3 per cent of evacuees had experienced high levels of distress and 17.2 per cent were diagnosed with post-traumatic stress disorder – higher rates than those recorded in 2011 and 2012 (Ohto *et al.* 2015).

Some organisations continue to focus on meeting the basic needs of those still living in temporary housing, especially the most vulnerable people – the long-term unemployed, elderly poor women, female-headed households and people displaced by the Fukushima nuclear disaster (Y. Suzuki, Executive Director, Sanaburi Foundation, personal communication 2015). These needs persist and, while the government is ill-equipped to handle recovery alone, due to the scale and complexity of the impacts, the socio-economic and demographic problems that have existed since before the disaster cannot be solved by local or international non-profit NGOs.

Impacts on the non-profit sector

The disaster's magnitude affected the work, scale and nature of many non-profit organisations. In the three prefectures worst hit by the disaster, the number of registered non-profit organisations increased by 40–43 per cent, compared with a rate of 27 per cent in the country overall (Japan NPO Centre 2014). Other organisations were established as 'general associations' under a 2008 law whereby registration could be completed at a notary's office in just a few minutes (Coalition for Legislation to Support Citizens' Organisations (C's) n.d.). Because no annual reporting is required and no central agency is responsible for collecting data on these groups, data on these organisations is lacking (T. Hayasaka, accountant, personal communication 2014).

Following 3.11, the Coalition for Legislation to Support Citizens' Organisations (C's), an alliance of non-profit and grassroots organisations, created in 1994, that had been instrumental in campaigning for the 1998 NPO Law, applied pressure on the government to make it easier and faster to realise tax credits and tax-exempt status for organisations (C's n.d.; Rossitto 2004).

Household donations in Japan rose impressively after the disasters. Charitable donations from fiscal year (FY) 1995 through FY2010, based on self-reported data (see Figure 11.1), remained constant at approximately 3,000 yen per household per year, but the figure rose to 6,579 yen in FY2011 (Government of Japan. Japan Statistics Bureau1995–2010, 2011). Based on data derived from individual interviews, the Japan Funding Association's annual giving report 2011 found an average closer to 14,000 yen. Of those interviewed, 76.4 per cent reported making charitable donations in 2011 (Japan Fundraising Association 2011). However,

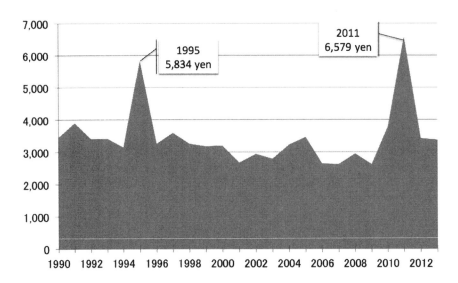

Figure 11.1 Household giving – annual donations (total)

Data source: Government of Japan Ministry of Internal Affairs and Communications 1995–2014.

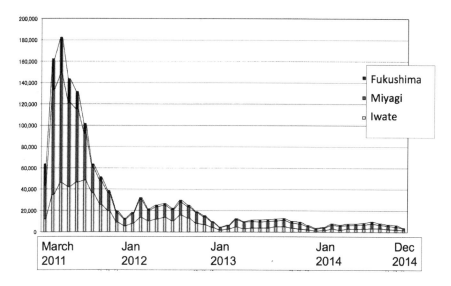

March 2011 to December 2014

Figure 11.2 Volunteering in the three worst-affected prefectures
Source: Government of Japan Disaster Volunteer Centre.

Tax Agency figures for FY2012 and FY2013 suggest that the increase in donations was short lived as average donations decreased to 3,400 yen per household.

It is not clear if a new wave of volunteerism has occurred because the data is neither consistent nor comprehensive. Disaster Volunteer Centres are set up by municipal Social Welfare Councils when a disaster strikes. They coordinate volunteer activity by linking people who want to volunteer with those who need volunteers to assist after a natural disaster. Their official data includes a calculation for 'volunteer days', indicating the number of days volunteers are placed. However, this only includes volunteer placements organised by the Disaster Volunteer Centres. Many large NPOs recruited volunteers in urban areas and online so they could carry out orientation, training and material preparation before dispatch to disaster sites. In addition, official data does not account for repeat volunteers because it measures days of work only. From 12 March 2011 to 31 July 2014 there were a total of more than 1.3 million volunteer days: 500,800 for Iwate Prefecture, 649,900 for Miyagi Prefecture and 186,000 for Fukushima Prefecture (Government of Japan Disaster Volunteer Centre 2014).

Volunteering data can be inconclusive on the question of long-term change in behaviour. In a 2012 Japanese Cabinet report on the status of NPOs, 27 per cent of the respondents said they had volunteered but only 3.2 per cent of them became interested in doing so after the 2011 disasters. A 2015 follow-up study showed only 0.1 per cent more people had volunteered over the past three years (see Figure 11.2).

It is too early to tell if the 2011 increases represent lasting changes in donor or volunteering behaviour or a short-term aberration. An increase of even 2 per cent in volunteering may bring about slow, sustainable change because an engaged population is more likely to be involved in charitable giving as well (Charities Aid Foundation of America 2014). Research done in 2013 by the Japan Funding Association indicated that people who volunteered tended to donate more (18,814 yen per person) than those who did not (11,161 yen per person). In some post-disaster contexts, volunteering stays at an increased level due to the expectations and character of those who become involved (Silva *et al*. 2009). This suggests we need to know more about the people who volunteer and what they hope to achieve in order to understand the long-term impact on civil society.

Environmental organisation case studies

In Tohoku, NGO activities were usually facilitated in coordination with government agencies (Leng 2015). In crisis situations where civic organisations work in concert with governments, sustainability and ongoing collaboration can contribute to the development of legitimacy and the capacity of civil society (Catholic Relief Services 2014). As people increasingly recognise the important role community organisations can play, their value rises and they assume visible and integral roles in the recovery process. By advocating for the people affected, they also gain public trust, becoming 'embedded in the public's psyche' (Choate 2011. See also Civicus 2013). This phenomenon can be seen in the rise in anti-nuclear sentiment and support for anti-nuclear groups after the Fukushima power-plant accidents as the public came to appreciate the important role civic organisations could and should play (Aldrich 2013).

After disasters, the inflow of resources – money, material and expertise – is often immense. For the Tohoku disaster, more than 160 nations provided more than US$1bn of support (Asian Disaster Reduction Centre 2015), including US$750m from the US alone (Japan Centre for International Exchange (JCIE) 2014). Local organisations with limited resources and/or experience had the opportunity to build their capacity by making use of this windfall.

Partnerships between local organisations and international humanitarian aid agencies provided opportunities for resource and capacity development. Knowledge and skills were shared to enhance future emergency response. Assessments conducted by Japanese non-profit organisations were made possible by international partners such as World Vision, Give2Asia and Mercy Corps. Lessons learned from collaboration and assessments led to the creation of policy recommendations for future disasters (Japan NGO Centre for International Cooperation (JANIC) 2013). Based on outcomes of the evaluation reports, training programmes attempted to meet the gaps in organisational capacity and individual skills by developing an understanding of the applicability of crisis response standards. The focus was on the value of standardised practices in needs assessment, inclusion of marginalised persons, security and safety, accountability to stakeholders and cash transfer programming as well as monitoring and evaluation (JANIC 2014).

The following case studies illustrate how Peace Boat and Greenpeace Japan, two organisations that were active both before and after the disasters in Tohoku, have been able to expand their programmes and approaches after 3.11 to engage the public more actively while linking with groups locally and internationally to improve local capacity.

Japanese INGO with a local partner: Peace Boat and Fukushima Action Project

Pre-disaster positioning in Japan

Peace Boat is a 30-year-old Japanese network of three separate but affiliated organisations. It was established by university students visiting countries in north-east Asia to develop better mutual understanding of their shared regional history in order to build a foundation for peace (Peace Boat 2015). Peace Boat the NGO focuses on the group's original aims of achieving peace and opposing nuclear power and nuclear weapons. Peace Boat ocean liner cruises circumnavigate the globe four times a year to promote understanding, involvement and peace. The organisation develops individual connections by sponsoring guest speakers, who embark or disembark at each port and speak on the theme of social justice.

The Peace Boat Disaster Relief Volunteer Centre (PBV) was established as a separate 'general non-profit association' in Ishinomaki, Miyagi Prefecture, for disaster response. While Peace Boat is generally regarded as a social movement organisation, since founding PBV it has expanded its profile by collaborating with a broader audience (T. Yamamoto, President, PBV, personal communication 2014). These organisations support and enhance each other's activities by drawing on local, domestic and international networks for information sharing, resource mobilisation and recruitment (M. Joyce, International Coordinator, Peace Boat, personal communication 2014).

Disaster activities

Although Peace Boat is not a humanitarian response organisation, it was able to draw on its long-established network, ability to activate and manage large numbers of volunteers and history of anti-nuclear activism to share information and mobilise volunteers in relief and recovery projects (Peace Boat 2011a; 2011b; 2011c). By the end of FY2013, PBV had recorded 87,500 volunteer work days, dispatching 14,759 people – including 3,510 non-Japanese from 56 nations and 8,288 people from 106 corporations, schools and other organisations – in PBV volunteer trips to Tohoku (Peace Boat 2015).

Building upon its network of experienced volunteers, PBV has developed a disaster training programme that develops the skills of volunteer leaders from across the country so that they are equipped to play a role in future disasters. As of spring 2015, more than 3,700 people have taken part in the volunteer training programme and 678 have become certified disaster volunteer leaders (Peace Boat 2015).

Themes for engaging the public

At the local, national and international levels, Peace Boat has been trying to stimulate public discussion on issues relating to energy, nuclear weapons and development. For example, in January 2012, in Yokohama, the group co-organised the Global Conference on a Nuclear-Free World to create a platform for a nuclear-free future and to build bridges between activists and ordinary citizens while promoting future leadership (Joyce, personal communication 2014).

The two-day event, the first of its kind in Japan, leveraged the momentum sparked by the disasters. Approximately 15,000 people – advocates, educators, members of youth and community groups, long-term activists and other concerned citizens – came together to share their thoughts. Half of the programme was devoted to workshops or discussion groups, creating a rare opportunity for members of the public to engage with environmental experts, nuclear experts and NGO leaders from around the world. It was the first time that groups opposing nuclear power and nuclear weapons had been brought together at a public event in Japan and the public was particularly receptive to these messages after the Fukushima disaster.

One of the outcomes of the conference has been the close collaboration between Peace Boat and the Fukushima Action Project (FAP), a local citizens' group comprising activists, residents and community leaders. Fukushima community leaders run the organisation and decide its direction, while Peace Boat continues to supply advice, technical assistance and occasional funding. FAP has focused on two areas – public engagement with government officials, and monitoring radiation levels and disseminating results (Joyce, personal communication 2014). Recently, FAP has begun focusing on the government's new educational curriculum in Fukushima schools, which, it believes, promotes the safety of nuclear power without explaining about radiation and the health risks (Joyce, personal communication 2014).

The global conference, FAP collaboration and volunteer programmes have been vehicles for engaging concerned citizens in dialogue and action, both domestically and internationally. Peace Boat has been able to improve its organisation-wide ability to regularly share information from overseas through seminars held in Japan and by developing materials about radiation, health issues, Fukushima updates and energy policy. At the international level, Peace Boat's participation in United Nations and international conferences enables it to share individual testimonies and involve FAP to ensure local voices are heard (Joyce, personal communication 2014).

PBV served as an organising partner for the Japan Civil Society Organisation Network, a coalition of more than 80 organisations, in preparation for the 2015 World Conference on Disaster Risk Reduction, held in Sendai in March 2015. The network aimed to share experiences of the multiple disasters to promote more disaster-resilient communities and to prepare for future disasters (Yamamoto, personal communication 2014). In collaboration with JANIC, Peace Boat played a key role in creating a booklet entitled *Ten Lessons From Fukushima*, which was disseminated at the conference.

Peace Boat's expertise and network allows it to raise awareness of contentious issues and encourage the public to transition from being distraught to being empowered to bring about change. Based on what was learned from the Tohoku disaster response and from Fukushima in particular, Peace Boat is publicising its model for activism, focusing on the importance of transmitting local experiences and knowledge through public engagement (Joyce, personal communication 2014).

INGO with a long-term presence in Japan: Greenpeace Japan

Pre-disaster positioning in Japan

Although Greenpeace Japan works on a wide variety of environmental issues, such as climate change, biodiversity and sustainable forest management, before 2011 it was mainly known in Japan for its anti-whaling campaign. Many Japanese regarded Greenpeace as a radical group that was generally critical of Japanese 'food culture'. However, this image does not reflect the fact that Greenpeace has served as a witness to environmental risks in more than 40 nations for more than 40 years. It employs non-violent direct action, advocacy and public education to inform the public, decision-makers and the media about environmental degradation. Such methods are sometimes not well understood in countries like Japan, where few organisations directly engage public dialogue to promote policy and social change (M. Reyes, COO, Greenpeace Japan, personal communication 2014). Since the 3.11 disasters, Greenpeace Japan has been focusing on three main campaigns: nuclear power and energy, seafood sustainability and sustainable agriculture.

Disaster activities

Greenpeace first focused its post-3.11 efforts on the Fukushima nuclear disaster but later broadened its efforts to issues more accessible to the public (Reyes, personal communication 2014; Greenpeace Japan 2014). Within days of the nuclear disaster, Amsterdam-based Greenpeace International dispatched experts to assist Greenpeace Japan with the monitoring of ocean radiation levels from a ship off the coast of Fukushima while also checking the terrestrial effects. Given the broad public concern and a lack of trust in the official government data, Greenpeace Japan was able to engage the public and media more directly than it had ever done before. Concerned that government radiation estimates were too conservative and were being released too slowly, Greenpeace Japan immediately shared its land and sea radiation readings with the government, media and general public (Reyes, personal communication 2014).

To increase public awareness, Greenpeace International has released several reports on the effects of the Fukushima disaster on the nuclear power industry, utility companies, energy and stock prices in Japan. It has also assessed the socio-economic and health impacts the disaster has had on the communities that depend on the nuclear power industry (Greenpeace Japan 2014). Greenpeace Japan has engaged policymakers, bureaucrats and corporate officials directly in dialogue on energy policy and nuclear power redevelopment. In sponsored public information sessions around the planned restart of the Sendai plant in Kyushu, Greenpeace Japan has shared information on evacuation and negotiation plans that had not been previously released to the general public. In 2014, Greenpeace Japan gathered 12,000 signatures in three weeks to a petition opposing the restart of Japan's nuclear power plants, which was an impressive response compared with the organisation's past experience in Japan (Reyes, personal communication 2014; Greenpeace Japan 2014).

Based on previous levels of public distrust, Greenpeace Japan decided to rely on volunteers rather than regular staff to deliver information to the public. For example, volunteers compiled local press advertisements promoting nuclear power and published them in a book to raise public awareness of pro-nuclear promotional tactics. Greenpeace Japan continues to monitor radiation in Fukushima and to publicise its findings through events and social media to keep the issue in the spotlight (Reyes, personal communication 2014).

Themes for engaging the public

Another recent Greenpeace Japan initiative involves advocating for changes in fishing policy to protect against over-fishing and dwindling fish stocks while informing and educating the public and working with producers. This is part of a broader regional campaign in north-east Asia that is being conducted in coordination with other NGOs, corporations and governments. In 2011, a Greenpeace Japan poll indicated that most Japanese respondents preferred to eat seafood that was sustainably fished to ensure that there would be healthy ocean and freshwater fisheries for the future. Respondents also wanted food labels to indicate fish species and sources more specifically to help them make more informed choices. In 2011, Greenpeace Japan released its first seafood ranking guide, listing fish species in danger of extinction, and then expanded the campaign to educate the public on seafood safety issues (Reyes, personal communication 2014; Greenpeace Japan 2014).

Greenpeace Japan is also using digital media in the hope that educated consumers will use their economic power to exert pressure on the fishing industry. The Green Shopping Guide is a smart-phone application that enables consumers to check the sustainability of different seafood products (Greenpeace Japan 2014).

Greenpeace is educating producers by involving corporations and representatives of fishers' cooperatives in dialogue to promote sustainable seafood practices. Whereas three years ago many corporations and fishers' associations would have refused a meeting, representatives now reportedly reach out to Greenpeace Japan for advice on improving sustainability practices (Reyes, personal communication 2014; J. Sato, Executive Director, Greenpeace Japan, personal communication 2015).

Since 2014, Greenpeace has been advocating for a national sustainability policy for all seafood sold in Japanese stores, with a primary focus on those fished and raised in Japanese waters. Greenpeace Japan conducted an investigation into the fish sold at supermarkets and ranked them based on five categories: 1) recognition of over-fishing; 2) procurement policy; 3) traceability, including fishing method and distribution channels; 4) information disclosure on environmental impacts; and 5) information on the sustainability of seafood used in seafood products (such as canned tuna or prepared foods) (Greenpeace International 2012). A leading Japanese nationwide department store, Aeon, is reported to be phasing in a more inclusive sustainability policy for seafood after consulting Greenpeace about the company's systems (Reyes, personal communication 2014; Sato, personal communication 2015).

Greenpeace Japan is also part of a global campaign on food sustainability aimed at ending the use of harmful chemicals in agriculture. Drawing on a growing public interest in food safety, Greenpeace Japan is focusing on the damaging effects of agrichemicals on health and biodiversity, and is promoting citizen pressure to change Japanese standards for toxins and harmful chemicals in pesticides and fertilisers as well as to reduce their use overall. Greenpeace Japan asserts that the Japanese public has become more interested in this campaign since 3.11 (Reyes, personal communication 2014; Sato, personal communication 2015).

Greenpeace Japan continues to promote civic action for health, food safety and sustainability, while recognising the economic interests of the energy, fishing and agricultural sectors. It hopes to change policy so that the sectors are more accountable to the public and practices are more transparent and compliant with international standards. These campaigns promote a more positive image in a society that formerly considered Greenpeace to be overly confrontational.

Both organisations, Peace Boat and Greenpeace Japan, have garnered media and public attention, promoting positive messages aimed at engaging the public to create a better future. Building on the post-3.11 momentum, they have developed new networks and built trust for future campaigns while empowering the participants in their capacities as consumers and citizens.

Conclusion

The case studies above illustrate how disaster responses can lead to enhanced public engagement, organisational capacity and expanded public awareness of issues as well as civil society organisations. Both Peace Boat and Greenpeace Japan have aimed to engage and empower individuals to be citizen activists acting for sustainability by transforming policy around energy, seafood safety and disaster risk reduction. Both organisations used the heightened interest in the environment, health and government accountability after 3.11 not only to transform their public image but also to engage broader sections of society in more issues.

It may be too soon to tell if the increased involvement by the public as volunteers or donors will bring about deep or lasting changes – the greatest challenge may be in maintaining the momentum as the events of 3.11 fade from the media gaze and public attention. Many may feel that the main disaster issues have been resolved, not realising that more than 200,000 people are still displaced.

Organisations like Peace Boat and Greenpeace Japan will need to continue sharing the experiences of people who are unable to forcefully represent their own interests, in order to help the general public make connections between sustainable recovery, sustainable energy policy and sustainable living. Perhaps this public mobilisation, rather than the occurrence of the disasters, will be the catalyst for the next phase of development in Japan's non-profit sector. Such engagement will be necessary to address pressing social problems, such as gender inequity, an ageing society, mental health and poverty.

References

Aldrich, D. P. 2013. Rethinking civil society–state relations in Japan after the Fukushima accident. *Northeastern Political Science Association Polity* 45(2), 249–264. (http://works.bepress.com/daniel_aldrich/25). Accessed 5 July 2015.

Amenomori, T. 1993. *Defining the non-profit sector: Japan. Working papers of the Johns Hopkins Comparative Non-Profit Sector Project.* Baltimore, US: The Johns Hopkins Institute for Policy Studies.

Asian Disaster Reduction Centre 2015. Tohoku disaster data (www.adrc.asia/nationframe.php?URL=./view_disaster_jp.php?NationCode=2011/03/11&lang=jp&KEY=1497). Accessed 2 July 2015.

Catholic Relief Services 2014. Understanding community perceptions of resilience (crsprogramquality.org). Accessed 5 July 2015.

Charities Aid Foundation of America 2014. World Giving Index 2014 (www.cafamerica.org/media/wgi-2014). Accessed 30 June 2015.

Choate, A. 2011. In face of disaster, Japanese citizens and government pull from lessons learned. *The Asia Foundation* (http://asiafoundation.org/in-asia/2011/03/16/in-face-of-disaster-japanese-citizens-and-government-pull-from-lessons-learned/). Accessed 30 June 2015.

Civicus 2013. The state of civil society 2013: creating an enabling environment (http://socs.civicus.org/?page_id=4289). Accessed 5 July 2015.

Coalition for Legislation to Support Citizens' Organisations (C's) n.d. (www.npoweb.jp). Accessed 15 August 2015.

Government of Japan 2010. Census. Japan Statistics Bureau 2013 (www.stat.go.jp/data/topics/topi672.htm). Accessed 26 February 2015.

Government of Japan Cabinet Office n.d. NPO Home page (www.npo-homepage.go.jp). Accessed 15 August 2015.

Government of Japan Cabinet Office 2004. Report on the status of non-profits and tax exemption. Tokyo, Japan. Accessed 26 September 2010 from previous version of website www.npo-homepage.go.jp/.

Government of Japan Cabinet Office 2010. Report on the status of non-profits and tax exemption. Tokyo, Japan. Accessed 26 September 2010 from previous version of website (www.npo-homepage.go.jp/).

Government of Japan Disaster Volunteer Centre 2014. (www.saigaivc.com/%E3%83%9C%E3%83%A9%E3%83%B3%E3%83%86%E3%82%A3%E3%82%A2%E6%B4%BB%E5%8B%95%E8%80%85%E6%95%B0%E3%81%AE%E6%8E%A8%E7%A7%BB/). Accessed 3 October 2014.

Government of Japan Statistics Bureau 1995–2010. 2011. (www.stat.go.jp/data/topics/topi672.htm). Accessed 1 March 2012.

Government of Japan Ministry of Internal Affairs and Communications 1995–2014. *Tōkei-kyoku* (statistics bureau) Family Income and Expenditure Survey (www.stat.go.jp/data/topics/topi672.htm). Accessed 26 February 2015.

Greenpeace International 2012. Lessons from Fukushima (www.greenpeace.org/international/en/publications/Campaign-reports/Nuclear-reports/Lessons-from-Fukushima/). Accessed 2 October 2014.

Greenpeace Japan 2014 (www.greenpeace.org/japan/ja/news/blog/staff/br/blog/50770/) (www.greenpeace.org/japan/ja/news/blog/staff/1024/blog/51009/). Accessed 2 October 2014.

Imidas 99, 1999. *NGO no kiiwado, shimin katsudou, Kokuren to kokusai kikan*, (NGO key words, civil society, the UN and international agencies). Tokyo, Japan:Asahi Shinbunsha.

Inoue, M., Matsumoto, S., Yamaoka, K. and Muto, S. 2014. Risk of social isolation among Great East Japan Earthquake survivors living in tsunami-affected Ishinomaki, Japan. *Disaster Medicine and Public Health Preparedness* August 8 (4), 333–40. doi: 10.1017/dmp.2014.59. Epub 2014 Jul 21. PMID: 25046222 (www.ncbi.nlm.nih.gov/pubmed/25046222). Accessed 30 June 2015.

Japan Centre for International Exchange (JCIE) 2014. JCIE special report: US giving for Japan disaster reaches $730 Million (http://2011disaster.jcie.org/philanthrophy/usgiving-2014/). Accessed 3 October 2014 and 30 June 2015.

Japan Fundraising Association 2011. Giving Japan 2011. White paper. Tokyo.

Japan NGO Centre for International Cooperation (JANIC) 2013. Presentation on NGO Response to the 2011 Great East Japan Earthquake. Tokyo.

Japan NGO Centre for International Cooperation (JANIC) 2014. Joint review report on humanitarian response to the 2011 Great East Japan Earthquake. Tokyo.

Japan NGO Network for CEDAW (JNNC) 1996. The summary report of the NGOs in Japan (www.jaiwr.org/jnnc). Accessed February 2000.

Japan NPO Centre 2014. NPO capacity development project. Project evaluation report. Tokyo.

Japan Platform 2015 (www.japanplatform.org/). Accessed 2 February 2015.

Leng R. 2015. Japan's civil society from Kobe to Tohoku: impact of policy changes on government-NGO relationship and effectiveness of post-disaster relief. *Electronic Journal of Contemporary Japanese Studies* 15(1): Article 2 (www.japanesestudies.org.uk/ejcjs/vol15/iss1/leng.html). Accessed 30 June 2015.

National Police Agency 2011. Monthly Suicide Report, May. As reported by the *Mainichi* Newspaper, 21 June 2011.

Nippon International Cooperation for Community Development (NICCO) 2013. Annual report (www.kyoto-nicco.org/whatisnicco/nicco2.html). Accessed 5 July 2015.

Ohto, H., Maeda, M., Yabe, H., Yasumura, S. and Bromet, E. E. 2015. Suicide rates in the aftermath of the 2011 earthquake in Japan. *The Lancet Correspondence* 385, 2 May (www.thelancet.com). Accessed 30 June 2015.

Orui, M., Harada, S. and Hayashi, M. 2014. Changes in suicide rates in disaster-stricken areas following the Great East Japan Earthquake and their effect on economic factors: an ecological study. *Environmental Health and Preventive Medicine* 19(6), 459–466.

Osa, Y. 2013. The growing role of NGOs in disaster relief assistance in East Asia, in Sukma R., and Gannon J. (eds) *A growing force*. New York, US: Japan Centre for International Exchange US (JCIE), 66–89.

Peace Boat Disaster Relief Volunteer Centre 2011a. Post-disaster programme report. Presented at Tohoku Rebuilding Japan conference. Temple University, Japan Campus–US Embassy, Japan collaborative event, 17 July.

Peace Boat Disaster Relief Volunteer Centre 2011b. 2011 Great East Japan Earthquake and tsunami: Peace Boat emergency relief operation. Peace Boat Disaster Relief Volunteer Centre (http://peaceboat.jp/relief/wp-content/uploads/2011/05/Tohoku-kanto-Relief-Apr21-eng.pdf). Accessed 30 June 2015.

Peace Boat Disaster Relief Volunteer Centre 2011c. Peace Boat 2011 Great East Japan Earthquake and tsunami midterm report. Peace Boat Disaster Relief Volunteer Centre (http://peaceboat.jp/relief/wp-content/uploads/2011/04/Ishinomaki-midtermreport.pdf). Accessed 30 June 2015.

Peace Boat Disaster Relief Volunteer Centre 2015. Annual report 2014 (http://pbv.or.jp/wp_en/wp-content/uploads/2014/09/2014-PBV-ANNUAL-REPORT-WEB.pdf). Accessed 30 June 2015.

Pekkanen, R. 2000. Japan's new politics: the case of the NPO Law. *The Journal of Japanese Studies* 26(1), 111–148.

Reimann, K. D. 2005. Gender and human rights politics in Japan: global norms and domestic networks by Jennifer Chan-Tiberghien, book review. *Pacific Affairs* 78(1), 138–139 (www.findarticles.com/p/articles/mi_qa3680/is_200504/ai_n14716220). Accessed 1 December 2008.

Rossitto, S. 2000. Development of Japanese non-profit NGOs. Presentation to Harvard conference on Japan studies, Harvard University, Cambridge, US, 8 April.

Rossitto, S. 2004. *NPO Seitei no katei to sonojyuyosei* (The significance of the process of the NPO Law development), in *Puro to shite NPO de hataraku, kakawaru: beikoku NPO intanshippu no kachi* (The value of US non-profit internships: working and committing oneself professionally to non-profit organisations). JUCEE, Tokyo, Japan: Shinpusya Publications, 16–17.

Schwartz, F. 2002. Civil society in Japan reconsidered. *Japanese Journal of Political Science* 3(2), 195–215.

Second Harvest Japan (2HJ) 2015. Annual report 2014. Available from http://2hj.org/english/about/pdf/ENG_2HJAR_2014_fix.pdf.

Silva J., Marks, L. D., and Cherry, K. E. 2009. The psychology behind helping and pro-social behaviours. In K.E. Cherry (ed.) *Coping with Katrina, Rita, and Other Storms*. New York, US: Springer-Verlag, 219–240.

Simon, K. W. and Irish, L. E. 2004. Legal and tax reforms for *Koeki Hojin*: discussion and comparative analysis (www.iccsl.org/pubs/reportforjapan.pdf). Accessed 30 June 2015.

Yeoh, G. 2012a. *Lessons learned from the March 11, 2011 disasters in Tohoku*. San Francisco, US: Give2Asia.

Yeoh, G. 2012b. *One year later: a report to donors and stakeholders*. San Francisco, US: Give2Asia.

Yeoh, G. and Rossitto, S. 2013. *Japan earthquake and tsunami disasters two years later: a report on ongoing recovery work*. San Francisco, US: Give2Asia.

12 A radical approach from the periphery

Informal ESD through rights recovery for indigenous Ainu

Fumiko Noguchi

Introduction

The path to sustainable development should start at the local community. Any theories and concepts for achieving stainable development are meaningless unless they are contextualised in real life at the community level. Ideas and concepts for sustainable development are realised only when people learn them by acting in a real-life context (Chris 1996; Fien and Tilbury 2002). Global organisations have also recognised the importance of taking a community-based approach such as Local Agenda 21, the UN-sponsored action plan for local autonomies.

International law and policy has also supported multi-stakeholder participation in development for a long time, as clarified by the 1986 Declaration on the Right to Development: 'Development is a process that aims at improved well-being of the entire population and of all individuals on the basis of their active, free and meaningful participation in development and in the fair distribution of benefits resulting therefrom' (UN General Assembly 1986). Marginalised people, in particular, must be at the centre of the search for sustainable development. Marginalised people are those who mainly bear the burden of being repressed historically, culturally and economically by those wielding power. In her 'endogenous development theory', Kazuko Tsurumi presented the goal of development as being 'no one's exclusion'. According to Tsurumi, the ultimate goal of endogenous development is to seek a process that will decentralise the system and create small mandala-like networks at the local level (a mandala symbolically represents the universe in Buddhist philosophy). She wrote that 'no one is excluded and no one is killed in the process of bringing the marginalised into the centre of each mandala' (Tsurumi 1999, 59). Tsurumi was trying to posit a non-western, non-violent model based on the history, traditions and ecological circumstances of a society at the grassroots level. She argued that repositioning the members of a society could transform the social system.

In reality, however, rapid economic development and modernisation have further marginalised already marginalised peoples. They are often the hardest hit by development-linked problems, such as rising inequality and industrial pollution, and are the most vulnerable to major crises such as wars, conflict and natural disasters. They are marginalised during the development process, where those in power, such as governments of colonising nations or developed countries, often make decisions. In any effort to achieve sustainable community development, a marginalised-people-centred approach is essential to share the burdens that marginalised people bear individually with all members of society. At the same time, marginalised people also need to be empowered to enable them to respond to the injustice they have suffered and its causes, so they can regain the rights and dignity they have lost. The process of social transformation is inevitably radical. It might present challenges of which most members of society or government are not aware or do not even want to admit are problems. It accompanies resistance, discomfort and pain, not only for the marginalised but also for the majority of society. However, without undergoing this process, no sustainable development can be achieved.

Educators have long drawn on the work of critical theorists such as Habermas to argue that environmental education (EE) and education for sustainability (EfS) can play a role in social transformation (Fien 1993; Huckle 1993; Huckle 1996), and this understanding is incorporated in the Education for Sustainable Development (ESD) concept (Hopkins 2012; Tilbury and Cooke 2005). ESD, by its very definition, aims to achieve social transformation through education. It aims to create 'a world where everyone has the opportunity to benefit from education and learn the values, behaviour and lifestyles required for a sustainable future and for positive social transformation' (UNESCO 2005), promoted through all forms of education through a life-long process, including formal, non-formal and informal education. Stakeholders from all fields and backgrounds can participate in the ESD movement. The value of ESD is shown when it broaches radical ideas that the majority do not want to face or question.

However, although ESD is, by nature, driven from the bottom up and centres on those who are marginalised, concepts like 'marginalised-people-driven' and 'radical' tended to be avoided in ESD policy implementation during the UN Decade of Education for Sustainable Development (UNDESD: 2005–2014). The UNDESD focused predominantly on formal education (schools and higher education) through a top-down approach (UNESCO 2012; 2014). It provided most of its funding and human resources for formal education and supported the establishment of a network and projects in the area of formal education, such as the UNESCO Associated School Project, the Promotion of Sustainability in Postgraduate Education and Research Network (ProSPER.Net) in Asia, Regional Centres for Expertise and the European Network on Higher Education for Sustainable Development (Copernicus Alliance).

Such imbalance in policy implementation has restricted the scope of ESD and promoted silence rather than calls for dramatic change. The UNDESD failed to integrate those community development stakeholders who are not in the education field but take community empowerment as the foundation of their efforts for sustainable community development. These stakeholders have also found that ESD prioritises formal and non-formal education, which has little relevance to their work. As suggested by Wals and Huckle (2015), without the involvement of these community development actors, the UNDESD was unsuccessful at redirecting ESD to address global realities.

What have been silenced are efforts that could be categorised as informal education in the community development field, conducted mainly by non-governmental and non-educational organisations. These stakeholders often tackle the problems that international and governmental educational organisations cannot address or may be reluctant to engage with as a result of political preferences and economic pressure. Because of its direct link with problems in a real-life context, informal education in a community development context can embody *praxis* (Freire 1972), which has been argued as being at the heart of critical approaches to environmental education and education for sustainability for the past 20 years (Fien 1993; Huckle 2002; Fien and Tilbury 2002).

According to Inoue and Imamura (2012), 'the debate on "sustainability" and "sustainable society" in environmental education can be realised only when the educators intervene in areas of effort that are often regarded as radical'. This assertion can be applied more broadly to ESD. How can ESD step into a radical area to engage effectively with the issues that humans face around the world? It is worthwhile to explore what has been left out so far.

This chapter reports on one ESD effort in this often overlooked area. It is an attempt to explore the role and meaning of ESD through the work of Mopet Sanctuary Network (MSN), a non-governmental organisation (NGO) seeking to achieve sustainable community development in Hokkaido, Japan. MSN was formed in 2009 to achieve sustainable community development by linking with the human rights recovery of the Ainu, an indigenous people of Japan. This chapter examines the period from the establishment of MSN until 2011. In particular, it shows how the problems facing one Ainu fisherman were shared with people in the wider community, and it investigates how residents learned and changed through this process, thus suggesting the significance and the role of informal ESD. This study employs critical ethnography, which takes the phenomenological approach of interpretive ethnography, as its method (Carspecken 1996). The chapter tries to understand the informal learning process of residents, marginalised people and community educators through their struggles and dilemmas in dealing with the issues of power, while aiming to bridge macro–micro gaps between current political and theoretical discourses on ESD and global and local practice, for both researchers and the participants.

Ainu people in the colonial history of Hokkaido

To achieve sustainable development in Hokkaido, it is essential to foster the participation of the Ainu people and recover their human rights. The Ainu people are the indigenous people of Japan, who lived in the Ainu *Mosir* ('Ainu's land' in the Ainu language) or *Ezo-chi* ('foreigners' land' in Old Japanese), the area currently encompassing Hokkaido, the Chishima (Kurile) Islands and Sakhalin. They have their own language, traditions and lifestyle, which are historically, culturally and physiologically distinct from those of the Japanese. Their land was colonised and possession divided as a result of negotiations during the latter part of the nineteenth century to determine the national border between Japan and Russia.[1] Subsequently, Ainu *Mosir* was named 'Hokkaido' by the Japanese government, which promoted modernisation and development of the region. The assimilation policy was continued until 1995.[2] Official recognition of the Ainu as an indigenous minority came about only recently, in 2008.[3] Under colonisation, their land was appropriated by Japanese settlers and all aspects of their culture were denied. They lost the right to access natural resources, including staple foods such as salmon and deer. Many issues created by the assimilation policy remain outstanding, including the provision of official apologies and compensation by the government, Ainu poverty, discrimination, the perceived need to hide one's identity, low self-esteem, endangered language and traditional knowledge and fragmented social and community ties (Yoshida 2011).

The sustainable development movement in Mombetsu

The sustainable community development movement in Mombetsu is rooted in the concerns of an Ainu fisherman, Satoshi Hatakeyama. Hatakeyama was born in 1943 and grew up facing poverty and discrimination. After dropping out of middle school, he hid his indigenous identity and worked as a fisherman. It was through his daily fishing activities that he became increasingly concerned about the negative impacts on the unique ecosystem in the Okhotsk region of industrialisation and commercialised large-scale fishing practices. He observed marine pollution, dumping of waste, malformation of fish and decreasing amounts of drifting sea ice year by year, caused by climate change. While coming to realise that these environmental problems were primarily caused by Japanese-initiated development, he became increasingly interested in his Ainu indigenous background. Hatakeyama was especially interested in the traditional Ainu value system, based on respect for nature, and how his people used natural resources sustainably. This was in contrast to the Japanese approach to development that had destroyed nature and decimated the Ainu people.

His concerns about local ecological problems, linked with indigenous rights issues, motivated him to publically reveal his indigenous identity as Ainu in the 1980s. When Hatakeyama turned 50 years old, he took the position of the chair of the Mombetsu Chapter of the Hokkaido Ainu Association, gaining the opportunity to link his journey in search of the meaning of Ainu rights recovery with his identity as a fisherman with wider local community interests.

Hatakeyama's main objective has been substantive rights recovery, or the recovery of rights granted by natural and substantive law, based on a holistic understanding of Ainu culture. He wanted to know what indigenous rights mean in a real-life context – in his case, in terms of his livelihood of fishing, not merely as words in legal documents. After he publicly proclaimed his indigenous identity, Hatakeyama began to study and learn from books and elders about the inter-relationship between cultural values, knowledge and practices and economic and social relationships. He reconnected then-fragmented information and his life experience as a fisherman. Hatakeyama developed his concerns about Ainu rights to access natural resources, such as salmon and whales.

Hatakeyama has been critical of the Japanese government's Ainu cultural promotion policy, which tends to further a narrow understanding of Ainu culture as mainly encompassing music, art, dance and craft.[4] Saying: 'I am a fisherman; I cannot dance or do embroidery', Hatakeyama argues it is the Japanese, not the Ainu, who determine these policies, which strongly reflect a Japanese view of Ainu culture. This bias has constrained the Ainu from establishing livelihoods based on indigenous values and economic self-sufficiency. Hatakeyama believes the concept of substantive rights recovery extends to achieving social transformation and that indigenous rights cannot be recovered without transforming Japanese society, which has colonised the Ainu people and developed Hokkaido to the benefit of Japanese economic and political interests.

He also started to study the indigenous rights to fish salmon and whales and advocated for indigenous fishing rights to the Japanese government, Hokkaido municipal government and Mombetsu local government. In 2000, he initiated a revival of the *Kamui Chep-nomi* at the Mombetsu River, an indigenous ceremony that welcomes the return of the sacred salmon to their original river in autumn before the salmon fishing season starts. This ceremony and fishing practice had been lost for many years – the ceremony was banned under the assimilation policy and the Japanese government prohibited salmon fishing and deer hunting to protect Japanese commercial interests. Furthermore, river fishing in general was strictly regulated by the law (Fisheries Agencies of Japan 1949).

In 2005, a critical event pushed Hatakeyama's Ainu rights recovery advocacy into the limelight. The local government decided to stop accepting industrial waste at the public landfill site because it estimated the existing site would be full within a few years. The food manufacturers' association, farmers' union, animal husbandry union and dairy union had to pay a fee to dispose of their waste in a waste management plant outside Mombetsu city. These industry groups put pressure on the local government and called for the construction of an industrial waste management plant in the city. The local government responded positively to this request, claiming it would help revitalise economic activity in the city. It planned the construction of a 41-hectare industrial waste management plant on a mountainside in the Toyooka district, which is the watershed area for the Mombetsu River, where Hatakeyama had been hosting the *Kamui Cep-nomi*. In 2007, the Hokkaido municipal government permitted the Mombetsu city government to construct the waste management plant.

Articulating what is necessary for ESD

Hatakeyama's individual activism took a major turn when, in 2008, he met a community educator, Masahiro Koizumi of Sapporo Free School '*You*' (SFY) in Sapporo, Hokkaido. Koizumi invited Hatakeyama to a workshop to share his knowledge of sustainable development issues in Hokkaido. Hatakeyama shared his life story and his concerns about indigenous rights issues linked to local sustainable development, particularly the construction of the industrial waste management plant in the Ainu ceremony area. His story inspired Koizumi and the other participants to plan a study tour to Mombetsu in 2009 to learn more about the issue. I went on this study tour and, since then, have joined Koizumi in committing to support Hatakeyama's activism while seeking to formulate the role of ESD in an informal, community development context. The 2009 tour activities included interviews with various local stakeholders, including local history and environmental conservation groups, Mombetsu City Museum and the Okhotsk Sea Ice Museum of Hokkaido, to understand Hatakeyama's concerns in the social, historical, economic and environmental context of Mombetsu.

The tour experiences helped us identify two major gaps in the residents' knowledge. The first concerned local historical knowledge. Japanese formal education and non-formal education at museums focus mostly on the history of Hokkaido after Japanese settlement and development promoted by the Meiji government in the nineteenth century. The area's ancient archaeological history is acknowledged in formal and non-formal education; however, Ainu history after colonisation was missing from the understanding of local history. Second, there are gaps in the knowledge of humans' relationship with nature. The rich biodiversity and unique climate of the Okhotsk Sea region have been widely appreciated by local residents. However, the local environment was mainly studied and understood by nature conservation groups and educators of the Okhotsk Sea Ice Museum of Hokkaido, who tend to understand the result of impacts on nature through scientific surveys, such as the study of sea ice change and ecosystem changes. Significantly, there was no way for local Ainu residents, who had a rich knowledge of local natural ecosystems and had adapted their practices to the local environment, to contribute to this knowledge base. Nature was regarded locally either as a resource (for example, when studying the history of the first settler fishermen) or as something to be observed or studied objectively. The lack of Ainu educational content and the long-standing assimilation policy were the main causes of these omissions. Ainu history is not taught in the schools and local Ainu elders have not prioritised passing their knowledge and memory on to the next generation. Traditionally, Ainu knowledge was passed on orally so today there is very little knowledge remaining to fill these gaps.

Sharing minority concerns with the wider community

Despite continuing efforts, Hatakeyama often struggled. He could reach very few people, in or outside Mombetsu, who shared his concerns. It was not easy to gain an understanding of his concerns from Japanese lacking knowledge of local Ainu history, or even from Ainu people affiliated with the Mombetsu Chapter of the Ainu Association of Hokkaido, who preferred to remain silent rather than raising issues based on a painful history of injustice that they wanted to forget. He also confronted the economic interests of local and national industries and challenged policies that sought as much profit for as many fishermen as possible, rather than protecting nature and the few indigenous people who argued their right to access natural resources.

Considering the knowledge gap among local community members, Koizumi and I felt that Hatakeyama's concerns and knowledge needed to be shared with the wider local community, so we organised a two-day workshop in Mombetsu in 2010. The event drew 50 participants, including residents, local supporters (organic farmers, dairy farmers and fishermen), Hatakeyama's family members from Mombetsu, Ainu people living within and outside Mobetsu, and researchers and NGO activists from outside Mombetsu. The workshop provided the opportunity to share and discuss Hatakeyama's concerns about local fishing industry issues, Ainu history in Hokkaido, international indigenous rights protection and the gap between international legal instruments and current Japanese law. While international laws, such as the UN Declaration on the Rights of Indigenous Peoples (United Nations 2008) and Article 8(j) of the Convention on Biological Diversity (United Nations 1992), acknowledge the right to self-determination of local indigenous people for community development, current Japanese laws do not currently recognise such rights.

The workshop discussion reached agreement on the following four points.

1   *The gap between 'legally defined rights' and 'contextualised rights'*
    The workshop highlighted the conceptual gap in comparing the global legal definition of indigenous rights with the local community context. The definition at the global level is too abstract to make sense in a real-life context, the participants noted. It can only have value if it is embodied in everyday life in a local community context. The discussion clarified the limitations of the international concept of 'rights' and the necessity of interpreting the concept based on concrete issues.

2   *Indigenous rights recovery as an underlying sustainable development concept*
    The participants recognised that the process of seeking solutions to Hatakeyama's concerns was also a search for an alternative pathway to post-modern development.

3   *Conceptually linking Hatakeyama's concerns to a bigger picture*
    The discussions enabled the participants to link the problems that Hatakeyama had suffered individually to wider indigenous rights issues and sustainable development problems in the local community to convey a bigger picture. From this understanding arose the 'Mopet Sanctuary Concept', a proposal by participants for sustainable development of the bioregion connecting Mombetsu Forest, the Okhotsk Sea, the Mombetsu River system and residents' lives and livelihoods.

4   *Forming a local group – Mopet Sanctuary Network*
    A major outcome of the workshop was the formation of the Mopet Sanctuary Network (MSN) to connect those who had expressed an interest in Hatakeyama's concerns. The workshop participants offered diverse expertise and networks and had the potential to contribute to Ainu rights recovery as part of sustainable community development in Mombetsu.

ESD: infusing educational elements into policy advocacy

The establishment of MSN expanded Hatakeyama's individual social activism into a collective action. Particularly at the initial stage, MSN concentrated much of its energy on opposing plans to construct the industrial waste management plant. MSN's activities included lobbying the local government (2007–2009), making an official statement to the UN Human Rights Council (UN General Assembly 2010), policy advocacy by the amassing of 56 petitions by domestic and international indigenous peoples' organisations (2010), and entering into arbitration with the construction company through the Hokkaido Industrial Pollution Examination Panel (HIPE) from 2010 to 2011. This resulted in the recognition of the Mombetsu Ainu as a stakeholder in the operation of the waste treatment facility, guaranteeing them the right to be informed about and to monitor the waste treatment facility operations.

A number of educational activities started after the establishment of MSN. Koizumi and I integrated learning activities into the group's policy advocacy efforts opposing the construction of the waste facility. We organised workshops and seminars to share MSN activities with the wider community, teaching at local schools and periodic local environmental and historical surveys. Hatakeyama and a member of MSN started a teaching programme in local schools, providing great opportunities for teachers and students to learn about local Ainu history and problems, long-ignored because Japanese schools are not compelled to include Ainu content in the educational curriculum. The results of the environmental and historical surveys were shared at workshops and seminars and the data helped to support our arguments in the arbitration process through HIPE. These workshops and seminars provided detailed and timely information on important policy issues, creating learning opportunities for residents about alternative opinions and approaches. While the local government, developers and industry supported the construction plan, creating strong political pressures, MSN provided an opportunity for previously silent local minorities, who were concerned about the construction plan, to participate actively and freely so they could express their thoughts and opinions and learn from each other.

The immediate impact of MSN was limited but its activities can be seen as an attempt to re-weave together disconnected community ties among the Ainu people, between the Ainu and other residents and between humans and nature. The participants learned about each other's experiences and concerns, searched for the best way forward and took action. This process generated dynamic learning among the participants, who tried to gain alternative knowledge, solve the problems of the marginalised and reorient their communities. This motivating impulse could be described as ESD.

Figure 12.1 illustrates my understanding of ESD in a local community context when I started to engage in MSN activities. It shows the specific social activism and learning activities involved in the MSN advocacy and how their combination generated a 'synergistic effect' that can lead to sustainable community development.

Social Actions

- Urgent request submitted to Hokkaido governor (twice in 2008–2009)
- Written statement submitted to UN Human Rights Council (2010)
- Request submitted to Hokkaido prefecture and Mombetsu city government with the petitions of 56 overseas indigenous people's organisations (twice in 2010)
- Official complaints regarding final industrial waste facility construction plan filed with Hokkaido Industrial Pollution Reviewing Panel (2011) and reviews held for settlement, conciliation and arbitration (six times: 2011–2012)
- Request submitted to Fisheries Agency of Japan for rights recovery of Ainu indigenous whaling (twice in 2011)

Synergistic effects towards sustainable development

Learning Activities

- Hatakeyama participates in ESD key players' meeting in Hokkaido, organised by *SFY* (2008, Sapporo City)
- *You* organises 'Okhotsk Mombetsu ESD Tour – Okhotsk forest, sea, history of Ainu, and now' (2009, Mombetsu City)
- ESD-J and *SFY* local community workshop in Mombetsu: 'Towards sustainable Mombetsu – what Ainu rights recovery movement tells modern society' (2010, Mombetsu City); MSN established
- Hatakeyama lectures at Ainu seminar (2010, Kobe City)
- MSN starts regular water quality study in Toyooka River; start of the salmon run (2010, Mombetsu)
- Hatakeyama participates in the side event of the Indigenous and Local Community group at UN conference on biodiversity (COP10) (2010, Nagoya)
- Hatakeyama lectures on Ainu rights and history at local primary and middle schools (2010–2011, Mombetsu)
- MSN organises ESD seminar in Mombetsu: Learning about the locality and its future – History, culture, environment and Ainu people (2011, Mombetsu)
- MSN coorganises seminar: Thoughts of an Ainu on sea, rivers and forests of Mombetsu (2011, Tokyo)
- Monbetsu ESD seminar: Listening to the sea and land – questions for us who survived 3.11 (2011, Mombetsu)

Figure 12.1 Synergistic effects of correlating social actions and learning

Key roles of informal ESD in the community development context

In 2012, the reconciliation process through HIPE was terminated. Although MSN could not stop the construction plan, the Mombetsu Chapter of the Hokkaido Ainu Association concluded an agreement with the developer that clarified the rights of the Mombetsu Ainu people to inspect the operation at any time and to receive regular monitoring reports on the operation of the waste treatment facility. The following analysis focuses on the nature of informal ESD, based on the author's experience of MSN engagement, particularly the HIPE process. I would like to identify two key questions for understanding informal ESD in the community development process:

1   Why is informal education critical here?
2   What challenges remain for effective implementation of informal education?

Why education is needed

First, education can help to bridge the gap between community stakeholders and initiate efforts to address existing conflict. I observed that many participants in MSN activities tended to depend on policy advocacy as the main avenue for restoring the rights of the Ainu people in order to solve their problems. They believe that policy advocacy will lead to policy change to improve the Ainu's situation through the recovery of their human rights. However, policy advocacy on its own is not likely to result in sustainable community development. The existing policy cannot be changed unless the majority of society changes its perception of the socially marginalised. Even if some social change is enforced administratively – through legislation or judicial decisions – some tensions among the majority of residents may continue, particularly if other residents also suffer from social, social, economic or cultural marginalisation. As an example of this tension, Hatakeyama heard other residents ask why the Ainu people seemed to be often receiving special treatment from the government.

Clearly, without community consensus and the support of the general community, those who are socially marginalised could be further isolated within a small community. Furthermore, social activism to support the claim of one's rights could ignore the complexity that exists within the local community, and might result in dividing local stakeholders into antagonistic pro or con opinions on issues. Educational approaches taken in MSN, such as workshops and seminars, provided a space to make visible the unrevealed opinions of the local community, and to raise residents' awareness with alternative data and information supporting the rights of marginalised people. Education can play a role in searching for an alternative path to understanding.

For example, the information given at the public hearing for the waste industrial treatment facility was provided by a contracted environmental assessment consultant. This information prioritised economic efficiency, emphasising the economic benefits promised by the construction and the low environmental impact of the facility's operation. Most residents considered the arguments for the proposed construction based on limited information. In this case, there was an obvious need for information backed by alternative data and research from an independent source.

The developer and the government have made decisions promoting local community development based on the efficiency sought by the majority of the local community. At the public hearing and during the MSN visit to the construction site, the developer was aware of a local Ainu elder, who used the lower stream of the river for a traditional Ainu ceremony. However, the developer and the government tended to take a utilitarian approach, seeking the greatest benefit for the greatest number. Seldom, if at all, did they take into consideration the views of minority residents.

The developers collected scientific and evidence-based data to support their argument so a lack of data and information from a local Ainu perspective strongly affected decision making. The lack of data and information reflecting the perspectives of the marginalised people motivated MSN members to conduct regular local environmental and fixed-point surveys of water quality along the Mombetsu River and Toyooka River. Others have conducted interviews with the local Ainu and experts in Ainu history in Mombetsu. The collected data and information helped to support Hatakeyama's claims during the arbitration panel meetings.

MSN provided education that is tailored to the diversity of the local community and that provides data and information, otherwise unavailable from conventional schools and media, to promote community development.

Continuing challenges for education

However, although education has the potential to transcend traditional approaches to rights recovery activism for MSN, some critical issues still need to be considered in planning and conducting ESD.

The first issue is the need to acknowledge that the knowledge and experience of indigenous peoples often do not fit neatly with modern knowledge systems. I often observed that Hatakeyama struggled to express his concerns to other MSN members and to the wider community. He sometimes became irritated or said things that other MSN members found to be unreasonable, and he sometimes asked other MSN members to articulate his concerns, his feelings and his goals for the group. This happened at both informal meetings and in formal institutional settings, including at workshops, seminars, and in policy advocacy to the government and the United Nations. Eventually, I realised that there was a big gap in vocabulary for expressing knowledge between Hatakeyama and other MSN participants.

On one hand, Hatakeyama's concerns about indigenous rights and local environmental and sustainable development issues emerged from his personal experience and feelings gained throughout his life as a fisherman in his local community. His concerns came from personal experience that was non-verbalised and anchored in a local community context. However, while he lacked knowledge of the Ainu language, he also felt a sense of inferiority in being poorly educated, which expressed itself in a resentment of those with more education. Thus he faced multiple difficulties in expressing himself, either in Ainu or Japanese, and other, more conventionally educated, MSN members tended to apply a logical framework based on universal, verbal-based rhetorical norms to try to understand Hatakeyama's concerns. Hatakeyama struggled with two different knowledge systems, two different languages and two identities, enmeshed in an unequal power relationship between Japanese and Ainu residents.

This experience provides two lessons. First, stakeholders, particularly those with a modern education, must appreciate that indigenous knowledge cannot be gained or understood through the perceptions and assumptions of modern knowledge.

Stakeholders with modern knowledge have a superior position in the power relationship for controlling and manipulating indigenous knowledge. It can be helpful in this instance to refer to decoloniality (Ndlovu-Gatsuheni 2013; Smith 2001) as a critical approach to informal ESD in community development, particularly in terms of knowledge and understanding. Decoloniality aims not only to identify the power issues relating to marginalisation from the perspectives of the marginalised, but also to establish an epistemology from their perspectives that will help to realise dialogue between the powerful and the marginalised. ESD may have a role to play in this process by enabling stakeholders with modern knowledge, including the educators, to understand indigenous knowledge from the perspective of indigenous people.

The second issue that must be considered in ESD in a community development context is the diversity of the residents of a community. At most MSN events, a diverse array of participants tended to prioritise their interests and rights over Hatakeyama's concerns. The participants could be roughly categorised as Ainu or non-Ainu but they could be divided further based on their interest in, and understanding of, Ainu rights recovery issues. They could also be categorised based on their diverse social, economic and/or cultural concerns.

Even the Mombetsu Ainu residents are not a monolithic entity. Not all local Ainu also wanted to recognise their indigenous identity or become involved in such issues. According to Hatakeyama, the majority of the local Ainu fear that Hatakeyama's activism could cause conflict within the community and affect their standing. Some did not want to express their opinions, even though they had the opportunity to share publicly the problems they were experiencing. They were not used to seeing problems from an indigenous perspective: a long history of assimilation predisposed them to adopt majority views and perspectives when considering issues. On the other hand, some non-Ainu individuals wanted to support claims for indigenous rights recovery. There were also silent non-Ainu residents, who understood the issues but could not support MSN's arguments because of conflicts of interest. Most of them were linked to the local fishing industries, which mainly support the waste treatment facility in Mombetsu as fostering economic growth because it reduces the cost of transporting industrial waste to facilities outside of Mombetsu.

ESD must not ignore the complexity and plurality of the local community. Every stakeholder needs a different type of empowerment that may require unlearning what they have learned through the school education system and everyday life, and unmasking expectations of behaviour to support economically driven development. This local diversity calls for various levels of empowerment and a variety of learning opportunities.

The way forward

One day I presented the MSN case at a workshop on ESD. After the workshop, a participant approached me and expressed doubts that the community activities I had described could be regarded as ESD because he could not find any elements that could be considered, conventionally, to be 'education'. He also wondered how many Ainu lived in Mombetsu. His comments questioned the very nature of ESD itself. The person assumed that education requires an organised and structured curriculum or teaching content, and so cannot occur outside educational institutions. He also thought it was not right for most people in a community to have to consider the benefit of a very few people, such as Hatakeyama. In the case of the waste management facility, the majority supported the construction plan because they thought it enabled sustainable economic growth.

What is the role of ESD and for whom does it exist? Concentrating on issues that affect the majority can result in further marginalisation and increased vulnerability of marginalised people. Shouldn't ESD respond to a situation where the interests of a small number of individuals are at stake? Education functions to effect social transformation, creating waves not only from the global to the local but from the local to the global and from the periphery to the centre. Education should not be treated as something that is fully defined but rather as something that creates a dynamic flow that can synthesise formal, non-formal and informal education, as in the MSN case study. ESD or sustainable development should not be promoted from a point of view prioritising social utility.

Solving the issues of the socially marginalised sometimes requires changing the social, political and economic system, which most people, especially those in authority, will not favour. ESD is not an educational approach that serves only the interests of the majority; it should function even in places where only a few minority residents oppose a proposed development. The marginalised should not remain silent in recognition of the decision of the majority.

Some questions remain to be tackled as we move forward. First, how do we evaluate a case like MSN from an ESD perspective? Is it possible to see it as a success by simply counting the increased number of residents who understand and take action to solve a problem? Second, can the increasing number of educated residents contribute to the empowerment of the socially marginalised? There is room for more research to understand ESD from the perspective of marginalised people, who have not yet been included in structured and institutionalised education.

Notes

1 In the 1850s, when western countries were competing against each to expand their colonies and procure much-needed resources, traders from England, America and Russia travelled to Japan and pressured the Edo Shogunate to open the country. These visits resulted in the signing of a number of official treaties between these countries during this period. During the negotiation process for the Treaty of Commerce and Navigation between Japan and Russia in 1856, the Edo Shogunate was compelled to determine the border between Russia and Japan. In order to justify territorial rights to these areas, the Edo Shogunate took a contradictory approach in dealing with Russia and the Ainu (Uemura 2008). The Japanese government argued with the Russians that the Ainu were under Japanese dominion; hence, their sphere of residence belonged to Japan. At this time, the government began to promote rapid assimilation of the Ainu to justify their territorial claims. On the other hand, the Japanese government did not recognise the territorial rights of the Ainu themselves. They regarded *Ezo-chi* as *terra nullius,* where no humans resided, insinuating that they did not regard the Ainu people as human and that the Japanese had territorial rights over this area. The Treaty of Commerce and Navigation between Japan and Russia confirmed that the Chishima islands were Japanese territory, while governance of Sakhalin island was shared by Japan and Russia. By creating national borders, the Edo Shogunate forced the Ainu people to adopt either Japanese or Russian nationality.

2 Subsequent to the enactment of the Hokkaido Ex-Aborigines Protection of the People Act in 1899, the Ainu were displaced from their ancestral land to infertile land. They were banned from using their own language and Ainu names and from conducting traditional practices and livelihoods. In order to conserve natural resources to be used for economic development, the Ainu were banned from fishing and hunting staple food, such as salmon and deer, and were excluded from economic opportunities. Ainu children were forced to receive a Japanese education and were legally considered Japanese (Momose 1994). The act was enforced until 1995.
3 The Ainu population in Japan is estimated to be about 50,000–200,000 (Chikappu 1998). No official population survey has ever been conducted at the national level. The Japanese government claims that a total of 23,782 Ainu resided in Hokkaido in 2006 (Hokkaido Prefectural Government 2006). However, this number and the survey method are problematic. The Japanese government requested that the Ainu Association of Hokkaido (AAH) report its membership in 49 chapters in Hokkaido and then merely added an estimated number of family members. However, this number does not include non-AAH members in Hokkaido or Ainu who live outside Hokkaido, including those residing in other parts of Japan or overseas.
4 See Government of Japan (1997).

References

Carspecken, P. 1996. *Critical ethnography: a theoretical and practical guide,* New York, US and London, UK: Routledge.
Chikappu, M. 1998. *1997 nen aki – ainu no jinken nitsuite omoukoto* (Fall 1997 – my reflection on the rights of the Ainu peoples), in *Hurights Osaka: Kokusai jinken booklet3: Asia taiheiyo no senjuminzoku – kenri kaifuku no michi* (Hurights Osaka: International human rights booklet3: Indigenous peoples in Asia-Pacific region – the path for rights recovery). Osaka, Japan: Kaiho Shuppan, 20–28.
Chris, M. 1996. *Resolving environmental conflict: towards sustainable community development.* Derley Beach, US: Lucie Press.
Fien, J. 1993. *Education for the environment: critical curriculum theorising and environmental education.* Geelong, Australia: Deakin University Press.
Fien, J. and Tilbury, D. 2002. The global challenge of sustainability, in Tilbury, D., Stevenson, R., Fien, J. and Schreuder, D. (eds) *Education and sustainability – responding to the global challenge.* Gland, Swizerland, and Cambridge, UK: International Union for the Conservation of Nature Commission on Education and Communication (CEC), 1–24.
Fisheries Agencies of Japan 1949. *Gyogyou hou* (Fisheries Act).
Freire, P. 1972. *Pedagogy of the oppressed.* London, UK: Penguin Books.
Government of Japan 1997. *Ainubunka no shinkou narabini Ainu no dentou nikansuru chisikino fukyuuto keihatsuni kansuru houritu* (Outline of Act on the promotion of Ainu culture and dissemination and enlightenment of knowledge about Ainu tradition).
Hokkaido Prefectural Government 2006. *Heisei 18 nen Hokkaido Ainu seikatsu jittai chosa houkokusho* (2006 Hokkaido Ainu actual condition survey report). Tokyo, Japan.
Hopkins, C. 2012. Reflections on 20+ years of ESD. *Journal of Education for Sustainable Development* 6, 21–35.
Huckle, J. 1993. Environmental education and sustainability: a view from critical theory, in Fien, J. (ed.) *Environmental education: a pathway to sustainability.* Geelong, Australia: Deakin University Press, 43–68.
Huckle, J. 1996. Realising sustainability in changing times, in Huckle, J. and Sterling, S. (eds) *Education for sustainability.* London, UK: Earthscan, 3–17.

Huckle, J. 2002. Education for sustainability. *Burning Issue Number 5*. National Primary Trust.

Inoue, Y. and Imamura, M. (eds) 2012. *Kankyokyoiku gaku – shakaitekikousei to sonzai no yutakasa wo motomete* (Environmental education studies – searching for social justice and well-being). Kyoto, Japan: Houritsu Bunka Sha.

Momose, H. 1994. *Hokkaido kyudojin hogohouno seirituto hensen no gaiyou* (Establishment of law to protect aborigines in Hokkaido and overview of its change). *Sion, The Historical Society of Rikkyo University* 55(1), 64–86.

Ndlovu-Gatsuheni, S. 2013. Why Decoloniality in the 21st Century? *The Thinker* 48, 10–15.

Smith, L.T. 2001. *Decolonizing methodologies: research and indigenous peoples*. London, UK and New York, US: Zed Books and Dunedin, New Zealand: University of Otago Press.

Tilbury, D. and Cooke, K. 2005. *A national review of environmental education and its contribution to sustainability in Australia: frameworks for sustainability*. Canberra, Australia: Australian Government Department of the Environment and Heritage and Australian Research Institute in Education for Sustainability.

Tsurumi, K. 1999. *Collection Tsurumi Kazuko Mandala IX: kan no maki* (Collection Tsurumi Kazuko Mandala IX: environment issue). Tokyo, Japan: Fujiwara Shoten.

Uemura, H. 2008. *Shitteimasuka Ainu people? – ichion ittou* (Do you know the Ainu people? Q&A). Tokyo, Japan: Kaiho Shuppansha.

UNESCO 2005. *UN Decade of Education for Sustainable Development: International Implementation Scheme (IIS)*. Paris, France: UNESCO Education Section.

UNESCO 2012. *Shaping the education of tomorrow: 2012 report on the UN Decade of Education for Sustainable Development*. Paris, France: UNESCO.

UNESCO 2014. *Shaping the future we want: UN Decade of Education for Sustainable Development (2005–2014) final report*. Paris, France: UNESCO.

UN General Assembly 1986. Declaration on the Right to Development. A/RES/41/12. New York, USA.

UN General Assembly 2010. Written statement submitted by the Shimin Gaikou Centre (Citizens' Diplomatic Centre for the Rights of Indigenous Peoples), a non-governmental organisation in special consultative status. A/HRC/15/NGO/24. New York, US.

United Nations 1992. The Convention on Biological Diversity. (www.cbd.int/convention/text/). Accessed 14 March 2016.

United Nations 2008. United Nations Declaration on the Rights of Indigenous Peoples (www.un.org/esa/socdev/unpfii/documents/DRIPS_en.pdf). Accessed 14 March 2016.

Wals, A. and Huckle, J. 2015. The UN Decade of Education for Sustainable Development: business as usual in the end. *Environmental Education Research* 21, 491–505.

Yoshida, K. 2011. *Ainu minzokuno hosho mondai: minpougaku karano kinjino yuushiki-sha kondankaihoukokusyono hihanteki kousatsu* (Compensation issues for Ainu people: critical review of the recent report by the Council of Ainu Policy Promotion). *Nomos, Kansai University Institute of Legal Studies* 28(2), 19–47.

13 The Tohoku Green Renaissance Project

Networking green rebuilding activities after a mega-disaster

Tsubasa Iwabuchi and Noriko Takemoto

Introduction

On Friday 11 March 2011, just before three in the afternoon, a magnitude-nine earthquake hit north-east Japan. The Great East Japan Earthquake – the country's most powerful to date – lasted about six minutes and triggered a massive tsunami. The impact was such that it moved the whole island of Honshu eastwards and shifted the earth on its axis. The National Police Agency (2015) reported 15,891 deaths and 2,579 people missing as of 8 May 2015. The tsunami reached a maximum height of 40m and travelled up to 10 miles inland. Structural damage included more than 100,000 partially or totally destroyed houses and 231,019 partially damaged homes (Ministry of Land, Infrastructure, Transport and Tourism 2011, 2).

At the time of writing, four years have passed since that Friday in March 2011. Tsunami wreckage has been removed from the coastal areas of Tohoku but, aside from flourishing weed growth, everything is much as it was. Rebuilding is slow. The reasons for this are: 1) the difficulty in persuading residents to agree on common measures for reconstruction, 2) the shortage of labour within local government, and 3) increased construction prices. The Tohoku area, traditionally one of the main suppliers of Japanese food, has a long and interesting history attractive to tourists but, like most rural areas in Japan, it is also burdened with a falling birth rate, growing numbers of elderly people and declining primary industries, such as fishing and farming. The challenges facing local fishing and agriculture have been exacerbated by consumer reluctance to purchase food sourced near the site of the Fukushima Daiichi nuclear plant disaster, although it now affects only the Fukushima coast. Rebuilding Tohoku means not only rebuilding the disaster areas but also rewriting mankind's 'contract' with the natural environment of the area. The phrase 'Green Renaissance' was coined to represent our work because we sought to conceive a programme for rebuilding a sustainable society.

This chapter describes our project activities related to green rebuilding, in the belief that restoration of biodiversity and ecosystem services will restore people's livelihoods, benefiting farming, fishing and the major industries of Tohoku. It is centred on a consortium of environmental organisations affiliated with the Tohoku University Ecosystem Adaptability GCOE (Global Centres of Excellence) programme, established in 2008, and it also involves non-profit organisations (NPOs), industry, local and national government and civic groups. The basic idea is that rehabilitation of a community cannot happen in a sustainable way without sensitive management of basic ecosystems.

The birth of the Tohoku Green Renaissance Project

After the earthquake, non-profit organisations (NPOs) with experience of the Great Hanshin-Awaji Earthquake of 1995 (Bochorodycz and Mickiewicz 2012) entered the disaster area, alongside official bodies such as the Japan Self-Defence Force, local fishing associations and agricultural support groups (see also Rossitto, this volume). At first, the Tohoku University GCOE group hesitated to become involved because it was reluctant to add to the burden of those affected by severe disruptions to transportation and insufficient water, food and energy. However, the director of a small local research institute for biodiversity and ecosystem services in rice paddy cultivation, NPO *Tambo*, convinced us that only with direct experience of the disaster could we advise others on restoring ecosystems in the long term.

On 17 April, with *Tambo* director Shigeki Iwabuchi as a guide, core members of Tohoku University GCOE, plus consortium members from Tokyo, visited the Ishinomaki coastal area, Onagawa and Minami Sanriku. It was clear that damage caused by the tsunami was worse than that caused by the earthquake, and that damage to coastal areas was greater than that found inland. Furthermore, damage to coastal rice paddies was significant. Salt deposition, building debris and even boats were dumped atop the paddies. Coastal forests, most of them artificial and designed to stop coastal erosion, were also affected.

Early removal of rubble and housing reconstruction were the most pressing problems for local government in the disaster areas, but there was also a need to ensure that rapid reconstruction and housing development did not further damage the natural environment. In discussions following the assessment exercise, Shigeki Iwabuchi asked our group to appeal to interested parties in the region using science-based arguments rather than short- and medium-term needs. In this way, the Tohoku Green Renaissance Project came into being as an umbrella organisation covering industry, academe, government and citizen groups.

Tohoku Green Renaissance Project declaration

Since there was serious infrastructure damage, it was hard for us to contribute in the short term so long-term restoration design became our target. On 22 May 2011 – World Day for Biological Diversity – the GCOE-led groups made a joint declaration at the United Nations University (UNU) in Tokyo. This was promulgated with the support of several Japanese NPOs, which had been active at the United Nations 10th Convention on Biological Diversity (COP10), held in Nagoya in 2010, Rice Paddies Network Japan, *Mori wa Umi no Koibito* (The Sea is Longing for the Forest) and the Tohoku Chamber for the Environment and Sustainable Solutions.

The Tokyo declaration was as follows:

> We believe ecosystem services connecting the ocean, the forests and rice paddies with human well-being are essential to rebuilding the Tohoku region. The massive earthquake and consequent tsunami of 11 March 2011 caused catastrophic damage to our homes in the Tohoku region. Rebuilding society and the economy of this region is a priority for Japan as a whole and of pressing interest to the international community. The area devastated was a harmonious natural mixture of riparian land, forest and ocean, and historically the population of the area has optimised ecosystem services for its livelihood. Rapid development of this area, without conducting environmental impact assessment and giving adequate thought to the biodiversity of its rivers, rice paddies and the ocean, may not only fail to repair the natural damage, but compound the losses already suffered. For this reason we believe a renaissance, or rebirth, of the area is necessary via 'green rebuilding' to enrich the ecosystems and nurture biodiversity. We affirm as citizens of the region that green rebuilding is necessary to regain and secure regional wellbeing and to strengthen our harmonious relationship with nature.

The declaration received support from many prominent domestic and international environmental actors, including the Institute for Global Environmental Strategies; Ramsar Network Japan; Environment Outreach Centre; General Incorporated Foundation; United Nations University Institute for Sustainability and Peace; United Nations University Institute of Advanced Studies; Think the Earth; Earth Day Everyday; Earth Watch Institute; Geo-ecological Conservation Network and *Egao-Tsunagete* (Smile Network) and, from the business sector, Regional Environmental Planning Inc, the Japan Business Initiative for Biodiversity and Tohoku Taskforce.

The first project meeting was held on 17 April 2011 at Tohoku University. The aim was to share information, discuss ecological and disaster risk reduction goals and draft a project declaration. Project members identified three goals. The first was to mitigate further disaster through ecosystem service management, including restoring coastal rice paddies and rejuvenating the diverse functions of wetlands. As part of this plan, tidal flats or coastal wetlands below sea level would be reassessed for exclusion from reconstruction development. The second goal was to mitigate risk by conserving flood plain basins or coastal belt zones for wetlands. The third goal was to develop sustainable livelihoods that fully utilised ecosystem services.

Overall, disaster recovery and prevention should not reduce ecosystem services. This means restoring original vegetation, land development with appropriate forest management and sediment discharge controls, conservation of marine ecosystems and assurance of water quality. Reconstruction should also take into account marine biological resources and animal migration routes, and the mitigation of tsunami or floods by smart construction approaches.

When redesigning local industry (agriculture, fishery, forestry, tourism and education), local culture and ecological resilience should be integrated and local residents should share in the process. Small-scale renewable energy sources, including biomass and hydroelectric power, should be used to promote self-sufficiency in energy. Use of geothermal power should also be promoted. Financial investment should support both rebuilding and biodiversity and should promote the rich local food culture and resources.

The role of the Tohoku University Consortium of Environmental Organisations in this project was to offer a place for sharing information and to act as a scientific think tank. As a so-called 'soft network', there were no rules as such and anyone who agreed with the project's aims could join, share their vision, develop strategy and introduce case studies for discussion. Meetings are now held every two to three months and there are usually about 40 people in attendance. The network is entirely voluntary and self-funding and has already, at the time of writing, lasted four years. The 'soft' structure makes it possible for governmental organisations, such as the Ministry of the Environment, local government and city representatives to communicate easily with the public. These bodies would refrain from participating in such unofficial meetings if they were closed and private. At regular meetings, members can hear ideas from ecologists or local government officers, for example, and engage with them in open and frank discussion.

Major project activities

As described above, the Tohoku Green Renaissance Project is a network of organisations and individuals that share common goals, and in this section we describe some of its major activities. The project addresses problems and challenges connected not only with sea defence but also with seaside forests, community development and other matters related to local communities, including Sendai, Natori, Minami-Sanriku, Kesennuma, the Urato Islands and other sites in northern Japan (see Figure 13.1 below). We have seen that a challenge in one place inspires people in another, and that people join together to tackle common difficulties.

Forest restoration in Natori

In addition to the loss of human life, the tsunami caused massive damage to coastal ecosystems. Many sandy beaches were swept away and intertidal wetlands thrust below sea level. Local vegetation was seriously affected, opening up land for opportunistic alien species. A local NPO, *Yuririn Aigokai* (Yuriage Coast Protection Group), has been dealing with the restoration of seaside forests. A major problem for vegetation restoration is the acquisition of seeds and seedlings. Bringing them from other places may cause genetic disturbance, while alien plants and civil engineering work may also affect on-site cultivation. The Yuriage Coast Protection Group unfortunately lacked both the people and skills to implement forest restoration effectively. However, at a meeting of the Tohoku

Figure 13.1 Tohoku Green Renaissance major project sites
Source: Adapted from map by Japanese Ministry of the Environment

Green Renaissance Project, the Yuriage Group, together with the Snow Brand Seed Company and Hokkaido University, agreed to cooperate on restoration. Seeds were collected from recovering native plants in Natori and grown on the Ishikari Coast in Hokkaido, while taking care to avoid their dispersion at the substitute growth site. When the seedlings were mature, they were then replanted on the devastated coast. However, the approach to the restoration of seaside forests differs from place to place and project to project. Some follow biodiversity guidelines while others do not. Our aim, therefore, is to open the Tohoku Green Renaissance Project to anyone who wants to learn how to approach restoration in an informed way.

Monitoring recovery of the damaged ecosystems

To assess the impact of the tsunami on ecosystems and their recovery status, research teams, led by Jotaro Urabe and Takao Suzuki of Tohoku University, have monitored biological systems in tidal flats, islands and rice paddies in Fukushima and Miyagi. While this work has been carried out in cooperation with Tohoku University, NPOs and business enterprises, the real force behind it is public participation via the Earth Watch Institute. This participation enhances the environmental 'literacy' of the public and brings about a better understanding of sustainable development in the devastated areas. To date, more than 300 people have joined a survey helping to identify variation in ecosystem recovery rates between sites. Differences in the mobility and life history of organisms may account for such variations (see Mukai *et al*. 2014).

Educating for sustainability through paddy field restoration

More than 20,000 hectares of rice paddies were damaged by the tsunami, and the annual crop in the damaged areas in 2011 was approximately 10 per cent of its normal size. The NPO *Tambo*, described above, was able to contribute to that 10 per cent by restoring paddies using volunteer labour, from local areas and from around the country, and by tapping ecosystem resilience without using chemicals and heavy machinery. *Tambo* has long-established expertise in ecologically sound local rice production. Before the disaster, it was active in promoting *fuyumizu tambo* (winter-flood rice cropping) as opposed to conventional rice growing. Under this system, paddies are flooded during the winter and organisms, including protozoa, sludge worms, waterfowl and others, help develop and fertilise the soil, promoting crops without the use of pesticides or artificial fertilisers.

The first step for rehabilitating the rice fields was to remove rubble by hand; volunteers even used hand sieves to remove tiny material fragments, such as broken glass, so the paddies could be worked with bare feet. Heavy machinery would have removed major rubble more quickly but it would have damaged the soil structure. A second step was desalinating the fields to help them recover from saltwater inundation. Since desalination agents affect the chemical balance of the soil and the surrounding ecosystems, the group flooded the paddies with fresh water. This both dilutes salt water and forces it into the soil below reach of a plough. According to Shigeki Iwabuchi, the chief director of *Tambo*, flooding is an established method for desalination in delta areas of Europe where the groundwater is salty. In the Camargue region in France, for example, farmers grow rice in flooded paddies before cultivating wheat and grapes.

Tambo has helped restore the rice fields in multiple regions, from Rikuzentakata and Iwate in the north to Ishinomaki, Matsushima and Miyagi in the south. The rice harvested from these paddies was marketed successfully as *fukkoh mai* – rice for 'restoration and happiness' – via multiple channels, including the World Wide Fund for Nature Japan. Since the *fuyumizu tambo* method requires extensive manpower, hundreds of volunteers – many from business – have participated as part of in-company training. Some fields have been returned to the original farmers. In other fields, even after full restoration, many volunteers continue to participate in planting and harvesting rice. Furthermore, it has given volunteers from urban areas, such as Tokyo, an opportunity to understand the real impact of the disaster on ecosystems. In this way, winter flooding has become an exercise in educating for sustainability.

Eco-friendly farming, including winter-flood farming, is attractive to consumers because information about growers and product safety appears on the food packaging or on marketing websites. Flooded paddies are also attractive feeding and resting sites for migrating waterfowl during the winter; thus the rice paddies surrounding Kabukuri-numa pond in Miyagi were designated a protected wetland site by the Ramsar Convention (2010). However, the method is not problem free. Japan's agricultural sector suffers from the issue of ageing farmers and a shortage of young successors. To tackle the problem, it is necessary to try to achieve sustainability for Japanese agriculture by creating high-value brands, developing new sales routes and other strategies.

Urato Satoyama-Satoumi Green Renaissance Project

The activities discussed above – rice paddy restoration, ecosystem monitoring and business partnership – have been implemented in the Urato Islands in the tsunami-hit Matsushima Bay in Shiogama city. Accordingly, the islands can be viewed as a working model for the Tohoku project as a whole. Long-standing prior research into the ecosystems of these islands, carried out by Professor Masakado Kawata, sub-leader of Tohoku University GCOE, and Professor Jun Yokoyama of Yamagata University, means that change wrought by the disaster can be viewed against substantial historical data.

Tohoku Green Renaissance Project launched the Urato Islands *Satoyama-Satoumi* Restoration Project in April 2012. Collaborators on the project included the International Partnership for the *Satoyama* Initiative (IPSI) of the United Nations University, the Ministry of the Environment, CEPA Japan and the Inkjet Cartridge *Satogaeri* Project (*satogaeri* means to return to one's hometown). The term *satoyama* signifies interaction between people and terrestrial–aquatic ecosystems, while *satoumi* signifies marine–coastal ecosystems. These two words are sometimes used together, *satoyama-satoumi*, to signify 'socio-ecological production landscapes and seascapes'. The idea is to highlight the roles of both society and ecosystems in traditional communities based on primary industries (Suzuki 2013). Since its introduction to an international audience at COP10, *satoyama-satoumi* has become a key concept in Japanese biodiversity efforts, connoting both conservation and the wise use of natural resources for a sustainable society.

It was difficult for partners in the restoration project to reach consensus on a rebuilding plan for the Urato Islands because the five administrative divisions across four islands had formerly acted independently and insisted upon their own policies and ways of working. The project hired two young workers to support the Urato residents immediately after the earthquake and to facilitate smooth communication between residents in Shiogama and supporters residing in and outside the islands.

Stakeholder discussions were held twice to forge an agreement between interested parties and eventually succeeded with a green rebuilding strategy that the mayor of Shiogama was asked to implement. The plan included a strategy for commercially developing Urato homemade delicacies, based on locally produced oysters, seaweed and yuzu citrus, which were market tested in Tokyo. In 2014, a new NPO, E-front, was established to continue such activities with residents.

The Urato Islands are typical of most rural areas in Japan. They have a falling birth rate, growing numbers of elderly people and declining primary industries, such as fishing and farming. Although they are located in Matsushima Bay, famous as one of the three most scenic sites in Japan and a popular tourist destination, they are not the most frequently visited because they lack a bridge to the mainland. The only way to get to the islands is by boat.

Unfortunately, many people left after the earthquake because of the lack of work. Furthermore, young people who might be attracted to fishing or agriculture in Urato often find it impossible to find accommodation because the islands are within a prefectural park with a landscape protected by strict building laws. The Tohoku Green Renaissance Project would like to continue supporting the Urato Islands in their efforts to rebuild their communities and industries.

One of the main activities of the project is branding local produce, such as oysters. Although Japan is not a large country, its food culture is highly diverse and each area or community has unique traditional produce. Although the local housewives of Urato have inherited traditional cooking skills and local dishes, they never thought these would appeal to people in big metropolitan areas, such as Tokyo. Intelligent marketing and branding can transform these traditions into added value for the local produce, which may expand the economic potential of these islands. Thus one of the first challenges for the project has been ensuring that local housewives understand and take pride in the value of their traditions, and exploring related business opportunities.

Koizumi education for sustainable development children's workshops

Koizumi district in Kesennuma, Miyagi Prefecture, is involved in a debate over the construction of a massive sea wall (to a maximum height of 14.7m) proposed by the local government in November 2011. A sizable number of residents disagree with the height and location of these walls. Furthermore, local households have already decided to move to higher ground so the new sea walls will protect only farmland and woodland. Nevertheless, many agreed to a buyout in order to promote the rebuilding of the Koizumi Coast.

A sea wall of such magnitude inevitably affects ecosystem services and effectively encloses the land like a fortress against the sea. It also restricts access to popular local beaches. Furthermore, such a fortress approach would make it difficult to view the sea from inland. In response to requests from local residents to reconsider the plan, the Renaissance Project members decided to support an education for sustainable development (ESD) programme known as Koizumi Children's Academy. This activity was intended not as political lobbying but as ecosystem education. The basic idea of the programme was to familiarise children and parents with major environmental issues relating to the natural world on their doorstep.

A graduate student of Tokyo University of Agriculture and Technology, Noriko Hata, devised the project with Associate Professor Satoko Seino of Kyushu University Graduate School of Ecological Engineering. The aim was to familiarise children from tsunami-affected areas with local ecosystem services and their importance for the future (Hata 2015). The programme was based on six concepts – diversity, reciprocity, limitation, fairness, collaboration and responsibility – all

Table 13.1 Koizumi Children's Academy in Motoyoshi-cho, 2014–15 programme

	Date	Contents
1	19 April	Examining the animal life of tidal flats (aquatic insects, fish, shellfish).
2	18 May	Examining the secrets of the forest (plant and insect life).
3	8 June	World Oceans Day 2014. Children's Environment Conference.
4	21 July	Play day at the Koizumi coast: making models and salt-making competition.
5	7 August	Discovering which local sea creatures come from the north, and which from the south of Japan. Sea shell art competition.
6	13 September	Examining the animal life of tidal flats (aquatic insects, fish, shellfish).
7	11 October	Examining the secrets of the forest (plant and insect life).
8	16 November	Examining the history and topography of rias coastlines.
9	7 December	Examining the animal life of tidal flats (wild birds).
10	14 December	Constructing a mini globe and planning the agenda for Motoyoshi Children's Committee for the Future.
11	11 February	Making a map for Motoyoshi Children's Committee for the Future.
12	14–15 March	Presentation by Motoyoshi Children's Committee for the Future members at the third session of the United Nations World Conference on Disaster Reduction. Excursion around Koizumi district for all participants.

identified as fundamental principles underpinning education for sustainability in a report from the National Institute for Educational Policy Research (NIER) (Kadoya and Goto 2013). Table 13.1 shows how the programme was organised.

According to Noriko Hata, although the whole of Koizumi district was devastated by the tsunami, a new wetland environment appeared after the disaster on the Sodeo River estuary. It was here that Koizumi Children's Academy held sessions for examining the animal life of tidal flats. The area is home to a number of endangered species, including Japanese eel, cherry salmon, benthic organisms, birds and algae. Furthermore, in the forest surrounding Kusushi Shrine in the Koizumi Coast hinterland, there survives a native species of *Camellia japonica*. According to Kikuo Haibara (2011), this flower species plays a significant role in Japanese folk customs, religion, literature, arts and crafts, fine art, flower arrangement and the tea ceremony. Other NPOs in Kesennuma have started to use the plant for sea coast protection because its root strength is comparable to that of Japanese black pine. The traditional shrines in distinctive natural surroundings, which survived the tsunami unscathed, represent an historical record of local wisdom about living with nature and its dangers. A Special Stories report, broadcast on 20 April 2011 by Tokyo Broadcast System Television, referred to this in an item entitled 'A warning from antiquity. Do tsunami stop in front of shrines?' Research revealed that 67 of 84 shrines in Fukushima survived the tsunami.

Historically, two great tsunami hit this coastal area in the years 869 and 1611. Constructed amid small groves that ameliorated the tsunami's force, the shrines served as visible, historical warnings.

The Children's Academy's first programme in April examined aquatic creatures, such as insects, fish and shellfish, and monitored the recovery of the damaged ecosystem. Children caught small insects, crabs and shellfish for 20 minutes, then identified them by species in an illustrated reference book. Professors and graduate students of Tohoku University treated the children as assessment partners by supporting them in this field work. The next step was to observe and draw shellfish. Crabs were the most popular creatures. This activity was again held in September with bird watching in December.

The second activity was discovering secrets of the forest, such as plants and insects. This was held in the area of the Kusushi shrine in May and October. Children had a lecture from the chief priest of the shrine and played a nature game devised by the Nature Conservation Society of Japan. The most popular creature was the spider. Drawing spider webs requires high levels of natural observation and technique, so the participating children were able to practise their concentration skills and eventually improve their drawing and oral skills. This proved a great surprise to parents and supporters alike.

In summer, activities were planned for a beach on the Koizumi coast for 8 June, World Oceans Day. However, rain meant it was held inside a junior high school with the support of CEPA Japan. The task was to examine several types of sand from Koizumi, Okinawa and other areas using a microscope to identify differences of shape, colour and size. All the participants, children and adults, were surprised by the glittering quality of the Koizumi sand that contained finely fragmented glass from the tsunami.

Other sea coast activities included observing shellfish, shell craftwork, collecting rubbish from the beach, creating models on the beach and so on. Project members and volunteers were concerned that the children might associate being near the sea with memories of the tsunami but this proved not to be the case. The following two remarks were noted by Noriko Hata (2015):

> My sons and I have changed dramatically. I never thought I would go to the sea with my sons and stay at the seashore for an hour. While we adults watched with trepidation, the children themselves were happily getting wet in the sea. I was deeply touched. It brought tears to my eyes.

> The sea takes life and brings life. I understood from a lecture that the sea gives us many precious things.

From December, the project members helped the children prepare for a presentation at a side event to be held at the United Nations World Conference on Disaster Reduction in Sendai in March 2015. The theme was Motoyoshi Children's Conference on Disaster Reduction. Noriko Takemoto introduced the Natural Step view of sustainability, a framework for strategic sustainable development that helps organisations make pragmatic decisions to move toward sustainability (The Natural Step 1989), and the children made a mini globe to understand the interconnections between nature and society. Afterwards, the children held a workshop to discuss the future they wanted to build or see in Motoyoshi. The day before the conference, a Motoyoshi area excursion was held with children acting as guides for 20 participants. As part of this, they visited the Rias Ark Museum of Art to receive a last lecture from the curator. At the conference the next day, the children made a 10-minute presentation to an audience of 130 people, in which they shared their ideas for a sustainable future for Motoyoshi.

A total of 80 children joined together with parents, local supporters, researchers and individual supporters from NPOs in Tokyo to provide public information. However, although the project was widely publicised by the local Board of Education and in community centres and schools, participation was poor. One reason for this was that construction work and heavy traffic near the Koizumi coastal area made it very dangerous for children to visit. In addition, although three years had passed since the tsunami and nuclear disaster in nearby Fukushima prefecture, parents in this area still worry about radiation. Furthermore, people were wary of approaching the coast and parents were fearful that beach visits would bring back traumatic memories of the tsunami. Others opposed the project on the grounds that it would be seen as an expression of opposition to building the new sea walls. However, members of the Renaissance Project did not necessarily disagree with the sea walls as such; they believed they were too large and should be set back inland to preserve important wetland biodiversity.

This sort of opposition and misunderstanding was not confined to this project. Parents kept children away from the seaside to save them – they said – from another tsunami. Some parents said they allowed children to play football, for example, or computer games instead. While this exaggerated fear is understandable, it may result in children being deprived of an understanding of their immediate natural world. The Koizumi ESD programme shows how parents and children can overcome their fears through well considered activities, but one cannot force people to confront their personal fears.

Another problem is how to continue the programme. Officially, it comes under the remit of Tohoku University, which then works with external researchers and local volunteers, but it has no established budget. In order to make a city sustainable, local residents need to continue their ESD programmes themselves, with professional support. It would be better to set up an organisation in the Koizumi area to take over the programme. A programme for children, run jointly with other NPOs, is already planned for the Sanriku area.

Concluding remarks

The green renaissance (green *fukko* in Japanese) concept is slowly but steadily influencing government attitudes and policy. For example, the Ministry of the Environment has used the term for the Sanriku Fukko National Park/Green Reconstruction Project.

The Tohoku Green Renaissance Project has drawn international attention at the second conference of the International Partnership for *Satoyama* Initiatives, led by the United Nations University and the Ministry of the Environment, Japan in March 2012 in Nairobi, Kenya, and at the UN Conference on Sustainable Development (Rio +20) in June 2012. The green renaissance concept was also included in the Charter of the First Asia Parks Congress in November 2013 in Sendai as a valuable approach to disaster risk reduction.

Yet, despite recognition of the project's merits, it is difficult to secure new funds to maintain activities run by NPOs and gather volunteers. Non-governmental organisations (NGOs) and NPOs have a relatively short history in Japan and attracted little attention before the Great East Japan Earthquake. Many Japanese traditionally leave social problems to the government to deal with (Kashimoto 2012). Furthermore, making private donations to NPOs that tackle social problems is not yet popular in Japan. This is partly because the tax system does not reward charitable giving, and partly because NGOs and NPOs are seen as a concept imported from the west (see the chapter by Rossitto in this volume).

Although many NPOs have made outstanding contributions to the recovery in the Tohoku region, most of them still lack true financial independence. Japanese government funding lasts for a maximum of three to five years so NPOs now need to find additional funding sources. For this reason, academic support has become more important in establishing an independent role. The networking of NPOs and other organisations is essential to achieve green rebuilding, and ESD activities should be carried out locally, involving parents, children and residents with an interest in the future of their own communities. In our own Green Renaissance project, the ESD activities for children were found to be as popular with parents, volunteers and project members as they were with the youngsters.

Rebuilding communities after a natural disaster like the one that struck Tohoku involves both short- and long-term measures, but the final aim is to build, through ESD, a sustainable society. Starting from scratch is not easy and there is a tendency to focus on the short term. Furthermore, the psychological trauma of a disaster that swept away everything one thought to be permanent may be overwhelming. For those affected, it may be tempting not to think about the future.

A huge sea wall may look like a fortress against future disasters but is also like the bailey of medieval castle – it isolates its community from outside dangers, in this case the ocean. But the ocean is where many residents earn a living by fishing. A sea wall provides a false sense of security. In Tohoku, in one or two decades' time, we may not see thriving communities but walled ghost towns. Such sea walls are designed to protect but they do not account for the livelihoods of those they are meant to protect. Fishermen do not usually live behind castle walls. It is obvious that recovery planning should truly reflect a community's needs and those needs should be supported through ESD projects. We all want Tohoku to recover rapidly and ESD should play a major role. Here we described the five major programmes of the Tohoku Green Renaissance Project – Natori forest restoration, ecosystem damage monitoring, business ESD partnerships, the Urato project including paddy restoration and, finally, the Koizumi ESD programme – all of which were local responses to disasters, and attempts to lead the renaissance of the damaged areas through education. While these were local ESD initiatives, they hold lessons for Japan as a whole. Japan is still a highly centralised country with little room for devolving power, so we must educate the next generation to appreciate and sustain their own communities and natural resources.

References

Bochorodycz, B. and Mickiewicz, A. 2012. Japanese NGOs during the Great Hanshin-Awaji and Tohoku Earthquakes: from civic revolution to policy advocacy. Paper presented in The Disasters in Fukushima and the Political Changes in Japan panel at the International Political Science Association Madrid 2012 conference (http://paperroom. ipsa.org/app/webroot/papers/paper_7903.pdf). Accessed 7 November 2015.

Haibara, K. 2011. *Camellia japonica.* Nature, Elekitel. (http://elekitel.jp/elekitel/nature/2011/nt_104_ybtk.htm). Accessed 19 November 2015.

Hata, N. 2015. The possibility and problems of environment learning and ESD in social education post 3.11 – case study of practical education focused on natural experience activities in a tidal wave disaster area, in the Japan Society for the Study of Adult and Community Education (ed.) *ESD as lifelong and social education: creating sustainable communities (studies in adult and community education No. 59).* Tokyo, Japan: Toyokan Publishing, 79–89.

Kadoya, S. and Goto, M. 2013. The past, present and future of ESD in Japan – how to develop and disseminate ESD at school with the network of the local community. *NIER Research Bulletin* 142, 47–58.

Kashimoto, S. 2012. History of NPO in Japan: problems of Japanese NPO with a historical perspective (in Japanese). *Bulletin of the Graduate School of Policy Science, Ryukoku University* 1, 187–189.

Ministry of Land, Infrastructure, Transport and Tourism 2011. Chapter 2: Impact of the Great East Japan Earthquake and challenges for reconstruction in *Land and Real Property in Japan* (http://tochi.mlit.go.jp/h23hakusho/02.html). Accessed 7 November 2015.

Mukai, Y., Suzuki, T., Makino, W., Iwabuchi, T., So, M. and Urabe, J. 2014. Ecological impacts of the 2011 Tohoku earthquake tsunami on aquatic animals in rice paddies. *Limnology* 3(15), 201–211. DOI: 10.1007/s10201–014–0432–5.

National Police Agency of Japan Emergency Disaster Countermeasures Headquarters 2015. Damage situation and police countermeasures associated with 2011 Tohoku district – off the Pacific Ocean earthquake, 10 September 2015 (www.npa.go.jp/archive/keibi/biki/higaijokyo_e.pdf). Accessed on 7 November 2015.

The Natural Step 1989. The Framework for Strategic Sustainable Development (www. thenaturalstep.org/about-us/). Accessed 24 November 2015.

Suzuki, W. 2013. Introduction: indicator approach to understanding resilience of socio-ecological production landscapes and seascapes. Convention on Biological Diversity, side event at 17th meeting of the Subsidiary Body on Scientific, Technical and Technological Advice, 15 October 2013, Montreal, Canada.

14 The importance of *genfukei* (memory of place) to citizen participation in community building in Zushi city

Koichi Nagashima

1. Introduction

A fundamental issue for Japanese society is how to attain a higher level of *shimin shakai* (civic society), given the country's feudalistic past and the more recent concepts of *kokumin* (members of the nation) and *kokka* (nation state) that emerged from the Meiji Restoration of 1868.

One of the most important means to achieve a viable civil society is to provide opportunities to self-generate or foster autonomous and self-motivated citizens. Involving citizens in the process of planning and designing their town offers a key opportunity to achieve this end. This chapter explains how civic participation in *machizukuri* (literally, town and community-making)[1] in Zushi, a small town in the Tokyo metropolitan region, has sought to preserve and promote Zushi's city-scape through the pursuit of *fudo* – the place where nature, manmade environment and human activities interact. Japan has seen many of its town and cityscapes destroyed by modernisation, war damage and an over-emphasis on economic achievement in the immediate post-World War II period, followed by the universal trend of homogenisation of lifestyle and urban environment caused by globalisation in more recent decades. City planners in Japan have singularly failed to identify viable goals and principles in building and rebuilding cities, disregarding the innate needs and aspirations of the people who live in those cities. In this context, citizen-led *machizukuri* efforts in Zushi to harness long-lost *genfukei* (literally, proto-landscape) as the memories – both conscious and sub-conscious – of *fudo*, offer a powerful means to create *fudo* that is worthy of *furusato* (home) – defined by philosopher Takashi Uchiyama as the place 'where one's soul wants to return' (Uchiyama 2015) – and, in so doing, enhance civic identity and a sense of belonging that contributes to the basic sustainability of a human settlement.

2. Historical overview of Japanese society since the Meiji period

2.1 Concept of 'citizen' unknown to Japanese before Meiji

In Japan, the words 'citizen' and 'nation state' did not exist until the Meiji Restoration of 1868, which restored imperial rule to Japan under Emperor Meiji.

The free city of Sakai emerged in the late sixteenth century as the foremost commercial city in medieval Japan to attempt to defy *daimyo* controls over commerce. However, its prompt repression and destruction by feudalistic samurai regimes, first under Hideyoshi Toyotomi and then under Ieyasu Tokugawa, left the citizen concept practically unknown to the Japanese until the country's reluctant opening up to relations with the world 250 years later, when the policy of *sakoku* (closed country) ceased with the demise of the Tokugawa Shogunate and the end of the feudalistic Edo era.

German economist and sociologist Max Weber once stated that 'there is no citizen consciousness in the East'. Certainly, civil society as it is generally understood today was created as a unique political and cultural entity particular to the west that dates back to Greek democracy. In Japan, the feudalistic social hierarchy of samurai (warriors – the ruling class), *heimin* (farmers), *shokunin* (craftsmen) and *shonin* (merchants), which prevailed throughout the Edo era, gave rise to the society of *chonin* (townspeople) consisting of merchants and craftsmen. Commonly credited as the creators and bearers of the flamboyant Edo culture, the *chonin* were given a limited amount of self-governance in urban local communities. In spite of this, the overall socio-political behaviour and ethos of *chonin* was fundamentally different from the idea and practice of modern civil society in terms of political freedom and autonomous governance.

Such was the situation at the beginning of the Meiji period. As yet in its infancy, with a history of barely 150 years, contemporary Japanese civil society is still growing through an experimental process involving trial and error in the operation of local communities as well as at the scale of a nation state, as will be shown in what follows.

2.2 Creation of the nation state and the emergence of kokumin

Nation state (*kokumin-kokka*) and citizen (*shimin*) were just two of the many new socio-political concepts and ways of thinking to be imported to Japan from the west during the Meiji Restoration. Japan had witnessed the military might of the nation states of the west during the battles between the British and samurai of the Satsuma-*han* (domain) during the Anglo–Satsuma War of 1863, which ended with the bombardment of Kagoshima and complete defeat for the Satsuma-*han*. Taught by experience that a single *han* could not deal single-handedly with the nation states of the west, Meiji Japan's new leaders – many of them reformists from the Satsuma-*han* and Chōshū-*han* – advocated forming a nation state under the *Tenno* or Emperor, the country's historic and symbolic ruler since ancient times, as Japan's best protection from western colonisation.

The basic concept of the new nation state of Japan was unique in that it replicated and expanded the concept of the feudalistic family system, with the *Tenno* governing as the family head and the *kokumin* – the legal members of the nation state of Japan – poised as the children of *Tenno*. With the abolition of the four classes, equity under *Tenno* and fraternity as a member of the nation state of Japan were recognised as the attributes of *kokumin*. People were encouraged to homogenise as *kokumin* under *Tenno* as a sort of clan rather than to pursue equity, individuality, local identity, political freedom, self-governance and fraternity. This was in no way a climate in which to foster citizenry or the ethos of civil society.

The process of creating a centralised nation state of Japan at the onset of the Meiji era involved the abolition of more than 300 *han* that had been enjoying some degree of local autonomy within the framework of the Tokugawa-centred feudal system. The existence of some 300 alternative draft constitutions – which mushroomed all over Japan as the country moved towards its first constitution, promulgated in 1889 – is one indication of just how much local autonomy carried over from the Edo into the Meiji era despite the Meiji government's determined efforts to form a homogenised *kokumin* and repress everything that was local on the grounds of its being backward and socially inferior.

One example of a draft proposal is the Itsukaichi draft constitution of 1881, created by a group of local intellectuals in Itsukaichi, 50km to the west of Tokyo. The town's location on the so-called Silk Road, connecting the Japanese port of Yokohama with inland silk-producing regions, had ensured that many silk merchants, foreign travellers and Christian missionaries passed through it. The Itsukaichi group of young intellectuals took this opportunity to acquire foreign knowledge and study new ways of thinking. They were duly stimulated to create a draft constitution to present to the central government during the process of creating the Meiji Constitution. However, their efforts were repressed in 1887 by order of the central government and their ideas disregarded. Some of the young and local idealists involved in the endeavour – Takusaburō Chiba and Yasubei Uchiyama among them – realised that most of the basic thought underpinning an ideal civil society is based on Christian values and they subsequently converted to Catholicism, brought to them by a missionary passing along the Silk Road.

2.3 Mixed messages from western civilisation: colonialism, Christianity and civil society

It is perhaps ironic that at the time when the democratic ideal of western civil society was introduced to Japan, the morality of the western nation states had been degraded. Instead of the idea of universal love (*agape*) brought to western civilisation by Christianity, the idea of fraternity (*philia*), promoted by the French Revolution in particular, contributed to the degradation of value systems of western society. The deed of love became confined to the same socio-cultural class, group and race – thus endorsing racism, colonialism and violent revolution. Negative consequences of the industrial revolution were also apparent in the conflict of interest between capitalists and labourers and the rush to secure and monopolise colonies as markets and supply sources for the products of industry. This mechanism made colonial incursions into the non-western world all but inevitable and, for the Christian churches, provided opportunities for worldwide expansion which, in turn, provided a convenient moral rationale for the colonialism of greed.

The emergence of the slogan *Wakon Yosai* – Japanese spirit, western means – at the start of the Meiji era is one response to the fact that from the time of the Opium

Wars onwards, unfair commercial treaties and greed were considered so much a part of western diplomacy and business that the Japanese could not see much morality associated with western civilisation. Conversely, although the spread of Christianity was limited in Japan at that time (even today, only one per cent of the total population is Christian), the progressive young intellectual elites of the day were impressed by the apostolic dedication of the missionaries and perceived common values between *bushido* – the moral code of the samurai – and gentlemanliness – fidelity to one's master and the sense of *noblesse oblige*. They managed to see beyond the immoral reality of colonialism prevailing in the non-western world, especially in Asia, to somehow identify with the ideals of the civil society and its fundamental values based on Christianity.

In spite of these somewhat contradictory messages from western civilisation, the *Jiyuu Minken Undou* or Freedom and People's Rights Movement, inspired by the modern democratic ideology of the west, flourished among the emancipated in the 1880s. The movement called upon the Meiji government to establish a National Congress consisting of elected representatives. These calls were only partially met when the Meiji Constitution was inaugurated in 1889 because only men of the one per cent of the total population who paid income tax above a certain level were eligible to vote.

The momentum towards human rights and democracy resumed with the so-called Taisho Democracy, a period of liberalism among the urban intellectual population during the reign of the Emperor Taisho (1912–26), and the proliferation of socio-political and cultural movements based on liberal thinking in the post-World War I period. These were both activated, in part, by the emergence of a new middle class. However, the Japanese people were prevented from achieving a new civil society and local autonomy because progress towards both floundered in the face of the rising authoritarianism associated with militarism that culminated in the Asia-Pacific War.

2.4 Post-war democracy introduced by the Allies

After the Asia-Pacific War, more substantial democratic systems were formally introduced to Japan during the Allied occupation. On the whole, these democratic systems and the ethos they promulgated enhanced the development of civil society in Japan that had its seeds in the aforementioned Freedom and People's Rights movement of the Meiji era and the Taisho Democracy. However, it was not the fruit of a genuine civil revolution initiated by the Japanese people. As such, it has the aspect of an artificial intervention – the temporary roots of which ought to have matured gradually as a result of the Japanese people's own enduring efforts and actual practices.

2.5 Kokumin consciousness and citizen consciousness

As seen above, Japanese democracy was neither autonomous nor consistently generated from a grassroot civic ethos or locally practiced autonomy. Instead, it was initiated by liberal intellectuals and political elites emancipated by new ideas and thought derived from western idealism before World War II and the promulgation of modern democracy after the war.

This may, in part, account for reactions to a protest that took place in Zushi in 1984. A number of Zushi housewives objected to the Ministry of Defence's decision to exhibit a scale model of a contentious housing development in a local Shinto shrine after Mayor Kiichirō Tomino refused to display it in the public lobby of the city hall. Mayor Tomino had come to power in 1984 on the back of a citizens' movement protesting against a government decision to convert Ikego Forest into a US military housing complex. He therefore had the people's mandate. However, the housewife-led protests in vindication of the mayor's action and against the government's subterfuge met with protests in turn, when a number of local men in their 60s castigated the women, shouting: 'You call yourselves *shimin* (citizens) but we are *kokumin* (people of the nation state)! How dare you raise your voices in protest against the national decision?'

These calls resonate with accusations of *Hi-kokumin* (non-*kokumin* or not worthy of *kokumin*), which were used often during World War II to condemn anyone perceived to be disobeying national decisions, with *kokumin* conceived to be the component of, and conditioned by, the framework of a nation state. At its simplest, the word 'citizen' means a person who is registered in a certain administrative boundary of a city, which is regarded as merely a small entity of the nation state. Therefore, it follows conceptually that a person who associates themselves with the larger entity of the nation state is superior to a person who associates themselves with a lower hierarchy within a nation state. Evidently, even at the time of the Zushi protests, 40 years after the end of World War II, 'citizen' and 'civil society' continued to have a fragile basis in Japan that could be easily abandoned or politically manipulated in the interests of nationalism or chauvinistic parochialism.

3. Enhancing *fudo* through civic participation: Zushi case study

Japan's interrupted progress towards an ideal civil society notwithstanding, ongoing *machizukuri* efforts by residents of the city of Zushi over the course of some 35 years display a level of participation and an enhanced civic ethos that look very much like the workings of a reasonable civil society. A summary of those efforts is given below.

3.1 People's movement to protect Ikego Forest

Zushi city, population 60,000, is located 60km south west of Tokyo, not far from Yokosuka Naval Base. Protests began in 1982 when the Japanese central government announced plans to construct a large housing estate for US navy personnel based in Yokosuka, which was destined to destroy Ikego Forest in Zushi. Protests spearheaded by specially formed citizens' associations to protect the greenery and children of Zushi were rooted in concerns about the validity of the planned development – citizens queried whether US military family members might not be better located in local communities accessible from the naval base, for example – and environmental concerns for the flora and fauna of the Ikego Forest, rather than in political concerns for Japan's defence and security relations with the US (Jain 1991, 559). For this reason, it has been called 'the first major green movement in Japan' (Ibid., 559).

The citizens' movement that followed the initial protest spanned 12 years and demanded considerable civic energy from those involved. Although, ultimately, the movement did not attain its goal of abolishing the housing scheme, it transformed residents into autonomous and motivated citizens able to participate and bear responsibility in forming and operating the city. Over time, the idea of participation has encouraged attempts to realise the city environment and local identity by drawing on and focussing people's innate desires, culminating in the creation of *furusato*. Citizens' personal and collective memories and desires associated with *fudo* (locality) were harnessed in participatory workshops to create viable city landscapes and urban spaces and applied over the course of decades of practical *machizukuri* activities in Zushi. These will be discussed in Section 4, which examines the role of *genfukei* as the memory of *fudo,* which residents drew upon when creating a vision for their city and making it a reality.

3.2 Five periods in the history of participatory machizukuri in Zushi

3.2.1 First period: the Save Ikego Forest movement

The early years of the protest movement coincided with a period of drastic urban sprawl for Japanese metropolises, including Zushi city, which caused fundamental disruption to local lifestyles, community structure and the natural environment. This period divided the residents of Zushi into two distinct camps: relatively young newcomers and long-term residents, many of whom were older. Since the newcomers tended to enjoy a rather different world outlook, derived primarily from the post-war democratic ethos, a mental and social schism inevitably opened up between the old and new inhabitants. Male newcomers were disparaged as *Zushi Tomin* (Zushi Tokyoites), who could not afford to put down roots because of their long working hours and lengthy commutes to and from the metropolis. Their experience contrasted sharply with that of their wives, many of whom sought to integrate socially, often through their roles as mothers and housewives, after recovering from the initial isolation of life in an unfamiliar physical and social environment. Although relatively highly educated – Motataka Mori's 1988 report on the Zushi residents' movement cites a survey of adult women in Zushi city, which found that city-wide only 15 per cent of women were university graduates while some 58 per cent of the women activists involved in the Ikego protest movement were graduates (Mori, cited in Hasegawa 2004, 139) – marrying young meant few of these women had had the opportunity to exercise their professional or intellectual abilities in the job market or social sphere. They were, therefore, eager to engage meaningfully in the social life of their community and to establish their own identities in relation to their new surroundings – both natural and social.

The period of the Ikego movement coincided with a period in which global eco-logical consciousness and environmental movements were gaining force. For this reason, Zushi citizens' associations set out to establish relationships with interna-tional environmental non-governmental organisations – many of them from the US. This state of affairs kept the citizens' movement viable from the 1980s into the 1990s.

3.2.2 Second period: progressive city administration under mayors Tomino and Sawa

The large-scale citizens' movement to protect Ikego Forest inevitably involved the local democratic political process during elections for mayor and other council members, which mandated them as the key decision makers on the part of the city to deal with the *machizukuri* issue. This led to a 10-year 'golden age', in which two progressive mayors were elected in succession. Kiichirō Tomino, in office from November 1984 to November 1992, was followed by Mitsuyo Sawa, Japan's first female mayor, who was in office until November 1994. Four female council members were also elected from among members of the movement.

These conditions resulted in a number of significant and innovative *machizukuri* undertakings aimed at creating a comprehensive development plan for Zushi. Initiated by the mayors, they inspired municipal officials at the city hall, who worked in collaboration with members of the *machizukuri konwakai* (discussion group) – a group of motivated and enthusiastic citizens, academics and profes-sional experts established as formal administrative machinery in the city hall. This was the first time citizens had participated and collaborated in city policy-making on the *machizukuri* issue anywhere in Japan and provided an example to the rest of the country.

At the same time, underlying changes in the national political climate were prompting calls for the establishment of a new model of city government pro-moting increased local autonomy as well as evidence of viable accomplishments in self-governance. A number of city governments, whose progressive mayors included Ichiro Asukada of Yokohama, later to become the secretary-general of the Socialist Party, proposed to 'surround the central government by a ring of progressive autonomous governments' to promote structural change (Watanabe 2015). This rebuke to an overly centralised Japanese political system, which did not allow substantial local autonomy, points to the fresh enthusiasm for a new civil society that prevailed at that time in Japan.

In Zushi, civic participation was advanced initially through the aforemen-tioned *machizukuri konwakai* and area meetings, set up to facilitate grassroot citizen participation in eight historical sub-community areas or *aza*. The *machi-zukuri konwakai* dealt with seven components of *machizukuri*: a *machizukuri* round table; information-sharing with the public; the provision and design of public facilities; a policy for environmental resources; environmental manage-ment; volunteer activities and an area information network. The group's members comprised one third citizens, who responded to a public announcement and were selected by a lottery, one third academics and professionals, and one third heads of relevant city hall departments. With the mayor present at all meetings, the well balanced personnel structure and scale ensured a platform for candid discussion. Meanwhile, the area meetings enabled the mayor and the directors of city hall to reach and engage with residents in the community. This consultative process fostered a number of *machizukuri* projects, which flourished in this period, including participatory workshops for citizens, the redesign of the Zushi railway station plaza, the provision of public toilets and improvements to neighbourhood parks.

Ultimately, as aforementioned, citizens' power failed to overturn the decision made by the nation state of Japan and the city was forced to surrender Ikego Forest for use as US military housing. The progressive and innovative city administration came to an end at the same time. The incumbent mayor was replaced by Yoshio Hirai (1994–1998), a local conservative politician, who had publicly expressed his acceptance of the central government's plans and decision. The four years of his administration saw the vigorous advancement of not only the Ikego housing development but also commercial housing developments all over Zushi. These quickly put the natural environment of the city under threat once again.

Efforts towards *machizukuri* continued, nonetheless. Citizens were, at least, invited to comment on the selected bids to build a civic centre complex in the town and the *machizukuri* movement was carried forward by 40 former citizen members of the *machizukuri konwakai* – abolished under the new administration – who came together voluntarily to form a *kenkyuukai* (research group). The group, led by architect Tamenari Nagahashi, held monthly meetings and research activities for the next 17 years. Zushi's current mayor, Ryuichi Hirai, in office since December 2006, and council member and architect Hiroshi Matsumoto are both former members of the group.

3.2.3 *Third period:* Machizukuri *Ordinance*

For some years after the surrendering of Ikego Forest and switch to a pro-development administration, the two camps of conservative and progressive citizens behaved as though – to quote Rudyard Kipling – 'East is East, and West is West, and never the twain shall meet'. Nevertheless, long-term engagement in the protest movement had nurtured a forward-looking and participatory habit of mind among Zushi citizens on the whole, spawning a variety of new citizen-led activities – cultural and otherwise – and enriching a civil society ethos. This was made possible by the natural social integration of the two camps over time and the neutralising influence of post-Ikego generations and newcomers who had not been involved in the conflict.

In 2003, under a new administration headed by Mayor Kazuyoshi Nagashima, in office from December 1998 to December 2006, preparations began for a *Machizukuri* Ordinance aiming to control the resurgence of new housing developments with the appointment of a citizen-led preparation committee. The committee consisted of 12 citizens – four who applied following a public announcement and eight representatives of various citizens' *machizukuri* activity groups (myself among them) – and three academics. The chairman, Professor Shigenari Kobayashi, former chair of the Grand Design Research Group formed during the offices of Tomino and Sawa to create a long-term (50-year) *machizukuri* vision for the town, was appointed to create the ordinance, with the city planning department acting as secretariat. Over a period of 14 months, 36 meetings were held, making it the most active committee ever to have met in Zushi city hall. It was also the most inclusive, in terms of citizen participation.

The draft Zushi *Machizukuri* Ordinance was completed in September 2005 and forwarded to the city council for approval. The draft was shelved shortly afterwards – partly because some council members were in favour of housing developments and partly as a result of misguided criticism that resulted from the draft not being examined properly. Frustrated and disappointed, the citizen members of the committee expressed their disappointment publicly in flyers distributed to every household in the city. Intense meetings were held with individual council members to promote a better understanding of the draft. Finally, a public meeting involving 200 citizens and a number of council members was held at the city hall. As the result of all these efforts, the city council ultimately passed the ordinance with few amendments.

Interestingly, in the following election, most of the council members who had shown a negative attitude to the ordinance lost their positions on the council. Zushi's small population of 60,000 once again was proving conducive to exercising due judgement and enhancing its hold on grassroots democracy.

3.2.4 Fourth period: Machizukuri *Basic Plan*

Citizen participation in creating the *Machizukuri* Basic Plan, expected to have a long-term perspective of 30 years, began in 2003 when a public announcement calling for committee members to prepare the plan attracted applications from more than 130 citizens. Operating on the premise that it would be far easier to work in a small task force than to organise such a large group, a preparation committee, comprising 20 volunteers from among the original applicants, worked for three months on the plan. Subsequently, five sub-groups – natural environment, urban landscape, transport systems, culture and community – were created to facilitate intimate and substantial discussion among all 130 members on subject matters identified by the task force.

The Citizen's Congress for the *Machizukuri* Basic Plan, which was subsequently formed by the whole membership under architectural engineer Michihiro Shiote, laboured over a draft of the plan for the next two-and-a-half years. The plan's completion in 2006 was the product of more than 300 meetings and large-scale workshops held among the 130 member citizens, adding up to some 9,000 man hours (Nagashima 2015a, 8).

3.2.5 Fifth period: Hototogisu-tai *and the Long-Term Comprehensive Plan*

It is not uncommon for long-term plans to be left to collect dust on shelves by municipal administrations – particularly during periods of administrative change in the mayor's office. This, indeed, had been the fate of the Grand Design.

To prevent this, citizens who had been involved in the formation of the *Machizukuri* Basic Plan formed a volunteer watch body, *Hototogisu-tai*, named after the lesser cuckoo, the city's mascot. The group negotiated with the city hall to hold two meetings a year to monitor and assess the progress of the project designated in the plan, with the attendance of all the department heads under the chairmanship of the mayor.

Under the supervision of Mayor Ryuichi Hirai, who assumed his third term of office in 2013, a Long-term Comprehensive Plan has been formulated. The city administration claims this plan assimilates the essence of the *Machizukuri* Basic Plan but citizens have expressed dissatisfaction with the planning process for not involving substantial public participation beyond the Committee for the Long-term Comprehensive Plan, which engages selected citizens and a few academics. Although calls for public comment to finalise the plan solicited some 1,606 public comments from citizens, only eight comments have been taken up for consideration so far. This has attracted criticism from the *Hototogisu-tai*, which feels the public comment process has been no more than a formality. However, hopes remain that enough citizenly energy is still latent among the people of Zushi to overcome some aspects of the present unsatisfactory situation. In Section 4.3, the notion of *genfukei* is presented as one way to stimulate and reinvigorate Zushi's citizens in their pursuit of the goals depicted in the *Machizukuri* Basic Plan.

4. *Machizukuri* by reviving and giving life to *genfukei*

Genfukei, by my definition,[2] is comprised primarily of memories, conscious or unconscious, of *fudo* – the place where natural and manmade physical environments interact with human activities. In this sense, *fudo* can be conceptualised along the lines of the micro civilisation shown in Figure 14.1, which depicts the intersections in a traditional Japanese rural coastal settlement between people and the rice fields, mountains, river and ocean from which they draw sustenance. *Genfukei* is also comprised of tangible clues, such as natural and manmade physical assets and events, that revive the memories of *fudo*. Mutual efforts to consolidate and comprehend people's perceptions of *genfukei* through participatory workshops for the *Machizukuri* Basic Plan proved fundamental to the *machizukuri* process in Zushi and are a valuable example for *machizukuri* efforts elsewhere in Japan.

4.1 Destruction of the identity of Japanese cities from Meiji onwards

'Everything seems to be being destroyed. And everything seems to be constructed anew at the same time. It is a huge movement!' (author translation). So exclaims Sanshiro, the 23-year-old eponymous hero of Natsume Soseki's masterpiece, first published in 1908. This comment captures the mood of the time, characterised – as shown in Section 1 – by an all-out national will to modernise Japan. It conveys a sense of excitement but also of alarm as continuity loses its value and respect for the valuable assets of the past is lost. It pinpoints the beginning of a time of flux, when Japan entered a state of upheaval as the country's leaders surrendered to modernisation and a mentality that put technology and the economy first.

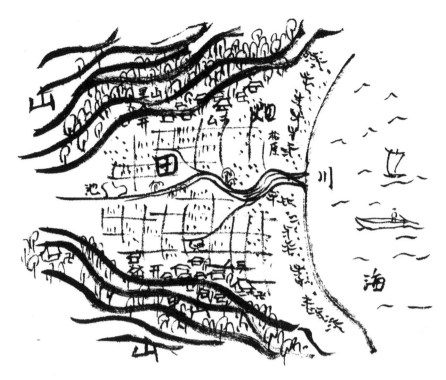

Figure 14.1 Typical structure of a traditional coastline settlement underlining Japanese
genfukei

Source: Koichi Nagashima

By contrast, the Edo period, spanning some 250 peaceful years preceding the
Meiji Restoration, was a unique period in Japanese history marked by self-
containment, self-reliance, self-sufficiency and environmental and economic
sustainability based on a frugal lifestyle. During this period – a period that has
been described as 'stable but not stagnant' (Yokoyama 2006, 41) – the indigenous culture digested and integrated hitherto imported foreign (mostly Chinese)
cultural elements, achieving a level of continuous refinement and sophistication
whilst being artificially insulated from the outside world. This period of peace,
frugality and moral integrity prevailed as Japan – a confined island community
at the time – embraced the notion of small local community and the influence
of Buddhism among the people and Confucian ethics among the ruling samurai
class that sustained the integrity of society. *Fudo,* the place where nature, manmade environment and human activities interact, was in a stable and refined state.
Architecture and urban design contributed to create beautiful *fukei* (landscapes)
and this still remains as the basis of *genfukei* for most Japanese people. The sense
of being secure in one's *furusato* was a given, at this time.

This situation changed with the onset of the Meiji period. The drastic transformation of Japan's traditional landscapes and urban environments is encapsulated, perhaps, by the ultimate *machikowashi* (destruction of human settlements) in air-raids during the Asia-Pacific war, which destroyed 75 per cent of the built-up urban areas of Japan. Haphazard rebuilding after World War II was based on all-out reconstruction and the expectation of high-speed, post-war economic development and population growth. Large-scale construction projects ran riot, without the pre-planning normally required in the implementation of building projects and with too few trained planners and architects available to rebuild and develop Japan properly.[3] Simplistic pragmatism and the neglect of cultural values became a habitual and accepted part of city planning. Excessive allowances were given to Urbanisation Promotion Areas, for example, in the volume allowance of floor area ratios and the unnecessary introduction of medium- and high-rise buildings in small and medium-sized cities became common (Nagashima 2010, 5). In short, blanket policies and principles for city planning, produced mainly by the central government with metropolises in mind, and implemented in accordance with merely quantitative and mechanical regulations, failed to consider qualitative aspects of culture and history, particularly with regard to small- and medium-sized cities.

Under these conditions, many traditional and indigenous buildings, refined over the course of history and a vital part of *fukei* and place, have been abandoned without regret. Various aesthetically inferior modern building styles – and synthetic building materials out of keeping with their local surroundings – are commonplace throughout Japan and contribute to the chaotic and characterless *fukei* that characterises Japanese urban landscapes today. The identity of a given place, which used to be derived from the individual characteristics of the *fudo* of locality, has been weakened, often beyond recovery.

There are, of course, notable exceptions to this trend. Architecture and urban spaces that have survived the test of time often depict *genfukei* – the memory of *fudo* – and, by doing so, continue to provide today's generation with a useful sounding board and norms to return to or reject. In 1996, Bunkacho, the government's Agency of Cultural Affairs, embarked on a system to register cultural assets of reasonably high quality (roughly equivalent to Grade II in the British heritage system), in an attempt to preserve Japan's architectural and cultural heritage. So far some 10,000 buildings and structures have been registered. However, in general, Japan's contemporary town- and cityscapes are lacking in physical natural or manmade historical and cultural assets and non-physical assets, such as *matsuri* (festivals) and other 'car free' street activities that, in comprising *genfukei*, act as clues to *fudo*. The resulting urban landscape is not what would enhance the identity of a place nor the cumulative identity of Japan as a whole. *Genfukei* – the memory of *fudo* and the means to recall *fudo* – remains an important but much neglected factor to those considering *machizukuri*.

4.2 The search for **furusato** *and the need to recover it*

Earthquakes, tsunami, air-raids and self-induced destruction through drastic urban development. These are just some of the causes of Japanese *furusato-soushitsu* (loss of *furusato* or home) in the span of only one century, compounded in part, perhaps, by the fact that the accumulation and continuity of manmade and natural landscape (*fukei*) has never assumed the same importance in modern Japanese culture as it has in other – for example, European – cultures.

It is normal for a society to change as time goes by. However, if the degree of change exceeds a certain limit, people may stop coping and find themselves falling apart. The vague feeling of dissociation and absence of meaning in one's life may be rooted in the instability of development without inheritance – the past disappears or collapses and the direction for the future is undetermined.

Feelings of loss and rootlessness surfaced after the earthquake and tsunami of March 2011, when various media – visual ones in particular – shocked viewers with the scale of the devastation of *fudo* in terms of the destruction of place and the loss of human life. In Japan, empathy for the dispossessed was expressed through charitable donations and volunteerism, as thousands headed to the afflicted areas to help out as best they could (see also Rossitto, in this volume). It was also evident, perhaps, in the revived popularity of an old primary school song entitled *Furusato*, composed in 1908. The song attests to a love of *furusato* and the desire to go back to it: 'Hills where I chased after rabbits/Streams where I fished *Kobuna*/Dreams still linger and take me back there/Ah! It is unimaginable to forget *furusato*' (author translation). Could it be that the disaster had confirmed something many Japanese had been feeling for some time, without realising it: the sense that they had lost their home? Had the terrible loss they had witnessed in Tohoku reminded them, in some way, of what they too had lost?

4.3 Lessons from Zushi: enhancing genfukei *as a new goal for* machizukuri

Hitherto in Japan, efforts to form urban landscapes have tended to focus on superficial beautification or the gentrification of the existing urban landscape. Little attention has been paid to the past and the lost fundamental assets of the place, or to the idea of developing the inheritances and memories of the place for the sake of present and future generations.

Awareness of *furusato-soshitsu* offers a new route to *machizukuri* that bases *machizukuri* on *genfukei* of the place, taken from people's memories of *fudo* over the course of participatory workshops. Here, the true and fundamental objective of *machizukuri* is to recreate *fudo* as a viable human habitat, which links the environment (natural and manmade) to human existence and time, and, in so doing, to rediscover *furusato*, the place of true identity 'where one's soul wants to return'.

4.3.1 Genfukei *as depicted in Zushi's* Machizukuri Basic Plan

The preamble to the Zushi *Machizukuri* Basic Plan, introduced in Section 3.2.4, summarises the heartfelt desires of the 130 citizens who helped to design it – desires explored and expressed over the course of numerous intensive participatory workshops held to discuss the contents of the plan. The preamble presents and

Table 14.1 Vision for Zushi outlined in the *Machizukuri* Basic Plan

Keyword	Description
Greenery	Sea of green covering every area of the city and including Ikego Forest
	Fukei (landscape) unchanged since Roka Tokutomi's *Nature and Life*
	Unspoiled green of hills and their ridges
	Well cared-for *satoyama* (community-managed hills and forests) with beautiful trees
	Forests full of life, particularly indigenous plants of the locality
	Green spaces throughout the town, created and tended by residents
	Walkways starting from ridges of hills and going down to the sea along the promenades of the rivers
Community	Nostalgia for the ancient past and creation of humane community
	Enhancement of *furusato*
	Maintaining pride in the refined and relaxing lifestyle of a resort town
	Place names that convey the geographical and historic characteristics of communities
	Small neighbourhood areas that enhance the daily activities of local residents
	Lifestyles accepting of slight inconveniences and frugality, based on warm human relationships
Transport	Freedom from excessive dependence on cars
	Priority given to pedestrians and bicycles
Low-profile cityscape	Refraining from high-rise apartment houses and mini-developments
	Graceful low-rise profile of townscape in harmony with greenery
Recycling	Realisation of a society that fully practises energy-waste circulation

defines five keywords as central to the citizens' vision for their town. These are shown in Table 14.1.

These keywords are primarily an extrapolation of *genfukei*, the memories of the *fudo* of Zushi. These memories are derived from citizens' personal experiences as well as the recollections of older relatives or friends who have since passed away. They are also memories of things the citizens may have read about in history books or seen in photographs and paintings. The participants were not really aware of taking part in the workshops for the purposes of extracting *genfukei* as such but, because they were free to express their thoughts and desires in terms of plans and proposed projects, they naturally reflected the contents of *genfukei*. This is perhaps the most significant learning from Zushi: citizens invited to design a blueprint for their city started out from *genfukei* – their personal and collective memories of the place in which they lived – and tried to make them real with a vision of *furusato* in Zushi that embraced both *genfukei* and *fudo*.

4.3.2 Rehabilitating genfukei *to enhance identity of place*

Zushi's example suggests strongly that the contemporary issue of *machizukuri* in Japan is whether existing *fukei* (natural and manmade landscapes) and patterns of human activity are capable of reflecting and expressing people's sensitivity to nature and enhancing their desire for *furusato*. This learning has major implications for efforts to rebuild townscapes in the areas devastated by the earthquake and tsunami of March 2011, where, if a substantial and genuine recovery is to be made, it could mean bringing the community back to the state where it used to be, a *furusato*, for the people who have been displaced. In Tohoku, more than anywhere in Japan today, the process of making planning and design systems that refer to *genfukei* offers substantial clues to reconstructing *furusato* and bringing about the genuine recovery of the disturbed and displaced psyche of communities that have been traumatised.[4]

4.3.3 Zushi examples for future practice

Engaging citizens in the *machizukuri* process is simple but requires time and energy, as Zushi's example has shown. Participatory workshops along the lines of those used to draw up the *Machizukuri* Basic Plan enable citizens to harness personal as well as collective memories regarding *fudo* of the place in which they live. As noted, memories of *fudo* are inevitably conscious and/or sub-conscious, private individual and/or group (collective), and include history and the verbal legacy of events and scenes that took place in that location in the past, stretching back for an indefinite length of time. The remembered and experienced – or imagined and idealised – aspects of *fudo* recreated in *genfukei* reflect residents' heartfelt longings rooted in the memories of their actual experiences and relate to the desirable conditions of the future of their habitat. As such, they can be interpreted – and ought to be integrated – as the goals and strategies for *machizukuri,* for materialisation later in the actual *machizukuri* activities of citizens and city administrations.

My own memories as a long-term resident of Zushi may be relevant at this juncture, to show how the process works. Table 14.2 lists my responses to three questions that might typically be asked in the workshops. These are framed to elicit *genfukei*, ascertain what has happened to *fukei* components of *fudo* in the town, and prompt citizens' opinions as to what should be done to preserve Zushi's cityscape.

My responses to Questions 1 and 3 resonate deeply with aspects of *genfukei* delineated in the preamble of the *Machizukuri* Basic Plan summarised in Table 14.1. This indicates the commonality of memory for many of the residents of Zushi – particularly where the residents are aged 65 or above, like myself – as well as the commonality of desires for the future of the town.

It is important to recognise that citizens involved in designing the *Machizukuri* Basic Plan were empowered by the participatory process of sharing memories and discussing their ideas for the city. For many citizens this was their first encounter with local politics. The demanding and rewarding process of interpreting *genfukei* in planning and design terms, vocabulary and proposals was an almost unconscious endorsement of the essence of the Ikego movement a quarter-century ago.

The citizens' efforts did not stop with the planning process that is fundamental to upgrade the democratic system of the society, however. In fact, the citizens have worked hard across the decades in Zushi – sometimes with, but often without, support from the local administration – to not only redesign but also to implement *machizukuri* for their town and community.

Table 14.2 Examples of *genfukei* in the case of Koichi Nagashima

Sample questions	Sample responses
Q1: What do you remember about Zushi that best expresses the essence of Zushi as a place?	View of Zushi Bay at sunset, looking out towards Sagami Bay with Enoshima Island, the Izu-peninsula and soaring Mt Fuji behind.
	The green hills that surround the city, reaching down to the river basin and the Zushi bay coastline, where a white sandy beach is flanked by pine groves.
	Natural boulevards made by rows of pine trees extending branches over streets in residential areas and *shourai* – the delicate sound that the wind makes, blowing through the pine leaves.
	Relaxing by the banks of the Tagoe river, among reeds and willows in the stream and the walls shoring up the river banks, made of local Ikego stones.
	Narrow streets and passages in residential areas, peppered by shops and low-rise one- to two-storey detached wooden houses surrounded by rich greenery.
	Two-storey shops along the main (high) street and summer retreat houses in Japanese-western hybrid styles, and the extensive use of natural materials for almost everything around me: e.g. hedges and fences made of fine local bamboo, wood and local Ikego stones.
Q2: What has happened to those fondly remembered elements of the city that are associated with the memories of *fudo*?	Housing developments on the surrounding hills have destroyed half of the green profiles. (Note: today, green coverage in the plain of Zushi is under 65 per cent, a rate that is lower than Setagaya ward in Tokyo).
	Loss of access to the sandy beach owing to National Route 134, constructed in 1964, which now cuts the beach off from the city.
	Loss of natural boulevards, with the felling of pine trees on both sides of the narrow streets.
	Scarcity of pine trees in the city making *shourai* a thing of the past
	Loss of cherry trees and willow trees along the riverbanks due to road widening.
	Spread of medium- and high-rise buildings with barren car parking where human-scale and low-rise buildings once stood and the loss of neighbourhood shops, replaced by convenience stores and supermarkets – most of them made of metal and concrete.
Q3: What measures can you suggest that might recover or improve the existing adverse/ deteriorating situation?	Overall re-planning of land use and down-zoning as part of a city-wide urban design.
	Strict height controls to maintain a low-rise urban profile.
	Creation of a green ordinance governing tree planting (especially pines) for greening the town.
	Provision of neighbourhood daily activity centres (day-care centres, nurseries, cafés, convenience stores, etc.).
	Campaigns and subsidies for the use of natural materials in building infrastructure and fences.
	Creation of a seaside promenade by partially re-routing Route 134 underground.

Innovative projects initiated and materialised by Zushi citizens include the *Machinami Keikan Sho* (prize for notable landscaping), awarded by members of the *Machizukuri* Research Group, who scour the city looking for examples of good landscaping. To date, they have donated 50 prize plates to various properties, providing examples to inspire the public. Residents have participated in the design of a number of small parks in residential areas, have had their say on the plans a new civic centre, a new recreational complex of pavilions and a local community centre. They have also initiated measures to limit the height of buildings in the Shinjuku 1-chome residential area.

Two groups – the *Hototogisu-tai* and the *Zushi Bunkano-kai* (Zushi Culture Association) – have been particularly active. The *Keikan* (landscape) group of the *Hototogisu-tai* has compiled and published a volume about *Machinami* (street) design in Zushi and *Hototogisu-tai* members have carried out maintenance work on the Wakimura house – a designated cultural asset – and its garden. The group is also responsible for the creation of *Inochi no mori* (living forest) in an unused plot of land in a primary school. Meanwhile, the Zushi *Bunkano-kai* has promoted *biwa* (traditional Japanese zither) concerts held in a private house (a designated cultural asset) and organised workshops led by craftsmen for repairing the *tatami* mats, *fusuma* (sliding paper doors), *shouji* (paper screens) and *nure-en* (veranda) of a city-owned traditional house in Roka park.

5. Conclusions

Machizukuri policies, strategies and measures rooted in the process outlined in Section 4.3 are essential to enhancing the sustainable development of a settlement, both in psychological and physical terms. They would also overcome the shortcomings of current urban planning and design, which is generally imposed unilaterally by outside professional experts and the technocrats of a city's administration (see also Nagashima 2011; 2015a; 2015b). Such *machizukuri* plans, which almost every city has at hand, tend to be universal and characterless, resulting in city landscapes lacking the identity of place.

There is little guarantee, however, that ideas and plans drawn up using the participatory process will be carried through to the next stage of implementation. In Zushi, as shown, the quest started by trying to identify commonly shared *genfukei* among residents of Zushi. The next step is to urge city administrations to put citizens' proposals into practice. Experimenting with ways to formulate a practical and methodological approach to environmental design that integrates *genfukei* – and to see it realised in life – is something that will require considerable administrative and financial input as well as planning and design efforts from professionals and policy makers working with citizens.

Fortunately, the emerging tide of citizen participation is on the side of Zushi's citizens. On the global stage, there has been a global paradigm shift from centrally governed nation states to decentralised autonomous regions and cities – recent examples being secession movements in Scotland, in the United Kingdom, and

Catalonia in Spain. More locally, numerous examples of *machizukuri* activities have emerged in Japan in recent decades. Citizen participation is increasingly becoming instrumental and indispensable to overcome the shortcomings of slap-dash 'legitimate' city planning. These have been particularly successful not only in Zushi, where the citizens who failed to stop a US military housing development and protect a much-loved forest went on to become part of the process to create an ordinance for their city, but also in Yokohama, where citizens have worked together with city officials and urban designers – myself and my wife as architectural consultants among them – from the 1980s onwards to plan and create parks and promenades such as Ooka River Promenade in 1982, Minami Ota Friend Park in 1989 and Tsurumi Machikado Hakkenjuku in 1990.

In both these cities and, indeed, in many others across Japan, the incorporation of citizens' wishes in planning decisions has offered a progressive direction towards sustainable socio-cultural development. However, the conscious integration of *genfukei*, as memories of *fudo*, into *machizukuri* to enhance the quality of *furusato* has yet to be achieved. Reintroducing elements reminiscent of *genfukei* into the landscape offers an opportunity to revive *genfukei* (memories). Ecologically sustainable lifestyles that enhance an ecologically sustainable environment, which incorporates the use of contemporary technologies as well as the wisdom of the past, would create a new viable breed of *genfukei* as a generative system.

* * *

It is time to put an end to development that pays no attention to the innate memories and desires of people – these feelings constitute an important part of their being as a whole. Even a decade ago, the idea of integrating *genfukei* into *machizukuri* might have been dismissed out of hand as incomprehensible, regressive and conservative nostalgia for a past that stands in the way of progress. Attitudes are shifting for the better, however. In part, this is because of the collective realisation of lost *furusato* brought to a head by the tragic events of March 2011, but it is also because of the end of drastic economic development. The younger generation is increasingly critical of the so-called *salarii-man* (literally, company man) lifestyle and vigorous in its pursuit of new lifestyles more conducive to sustainability – ways of living that have space for ideas such as *machizukuri* based on the enhancement of *genfukei*. Material affluence brought about by economic development is no longer the significant *ikigai* (life's purpose) for the younger generation.

Zushi's example proves that people's participation in the process of planning and implementation is an effective tool or experience to foster a higher level of *shimin shakai* or civil society. At the same time, a higher level of civil society, secured through a holistic process of mutual sharing and exploration based on locality and indigenous knowledge, contributes to the preservation and promotion of *fudo* in a Japanese context. In doing so, it fosters and promotes a higher quality and more sustainable level of both *fudo* and local civilisation. In short, a *machizukuri* process generated by *genfukei,* when integrated at the city-wide level, offers a means to attain both physical and socio-cultural sustainability for human settlements, and a genuine identity of the city that is conducive to being *furusato*.

Notes

1 *Machizukuri* – a term coined in Japan in the 1960s and 1970s 'to refer to a civil society reaction to the negative environmental and social consequences of rapid economic growth and the centralised control of the development associated with that growth' (Woodend 2013, 9) – is generally understood to mean urban community (*machi*) building/making (*zukuri*). Today, as Woodend explains, the term *machizukuri* is used in the relatively limited English language literature on the topic to refer to and encompass a wide range of activities, including community involvement in planning and the work of citizens' environmental and social movements in a diverse range of community, social, economic, environmental and urban change issues.

2 There is no directly equivalent term for *genfukei* in any of the five European languages that I have investigated – English, German, French, Spanish and Italian. The Latin term *Genius loci* – which translates as 'spirit of the place' in English and as 'holy power living in the land, or ancestral mind alive in customs and traditions' in Japanese (Fr. Michitaka Yamaguchi, cited in Nagashima 2015a, 10–11) perhaps comes closest.

3 This is in contrast to the European situation, where, after two world wars, the consensus seems to be that recovery primarily means restoration of the original state of physical assets (environment). In Paris, after World War II, 20 per cent of buildings were replaced by new ones that, to outsiders, were hard to recognise as being new. Another example is Rothenburg in Germany, which was restored almost precisely to its original condition. Meanwhile, in the UK, 55 per cent of architectural commissions are based on renovation, rather than building anew (according to the Royal Institute of British Architects president, Rod Hackney, speaking in Tokyo at the Japan Institute of Architects (JIA) in Tokyo,1994).

4 To this end, urgent calls have been heard from architects – myself among them – seeking to rebuild Tohoku in ways that are sensitive to people's memories of place (see, for example, JIA Design Department (2012) and Nagashima 2013; 2014; 2015b). Although, unfortunately, these calls have been for the most part disregarded, 'it is not yet too late: one round for *machizukuri* is 25 years'. (Nagashima 2015a, 9).

References

Hasegawa, K. 2004. *Constructing civil society in Japan: voices of environmental movements.* Melbourne, Australia: Trans Pacific Press.

Jain, P. C. 1991. Green politics and citizen power in Japan: the Zushi movement. *Asian Survey* 31, 6, 559–575.

Japan Institute of Architects/Design Department (JIA) 2012. *3.11 and glocal design: a message from the UIA.* Tokyo, Japan: Kajima Publishing.

Nagashima, K. 2010. Creating local identity of Asian small and medium cities through recovering proto-landscape. Conference paper, given at the World Conference of Historic Cities, Nara. Available at (http://rdarc.itakura.toyo.ac.jp/webdav/ask/public/ACP2010/5.pdf).

Nagashima, K. 2011. The International Competition for the Disaster Recovery Plan after the Great East Japan Earthquake. Competition entry document in *Chie to yume no shien sakuhin shuu* (Wisdom and dreams: community design for children's future), *Kodomo Kankyo Gakkai* (Institute for Children's Environment), 25 September 2011.

Nagashima, K. 2013. 3/11 and glocal approach: an evening talk. Presentation to the Royal Institute of British Architects, London, 18 June.

Nagashima, K. 2014. *Watashi no shiten. Shinsai fukkou jigyou: Genfukei ikasu machizukuri wo* (My perspective. Towards recovery for the tsunami disaster zone: *machizukuri* through the activation of *genfukei*). *Asahi Shinbun*, 24 July 2014.

Nagashima, K. 2015a. *Kono hito ni kiku. Nagashima Koichi shi: Fudo no kioku, genfukei no fukusou suru dezain no toshi e* (Towards urban design where *genfukei*, the memory of *fudo*, plays a viable role). Interview in *Kenchikushi, Nihon Kenchikushi-kai* (JIA). July, 6–11.

Nagashima, K. 2015b. *Senmonka shuudan ga sougou teki handan wo* (A group of [third-party] experts lend their comprehensive judgement [to the project]), *Asahi Shinbun*. 5 September.

Uchiyama, T. 2015. *Uchiyama Takashi Chosaku-shu* (Takashi Uchiyama anthology). Tokyo, Japan: Noubunkyou Shuppan Co.

Watanabe, N. 2015. *Kanagawa no kioku* (2): *Kakushin jijitai doko ni* (Kanagawa recollections (2): where is progressive self-governance?) *Asahi Shinbun dijitaru* (Asahi Newspaper online). 10 October.

Woodend, L. 2013. The George Pepier International Award: a study into the practice of *machizukuri* (community building) in Japan. Sponsored by the Japan Foundation and the Royal Town Planning Institute. (www.rtpi.org.uk/media/665448/Japanreport1. docx). Accessed 2 December 2015.

Yokoyama, T. 2006. Even a sardine's head becomes holy: the role of household encyclopedias in sustaining civilisation in pre-industrial Japan. *Sansai: an Environmental Journal for the Global Community* 1, 41–57. (http://repository.kulib.kyoto-u.ac.jp/dspace/bitstream/2433/108259/4/SANSAI1_41.pdf). Accessed 23 October 2015.

15 Exploring the values of rural communities through place-based education in Niigata prefecture

Takako Takano

Introduction

Today, 'sustainability', which embraces aspects of the environment, socio-politics and economy, has emerged as an increasingly important goal for all people and all nations to pursue. Ecoplus, a small educational not-for-profit organisation that was founded by the author in 1992, addresses the relationship people have with nature in the context of sustainability through a wide range of educational programmes.

While the increasing populations of developing nations in Africa and Asia continue to make a global impact on energy, food, water, waste and environmental degradation, Japan's decreasing and ageing population is posing serious challenges for the country. These phenomena are particularly prominent in small, rural villages that have so far managed to sustain themselves for hundreds of years. In communities where the local economy remains strong, many residents continue to maintain a semi-subsistence way of life, growing their own rice and vegetables, harvesting edible wild plants and fungi, hunting wildlife for meat and foraging for wood in adjacent forests to make their tools and household necessities. These people can be independent even at times of emergency because they know where to find fresh water, bio-fuels for cooking and heating, and medicinal herbs. Village elders tend to have the traditional and ecological knowledge and skills to make such a lifestyle possible.

Ecoplus's activities are based on the assumption that because those old communities have continued over hundreds of years, the residents, especially the elders, are the bearers of knowledge – passed down through generations – that enables them to live in harmony with their natural environment (Iwasaki and Takano 2010). These communities, therefore, can pass on their wisdom to help Japanese society as a whole move towards sustainability. As the population of Japan's rural communities continues to decline, the opportunities for direct learning experiences in those communities will decrease. If designed well, educational initiatives bringing city dwellers into those communities offer an opportunity to re-evaluate what such communities and local individuals have, and to explore their meaning in the context of sustainability.

This chapter introduces the Tappo Minami Uonuma School of Life and the Environment (hereafter the Tappo project), which was established in 2007 by Ecoplus in cooperation with villages in the mountainous areas in Niigata prefecture to explore the educational values of rural communities. The chapter starts with an overview of some of the problems faced by rural communities in Japan and a discussion of the importance of place and place-based education, before introducing a number of flagship Tappo project programmes. It concludes that place-based education programmes in rural communities, such as the Tappo project, can lead residents and visitors alike to reconsider values that promise to revitalise all communities by placing sustainability at the centre of society.

Countryside in crisis: the challenges facing Japan's rural communities

Among the world's industrialised nations, Japan is the recognised frontrunner in facing the challenges of ageing and depopulation. After losing nearly one million people in the four years from 2010, the Japanese population stood at 127 million in June 2014 (Ministry of Internal Affairs and Communications 2014). Projections of a further 61 per cent decline by the end of this century would bring the population down to below 50 million, with 41 per cent – or one out of every 2.5 people – being older than 65 (National Institute of Population and Social Security Research 2014).

In Japan's countryside, especially in the areas known as *chu-sankan-chiiki* (semi-mountainous regions), the depopulation issue threatens the survival of rural communities. Semi-mountainous regions, as defined by law, occupy 73 per cent of the Japanese archipelago. It is here that 40 per cent of Japan's agricultural land is to be found, along with 52 per cent of its farming communities (Ministry of Agriculture, Forestry and Fisheries n.d.).

The Japanese government conducted a nationwide survey of communities in depopulating areas in 1999 and 2004, with a follow-up survey in 2010. The most recent report identified 64,954 communities in depopulating areas, of which 10,091 – or 15.5 per cent – have more than 50 per cent of residents aged 65 years or over, while 575 communities have residents who are all older than 65 years (Ministry of Internal Affairs and Communications 2011). Those communities whose residents are all older than 65 years – defined in the report as being in a 'super-ageing' condition – are concentrated in mountainous rural areas. Some 191 communities had disappeared between 1999 and 2004, and the number of communities deemed likely to disappear in the next 10 years had increased.

The depopulating and ageing crisis affecting Japan today is commonly attributed to Japan's low fertility rate, coupled with the global trend towards urbanisation. The consequences for Japan's rural communities in particular are profound and far reaching. The government report mentioned above outlines the impact made on natural surroundings when communities disappear: the abandonment of crop fields and rice paddies causes embankments to collapse, triggering landslides; the proliferation of trees and bushes further contributes to landslides by affecting soils and waterways; wild animals become a problem in villages and towns and biodiversity declines. In addition to environmental factors, the ageing populations of semi-mountainous regions affect Japanese food security – already compromised by decades of cheap food imports – as the number of communities engaged in agricultural production dwindles ever further.

Ecoplus has conducted educational programmes in a number of small rural communities facing the possibility of closure due to ageing and depopulation in Minami Uonuma city. With the advent of the Tappo project, Ecoplus began to encourage more people to think about the current situation of rural communities in a wider sustainability context. The word *tappo,* meaning rice field in the local dialect, is symbolic of all the activities carried out by Ecoplus and its partner communities in Minami Uonuma city under the auspices of the Tappo project.

The importance of place and place-based education

The concept of place has received attention in many disciplines. Gieryn's sociological analysis of literature states that place consists of geographic location and material and is invested with meaning and value (Gieryn 2000). As such, place is not just a space defined by abstract geometries – it carries active meanings for social life because it also comprises people, practices and cultural interpretation. Cultural geographers conducting phenomenological studies of 'rootedness' and 'sense of place' are influenced by Heidegger's ideas of 'dwelling' or 'being in the world' (Heidegger 1993, 55). Considering 'dwelling' as inseparable from other activities in life, Heidegger emphasises the importance of engagement with place to people's wellbeing and existence as a whole (Casey 1996; Massey 1993). Malpas explains that, for Heidegger, it is not merely human identity that is connected with the land but the very possibility of being: of being an individual that can 'engage with a world (with the objects and events within it), that can think about that world, and that can find itself in the world' (Malpas 1999, 8).

Others have pointed to the importance of 'place as experience' (Basso 1996; Kahn 1996; Relph 1989) and the multiple 'psychical, physical, cultural, historical and social' dimensions of place (Casey 1996, 31). Kahn suggests that places 'represent connections between people and their common past, individuals and their group, or sources of individual or shared identity, rooting them in the social and cultural soils' (Kahn 1996, 194). In short, place is 'what makes possible the sort of life that is characteristically human, . . .[and] human identity' (Malpas 1999, 13).

The notion of place used in this chapter implies relationships and social aspects inseparable from a notion of 'community', as well as geographical place, as suggested by the above literature. A community can be defined in terms of outward aspects, such as its administrative framework, population or economic structure. From the inside, however, a community is defined by its relationships with the natural surroundings and its history, as well as the relationships within and between families and other individuals.

Although communities naturally exist in both urban and rural environments – and it is important that a notion of place includes cities – this chapter focuses on

Japan's rural areas, for which the relationship with the natural surroundings is particularly important. In Japan, all members of a rural farming community are expected to take part in community activities – these may include maintaining the village environment and tackling any problems linked to the community – in addition to dealing with their own family matters and work. For example, an individual who engages in farming will be expected to work with other villagers to maintain healthy forests on mountainsides and waterways. Even children are expected to take part in some communal activities, such as cleaning up waterways and weeding village pathways. In cities, communal responsibilities and tasks, such as picking up garbage along the street and cleaning gutters along the roads, are principally shouldered by municipal governments or designated organisations, rather than by residents. However, life in a rural community, which is rooted firmly in its relationship to time, place and people, requires residents to accept responsibility for all communal activities. It is not uncommon in Japanese rural communities to find families that have protected their land and family graves, in obligation to their ancestors, for centuries. In return, residents have the security of knowing that they and their direct family line may continue to live in that place as long as the community exists. Only in recent years have these common beliefs begun to fade and with them the communities themselves, along with their long histories.

In the past decade, in recognition of the importance and meaningfulness of place with regards to sustainability, Ecoplus has focused increasingly on place-based education that seeks to achieve a 'greater balance between the human and non-human' and provide a pathway 'to foster the sets of understanding and patterns of behaviour essential to create a society that is both socially just and ecologically sustainable' (Smith and Sobel 2010, 22). Since the inauguration of the Tappo project in 2007, Ecoplus's undertaking of place-based education has expanded to make the organisation an example to other organisations and communities working across Japan to revitalise community. Based in Tokyo since its establishment in 1992, Ecoplus opened a second office in one of the communities in Minami Uonuma at the inception of the Tappo project to provide a secretariat for the charity's activities in the region. The following is an explanation of where and how the project began.

Introducing Minami Uonuma city

Increasing centralisation in Japan over the past 130 years has seen many small villages and farming communities merge into larger administrative units. In 2005, Minami Uonuma city was formed by the merger of three towns, already composed of many rural communities. The city is located in the southern part of Niigata prefecture, known throughout Japan as 'Snow Country', approximately 200km north-west of Tokyo. It is situated in a valley surrounded by mountains and experiences heavy snow in winter. The mountainous areas are typically covered with more than 3m of snow for four months of the year although the snowfall has decreased in recent years. Average temperatures range from 26°C in the summer to −1°C in the winter.

Although the entire area occupied by the city is designated semi-mountainous, it includes a number of urban or non-agricultural districts with shopping areas and hospitals, located in a flat basin along the Uono River. In all, the city comprises 135 communities that pre-date a series of municipal mergers (some original settlements are 150 years old), each with its own distinct boundary, community name and community self-government.

Niigata prefecture is known for rice farming. Minami Uonuma is particularly renowned for *koshihikari*, a local variety that is Japan's top selling and most expensive type of wholesale rice. Some 60,000 residents and 19,650 households – a quarter of all households in the city – were engaged in rice farming in 2014; many of them also having other paid work in town (Minami Uonuma City, n.d.). Its *koreika-ritsu* or ageing rate – the percentage of people older than 65 – stood at 28.2 per cent at the end of 2014, up from 27.8 per cent just one year earlier, in July 2013 (Niigata Prefecture Minami Uonuma Regional Promotion Bureau, n.d.). The proportion of people older than 65 in Minami Uonuma in late 2014 exceeded the national average (25.1 per cent in late 2013) and was similar to the prefectural average (28.1 per cent in October 2013) (Cabinet Office Japan 2014).

Although the Tappo project extends to several communities, its main activities take place in two mountainous villages – Tochikubo and Shimizu – located on opposite sides of the Uono River basin. Situated at about 550m in elevation, the rice farming community of Tochikubo had a population of 176 in March 2014, of which 36.9 per cent were 65 or older. Shimizu, at about 650m in elevation, used to have forestry as its main industry and is now home to 57 registered residents with an ageing rate of 38.6 per cent (Minami Uonuma City n.d). The ageing rate in these villages is noticeably higher than the city average, with more than one in three people being older than 65. In winter, both communities have much more snow than other areas in the city and two ski resorts are located in the immediate vicinity of Tochikubo.

Although there are no official records of when these communities were established, historical documents and cultural heritage statues suggest the villages have existed for more than 600 years. Remains found in the vicinity suggest humans have lived in the area since the Jomon period, about 15,000 to 3,000 years ago.

The beginnings of the Tappo project

In early summer 2006, the then village leader of Tochikubo approached Ecoplus with his concerns for the village primary school, which was threatened with closure by the city government because of a lack of pupils. As Ecoplus's founder and a native of Minami Uonuma city, I had already initiated a number of Ecoplus programmes in Tochikubo over the years – nature camps for children among them – before returning to live in Minami Uonuma in 2005. Encouraged by his personal ties with the author and his acquaintance with the activities of Ecoplus, the Tochikubo chief wanted to know if anything could be done to save the village school.

Residents in Tochikubo recall that, at one time, there were more than 100 pupils in Tochikubo's primary school, which was first established in 1879. However, by 2006, only 10 pupils attended the school across all six grades and were being taught in just three classes that combined grades 1–2, 3–4 and 5–6. The number of pupils fell to nine in the school year starting in 2007.

Records show that the community comprised 305 people and 61 households in 1876 – a figure that increased to 513 and 83 households in 1953 and peaked in 1955 with 86 households (Hosoya 2003). Since then, the population of Tochikubo has decreased rapidly, with the school coming under pressure of closure in the early 1990s.

Tochikubo's residents have worked hard to save their school in recent decades, forming a School Continuation Committee in the 1990s to fight local government plans to merge it with a larger school in town. The residents have managed not only to keep the school but completely rebuild it in 2004, in order to meet new government standards for earthquake resistance. Unfortunately, pupil numbers continued to fall and the Japanese central government maintained pressure on local authorities to merge small schools to maximise managerial efficiency, bring down costs and encourage the personal social development of school children by enabling them to interact with larger peer groups.

It was at this juncture that the village chief – acting also as chair of the School Continuation Committee – first approached Ecoplus to discuss what might be done for the school. While both parties agreed that a school merger should be avoided at all costs, Ecoplus was also interested in the implications of keeping the school open in terms of sustainability and the community's vision for the future. Ecoplus proposed the Tappo project in 2007 with not only Tochikubo, but also other rural communities in the region where depopulation and ageing are prevalent, in mind.

The aims of the Tappo project

To better identify the aims of the Tappo project, in 2008 Ecoplus distributed questionnaires to all Tochikubo and Shimizu residents above seventh grade (usually 12 or 13 years old). Two hundred and forty questionnaires were distributed in total. The residents were asked to identify the problems and potential in their communities and to share their vision for the future of their villages. In total, written responses to some 148 questionnaires were collected. The results showed that although 70 per cent of the respondents considered ageing to be a challenge, the residents remained hopeful for their villages' future and had a clear picture of what they wanted their communities to look like. In Tochikubo, for example, one man in his 30s commented that growing crops unique to the area would create income opportunities for villagers that would 'make the community more lively', and a woman in her 40s stated that she wanted to 'make the village's natural surroundings more beautiful to make visitors feel relaxed'. In Shimizu, a man in his 40s responded that he wished for a village where 'our children can continue to reside'. Ecoplus's analysis of the questionnaire results showed that the residents considered it important to generate more income as well as attract more visitors. Meanwhile, 'nature', 'food', 'people' and 'health' emerged as key words for vision making. These words have become the core principles of the Tappo project, guiding programme design and goal setting.

The Tappo project is led by a steering committee comprising community leaders, elders, the principals of a number of small primary schools in Minami Uonuma city and city officials. Ecoplus serves as its secretariat. The project's guiding mission – as agreed with the committee – is to explore the values of rural communities in mountainous areas and link these to the concept of sustainability by using the whole of the rural Minami Uonuma region as a mutual learning space for the local residents, children and urban dwellers who participate in its place-based and experiential programmes.

Tappo's programme goals are defined as follows:

1   To encourage residents to re-evaluate the values embedded in their community, thereby increasing residents' sense of wellbeing, happiness and hope.
2   To contribute to children's sense of identity, belonging and personal growth by encouraging them to learn more about the place in which they live and to take pride in their village.
3   To ensure the external visitors who participate in the programmes and events come as contributing members rather than as consumers buying certain services.
4   To generate small businesses in the communities in line with residents' hopes for their village's future.
5   To enhance biodiversity as the basis of life itself as well as residents' livelihoods.

(Iwasaki and Takano 2010)

As shown above, Tappo emphasises a re-evaluation of what the community already has, prioritising residents' pride in their way of life and their hopes for the future above all other goals. In encompassing all aspects of sustainability, including the economy, environment, socio-political structure and culture, the five goals above propose a way to sustain community in a manner that is meaningful to the residents of Minami Uonuma city. The goals also have implications for wider society by encouraging visitors to Minami Uonuma to think not only about what constitutes a sustainable community in a rural setting but to question the sustainability of their own, predominantly urban, communities as well as the values that underpin the urban way of life.

Tappo project programmes

Learning from nature

Initiated in 2007, the Tappo project's first programme set out to identify local wildlife in Tochikubo and help residents better know the place in which they live, in accordance with four of the project's goals. Local adults and children walked around their village in the company of an expert – most often a local high school biology teacher but sometimes an entomologist or an ecologist from Tokyo. The two-hour nature walks covered only short distances because the participants stopped to look at interesting things they found along the way. The participants carried field notebooks to record what they found or noticed with the help of their guide. After each session, the Tappo office and the expert made a list of the living creatures recorded with photos and text. The findings included several species on endangered lists drawn up at the national and prefectural level.

'Usually, I drive everywhere so I would never take the time to walk on the road like this, were it not for this activity'. Thus remarked one resident in his 40s during the walk, recalling his pleasure on looking for the first time through a field-scope at birds whose songs he had often heard. In the built-up areas and the flatter areas of Minami Uonuma used for farming, many creatures once common in rice paddies have disappeared as a result of changes in agricultural practice in the late 1960s, such as the use of chemical pesticides and fertilisers, straightening and concreting of waterways and riverbanks and the transfer to machine-based agriculture. By contrast, a number of rice paddies in Tochikubo remain unchanged over time – while many are fallow, these wetlands provide pockets of land in which certain animals and seeds can thrive.

The walks took place on a monthly basis (but not in the winter) for six years. Yearly reports compiled using the data accumulated by the villagers attest to a high degree of biodiversity in Tochikubo and this has been confirmed by the director of the prestigious Nature Conservation Society of Japan – himself an enthusiastic participant in Tappo project programmes. The data provides an important knowledge base for the local people when they show visitors around their village. Perhaps equally important, in terms of the Tappo project's goals, are the changes that took place in villagers' minds as a result of observing nature. Speaking with the author in July 2008, the man in his 40s quoted above explained how his view of the village and natural world changed over the course of the programme. He said he felt himself becoming much more attached to the place in which he lived and was surprised to find himself caring for frogs – something he had never done before – and 'talking to his children with joy' about wildlife in the village.

Learning from agriculture

The long-standing ABC in a Rice Paddy programme supports the villagers of Tochikubo in their commitment to growing rice safely and naturally without the use of chemicals and machinery and helps them keep farming in mountainous areas economically viable. The programme brings villagers and visitors together for a series of weekend exchange activities focused on the process of organic rice growing, and features lectures by farmers as well as opportunities for visitors to work alongside the farmers. The exchange programme provides an invaluable learning space for participants and locals to think about their lifestyles and values over the course of one year in the agricultural calendar. The calendar starts with the planting of young rice seedlings in May, proceeds through the weeding and cutting of grass in June and July and harvesting in October, and ends with the harvest festival and ploughing for the next season in November.

Each weekend itinerary starts with the arrival of the visitors at around noon on Saturday. After a short orientation there is a village walk, led by a local resident, usually a village elder. During the walk, the guide will talk about local features unique to Japan's Snow Country or aspects of Tochikubo's history, traditions and customs, wildlife and village life, depending on the interests of visitors and the season. After their walk, the visitors settle down in a large *tatami*-mat room at the community centre to listen to a short lecture from a Tochikubo farmer on various topics linked to rice farming in the region and Japan. The lively discussion that invariably follows spills over into dinner, which is prepared from locally grown vegetables by a chef who runs the only guest house in the community. The residents and visitors enjoy this shared opportunity to contemplate how 'rich' life lived close to the land can be, and the evening passes quickly as the visitors socialise with the residents over local sake (rice wine) – another natural product – gaze up at Niigata prefecture's star-filled skies and enjoy a soak in a Japanese cypress bath tub.

The greater part of the second day is spent in the paddy fields, except for an outdoor lunch beside the rice field (weather permitting) of organic rice balls, which the participants enjoy while looking at a panoramic view across the river basin. Although rice farming is demanding work that requires participants to walk ankle deep in, and put their hands into, the mud, the village children and young people also participate in the work. For many of them, it will be the first time they have engaged in rice farming without the use of machines and chemicals.

Over the course of the day, the rice field becomes a space for communication bridging generations, social backgrounds and occupational divides. Even in Tochikubo, residents lament that their young children have little to say to their grandparents and shun the outdoors to stay inside with computer games. On this day, however, for village children and young visitors alike, the village elders are the honoured knowledge keepers and teachers in the rice paddies, who can do everything better than everybody else. Dialogue starts naturally between the visitors and villagers, the young and the elderly, and relationships start to shift.

The written responses to questionnaires distributed to all participants at the end of the weekend's activities suggest that the impact of the agricultural experience exchange programme on participants is profound. In early July 2014, a group of 12 international university students who came to Tochikubo for field study shared their reflections after participating in a weeding session offered as part of the programme. One student from Singapore wrote: 'It was a very unique and valuable experience for a city dweller like me. The programme shows us the rural lifestyle of Japan, something more down to earth. My father has always taught me that food is very valuable – that when we eat, we must think of all the hard work the farmers have put into growing the food. This opportunity confirmed the fact that all this food does not come easily.' A Bosnian woman in her 20s, who attended the programme's harvesting session in October 2014 with colleagues from a Tokyo-based bank, said the weekend she had spent bringing in the harvest with villagers was '[my] happiest moment since I came to Japan', owing to the pleasure of engaging in physical work with other people in the fresh air as well as the joy of eating lunch outside. One of her colleagues – a Nepalese woman in her mid 40s – explained that what impressed her most during her two-day stay in Tochikubo was the 'simplicity of the place and people' and the delicious food. Japanese participants in the group were also deeply affected by their experiences, one stating simply: 'I began to feel affection for rice plants' and another admitting: 'I thought I knew a lot but I realise I know nothing'.

These comments and many more like them indicate the respondents' passage from new understanding to a deep shift in values after their primary experience of engaging with nature and growing food with local farmers. Whether the shift in values noted by the participants affects their respective actions – and for how long – has yet to be seen. However, although accumulated studies regarding the long-term impacts in experiential, environmental and outdoor education suggest that learning through experience can take various forms (Takano 2010; Asfeldt and Hvenegaard 2013), it can – at its deepest level – form the basis of a life philosophy (Takano 2010), which is closely linked to individual decision making on a daily basis. The body of 'significant life experiences' research, in particular, suggests that childhood experiences in the outdoors are the single most important factor leading individuals to take pro-environmental pathways that may be sustained over a lifetime (Chawla 1999; Palmer *et al.* 1999; Tanner 1998).

Learning from daily life and community works

Between 2007 and 2014, Tappo conducted more than 170 different events in different areas of Minami Uonuma city for more than 3,500 people. Most of the events centred on giving visitors an opportunity to experience daily life in rural communities.

In Shimizu, for example, between 2008 and 2010, a programme of mountain hamlet workshops organised two to four times a year brought visitors in as volunteers to help locals with simple maintenance tasks ordinarily carried out by villagers. These tasks were predominantly seasonal community activities, such as removing mud from watercourses and trimming back trees where branches obstructed roads and paths. Although the work could have been accomplished much more quickly by experienced locals without the help of the enthusiastic but inexperienced visitors, the locals were greatly cheered by the visitors' willingness to help and learn from them. For their part, many visitors arriving with a gloomy image of a marginally viable community crippled by an ageing demographic, found themselves energised by the spry and skilled elderly residents who led them in their maintenance chores.

A workshop held in September 2009 in the village of Shimizu for four women from Tokyo was typical of the kind of event implemented under this programme. On the first day, under the supervision of the local people, the visitors used sickles to cut grass away from the logs in the beech forest, where villagers had planted *nameko* fungi four months earlier in May. The only two middle-school students in the village community joined in. As well as cutting grass, the visitors and locals harvested wild grapes, *akebi* fruits and honey mushrooms on their way to and from the site. These were made into a nourishing soup in the evening and offered the visitors and villagers alike a moment to count the village's natural blessings. The second day was spent maintaining a 2km stretch of waterway that feeds the village from the mountain above. The work consisted of removing weeds and small branches from waterside ditches and cutting back overhanging trees and weeds growing in the waterway to allow the water to reach the village unimpeded.

As for all Tappo project programmes, the participants were handed a questionnaire to fill in at the end of the two-day programme and invited to share their thoughts on their experiences. One graduate student in her 20s stated that the two-day experience had made her acutely aware of her mental and physical isolation in Tokyo and had helped her recognise the importance of the connections between people in a community. She expressed her admiration for the residents, for whom watercourse management is just one of the many ways in which they support village life. She continued:

> Community life was very different from what I had imagined. Maintaining a watercourse is something I could never do anywhere else. There is no experience like it. In a way, it is the complete opposite of the world where you can always buy the same product in exchange for money.
>
> (Extract from questionnaire, author translation)

The young woman's revelation – that there are some things money can't buy – carries with it the implication that rural communities have values that are non-exchangeable with money.

Where people live next to nature, as they do in Shimizu, it is easier to see the connections between them and to appreciate nature more. Whereas life in a busy metropolis like Tokyo separates people from nature, opportunities to experience village life such as this one prove a poignant reminder to city dwellers of the principles that have supported human life for centuries.

Effects of the Tappo project on local residents

Speaking at a symposium held by Rikkyo University in Tokyo in 2010 on the theme of nature, school and sustainable society, a resident of Shimizu village said: 'I am not sure what you mean when you talk about success linked to community revitalisation. But one thing I can say for sure is that our village is certainly changing with involvement in the Tappo project. The community has received energy from visitors.'

Some 10 days earlier, a village-building meeting had been held in Tochikubo by members of the village community, with support from Ecoplus. These meetings were held two or three times a year between 2008 and 2012, and this particular one had been called by the village chief, who was seeking to increase residents' participation in the Tappo project. Sharing personal reflections of her involvement in the project activities and her commitment to the project, a woman in her 60s commented: 'Although I sometimes get nervous, it makes me very happy when people come from other places. I have to think hard about what meals to cook with the vegetables I have there and then. This project is my source of energy.' She has been one of the main actors in a group called Tochikubo *Kahchans* (mothers), which comprises local women (and some men) who cater for the visitors during programmes and events. This group began as a small business scheme and has since opened a local café, which operates seasonally and plans to expand in the near future.

The woman's comment and her group's plans for the future suggest the Shimizu resident who spoke out at Rikkyo University is not alone in finding his community 'energised' by its involvement in the Tappo project. Several villagers have told Ecoplus they feel proud when hearing people talk in the town about their village. One father in his 50s confessed that, for the first time, he had encouraged his son to come back to the village after finishing school because 'this is not a bad place'. The father had returned to the village reluctantly some 30 years previously, obliged by his family to quit his job in a city and come home because he was the eldest son. Years of regret had left him determined that his children should live in the city, should they wish to do so. He had often admitted to the author that he found it hard to think well of Tochikubo, no matter how often visitors praised the village to him. However, something inside him changed over the course of his involvement in the Tappo project and he now says he is more proud of his village and feels a sense of hope for its future.

Positive signs for the future

In the summer of 2011, Minami Uonuma city was pounded for several days by record levels of heavy rain that caused large-scale landslides and widespread flooding. In Tochikubo, the main road collapsed, several houses were affected by falling rocks and mudslides, and many rice fields were buried beneath rocks and debris.

With the rice harvest due in just two months' time, Minami Uonuma's problems extended far beyond any immediate damage. Fallen rocks and debris made harvesting machines unusable in certain paddy fields and mudslides made the soil in fields very deep and soggy. In many cases, the surrounding ridges of paddies, many of which were terraced, were broken, leaving the paddies misshapen and the use of machinery impossible. The only way to harvest rice was by hand – an impossible feat for any farmer working his or her fields alone. Farmers, who had tended their fields for months, watched in dismay as the surviving rice crop grew tall in fields that they had no way to work, fearful for the income they would lose should the harvest be lost and desperate to gather even a portion of the crop to feed their own families.

Responding to the farmers' need, Ecoplus sent out an urgent call for volunteers to help bring the harvest home in time. Over the course of 13 days, 300 people – from children of middle school age to adults in their 60s – came from all over Japan to work on 50 paddies in various villages, including Tochikubo. Notably, some 40 per cent of the volunteers who came from outside Niigata prefecture were previous Tappo programme participants and their friends. This would not have been the case had Tappo's programmes been conventional tourism ventures exchanging services for monetary gain, rather than exchanges that set out to build relationships between participants, places and locals through mutual learning. The former participants had returned because of the relationships they had built with the people and the land as a result of the Tappo project.

Remaining challenges for the Tappo project

Tappo programmes have contributed to community development as well as learning for sustainability for many people. However, the ageing trend continues and the survival of the Tochikubo primary school depends on students who come there from outside the village. In April 2015, at the start of a new school year, the school had 11 pupils registered from Grades 1 to 6; just six of these children are from Tochikubo.

Interactions with villagers of different ages and observations of the Tappo programmes show clearly that traditional knowledge and skills have not been passed on to the younger generation. It is also clear that the younger generation will never attain the same level of knowledge and skills possessed by their elders, given their very different lifestyles and the subsequent lack of time invested in honing those skills and knowledge. The organisers of the Tappo project now need to assess carefully the important things to carry on across the generations, and to determine what the next generation can do to continue the project's mission to explore the values of rural communities in mountainous areas in terms of sustainability. This includes seeking new ways to involve young locals – most of whom naturally tend to focus on their jobs and families – in its programmes.

Meanwhile, with the number of non-Japanese participants in Tappo programmes on the increase, the organisers are well placed to bring global perspectives to bear on the challenges of sustaining Japan's rural communities and to bring fresh eyes to see their value. There are no simple solutions to the problems of ageing and depopulation. Community issues are also highly complex – residents have various opinions on them and disagreements flare frequently, often for emotional reasons. No one involved in the Tappo project felt able to protest when one of the young leaders in Tochikubo elected to leave the village after his marriage because his wife did not want to live there with her in-laws as well as a great grandmother. On the other hand, the addition of a new family with small children, who moved into Tochikubo in 2014, was welcomed by villagers and Tappo project participants alike. The mother – originally from the village – had decided to raise her children there. The villagers celebrated her return, happy in the knowledge that as long as the family stays, their school will remain safe.

Conclusion

Rural communities provide a learning space in which to understand the processes of living – processes that in city life are sacrificed in exchange for convenience but that are, arguably, necessary if we are to recognise what is important in life. The educational power of rural communities, therefore, lies in their implications for current society as a new – or perhaps old – social paradigm that questions materialistic civilisation, promotes diverse forms of economy and necessitates a shift in values. Since the Tohoku Earthquake in 2011, scholars such as Uchiyama (2011) state that an increasing number of Japanese people have shown an interest in human–nature and human–human connections as well as exploring a different form of society.

The Tappo project is one of a number of experiments seeking to test the direction in which Japanese people want to move, and to inform citizens what they can do to come closer to a sustainable society. Addressing the issues and tackling the challenges in rural areas helps people to find new values and has deep relevance to the future of the partner communities. The key here is the residents' willingness to make efforts to change the present situation. Without this, the positive effect of any external intervention will be short lived. In Japan, it is said that there are three things needed to enhance a community: *wakamono* (a youth), *bakamono* (a fool) and *yosomono* (an outsider). Real change may begin with the belief that *irumono* – literally, those who exist there – can make a difference by taking actions together with the outsiders using the skills and knowledge based on the unique assets the community members already possess.

References

Asfeldt, M. and Hvenegaard, G. 2013. Perceived learning, critical elements and lasting impacts on university-based wilderness educational expeditions. *Journal of Adventure Education and Outdoor Learning*, DOI:10.1080/14729679.2013.789350.

Basso, K. 1996. Wisdom sits in places: notes on a western Apache landscape, in Feld, S. and Basso, K. (eds) *Senses of place.* Santa Fe, US: School of American Research Press, 53–90.

Cabinet Office Japan (ed.) 2014. *Koreishakai Hakusho Heisei 26 nendo ban* (Annual report on the ageing society: fiscal year 2014). Nikkei Printing.

Casey, E. S. 1996. How to get from space to place in a fairly short stretch of time: phenomenological prolegomena, in Feld, S. and Basso, K. (eds) *Senses of place*. Santa Fe, US: School of American Research Press, 13–52.

Chawla, L. 1999. Life paths into effective environmental action. *Journal of Environmental Education* 31 (1), 15–26.

Gieryn, T. 2000. A space for place in sociology. *Annual Review of Sociology* 26, 463–96.

Heidegger, M. 1993. *Basic writings: from 'Being and time' (1927) to 'The task of thinking' (1964)*, trans. D. F Krell. London, UK: Routledge.

Hosoya, K. (ed.) 2003. *Toge no mura* (Village at the pass). Shiozawamachi Rekishishiryou Kankokai (Shiozawa Historical Document Publishing Committee).

Iwasaki, M. and Takano, T. 2010. *Ba no kyoiku – tochi ni nezasu manabi no suimyaku* (Place education – trend of place-based education). Tokyo, Japan: Nobunkyo.

Kahn, M. 1996. Your place and mine: sharing emotional landscapes in Wamira, Papua New Guinea, in Feld, S. and Basso, K. (eds) *Senses of place*. Santa Fe, US: School of American Research Press, 167–196.

Malpas, J. E. 1999. *Place and experience*. Cambridge, UK: Cambridge University Press.

Massey, D. 1993. Power-geometry and a progressive sense of place, in Bird, J., Curtis, B., Putnam, T., Robertson, G. and Tickner L. (eds) *Mapping the futures: local cultures, global change*. London, UK and New York, US: Routledge, 59–69.

Minami Uonuma City n.d. *Jinko tokei* (Statistical information) (www.city.minamiuonuma. niigata.jp/). Accessed 10 November 2014.

Ministry of Agriculture, Forestry and Fisheries n.d. *Chusankan chiiki towa* (Explanation of semi-mountainous regions) (www.maff.go.jp/j/nousin/tyusan/siharai_seido/s_about/ cyusan/). Accessed 22 January 2015.

Ministry of Internal Affairs and Communications 2011. *Kasochiiki nado niokeru shuraku no jokyonikansuru genkyohaaku chosa hokokusho* (Report: present situation of communities in depopulating areas) (www.soumu.go.jp/main_content/000113146.pdf). Accessed 22 January 2015.

Ministry of Internal Affairs and Communications 2014. *Jinko suikei* (Population estimate statistics) (www.stat.go.jp/data/jinsui/new.htm). Accessed 10 November 2014.

National Institute of Population and Social Security Research 2014. *Nihon no shourai suikei jinko* (Population projection in Japan) (www.ipss.go.jp/syoushika/tohkei/new est04/gh2401.asp). Accessed 10 November 2014.

Niigata Prefecture, Minami Uonuma Regional Promotion Bureau n.d. *Kannai no gaiyo* (Overview of the area under its control) (www.pref.niigata.lg.jp/minamiuonuma_ seibi/2_kannnainogaiyou.html). Accessed 25 November 2014.

Palmer, J., Suggate, J., Robottom, I., and Hart, P. 1999. Significant life experiences and formative influences on the development of adults' environmental awareness in the UK, Australia and Canada. *Environmental Education Research* 5 (2), 181–200.

Relph, E. 1989. Geographical experiences and being-in-the-world: the phenomenological origins of geography, in Seamon, D. and Mugerauer, R. (eds) *Dwelling, place and environment: an introduction*. New York, US: Columbia University Press, 15–31.

Smith, G. and Sobel, D. 2010. *Place- and community-based education in schools*. New York, US and London, UK: Routledge.

Takano, T. 2010. A 20-year retrospective study of the impact of expeditions on Japanese participants. *Journal of Adventure Education and Outdoor Learning* 10 (2), 77–94.

Tanner, T. 1998. On the origins of SLE research, questions outstanding, and other research traditions. *Environmental Education Research* 4 (4), 419–423.

Uchiyama, T. 2011. *Bunmei no saika* (Disaster of civilisation). Tokyo, Japan: Shinchosha.

Postscript

Reflections on visions of rebuilding Tohoku and the future of ESD as a response to risk in Japan

Yoko Mochizuki with Makoto Hatakeyama

Kesennuma and its significance for ESD in Japan

The city of Kesennuma, located in Miyagi prefecture on the Sanriku coast, was hit severely by the tsunami of 11 March 2011. Its fishing port was completely destroyed, not only by the tsunami but also by a fire that erupted because of gas leaking from wrecked fuel ships in the harbour. As one of the most devastated tsunami-affected areas, Kesennuma received substantial media coverage. Vast numbers of volunteers descended on Kesennuma and helped clear mud from the roads, remove the wreckage and debris, serve food and water to evacuees, sort and distribute relief supplies and provide psycho-social support to residents, such as entertainment, counselling, discussion groups and other interactive activities.

From the perspective of schools-based ESD, the Kesennuma Board of Education is well known for having taken the lead in encouraging schools to join the UNESCO Associated Schools Network (ASPnet), which led to all Kesennuma primary and secondary schools becoming ASPnet schools in 2008. As pointed out by Sakurai and Shaw in Chapter 2 of this volume, there were no casualties on school compounds across Kesennuma. This was viewed as an indication of the success of ESD in fostering school–community partnerships that, in turn, facilitated a quick and effective education sector response to the disaster (Oikawa 2014a; 2014b). After the tsunami, Kesennuma was showered with various education initiatives designed for disaster-ravaged Tohoku. These included a collaborative disaster education programme, supported by Kyoto University and the non-governmental organisation (NGO) SEEDS Asia (2013). Another was OECD (Organisation for Economic Cooperation and Development) Tohoku Schools (OECD Tohoku School n.d.) – a two-and-a-half-year education recovery project commissioned by Japan's Ministry of Education, Culture, Sports, Science and Technology (MEXT). This engaged 100 secondary school students from disaster-struck areas in Fukushima, Miyagi and Iwate prefectures in project-based learning to envision a 'new Tohoku' through intensive workshops and local school activities.

In addition to the efforts of the formal education sector, local NGOs and communities have been active in responding to the 3.11 disaster in Kesennuma. Indeed, along with the well documented case of Kesennuma's disaster preparedness and response through education, local efforts to fight against disaster recovery projects that will have a long-term negative impact on the local environment and quality of life provide significant lessons on how to build back better – and to put Japan on a more sustainable development path. This Postscript combines my reflections and those of Kesennuma fisherman and activist for ecologically integrated natural resource management, Makoto Hatakeyama, on visions of rebuilding Tohoku and the future of ESD. It centres on actions Hatakeyama has taken to address the challenges posed by unsustainable disaster recovery projects and his reflections on what kind of education is needed to shape a more sustainable society. His actions and reflections – as a tsunami survivor, local resident whose livelihood depends on the sea, environmental educator and activist – are compelling and valuable in envisioning a more sustainable future for disaster-ravaged Kesennuma and Tohoku as well as for Japan at large.

The sea is longing for the forest, the forest is longing for the sea

Makoto Hatakeyama's father, Shigeatsu Hatakeyama, is an oyster farmer and activist. He started an environmental movement called *Mori wa Umi no Koibito* (literally 'The forest is the ocean's lover' or 'The sea is longing for the forest, the forest is longing for the sea') in 1989 to restore a symbiotic forest–marine coastal ecosystem that had deteriorated during the high-growth period of the Japanese economy. He highlighted the importance of restoring mountain forests upstream, which would then help reduce pollutants flowing into the sea and breathe life back into oyster farming. This served to revive, albeit on a small scale, Japanese fishermen's tree-planting tradition. Traditionally, fishermen across Japan planted trees so their children and grandchildren could build fishing boats from the timber, but this tradition became obsolete about 40 years ago as fishing boats came to be mass produced from metal and fibreglass. Shigeatsu Hatakeyama's movement has spread nationally and grown into a symbolic movement combining reforestation activities by fishermen, raising awareness of the intricate links between the ocean and mountain forests, and experiential environmental learning for children. Shigeatsu Hatakeyama gained more attention in 2011, when his entire aquaculture oyster farm in Kesennuma was washed away by the tsunami. In 2012, the United Nations Forum on Forests Secretariat named him a winner of the Forest Hero award for recognising and promoting the vital connection between forests and oceans for the coastline in post-tsunami Tohoku. In 2015, he won the sixth Earth Hall of Fame Kyoto award, which put him in the ranks of great environmentalists such as Wangari Matthai, Gro Harlem Brundtland and Vandana Shiva.

Rebuilding Tohoku

In his role as a community leader, Shigeatsu Hatakeyama has questioned whether a technologically driven approach to rebuilding Tohoku is the best option, exploring how forestry workers, farmers and fishermen along the rivers upstream of Kesennuma can join forces to help to rebuild the tsunami-ravaged community (UNU Media Centre 2011). Following in his father's footsteps and as a young activist in his 30s, Makoto Hatakeyama has advocated the need for a sustainable recovery process. When the earthquake struck, he was shucking scallops in a factory on the coast. He immediately took his most valuable fishing boat and headed straight out into the bay to prevent it from being destroyed or taken away by a tsunami. It is fishermen's traditional wisdom to head into open sea in the event of a tsunami but his boat slid down the big waves and became temporarily submerged. Knowing that a tsunami hits repeatedly, he abandoned the boat, jumped into the sea and swam towards the coast, avoiding the debris and buoys that had come loose in the water, and miraculously made it to nearby Oshima Island. When a Self-Defence Forces helicopter took him back to Kesennuma four days later, he learned that the tsunami had destroyed his house, factory, oyster cultivation farm and one of his fishing boats and killed his grandmother.

In the pages that follow, I introduce Makoto Hatakeyama's observations and reflections on the ongoing recovery process in Kesennuma. The interview focuses on his reflections on the recovery process after the emergency relief phase in order to draw lessons for the future of ESD in Japan. Makoto Hatakeyama advocates a future-oriented, sustainable recovery process that embraces and establishes harmony with the natural environment for current and future generations.

Transforming abandoned arable land into a space for environmental learning

YM: Please share your views on the ongoing recovery process for the city of Kesennuma.

MH: On the coastlines of Tohoku, various government agencies have carried out a range of disaster recovery projects that aim to restore damaged public properties, such as roads, guard rails and coastal embankments, to their original condition. Although certain public works projects are important in the recovery process, there are many that seem to be extremely useless. Agricultural land restoration projects are a case in point. Since agriculture is designated as a key industry, the government has measures to subsidise replacing soils damaged by seawater as long as a piece of land has been registered as agricultural land. This is leading to a wasteful situation where taxpayers' money is being used to restore long abandoned farmland that has little likelihood of being used as farmland in the future.

YM: Could you elaborate on the implications of agricultural land restoration projects?

MH: In the Sanriku coastal area, where flat land is limited, abandoned arable land is concentrated near the beach. The huge force of the Great East Japan Earthquake lowered the ground level. Since then, some nearshore abandoned arable lands filled with seawater at high tide. This has transformed them into salt marshes and tidal flats, which provide a habitat for juvenile fish, meiobenthic species (small benthic invertebrates that live in both marine and freshwater environments), *unagi* (a Japanese eel specified in 2014 as an endangered species by the International Union for Conservation of Nature), clams and so on. In addition, the strip of land connecting the seawater wetland to the dry land often has fresh spring water, providing a habitat for species such as *Minami* killifish (*Oryzias latipes*), salamanders and frogs. An integrated ecosystem combining a continuous flow of fresh water, brackish water and seawater has been restored, reviving rare seaside plants and providing a feeding ground for wild birds.

Although the value of newly created salt marshes and tidal flats is immense from the perspective of restoring biodiversity, the government is mechanically dumping soil on top of them if a landowner applies for an agricultural land restoration project, without setting forth guidelines for land restoration based on integrated and long-term perspectives. It is regrettable that these pieces of land, even restored as farmland, are not likely to be farmed. Perhaps because residents in Sanriku are used to the rich natural environment, few seem to understand the value of ecosystems regenerated by the tsunami. Some landowners have said that they would like to restore the original condition of the precious plots of land inherited from their ancestors, but it is often the case that this is reclaimed farmland that used to be tidal flats in the first place. In this sense, the earthquake and tsunami have restored the nearshore landscape to its original condition.

YM: Have you taken any action to conserve the restored salt marsh?

MH: To protect and hand down this rich natural capital to future generations, I came to the conclusion that there is no other way than to purchase the reverted wetlands. I considered applying for support provided by the Japan National Trust and other organisations. However, administrative procedures were time consuming and time was against me because the government was moving quickly to put soil into the restored wetlands as part of a disaster recovery project. In consultation with members of *Mori wa Umi no Koibito*, I proposed to use my father's savings – intended for investment in our family fishery business – to purchase pieces of land that had been abandoned farmland for more than 40 years. I respect my father for readily accepting this proposal, which could hinder the recovery of our family business. The area of land I purchased – about 10,000m^2 – is, of course, tiny in comparison to the entire coastal areas affected by the tsunami but I plan to transform it into a space where everyone can be in touch with nature.

Protesting against sea wall construction

YM: I understand that you are protesting against the building of gigantic sea walls that are being dubbed 'Great Walls of Japan'. As a tsunami survivor, could you explain why you are against it?

MH: Constructing gigantic sea walls is definitely one of the Japanese government's most controversial disaster recovery projects. This concerns not only the tsunami-struck coastal areas of Tohoku but also coastal areas across Japan in the long run because it kickstarts a larger national project to build concrete sea walls along the coastline of Japan. This is a life-and-death matter to residents like me, who have always lived in harmony with the sea.

On the Sanriku coast struck by the tsunami, a 14.7m high concrete sea wall – the highest in Miyagi prefecture – is planned at the waterfront of the Koizumi district in Kesennuma. This is planned mostly on the flat coastal areas and will destroy sand beaches that are gradually being restored after the tsunami. In principle, private houses cannot be built in the areas inundated by the tsunami. Therefore these walls – supposedly meant to protect 'Japanese citizens' lives and properties'– in reality will be protecting mainly public properties like roads and guardrails, which also constitute 'Japanese citizens' properties'. Massive amounts of taxpayers' money will be used to implement this project without any regard for cost-effectiveness and cost-benefit considerations. Most planned sea walls are meant to protect against a level-one tsunami, which is likely to occur once in several decades or once in 100 years. They cannot resist a level-two tsunami like that of 2011, which occurs once in 1,000 years. They will, therefore, be quite useless if a tsunami as big as the one in 2011 is to hit other regions of Japan.

YM: You seem to be implying that constructing sea walls is not only wasteful but useless.

MH: Although a disaster recovery project should be implemented based on the principle of multiple protection, which combines 'hardware', such as drawing up hazard and evacuation maps, with 'software', such as disaster education, most funding for a disaster recovery process is allocated to infrastructural development. For me, this emphasis on infrastructure is alarming because it encourages people's inattention or carelessness to natural disasters. The 2011 earthquake and tsunami taught us in the most painful way possible that it is dangerous to indulge in uncritical thinking, such as 'we do not need to worry about a tsunami because we are protected by a sea wall' or 'we are safe only if we get to an evacuation tower'.

YM: If it is wasteful, useless and even potentially harmful from the perspective of disaster preparedness, why can't the plan to construct a sea wall be stopped?

MH: The plan reflects the power of the Ministry of Land, Infrastructure, Transport and Tourism (MLIT) and the powerlessness of the Ministry of the Environment (MOE) in terms of budget size. The MOE's entire annual budget is about the same size as just one project managed by the MLIT. The plan to construct sea walls in Kesennuma was drawn up by Miyagi prefecture, and includes a plan to destroy an existing facility managed by the MOE. This reflects the relative powerlessness of the MOE budget, even in relation to a municipal government. In a similar vein, environmental assessment in Japan is basically conducted by the project implementer and rarely results in a project being revised or cancelled. If a rare species is found on a project site, it will be simply moved to another site. If rare wild birds are found, bird houses will be set up. Project developers are not even required to put aside an alternative site for conservation – even when a valuable wetland is destroyed by a construction project. The construction of sea walls is mechanically proceeding as though it were a standard operational procedure, without any consideration for the expressed concern that they would become a negative heritage for future generations.

YM: What are the financial implications for local communities of building sea walls?

MH: Although the construction of the sea walls will be financed primarily by the national government, they will require regular maintenance, the cost of which is to be borne mainly by local government. In Japan, various entities – state, prefecture, city, town, village, etc. – manage coastal lands and there are seven entities that are in charge of coastal lands in the City of Kesennuma. This is bringing extra confusion to local governments struggling after the disaster.

YM: What would be a long-term economic and ecological impact of sea wall construction?

MH: I am afraid that the construction of sea walls will bring about a decline in the Japanese fishing industry. Japan is an island country rich in fishery resources. These are supported by abundant forests, which produce nutrient salts and micronutrients essential for the growth of marine phytoplankton, and by rivers that carry these nutrients into the sea. However, it is not enough to conserve forest and river ecosystems. For example, recent studies show that groundwater in coastal areas contributes to marine ecosystems significantly. Rainwater flows downstream from forests through rivers to the sea but a substantial amount of rainwater filters underground and springs forth from the seabed in the coastal areas. This groundwater contains much more nutrient salts and micronutrients than river water.

We also have to consider that the geological formation of a beach tends to be a soft foundation that can go as deep as 30m. Therefore, sea walls, revetments and coastal roads are usually built on a series of steel sheet piles, hammered into the soft foundation. This construction method has major implications for the marine ecosystem because it stems or changes the flow of groundwater.

According to the current law, environmental assessment is not required for a disaster recovery project. Since the evaluation of impact on ecosystems does not need to be considered, the potential negative impact on the local flora and fauna and the aquatic product industry is virtually ignored. We need to be very careful about the 'fake', as opposed to genuine, environmental considerations that are being put forward. A gigantic concrete sea wall will be built on a steel sheet pile foundation, and sand and rocks will be placed artificially inside the wall to give an illusion of a natural beach. There's nothing natural about it.

Building a vision for sustainable Kesennuma: education for the future

YM: How have local residents reacted to this plan to build a gigantic sea wall?

MH: I'd say that 60 per cent of the residents are indifferent or have no opinions at all, 30 per cent are perhaps sceptical of the project but are being careful not to take sides, and only 10 per cent are fiercely opposed to the project. Generally speaking, Japanese are not inclined to organise themselves in demonstrations, perhaps as a result of school education that discourages people from taking such action. The reality is that most residents are indifferent to a problem that will have major implications for their own futures. I believe one of the biggest obstacles to recovery from the earthquake and tsunami is the sheer indifference of local residents to important issues.

Another bottleneck is the gap in what is valued by different age groups in the tsunami-ravaged areas. Those over 50 tend to want life to return to how it was before the disaster, while younger adults tend to want to transform their community, which was in steady economic decline. I am one of those who acts to create a sustainable local community where future generations can live a healthy and happy life. What do we want to hand down to future generations? Do we want a sustainable society supported by a rich natural environment? Or do we want gigantic concrete sea walls and massive public debt, supported by the unbridled issuing of government bonds? To me it is crystal clear which option is more future-oriented.

YM: One challenge seems to be to build a shared vision of the future of Kesennuma. What challenges to community-based decision making or consensus building have you observed after the tsunami?

MH: Consensus is a tricky word. When most of the residents are in agreement, those who disagree tend not to voice their opinions in fear of creating tensions within the community. Expressing one's own ideas, listening to others and having constructive discussion is not really rooted in our culture. I believe this is deeply linked to the kind of education we receive. In my opinion, we are taught that there is only one right answer to everything in school education. This encourages a collectivist tendency that respects and reinforces a group's interests over individuals' views. Of course, if all individuals share the same purpose, this type of education can maximise outputs. At the same time, it cannot foster diversity in values and opinions, making it difficult to cope flexibly with complex and uncertain problems, such as recovery from the Great East Japan Earthquake. This is not simply a personal problem but a fundamental problem of contemporary Japanese society, which is eroding corporations and other groups. I feel this might be one of the reasons for the lack of flexibility and vitality we see in Japanese society today. I am hoping that the post-3.11 recovery process provides an opportunity for us to break away from this stagnation.

YM: In your view, what kind of education is needed to shape a more sustainable future?

MH: I am still searching for answers myself but I feel that childhood experiential nature learning is the key. Experiencing wonders and discoveries and playing creatively in nature – these experiences promote social and emotional development and help children to grasp connections between the natural environment and their life. Children today are not allowed to play in nature because it is considered dangerous. For example, suppose that children are playing in the river by themselves and one of them almost drowns. The 'dangerous' river becomes off-limits to children with the installation of a no-trespassing sign, and children will forever lose an opportunity to learn how the river really looks and feels and how it functions. This approach has parallels to the plan to construct sea walls to protect us. We cannot secure our lives and livelihoods by separating ourselves from nature. Our life is embedded in nature and it is we – people living in the natural environment – who understand it and determine in what shape we want to hand it down to future generations. If we would like to build a sustainable society, we have to live our lives asking what we should leave behind. In my case, I would like to leave behind social mechanisms and spaces that allow future generations to think and act outside the box. We need an integrated, rich natural environment and a society open for discussion, not a concrete structure with high maintenance costs and a stifling society with too many regulations. I would like to hand down sites or fields for experiential nature learning.

Final thoughts: connecting the dots

What Kesennuma is undergoing today is not an isolated phenomenon in the tsunami-struck area but symbolic of Japan's post-war development projects, which have transformed Japanese people's relationship with nature. Although Japan is a small industrialised nation, it is a country of abundant forests and coastal ocean – two-thirds of its territory is covered with forest and its coastline is longer than that of China. As the Japanese economy grew, however, rich connections between humans, forests, rivers and oceans were severed in many regions. Hatakeyama has advocated the need for a sustainable recovery process that restores these connections and reflects on how education can help shape a more ecologically balanced era post 3.11.

Like the environmental scandals of the 1960s that prompted Japan's proposal for the UN Decade of Education for Sustainable Development (DESD), armouring Tohoku's pristine coastline with concrete might be a Japanese 'mistake' that will show the rest of the world the negative impact of technology-driven and ecologically unsound solutions to risks in the near future. Having characterised the latter half of the twentieth century as a period when education evolved 'as a response to emerging risk within the modernist project', O'Donoghue (2014, 8) explores the expanding contours of ESD at a time when 'socio-economic and environmental issues escalated into a polycentric global crisis'. This characterisation of ESD as a response to risk helps us understand ESD in Japan and reflect on its future.

Following the global financial crisis triggered by the collapse of Lehman Brothers in 2008 and in light of the combined crisis of natural resource degradation, climate change and food security, the UNESCO strategy for the second half of the DESD (UNESCO 2009) prioritised addressing global sustainability challenges through ESD by focusing on three key action themes: climate change, biodiversity and disaster risk reduction (DRR) and preparedness. The Great East Japan Earthquake highlighted the already recognised links between ESD and DRR education. Following 3.11, the government of Japan hosted the UN World Conference on DRR in Sendai, Tohoku, in March 2015, giving an additional impetus to put Japanese DRR education on the global map. DRR education (see Chapter 2) is one of the most straightforward examples of ESD as a response to risk.

German sociologist Ulrich Beck, a populariser of the concept of risk, views risk as the product of the process of industrialisation underpinning modern society's material prosperity (Beck 1992). A nuclear accident is a prime example of Beck's notion of risk in that it is unpredictable, potentially global and catastrophic, even affecting the citizens of countries that do not use nuclear power (Ibid., 35). Effective, balanced radiation education (see Chapter 6) is a clear example of ESD as a response to the risks posed by the construction of 54 nuclear reactors in one of the world's most seismically active nations. In addition, while not as straightforward as the cases of DRR education and radiation education, various community-based initiatives encouraging local residents to take pride in their community or local region can be understood as a response to one of the greatest risks faced by Japan's 'super ageing' (Muramatsu and Akiyama 2011) society – that of demographic risk or the very survivability of Japan's declining population (see, for example, Chapters 9 and 15). Closely linked to a population crisis are the risks of losing local cultures, local identities and livelihoods based on place.

Japan's pollution scandals in the 1960s were a matter of life and death because of the direct health implications for those affected. Drawing a line between right and wrong or good and evil was, therefore, relatively straightforward. By contrast, the current controversies surrounding the 'Great Walls of Japan' are much more complex and nuanced. Who is the villain in this scenario? Sea walls are being built to 'protect' residents from future tsunami yet Hatakeyama and others are warning of the possibility that they will make a negative impact on local ecosystems, local residents' disaster awareness (hence increasing vulnerability to future disasters), livelihoods (considering the immediate impact on local tourism and the longer-term impact on the viability of local fisheries) and the overall quality of life and identity of the place. For those whose livelihoods and identities depend on living in harmony with the sea, the construction of sea walls means the slow and inevitable death of their local communities – and not fighting against it cannot be right. Hatakeyama's criticism of disaster recovery projects is levelled not only against the Japanese government's conventional public works projects but also against the Japanese people's unreflective conformity to rules and regulations, majority opinions and the way development projects have always been done – 'business as usual'.

The 3.11 triple disaster, dwindling birth rate, ageing population, weakening communities, exhausted countryside, battered Japanese economy, more frequent and intense natural disasters and transboundary environmental issues are threatening the sustainability of local communities, which support the lives, health and livelihoods of people residing in Japan. The 3.11 triple disaster has revealed the limitations of science and technology in a knowledge-based society, led to disillusionment with the myth of nuclear safety and exposed the 'oppressor–oppressed' (Sato 2015, 3) structural relationships between the metropolitan 'centre' and Tohoku. It has also confirmed the remarkable resilience of a deeply entrenched power structure that has undergirded the safety myth and Japan's self-strengthening nation-building project.

The case of sea walls vividly shows that building back better and transitioning to sustainability are not primarily about technological solutions. Rather they require informed and empowered citizens, who have a deep understanding of their place within the ecosystem – citizens who know that they survive and thrive through their connectedness to each other and the ecosystems that support them. This is true about Kesennuma and other disaster-struck areas of Japan as well as the country as a whole. What needs to be challenged is not just unsustainable development projects – be they unneeded infrastructural projects or unsound industrial or agricultural projects – but indifference, unawareness, uncritical and non-systemic thinking and unreflective conformity to business as usual – both on the part of the decision makers and the local communities that will suffer the consequences of these projects. This is where ESD has a crucial role to play – and is where the future of ESD lies.

References

Beck, U. 1992. *Risk society: towards a new modernity*. New Delhi, India: Sage (Translated from the German *Risikogesellschaft*) 1986.

Kyoto University (Graduate School of Global Environmental Studies) and SEEDS Asia 2013. *Kesennuma-shi ni okeru aratana bosai-kyoiku no torikumi* (Exploring innovations in disaster education in Kesennuma 1). Mid-term review of the project jointly implemented by Kesennuma Board of Education, Kyoto University and SEEDS Asia. (www.preventionweb.net/files/32237_32237kesennuma17.53.20.pdf). Accessed 11 March 2016.

Muramatsu, N. and Akiyama, H. 2011. Japan: super-aging society preparing for the future. *The Gerontologist* 51 (4), 425–432.

O'Donoghue, R. 2014. Re-thinking education for sustainable development as transgressive processes of educational engagement with human conduct, emerging matters of concern and the common good. *Southern African Journal of Environmental Education* 30, 7–26.

OECD Tohoku School n.d. About OECD Tohoku School (http://oecdtohokuschool.sub.jp/english.html). Accessed 12 March 2016.

Oikawa, Y. 2014a. Institutional response in education sector in Kesennuma City, in Shaw, R. (ed.) *Disaster recovery: used or misused development opportunity,* Tokyo, Japan, Heidelberg, Germany, New York, US, Dordrecht, The Netherlands and London, UK: Springer, 89–113.

Oikawa, Y. 2014b. City level response: linking ESD and DRR in Kesennuma, in Shaw, R. and Oikawa, Y. (eds) *Education for sustainable development and disaster risk reduction,* Tokyo, Japan, Heidelberg, Germany, New York, USA, Dordrecht, The Netherlands and London, UK: Springer,155–176.

Sato, K. (ed.) 2015. *Chiiki-gakushu no sozo: Chiiki saisei e no manabi wo hiraku* (Dynamics of community-based learning for social revitalisation). Tokyo, Japan: University of Tokyo Press.

UNESCO 2009. UNESCO Strategy for the Second Half of the UN Decade of Education for Sustainable Development. Paris, France: UNESCO (http://unesdoc.unesco.org/images/0021/002154/215466e.pdf). Accessed 22 March 2016.

UNU Media Centre 2011. From mountains to sea: a vision to rebuild Tohoku (video clip) (http://unu.edu/news/news/from-mountain-to-sea-a-vision-to-rebuild-tohoku.html). Accessed 10 March 2016.

Index

Note: The following abbreviations have been used – f = figure; n = note; t = table